Handbook of LAN Technology

Handbook of LAN Technology

Paul J. Fortier

Intertext Publications
McGraw-Hill, Inc. New York, NY

Library of Congress Catalog Card Number 87-090933

Page composition in TₑX by Frank Lusardi.

10 9 8 7 6 5 4 3 2 1

ISBN 0-07-021623-1

Intertext Publications/Multiscience Press, Inc.
One Lincoln Plaza
New York, NY 10023

McGraw-Hill Book Company
1221 Avenue of the Americas
New York, NY 10020

Contents

Part One
Local Area Networks: Overview and Perspective

Part Two
Communications Technology

Part Three
Local Area Networks: Topology Considerations

Part Five
Local Area Network Security

Part Six
Modeling and Analysis of Local Area Networks

Part Seven
Systems Management

Part Eight
Examination of LANs in Use

FIGURES

CONTRIBUTORS

Dr. Jan Bergandy
Southeastern Massachusetts University, North Dartmouth, Massachusetts.

Part Five: Local area network security.

Robert Charette
Itabhi, Inc., Fairfax, Virginia.

Part Three: Local area network topology.

Douglas Dauphinee
General Dynamics, Inc., Middletown, Rhode Island.

Part Two: Communications technology.

George Desrochers
TASC, Inc., North Reading, Massachusetts.

Part Four: LAN standards.
Part Eight: Examination of LANs in use.

Paul Fortier
University of Lowell, Lowell, Massachusetts.

Part One: LAN considerations.
Part Four: LAN control.

Daniel Juttelstad
Naval Underwater Systems Center, Newport, Rhode Island.

Part Six: Modeling and analysis of LANs.

Dr. Hideyuki Tokuda
Carnegie Mellon University, Pittsburg, Pennsylvania.

Part Seven: Systems management.

Preface

Local area networks are becoming a central component of the computer resources of almost every company. Consequently, among all those individuals involved with LANs—designers, users, students, managers—the need has grown to acquire a better understanding and appreciation of the design, analysis, and services for this critical area. *Handbook of LAN Technology* is meant to provide a solid foundation in the technology utilized in the design and use of LANs. Of equal importance, *Handbook of LAN Technology* serves as a concise source of the pertinent information a user, designer, or manager of LAN systems is required to know in the performance of his or her job. As the vehicle for connecting various informational sources together, LANs make possible the sharing of all software and hardware resources. By providing such access, LANs allow users dramatically to expand their use of up-to-date information, thereby enhancing the performance of their tasks with a higher degree of accuracy and timeliness. In various applications—transmitting digital data for data processing, video presentation, voice presentation, to name a few—LANs have shown their effectiveness. And, the LAN has provided the impetus for the development of many new applications of computers in business, education, finance, and government and clearly will continue to do so into the future. The need for connectivity and the knowledge of how to use it has become a fundamental fact in modern enterprise.

This book is broken up into eight sections, each dealing with a different aspect of LAN technology. Section One constitutes an introduction to LANs and defines what they are and how and where they can be applied. Section Two deals with communications technology and error correction and detection schemes. Section Three addresses the issues and technology associated with LAN topology. The fourth section examines the control protocols found in LANs and the emerging standards being applied to them. Section Five covers the technology and issues surrounding the security of LANs, an important issue in this time of increased reliance on information in everyday dealings. Section Six provides a view of the issues and techniques involved in the selection and performance evaluation of LANs. Section Seven addresses the details of LAN management, presenting in particular the technology applied to the construction of operating systems and their environments for the LAN. Section Eight examines presently available LANs and their technology. Each section is complete with its own references, and a comprehensive reference section concludes the book.

Handbook of LAN Technology could not have been realized without the great efforts of many people. I wish to extend my deepest gratitude to the authors of the various sections, and to the group of individuals who pulled the components together into this final form. In particular I want to thank Lloyd Watts and Bonnie Netten Reily for the typed text, Celeste Fortier and Chris Santos for their superb artwork, and—as always—my wife Kathy and children Daniel, Brian, and Nicole for their encouragement and support.

Paul J. Fortier

PART ONE
Local Area Networks
Overview and Perspective

1. Introduction

The information community's insatiable appetite for timely information has led the push to the development of local area networks (LANs). LANs have been developed to link industrial plants such as banks, schools, offices, etc., together. These networks provide resources and information to their users in greater volume and faster than earlier methods did. LANs provide a means for these users to interconnect a wide range of devices together into united geographical resource-sharing systems. A LAN generally provides for high bandwidth communications over relatively inexpensive transmission media. A LAN is mainly composed of three parts: (1) the transmission media, (2) the mechanism of control, and (3) the interface unit to the network. These provide the mechanisms to transport information to and from remote devices. Generally, any network must have a transport capability, an internal switching mechanism, and an ultimate consumer (see Figure 1.1); all are controlled through having an overseeing construct (the control).

Many examples of networks can be found in nature, such as the human nervous system which communicates stimuli via the synapse from the sense organs to the brain or the human circulatory system which transports blood laden with nutrients under the control of the heart to the organs via capillaries. Other examples are the railway system that transports freight from source points to destination points and is controlled by the railroad yards that perform the switching. The phone and power grids are also networks that provide for distribution of commodities to users. In all cases, these examples illustrate the basic notion of a network: the transfer of some commodity under control of a switching center from one site to another.

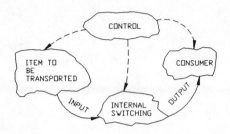

Figure 1.1   Network transport and switching.

Computer networks are no different. That is, they possess sources and sinks and a commodity to transfer (control data or program information) under the control of a "controller" (hardware, software, and a protocol).

Communications from the source host to the sink or destination host occur through the interaction of the two machines through their interface units under a structured set of operations referred to as a protocol. For example, if host A wishes to send a message to host D, the the following must occur (see Figure 1.2):

1. Host A must formulate a message to transfer.
2. Host A issues a send request to its network interface unit (NIU).
3. Host A's NIU forms a message transfer unit for transmission over the network.
4. Host A's NIU sends the message over the network to logical host D.
5. Host D's NIU recognizes the message as addressed to it and reads it in.
6. Host D's NIU strips off the network control information and, if the message is okay (at this level), it sends an acknowledgement to host A's NIU.
7. Host D's NIU sends the message to its host.
8. Host D strips off the remaining control information and, if okay, issues a final acknowledgement.
9. Host D's NIU ships the acknowledgement over to host A's NIU, which sends it to its host.
10. At this point the communication is complete.

This sequence is generic and has many variations in real networks. Some protocols will not require an end-to-end acknowledgement or even a NIU-to-NIU one. Others will break a message up into equal chunks called "packets"

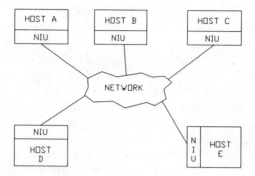

Figure 1.2   Network protocol.

and send these over the network or will form physical conduits to destinations to send the information over the network. Details of these issues will be seen later in this text.

1.1   Network Evolution

LANs are an outgrowth of their long-haul network ancestors. The technology and structure of LANs is rooted in that of the early packet communication networks and computer buses. The evolution and refinement of these technologies as well as hardware technology provides the basis upon which the early LANs arose.

Packet communications networks began with Arpanet in 1969. This and other early networks provided the vehicle to research many of the issues in intercomputer communications and to set the groundwork to provide the stimulus to researchers to refine techniques seen in these networks.

The road to these early networks began in the early 1960s. The major event viewed as the beginning of the technology and the reason for networking was the necessity to share expensive resources more effectively. The technology that first arose to meet the need was time-sharing operating systems. These early systems (RTOS for the IBM 360, GECOS III for the Honeywell 600, Demand for the Univac 1108, and TSS/8 for the PDP 8) provided a means by which users could simultaneously (from a user's perspective) share and use the expensive central processing unit (CPU) and its associated resources. These early developments made computers more accessible to a wider number of individuals.

The second event in the timeline to networking was the development and introduction of communications-oriented software and hardware components such as asynchronous line protocols (start/stop), synchronous line protocols (SDLC, Bisync), intelligent terminals, and line concentrators. These developments provided the capability for computers to transmit information from one site to another. This event, coupled with the evolving time-sharing systems, provided a means to develop large disjointed systems such as the airline reservation system, credit reporting and information systems, banking information systems, and remote booking and point of sales systems. These still though were not true networks. They were disjointed systems that communicated sporadically using leased lines or telephone circuits to transfer information.

A feature that ultimately provided the economic reason to interconnect computers to fixed networks was the dramatic drop in computer equipment cost and the improvement in its performance. When taken together, these factors resulted in the inception of the early networks.

The goal of early networks was to provide more effective use of the various computer resources via resource sharing and to provide for effective dissemination of information and more computing power to users.

As previously stated, the first operational network was Arpanet (Advanced Research Project Agency NETwork). Arpanet was constructed by Bolt, Beranek, and Newman of Cambridge, Massachusetts, under a contract to Arpa and came online in 1969. The first configuration had four nodes located in four widely dispersed geographic areas (University of California at Santa Barbara, Los Angeles, SRI, and Utah). From this early start, Arpanet has now grown to a network consisting of hundreds of host machines extending from Hawaii to Europe. This network provided the vehicle for early pioneering efforts in the research and development for network:

- Topologies
- Protocols
- Flow control
- Routing
- Performance analysis
- Communications

1.2   Network Communications

The early systems developed mechanisms and techniques for interdevice communications. The basic components for this communication are circuits, modems, terminals, multiplexers, concentrators, and control procedures. The circuits consisted of conductors or wireless transmission media. Typical of these were metallic conductors twisted pair, multipair, coaxial cable, and waveguides. Also used are optical fibers, microwave, and satellite links. These represented the technology used to transmit information from source to sink. The signalling rate, or the information transfer rate,

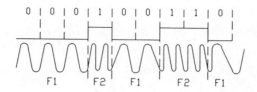

Figure 1.3   Signal frequency shifts.

on these media ranged from 45 to 500,000 bits per second (bps), with delays
for long-haul transfer (across the country) of from 0.016 to 0.25 seconds (s).

Modems provided the techniques to convert and transfer digital logic
signals over analog (telephone) transmission lines. The main techniques
used for the conversion are frequency modulation, amplitude modulation,
and phase modulation. In frequency modulation, the transition of a digital
signal from 0 to 1 or 1 to 0 is handled by changing the frequency sent over
the channel. For example, if we wish to send 000100110 over a channel,
it would be necessary to reformat the digital signal into an analog one
consisting of two frequency shifts as shown in Figure 1.3.

By sending a different frequency to represent the transition, the modem
on the other end can decipher the signals into the proper sequence of 1s
and 0s. In amplitude modulation, the digital signal is transferred into
analog transitions using the waveform amplitude as the differentiating item.
For example, to transmit the same digital sequence as before, this method
produces the waveform seen in Figure 1.4.

In the example, the transition from a quiescent state to the waveform
of higher amplitude signals the transition from a 0 to a 1. Using this
technique, any sequence of 0s and 1s can be encoded.

The last technique is phase modulation. In this technique the transition
from a 0 to a 1 or vice versa is recognized by a phase change. A phase

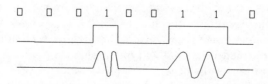

Figure 1.4   Amplitude modulation.

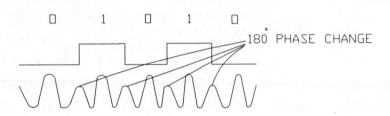

Figure 1.5 Phase modulation.

change is one in which the waveform changes its direction from the simple sinusoidal to a reversed sinusoidal as shown in Figure 1.5.

In all these examples, another important aspect is that there must be known timing intervals for a single bit. This is required so that the signals can be easily encoded and decoded. Additionally, to initiate a sequence, the devices must know where to begin and end decoding. This requires a form of synchronization such as start and stop sequences or quiescent state to active state transitions, etc. More will be said later in the text about these and other transmission techniques.

The next component in the communications technology is the terminal. This represents the end device that translates the computer internal representation to the end user representation. The terminal represents devices such as user operator consoles, intelligent workstations, disk drives, line printers, tape drives, etc. These devices are the end users of the communications channels and the attached machines.

To make networks and computers more accessible to more users, the concepts and devices for multiplexing and concentrating communications arose. Multiplexers provide a means to take multiple inputs (fixed) and provide a sharing of the end media to the N users (see Figure 1.6).

Multiplexers provide for fixed capacity division, are hard wired (meaning that there can only be N devices, no more once all the lines are consumed), with no growth available beyond the designed limit. The capacity of the high-speed line is equal to the sum of the low-speed lines connected to it. No intermediate storage is provided, all switching is circuit switched, and control is performed via sampling type mechanisms.

A concentrator, on the other hand, provides an adaptive-type sharing of the channel. It is programmable and can adjust its service to user terminals based on the statistical loading being provided to it. Concentrators provide a capacity that is less than the aggregation of its terminal links capacity;

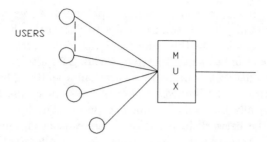

Figure 1.6   The multiplexer.

but through dynamic linking, less than full loading levels, and varying usage patterns, adequate service is provided to all. It provides for store and forward transmission, allowing it to take on more information than it can put out. The final component of network communications is the control procedures. These provide the services necessary for the remote devices to use the network communications components in communicating with one another. These control procedures provide for error detection, error correction, flow control, and synchronization. These will be covered in detail in following chapters.

1.3   Network Topology

Research in early networks in this area looked at schemes for connecting network components together to provide reliability, availability, computing power, information transfer throughput, etc. The topologies examined included fully connected, mesh or irregular, star, ring, bus, tree, and hybrids containing subsets of one or more of the above interconnection schemes. The selection of the interconnection scheme provides a means to establish the basic capabilities for reliability, availability, and throughput that the system will possess. For example, if a simple point-to-point scheme is used in which nodes are connected to all others, any node can talk to any other by communicating over its dedicated path. Additionally, if we add intelligence to the routing algorithm, if the dedicated path should fail, there still would be $N - 1$ possible ways to get to the other site via a single hop (see Figure 1.7).

If link 1 or 2 failed, node 1 could talk to node 2 by sending the message to either site 3 or 4, which could then ship this message forward to site 2. The extra delay would be acceptable if the communications must get through.

Conversely, if we used an irregular topology, the loss of a link could jeopardize its ability to get from one site to another with a message (see Figure 1.8). To alleviate this, one may wish to enforce some minimum number of links from any site, thereby providing for alternate paths. Additionally, such a network is prone to separation or splitting because of node failures. Because of the limited number of links and connectivity, a single point can typically be used to unite two parts. The loss of such a node would cause the network to partition, thereby isolating one set of nodes from another. Networks that have grown uncontrolled (such as Arpanet) topologywise are typically of this class. Alleviation of these problems would require additional links and intelligent routing algorithms and information.

Another early network topology was the star, or central switch. In this type of network, a central host acts as the switching center for the users. Requests for data exchange are directed to the hub, which will determine the route and send the message on its way. The typical topology of wide area networks with this topology is represented as a set of stars (see Figure 1.9).

Additional topologies developed during the early days of networking included the ring and bus structured topologies. These are more affiliated with local area networks, though they still have their basis in wide area networks. More will be said later in this text regarding these topologies and the variety of configurations and protocols developed for them.

1.4   Network Protocols

Protocols represent the means agreed to for transferring information. Because of the point-to-point topology of most early machines, these control protocols tended to be quite simple. The network's problem lay more in

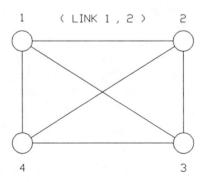

Figure 1.7   An intelligent routing algorithm.

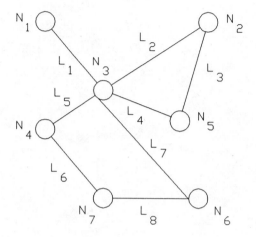

Figure 1.8   An irregular topology.

the routing and flow control for messages. These control protocols become much more of an issue and have many more variations within the shared media of the local area networks, as will be seen.

Protocols in a network exist to provide for the establishment of:

- Standard data element (format)
- Necessary conventions
- A standard communications path

That is, the protocol provides the mechanisms necessary for the orderly exchange of data between computing elements.

One of the primary functions of network computer communications protocols is to establish a standard communications path between the communicating computers. This communications path represents a virtual communications media dedicated to the interacting sites, and it is embodied with known desirable characteristics. It provides the physical media with a character more amenable to the interacting peer processes via the physical media intricacies. The virtual communications media, set up by the protocol, provides for the establishment of addressing mechanisms, sequencing, priority, error control, and flow control; most importantly, the setup provides for the virtual channel from the source node to the destination node(s).

The protocol provides to the users capabilities for communicating information. Or put another way, a protocol provides users with standard conventions to use in their conversations. For example, it provides the means

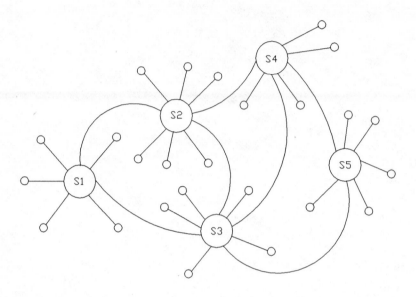

Figure 1.9   A wide area network topology.

for one device to understand what it is receiving from another through the use of a standard format. The format describes what constitutes the start of a message, any control information necessary to read the message, and an end-of-message marker. Protocols additionally set up standards for code sets to be used, speeds of transmission, formats, and meanings of control messages.

Elaboration on the representation of the data will provide another important point. Data is represented in many forms between users. Some examples are:

- Characters
- Messages
- Packets
- Files
- Jobs
- Images
- Instructions

All these data items have specific representations that must be understood on both ends of a network transfer for the item to be recognizable and useable.

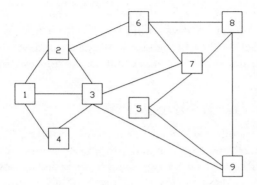

Figure 1.10   A simple irregular network.

More details on protocols, conventions, and standards will be shown in the forthcoming chapters.

1.5   Network Flow Control

Another contribution to the state of knowledge in networking that resulted from the early wide area network research was flow control. The problem addressed here was how to provide mechanisms which would prevent saturation of transmission components, loss of information, or blockage of information paths, that is, how to match the sender's rate with the receiver's rate of transmission. Early system researchers dealt with this problem with new concepts to control the flow of information. Typical of the solutions applied were techniques for preallocation of resources or feedback loops.

In preallocation schemes, traffic on the networks is minimized by requiring that communicants acquire storage space at receptors before they begin transmission. This requirement to acquire the needed storage space before transmission causes more control messages to flow within the network, but a much more bounded flow of data messages is seen. This ensures that receivers will not be swamped with more messages than they can handle.

Another well-known flow control technique involves a concept referred to as a "sliding window." This protocol provides each of the sender and receiver pairs with windows of allowable frames that a sender can send, and the receiver maintains a window of frames it can accept. By using these, they limit the amount of information they are allowed to send over the network. Details of this can be found in Tannenbaum [1981].

The final general form of flow control is called "feedback." In this form of flow control, the receiver performs some action when it cannot receive any more information. This action may be in the form of choke packets, which tell the sender to stop sending so much packet traffic, or in some other form of action that the sender would sense and act on, based on the feedback algorithm in place. Later chapters will address this issue in more detail.

1.6   Network Routing

An important requirement in early computer networks, which was caused by their irregular topology, was how to route messages. Routing messages is concerned with how to direct messages to their destinations with requirements to minimize transit delays, equalize loading on circuits as much as possible, and adapt to component failures.

In the irregular topology of early networks, routing was of the utmost importance. If a poor route is chosen, network performance falters. If a good route is chosen, the network performs up to expectations. For example, a simple irregular network is shown in Figure 1.10. If we wish to transmit a message from node 1 to node 6, many paths could be chosen. Some paths are:

- Node 1, node 2, node 3, node 7, node 8, node 6
- Node 1, node 3, node 7, node 5, node 9, node 8, node 6
- Node 1, node 4, node 3, node 9, node 8, node 6

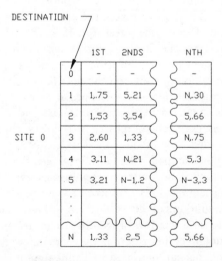

Figure 1.11   Directory routing.

- Node 1, node 3, node 7, node 6
- Node 1, node 2, node 6

It can be seen from this simple example that if we assume all link delays are equal, the best route to take would be route 5. This is because of the requirement for a message to transverse just two channels instead of the seven in one of the worst cases. Choosing a route for a message to traverse requires that the network possess intelligence in the form of routing algorithms and link-status information.

Two major classes of routing exist; they are static and dynamic. Static (or nonadaptive) routing refers to routing that is performed once during the network-up period. The major form of this algorithm is called directory routing. This algorithm consists of a fixed table that contains routing information for destinations with 1 to N choices for possible paths and probabilities, or weights, to be used in determining which path to use (see Figure 1.11).

When a message is to be sent to a site, say site 2, the routing algorithm looks at the table in location 2 and then generates a probability between 0 and 0.99. If the number is greater than 0.66, it chooses path N; if it is 0.53 or less, it chooses path 1, and so on. It is not the best algorithm for computing minimum route delays, but it does work.

The other form of routing, called "dynamic" or "adaptive," has a much wider range of algorithms that have been developed. They include:

- Flooding
- Centralized
- Isolated
- Delta
- Distributed

Flooding takes in a message and sends it out on every free link except the original receiver. This algorithm causes a lot of extra traffic over the network, but by exhaustive search it finds the best route. It also wastes large volumes of link capacity and requires nodes to remove messages they hear again.

Centralized routing is a dynamic version of the static algorithm. In centralized routing, a central site is selected as the routing control center. Periodically, each of the network nodes sends status to routing central on its known environment (uplinks, capacities, utilizations, etc.). This information is collected and collated by routing central, which then recomputes optimal routes from every node to every other node. These new routing tables are then distributed out to the remote sites. This will provide some level of resiliency to failures, though it still does not provide quick response to failures or peak load conditions.

Another form of adaptive routing is isolated routing. Algorithms that fall into this category make their routing decisions based on information they have gathered themselves. One example of an algorithm of this type is the hot potato algorithm. This algorithm attempts to get rid of incoming messages it is handling for others as fast as possible. This is accomplished by selecting the shortest output queue and putting the message out on that link. Other algorithms of this class include delta route (in which path costs are determined and distributed for routing use) and backward learning (in which information about where packets have been is used to glean routing information). More will be said later about these algorithms. Additional information may be found in Tannenbaum [1981].

Distributed routing algorithms do not have a central host from which it can condense network information. Instead, the neighbors are used. Routing information is passed to the nearest neighbors who, in turn, adjust this information based on their knowledge and pass this on to their nearest neighbor and so on. Details can be found in Tannenbaum [1981].

1.7   Network Performance Analysis

As the development of networking progressed, so did the science of evaluating networks using mathmatical means. As more nodes were added to networks, it became apparent that a means to assess the impact of growth on the network's performance was needed. Typically, the measures of highest interest in the early systems were delay, throughput, cost, and reliability. These in turn could be applied to solutions for:

- Line capacity assignment
- Flow assignment to lines
- Flow and capacity assignment
- Topology, flow, and capacity assignment

There are some excellent examples of these problems and their solutions in Schwartz [1977] and Kleinrock [1975a and 6]. Further details on network performance analysis for local area networks will be provided in Chapter 6.

1.8   Conception of LANs

The development of the early networks provided the seed for the inception of LANs. That is, once the concept of the wide area network was accepted and it proved its worth, developers began to see the need to provide higher-speed services (similar to those seen in the wide area network) to locally clustered groups of users. Additionally, pressure was exerted by users of local computer sites for more services than were available on a single site. The evolution from central computers and wide area networks was fed by

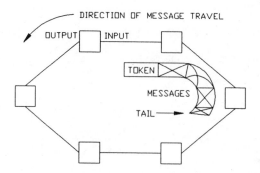

Figure 1.12 The ring topology.

the increased availability of high-performance, low-cost hardware and the technology developed in wide area networks for communications.

LANs have provided the bridge between a single computer and the corporate system. That is, LANs were initially conceived to provide interconnection of computing assets available at one site (building, cluster of buildings, etc.). LANs provide a high data rate, low-cost communications media for these machines. The low cost is in relation to wide area networks in which minicomputers are used for network interconnects. In LANs the interconnects require little extra hardware along with some associated software. The geographic characteristic of local area networks lend themselves to the use of inexpensive media. For example, a simple twisted pair can be used to support point-to-point or broadcast communications with data rates of 1 to 10 megabits/second (Mbps) ranging in distance from 1 to 10 kilometers (km).

Typical of this media is the use of baseband signaling to transmit the digital signals directly on the medium instead of with the modulation techniques required on long-haul networks.

Early local area network researchers focused their efforts on developing the technology for communications within the LAN environment. Included in this were topology and connectivity research, control protocol, and addressing research. The major topologies researched for LANs were the ring, bus, and star configurations. The ring topology connects nodes together with a path that travels from node to node, ultimately returning back to the originator. The link goes only from a single source to a single destination. Each node has an input link and an output link (see Figure 1.12).

Control in local area network rings is typically achieved by using a rotating token (a special character string indicating the head of the message

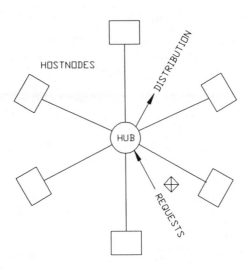

Figure 1.13 The star topology.

train). When the token is received into an interface unit, it can insert its message into the train before the tail indicator.

The star topology is configured as a central hub with all nodes hung from it (see Figure 1.13). The central hub performs all routing of messages between sites. Control of the media is performed by the active star, which takes in requests for transmission, determines if it can do it, and then performs the linkup to the destination. The linkup can be either circuit switched, packet switched, or message switched based on the active star's technology and protocol used.

The final major topology is the bus structure. In this topology, nodes are strung on a global bus (see Figure 1.14). Communications are performed by the acquisition of the media and by the transmission of the information to the designated site(s).The acquisition process in this architecture has many forms; it could be performed via a slotted token scheme (HXDP), or a rotating token (sent from host to host), via contention (in which all vie for control through some interactive mechanism), or by a centralized host that accepts requests and grants service based on some selection algorithm.

The major research issues addressed during these early studies addressed what media was appropriate for the topology (twisted pair, coaxial cable, optical fiber, radio, etc.), what types of control protocols could be implemented using the topology and media (polling, daisychaining, contention, etc.), and how to name and address sites on the network.

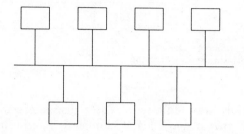

Figure 1.14   The bus structure topology.

Naming and addressing usually was performed by a combination of process designator and a site, or host, designator. Many used logical designators, which were then turned into an address with a physical process identifier part and a node address part (see Figure 1.15).

Once LAN researchers had a good handle on communications technology (topology, protocol, addressing) for LANs, they began to more strongly aim their efforts at providing a higher level of control and services to users. This represented the trend toward loosely coupled operating system environments and resource-sharing services for the LANs (the office automation environment). The goal was to share mostly data among the users of the networks. This provision required cooperating operating systems and information management software. Therefore, the efforts were directed into the development of these services. The initial thrust in these areas, though, led to further avenues—into fully integrated environments. That is, users began to request further services, requiring tighter synchronization and cooperation among the network resources. The avenue is leading into tightly coupled, distributed processing environments controlled via a unified distributed operating system [Fortier, 1986].

Beyond these highly integrated, high-speed local area networks are interconnections of many networks into metropolitan networks, national networks, and, ultimately, global networks providing various levels of service to users (see Figure 1.16).

1.9   Book Summary

The remainder of this text covers the various aspects addressed in Chapter 1 in much greater detail. Part 2 addresses the basics of communications technology. Specifically, this part covers elements of digital communications, transmission rates and drivers of same, and modulation techniques used. Specific coverage of broadband transmission media technology and

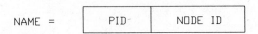

NAME = | PID | NODE ID |

Figure 1.15 Naming and addressing.

fiber technology is also addressed. These discussions are followed by a presentation of error management techniques. Specifically, this looks at techniques for linear and cyclic coding technology.

Part 3 expands on the presentation of Part 2 by looking into topologies used in connecting components into LANs. In particular, the major classes of LAN techniques—ring, bus, star, and mesh topologies—are covered in terms of characteristics, technology, and operations for each.

Beyond these basic topological considerations, this part examines topology characteristics and how these can be matched to system requirements and aid in systems design and specification. This discussion directly leads into examinations of techniques for automatically generating topologies from requirements and the analysis of these topologies in terms of reliability, availability, capacity, performance, and recoverability.

The goal of Part 4 is to address control of local area network communications and standards related to the same. In particular, this part addresses aspects of control theory for LANs, addressing, and routing flow control. These are addressed in generic form, then specifically in terms of

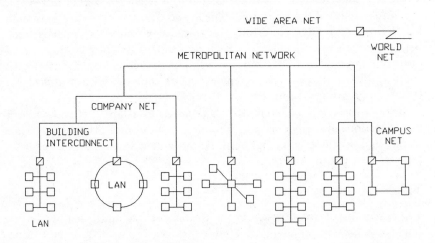

Figure 1.16 Interconnected networks.

the IEEE 802 standards committee. This is followed up by discussions on other standards work such as FDDI, Safenet, and SAE LAE-9B. Typical devices available that implement these standards are also addressed.

Part 5 presents the basics of security for LANs and the technology and techniques applied to this problem. In particular, this part introduces the concept of security, why it is needed, and the applications it supports. This discussion flows into a presentation of basic security measures such as physically protected environments and protection methods for software. These are best done before purchase to determine if the LAN can meet requirements and after purchase to evaluate how well it truly meets the needs for which it was acquired.

Part 6, on performance evaluation, provides a tool to look at how to best evolve the system we have now and what this evolution does to all aspects of operation. In particular, this part looks at techniques for analysis including analytical techniques, simulation techniques, and operational analysis techniques presently in use to evaluate systems performance. Specifically geared to networks, this evaluation process addresses the metrics used to evaluate these systems and their particular definitions. These test points are looked at and discussed in terms of their importance to overall network assessment.

Part 7 places major emphasis on addressing overall network management issues, theory, and technologies. Specifically, this part examines the aspects of centralized versus distributed control concepts associated with physical and logical decentralization and resource management issues. Details of decentralization control algorithms are presented followed by examples to solidify concepts. The part closes by introducing and examining the computational paradigm from a server abstraction model into the three basic models of operating systems structure: the procedure, message, and object-based paradigms.

Part 8 examines the state of a variety of LANs available for use today. The examination addresses the features that make the LAN unique, along with details of communications protocol, available devices, topology, performance characteristics, software support, interfacing requirements, and application discussions.

1.10   Summary

The goal of this chapter was to provide a high-level vista of the concepts associated with LANs. This coverage included definition of technologies associated with organizational issues. The goal was to bring the reader into an overall understanding of the concept of LANs in order to make the transition to the other chapters much cleaner.

1.11   References

Fortier, P. J., *Design of Distributed Operating Systems: Theory and Concepts*, Intertext, Inc., McGraw-Hill, New York, 1986.

Kleinrock, L., *Queueing Sytems: Vol. I, Theory*, John Wiley & Sons, 1975a.

Kleinrock, L., *Queueing Sytems: Vol. II, Computer Applications*, John Wiley & Sons, 1975b.

Schwartz, M., *Computer Communications in Network Design*, Prentice Hall, Englewood Cliffs, NJ. 1977.

Tannenbaum A., *Computer Networks*, Prentice-Hall, Englewood Cliffs, NJ, 1981.

2. Why Local Area Networks?

2.1 Needs Served

If you were to query every user who presently has a LAN installed why it was installed, you would receive a wide variety of reasons. Upon detailed examination, all these reasons can be categorized into roughly three major areas:

- Organizational
- Financial
- Technical

2.1.1 Organizational Benefits

These three major categories can be additionally broken down into a few trends, as will be seen. Organizational reasons for wanting to acquire and install a network fall into one or more of the following:

- Coordination
- Centralization
- Decentralization
- Data and program sharing

Coordination in business moves is essential to properly time these actions. Typically, coordination activities mean meetings and frequent correspondence. To provide better means to synchronize these activities, local area networks were brought into use. Coordination also implies the knowledge of one individual's action so as to direct another's. For example, if

one plant is producing item x and another is also producing that item, it
would be to their advantage to coordinate the activities associated with the
two facilities to economize efforts and maximize the value of the company.
LANs provide a means for managers, schedulers, workers, etc., to quickly
obtain up-to-date information to use in the coordination of their business
activities.

Centralization of operation is another operational means for incorporating LANs into the computing environment. Many organizations wish
to control operations from a central site. If the business is physically dispersed throughout some geographical area, performing this central function
will require that the remote sites periodically dump the contents of their
operational database into the central site for processing and action. Doing
this may require that the remote sites dump files to tapes and have them
brought to the central site or that they phone in the information using a
modem to dump the data into a file. Once the data is received at the central site, processing is performed based on the job to be done, for example,
payroll, accounts receivable, accounts payable, inventory, production, etc.

When the central site has completed its function, new data files and
management orders must be reissued to the remote sites for continued use.
By incorporating a network into such an environment, the company can
have its centralization but with a much more efficient means to collect and
distribute information, programs, etc.

Another organizational objective may be to disperse or to distribute
operations. A company may have five major departments (engineering, research, production, sales, and employment), each with its own function; but
because of dispersion of the facilities, each has its own autonomous computing, though they need information facilities with copies of each major
process from all the sites to properly perform their tasks (see Figure 2.1).
In an old environment, that is, one without a network, the departments
would rely on hand-carried hardcopy or on telephone means to distribute
information to and between the sites. To provide for better interaction
while keeping their autonomy, a local area network is used. This network
provides a means to further separate, or specialize, the computing sites
while maintaining their ability to be cognizant of the others' states. For
example, instead of having a piece of each major job (process) on each site's
machine, we could specialize each site's system to its major function; for
example, a sales site would allow access to the others during the few times
they required access to this function.

The last major organizational reason for including a network into the
data processing arena is to provide for the sharing of programs and data
between the remote sites. This is significant when we think about the need
for specialized devices or programs that require a specific machine. Instead

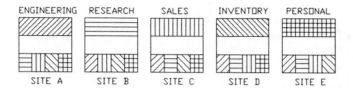

Figure 2.1   Distributed operations.

of going to the next building, finding a free terminal, and doing our job, we simply log onto the other machine via the network, perform our task, and then exit the system back to our own machine. This sharing of the programs on one machine with another is important when we consider the volume of software that is licensed for use on one machine. This machine must be used to perform the specific task. No other machine is legally able to do the job. LANs provide a means for users to easily ship their data down to the proper machine, let it be processed, and later receive the processed information back. Data sharing is essential in all aspects of business, and LANs provide for easier mechanisms for various machines to share the corporate information they process and manage.

2.1.2   Financial Benefits

A second major driver of why organizations (political, economic, educational, business, military, etc.) select and use LANs is economics or finance. For small companies who presently do not own computers, the attachment to a LAN for local computer resource sharing is a very cost-effective means to acquire just the needed computing at only the cost of a terminal, interface unit, and usage charges. Additionally, if you have an organization with computers that need larger machines (more computing cycles), connecting to a local area network resource-sharing network can cheaply provide access to possibly a super computer, or tons of machines, to enhance your computing capability. Again, you only pay for what you uses.

Another good cost advantage of a LAN connection is for the organization that wants computing power but does not want to operate a computer center. A LAN resource-sharing network will provide all the services it requires but without the headaches of owning, operating, and maintaining the computing resources. These represent some very important organizational cost drives for linking to LANs for the acquisition of computing resources.

Another group of cost-related reasons for acquiring a local area network for a company that already owns computers is:

- Consolidation
- Data exchange
- Backup
- Distributed processing
- Specialization
- Sale of services

Consolidation refers to the organization's ability via the network to consolidate the financial aspects of running the system. Consolidation via the network provides a means to better manage and monitor operations while providing better service to users. The network provides a means for distributed users to easily and inexpensively communicate information to one another. The network additionally supplies a means to increase the reliability of the information through the use of backups. Information can be backed up in real time providing alternative sources of information when failures affect a site's ability to get to wanted information.

The network provides more computing resources to each individual than was previously available at that site. A user at site A can use the resources at all other sites, thereby increasing performance capability drastically. This is the notion of distributed processing.

An organization, by linking up all its machines into a cohesive network, can provide more specialized optimal services to users. This can be done, for example, by consolidating all of a particular function at one site and allowing the other sites to use this site as the point to provide the service. For example, accounting, sales, inventory control, personnel, etc., could each have a dedicated machine instead having them all reside at each site. This provides an avenue for consolidation of personnel at each site. With centralization and specialization, possibly less of each type of job category would be needed.

Finally, another important financial reason for an organization that owns many computers to link up into a local area network is to sell their excess computing power to others who cannot afford to own their own systems. The owners can become computer service vendors providing machine cycles as a saleable commodity.

2.1.3   Technical Benefits

As there are many financial and organizational reasons for linking computers into local area networks, there are also many technical factors that add fuel to the argument for purchasing, designing, and installing a LAN into one's computing environment. The technical drivers seen as common reasons for migrating to local area networks include:

- Faster turnaround
- Higher availability
- More potential growth
- Load balancing

Organizations are always looking for ways to more efficiently and effectively perform their data processing tasks. This is because of the time value associated with getting information to the end sources in real time. This, in turn, permits better control of organizations and provides sufficient time to react to information. LANs provide for this more real-time distribution and access to information which in turn provides the previously indicated features.

Additionally, from an efficiency and productivity view, faster turnaround of processing jobs will better serve organizational goals of increasing their measured performance. A LAN provides an organization with greater integrated online computing capacity without purchasing new computing assets, thereby providing for the ability to increase the turnaround time of jobs.

Another technical driver for connecting an organization's computing assets to a network is availability. By connecting the organization's computing resources (terminals, workstations, PCs, minicomputers, tape units, disk drives, etc.) to the network along with the proper operating system services, users have a higher availability of these assets. That is, if they cannot get to one machine, they have the option of many others that they can use. Failure of one device does not bring all computing to a standstill; others can pick up the slack, thereby providing a higher degree of reliable service to the user community.

A LAN also provides a means for the growth of computing resources as needed for all instead of one site at a time. For example, in a traditional organization with five sites, each with its own computing resources, if all need to increase their processing capacity, each of the five sites will need an additional computing engine that costs 5 times the cost of one machine, whereas in a computing environment connecting together all five sites by a LAN, increasing the capacity may only require the addition of one computer, a savings of four machines. If the company wished to spend the same amount, five machines could be added, allowing each site to view an increase of five machines rather than one.

A side issue intertwined in all of these technical reasons for a LAN is one of efficiency. If the same company discussed above has five sites with only two heavily loaded and the the others slightly used, it is not optimizing its resource usage. In fact, the company is wasting money by having three sites only slightly used. A LAN provides the capability to more evenly balance the processing load onto all the machines, thereby increasing throughput,

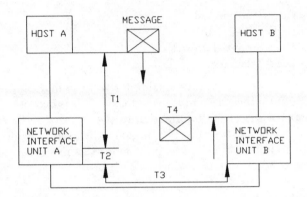

Figure 2.2   Timeliness of communications.

lowering turnaround time, and at the same time more cost effectively using the computing resources. These represent but a few of the myriad motives for organizations migrating toward local area networks.

Once an organization has decided it wants to either purchase, develop, or link into a local area network, it must review and analyze its objectives for getting online. The major objectives deal with performance, service, applications, and cost effectiveness of the local area network.

Performance objectives deal with the organization's goals for the operational level that the local area network must provide. The main measures looked at in performance objectives for LANS are timeliness of communications and services provided.

The timeliness of communications has two major components, delay and throughput. Delay is defined as the time between the presentation of a message for transmission and the reception of the first bit. This measure has many components including delay associated with acquiring the network media for transfer, queuing delay waiting for each turn to attempt to acquire the media, propagation speed down the media from the source to the sink node (see Figure 2.2). As was stated before, delay has three main parts:

- Queuing
- Contention
- Transmission

The queuing delay is computed from the time the message is presented to the interface unit for transmission until it is removed for active acquisition of the media.

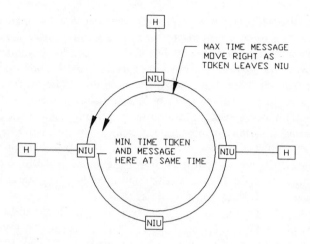

Figure 2.3   Contention.

Contention or acquisition delay is comprised of the time from which you become the next in line at your host to be transferred until you actually win use of the media. For example, in a ring architecture, this delay could range from a low of zero (if the token arrives at your node at the same time you become available for acquisition of the link) to a maximum of an entire sequencing through all the other hosts (see Figure 2.3).

The last component of delay is the physical propagation time down the media (the transmission time). This time is dependent on the technology used; for example, the coaxial cable has transmission delays in the order of 0.01 s and satellites are the in the range of 0.25 s or greater. The propagation delay is computed as the time the first bit is placed on the physical transfer media until it is received at the destination.

The important aspect of performance in terms of delay from a user's perspective is the aggregate time. User applications will drive the need for more expensive media and protocols which minimize the delay component. For example, if users of the LAN want near real-time responsiveness, they will need a LAN with low overall delay. This will allow the users to react to data and initiate proper responses as if they were directly physically connected to the device under control. Additionally, for example, the LAN, if it provides low delay, can support interactive applications running between machines or distributed database inquiry and response.

The second component of the timeliness of communications measure is throughput. Throughput deals with the number of bits that can be clocked and sent over the channel per second. That is, it represents the effective traffic rate in bits per second over the media. Throughput is equal to the number of bits sent over the link beginning after time T2 until the entire message is received at T4. As an example to illustrate this for an Ethernet-type system, the clocking rate is 1 to 10 Mpbs. What this means is that the clocking and receiving capability of the media and processors can provide up to this number of bits transferred from source to sink once the first bit is received. Throughput is an important measure in terms of the actual information content that can be transmitted. For example, if the system under consideration to add a LAN to has requirements for high information transfers (database files for example), it would be beneficial to have high throughput even at the expense of having high delay in initiating and receiving the start of the message.

Delay and throughput are measures that must be addressed in the selection of a LAN, and they must be weighed against their cost versus performance in meeting the users requirements. Low delay is needed when a LAN is going to use many short messages in its operation, whereas high throughput requires large messages to minimize overhead and minimize information flow.

2.2   Services

The next feature that a new, potential user of a LAN must examine before making a selection is services provided. The service measure examines the capabilities that the LAN provides in data representation, data transfer, and network characteristics.

2.2.1   Data Representation

Before deciding which LAN to use, a user must be sure that its operational capabilities match the devices to be connected to it. In data representation, the services one must be cognizant of in selecting the LAN are the information codes supported, the information formats, and content. Codes refer to the representation by which information will be interpreted. For example, the network may support limited data representation such as ASCII or EBCIDIC or it may be unstructured and accept binary transitions with no interpretation, leaving it up to the users to do this task.

Format in data representations refers to how the data is interpreted; for example, does the data have a fixed length and fixed field to describe it, or it is unstructured, having no restrictions on size, etc?

The final variable in data representation to consider is content. What this refers to is how the network delivers the information. Does it provide all conversions and interpret the data, or does it transfer it in a transparent fashion as if it was a direct point-to-point link with no protocol?

2.2.2   Data Transfer

The second major variable one must examine when looking into the acquisition of a network is data transfer. This measure encompasses features such as error control, addressing, priority, and security of the network. These all address the issues in getting data from one point to another.

Error control is a system service that provides either a bare wire (no error control) or up to fully guaranteed services. Techniques used include parity bits, checksums, encoding, and decoding schemes to add correctability to words, error detection, and retransmission for guarantee of correct reception. Another important variable in data transfer is the addressing capability supported. That is, if the network forces users to know physical addresses of nodes and processes on them, this greatly restricts the flexibility of users to port code or change operations easily. Additionally, the addressing modes supported are extremely important. For example, if the network only supports one-to-one linkage, a multiported broadcast-type message must be sent. The sender would have to form multiple messages (one for each node in the network for broadcast) and send them serial to the receptors. This adds extra overhead to operations. If broadcasts and multipoint messages are common in any application, a network with only point-to-point addressing will be a poor choice.

Once the addressing is known, the next important variable is priority support. For real-time systems, the ability to override the sequential communications scheduling service is essential in order to guarantee service to system-critical messages. When a high-priority condition arises, it is essential that the information associated with it is dispersed in a timely fashion. A LAN with priorities and preemption built in can provide such services, whereas one without priority built in can only provide service in the order of arrival—not an optimal condition for users who require such a feature.

A final consideration for data transfer is the security of the communications. If the network is handling company proprietary information, we do not want the competition to be able to get into the network and read our data files or intercept messages in transit. Security within a network can be as simple as once you get in, everything is accessible, or as complicated as multiple levels of access authorization and message scrambling and descrambling. The depth of the services provided will be dependent on what the users are willing to pay for. Security is not cheap. More will be said on this issue in Part 5.

A final component of data representation in determining which LAN to acquire deals with network characteristics and services. This measure of network performance uses information on levels of service in analyzing a LAN's capability for an application. Types of services within this measure include:

- Class of communication service
  a. First come, first served
  b. Prioritized
  c. Fairness
  d. Guaranteed
- Acknowledged transmissions
- Guaranteed transmissions
- Traffic analysis
- Dynamic reforming

These measures look at the additional services added to a LAN that provide users with a transparent system. That is, these provide the users with a view of a virtual, large uniprocessor computer system with all its capacity available to them. These services provide the network user with tailored operations for access, reliability, and management. The network is brought into the system environments; instead of being a peripheral service, it becomes an integral and controllable part.

2.2.3   Network Characteristics

The third component of the selection process for determining which type of LAN is applicable for our needs is applications support. It is necessary to define what applications will operate on the future network; this in turn will help drive the selection process.

The selector or designer of the LAN must address questions dealing with the potential users' current computer resources and applications. The issues deal with saving initial investments while not limiting future growth. The questions to examine include:

- Must existing hardware be supported?
- Must existing software be supported?
- Must existing protocol be included?
- Must existing interfaces be supported?

However, this is only a partial list. Beyond these readily available questions are a number that more clearly deal with issues of supporting present applications. The applications envisioned for a computer system will greatly affect the resources and services necessary to realize an effective implementation. For example, if the major function is video information transfer, the LAN should be a video-grade media with services directed to supporting video signal transfers. Applications include:

- Interactive terminals (point of sale, etc.)
- Query and response (information services)
- Data entry (accounting, etc.)

- Message processing (electronic mail)
- Financial processing (banking machines, electronic transfer of funds)
- Information banks (distributed database)
- Real-time command and control (robotics, nuclear power station)
- Remote job entry
- Resource sharing

Not only must the selection of a LAN take the present applications into account, but it also must be cognizant of trends and potential future applications which will be applied to the network environment. The nature of these applications and their possibly unique processing requirements will drive LAN technology that must be put to use in servicing the needs properly.

The final issue in the selection of a LAN is the cost factor. This measure implies the obvious: Does this LAN meet our needs while not costing us an arm and a leg? Measures examined at this level deal with cost versus performance.

A LAN designer must look at the present computing situation and assess whether the addition of the LAN will pay for itself; that is, will the cost of the LAN be offset by the reduced cost of intersite data transfer compared to the old way of transfer (carrying tapes, mail). Another way of viewing cost is: Does the addition of a LAN increase our efficiency? The important views to examine are based on relative costs (less than we pay now), absolute costs (the LAN cost x, the nine couriers now cost y), and incremental cost (linking into this LAN will cost us X dollars per month versus our old outlay of Y dollars per month).

Additionally, the LAN selector or designer must examine other measures such as the cost of:

- Service
- Adding users
- Increasing message flow
- Adding application
- Adding new locations
- System operations
- Installation

The analysis of these costs takes the form of examining short-term costs over the long-term return based on the costs, as well as determining the incremental or average costs associated with the LAN's operations. The LAN selector or design must formulate tradeoff or performance assessment criteria upon which to select the best system for the dollar. All of these measures must be incorporated into a cost model so that the proper LAN (performance and cost) can be selected.

2.3   Summary

This chapter provided insight as to why local area networks evolved as well as reasons why they are used by enterprises. As was shown, the reasons for selecting a network are varied as are their uses. Companies select local area networks mainly to provide a better means to access and share information and resources. The selection is performed using the organization's posulated needs as the requirement's source. These requirements in turn provide a network administrator with the metrics to use in selecting a LAN that best meets the needs of the company. The focus of this selection process and the driving forces behind it were described in this chapter.

3. Information Industry LAN Users

Local area networks have opened up an entire new arena for information management. As organizations have grown, and their appetite for timely information along with them, they have pushed for means to more effectively acquire and use information. Companies today need to have up-to-date information to judge the market and make business decisions. The victor in business today is typically the one with the most up-to-date information to base business moves on. LANs have aided in and fed the voracious growth in information flow and usage. The evolution of LANs from simple connections of multiple machines into metropolitan networks has provided unending information and capability to the user willing to determine new applications for its use. Industries have grown out of the LAN technologies' emergence, and continued growth is projected into the future.

The users and uses of LANs are many and very diversified. LANs can be found in the home, office, hospital, factory, school, underwater, and in space. The possibilities are limitless.

As can be seen from the brief list above, LANs are found in most environments and organizations today. If a company does not have one now, it is probably thinking about one for the near future. All facets of civilization use LANs, as will be seen.

3.1   LANs in the Government

The government utilizes local area networks in many aspects of management and technology. The major categories where LANs can be found are:

- Military
- Domestic service

● Controls

The military utilizes LANs in a wide range of applications from resource networks to life-critical tactical real-time networks. Typical of the military use of networks for shore-based facilities are:

- Information network
- Resource network
- Trainers
- Test beds
- Facility linkage
- Single site
- Multiple sites

Information networks provide a means to link up a site's mainframes into a single large database system with information available to users with the proper level of access. This provides, for example, the ability to query the central libraries' databases to determine if information on a particular topic can be found at this site or another. It could be used by management to integrate the knowledge of all departments within a facility to glean out a total site profile. Additional use of the LAN as an informational network is for transfer of reports, graphic presentations, mail memoranda, and notices,

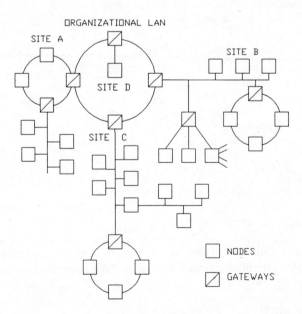

Figure 3.1   Information network for organization.

to name a few. The information network provides the means to connect an entire organization versus a building or laboratory. It represents the point used to link multiple subnets together. The media for integrating the entire organization's computing facilities is found in Figure 3.1.

The goal of the information network is to make available to those with the need to know all the information known to the organization.

A resource network, on the other hand, provides to the organization access to all its computing resources from all others. Typically, the type of services provided here are remote log-on and operation of programs and data on other machines. This class of service would usually be limited to a single site and typically a single building, though there is no real limitation other than turnaround time. Many of the government research and development laboratories possess networks of this type to allow researchers access to limitless computing power in performing studies. Such networks provide a wide range of devices to users in performing their tasks. For example, if a user on a VAX machine wishes to execute a computationally expensive simulation task, he would ship it to a specialized device such as a CRAY for its powerful computing capacity (VAX is a trademark of Digital Equipment Corporation; CRAY is a trademark of the CRAY Computer Company), instead of bringing his local machine to a halt. The CRAY can better perform the wanted application and do so within a shorter period of time.

A significant need exists on shore-based military facities for training. Training facilities provide for realistic conditions without the expense of utilizing the real hardware under real situations. Many trainers are comprised of suites of hardware linked together via LANs (Figure 3.2).

The use of a LAN allows for a single event simulator and controller to provide the stimulus for the multiple training stations. It provides a vehicle for setting up team training and keeping all the sites and users linked up with the situation being modeled.

As a research and development tool, LANs provides test beds for examining the gain from connecting varying devices together into a real-time computing facility. This provides, for example, a way to easily test the use of different graphics devices, processors, storage devices, or sensors in a wide range of configurations to get an optimal mix, or to study the concepts in distributed computing such as programming languages, algorithms, distributed operating systems, or distributed data base management, etc.

Finally LANs provide the military organization with a means for link-up of the computing resources at its site or at other sites, along with any of the aforementioned or unspecified reasons.

A more interesting use of LANs by the military is found in their military hardware. LANs can be found on board surface ships (AEGIS), submarines

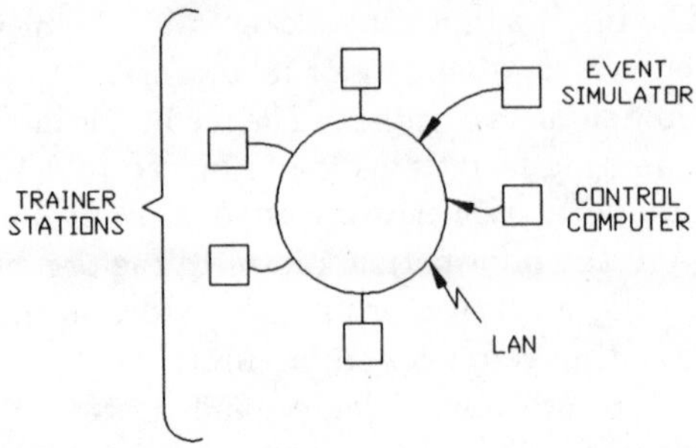

TRAINER
STATIONS

EVENT
SIMULATOR

CONTROL
COMPUTER

LAN

Figure 3.2   Land-based training facility.

(BSY-1), aircraft, space vehicles, armored vehicles, ground stations (missiles), and command and control hierarchies.

The variety of topologies span the spectrum as well as the sophistication. LANs within these systems have three major classes of function or processing, namely,

- Interactive
- Background
- Real-time

The real-time component provides the interface between the real-world system and the LAN-controlled environment. On a ship, this component is the sensor and real-time controllers. These devices accept sensor information (radar, sonar, etc.) and distribute this to the various processing sources to be examined, deciphered, and reduced into information that can be utilized within the system. LANs at this level of a system must be high speed and event schedulable. This implies that the network must be some form of contention-based system that can readily act upon specific stimulus and provide service (network transmission) to the highest valued event and process. Networks being built or in service for such uses are typically wire based and bus structured.

The background component provides the backbone processing for the systems. It takes reduced information from the real-time component and performs various background processing tasks like pattern recognition, correlation, state analysis, etc.; on the other side they also support the interactive tasks which will periodically, or on event, extract out the state of the running process or initiate some new process. The networks seen at this level are either star based, mesh based, ring, or bus structured. They are supported by a few but powerful computing components with lots of storage capacity.

The interactive component represents the end user graphics input/output devices. These devices are either dumb terminal-type devices or high powered workstations. The trend is to move more into the latter technology. The workstations will be configured to run interactive software almost entirely in a stand-alone mode, only going outside to kick off processes and extract or receive information.

Networks for these devices need to be high speed, but do not need to be as robust a protocol. Typically, either bus or rings are used at this level.

3.1.1   Domestic Services

We all know of the problems with the IRS computers of late. They had software problems that were causing delays in processing. The IRS, as well as many other government service organizations, makes phenomenal use of computers in performing their information-processing tasks. The many government agencies such as social security, IRS, banking, forestry, Medicaid, census, etc., utilize computing to effectively perform their tasks. The major functions of these machines is in data processing, word processing, forms production, and file manipulation. The volume of data that needs to be crunched at each of these organizations, as well as the need for cross-correlation of data, cries out for networking. In some cases the government machines are linked together to form their tasks, while in others, only plans exist. The most significant use of LANs in these organizations to date is to link local site machines together to provide for more readily accessible information and processing capacity.

3.1.2   Controls

The "long arm of the law" and the executive level of government comprise the controls portion. The goals at this level are to share information in performing their tasks. Cross correlation is data matching of findings to known information, collecting statistics, or collecting evidence. All of these activities are involved with the manipulation of data. The data is collected and stored in many sites world wide, nationwide, organizationwide, and needs to be acquired for use by any and all agencies in performing its controls function.

The users of this collection of data utilize computers connected via networks to provide the necessary services. Though the systems are not as automated as they would like, users include:

- Drug enforcement agencies
- Federal Bureau of Investigation

- Defense Intelligence Service
- National Security Agency
- Central Intelligence Agency

The executive branch of the government utilizes computers to analyze information on defense, economic, and social issues. Again, the suggested need is to share and be able to access as much information as possible to allow the most optimal solution to be made. LANs will, in the future, play a much greater role in linking the various governmental agencies together.

3.2   LANs in Industry

The industrial use of local area networks is no less dramatic than that of the government. Industry also, possibly even more so, has an insatiable appetite for information. LANs provide to industry many possibilities for information transfer and equipment interconnections. The business possibilities are awesome and continue to expand daily.

Major areas where networks have emerged include:

- Financial organizations
- Informational organizations
- Business organizations
- Medical organizations

The reasons for each industry to evolve into using LANs have been varied. The financial organizations went toward networks to provide more services to consumers and to streamline operating practices. Informational organizations found a means to distribute data to users more effectively and to open up more business avenues. Basic business activities, such as manufacturing, found networks conducive to more tightly integrating and controlling plant activities, thereby increasing productivity. Finally, the medical field saw LANs as a means to provide doctors with more ready access to medical data (diagnostics, donors, procedures, etc.). The common thread, though, is to move information among multiple users in a more efficient and timely fashion than was previously available.

3.2.1   Financial

Financial organizations began to embrace LANs as a necessary part of business to support a more mobile group of clients. Banks found that, through the use of computers and LANs, they could better manage multiple sites along with the people who use them. Additionally, as banks progressed in their use of networks, technology brought in new uses for the environment. Electronic transfer of funds is such an example. LANs provided a way to easily and quickly transfer funds from site to site, eliminating the need for paper checks and the additional processing overhead associated with them.

The advent of banking machines and the national networks such as CIR-RUS all have their existence due to LANs. Without LANs and the service they provide, these could not exist. Banks do not hold all the cards in the financial arena. Other important players are insurance companies, securities firms, and lenders, for example. All of these types of financial organizations have also grown up into having LANs as part of their information processing repertoire. Insurance companies rely on LANs to provide their organizations with integrated, up-to-date access to corporate information. They rely on these for access to information on accounts and investments, all necessary to make them viable business entities. The securities companies that exist all over the country use networks and LANs to provide them with accurate up-to-date market information and accounts information. The LAN provides a means for brokers to easily share information with each other, thereby potentially increasing their effectiveness. Lenders use LANs to coordinate activities among cooperative siblings and to acquire and use information on prospective consumers.

3.2.2   Informational Industry

What about the clearinghouses for information? How do they utilize this technology in their interests? This is a multi-faceted question and will be addressed in the coming paragraphs.

Informational industries cover a wide spectrum of vendors and services encompassing on-line news systems, television, books, advertisers, telephone. The thrust in their industries began migrating towards LANs due to market forces calling for more services. Television viewers wanted more services in the form of more stations. Beyond providing television viewing stations, the information services began to move in. The media provided a way to supply extra services; for example, news in the form of rotating text (newspaper in video), shopping by network video marketing surveys, etc. Beyond video, the information industry most recognized in textual form are books. This segment of the industry is also looking toward the future. The use of LANs and database technologies can provide the media for books to be accessed and read in video format.

3.2.3   Business

The business community, including manufacturing services, suppliers, and retailers, have all to some extent begun to utilize LANs in their business activities. In all cases the goals are to better utilize the information available to them in order to make more optimal business decisions.

The first inroad into business was in the office. The LAN was seen as a way to link up a corporation's manufacturers in order to better utilize the corporation's entire data bank. With the advent of intelligent terminals came a need for more integration. LANs provided the means to link the diverse information sources together. The main emphasis in this class of LAN application was management. That is, these LANs provided information for the corporate decision makers. The use of this technology migrated from the corporate managers' offices to the lower management ranks, and finally out into the other sections of the corporation. The company production organization saw a use for LANs to manage and control the manufacturing process controlled by computers. LANs were used to collect statistics on production. They are used to distribute information to remote robotic manufacturing endpoints or on a line to control and coordinate the actions of the line elements. LANs have provided a new dimension to the control of the manufacturing process. Another benefit of LANs to the manufacturing process, as well as service sectors, was to provide a capability for remote diagnostics of equipment. Health checks and fault isolation checks could be run on all sites under control of one host site on the LAN. It was inevitable once LANs found their way into manufacturing that the other levels of production support would also utilize this new media. The plant accounts, personnel, salesmen, suppliers, and retailers also began to use LANs to better control their type of information.

The plant accountants used LANs to better manage the inventory of products produced by their company. The LAN provides to them the ability to quickly and easily acquire inventory balances and orders on all products in stock at all sites linked to the network. This is a great improvement from the earlier days when such statistics would take days, even weeks, to compile together and distribute. Additionally, by the time the manual process was done, it was no longer up to date.

The sales groups also could use the same type of information over the LAN to acquire status or availability of a product and delivery time statistics, etc. This enabled them to provide a better service to their customers.

Likewise, the distributors could use a LAN in their end sales plants to keep their stock information up to date and consistent with customer demands. This is accomplished best by having the end sales points, the registers, as part of the network to provide a total view of the entire process from manufacturing to sales (Figure 3.3).

The future of LANs in business is bright. They are finding their way into more diverse applications as their value is proven. Law firms have begun to utilize computer technology and LANs to provide their law clerks the ability, from workstations on a LAN, to search a diverse set of case histories for planning defense and prosecutions for judicial cases. The potentials are enormous.

3.2.4   Medical

The medical service industry has begun to see an increase in the use of computers and also LANs. The major uses of LANs in the medical field is to share information, providing doctors quick access to large banks of data for case histories, diagnostic profiles, procedures, analysis of data, drug surveillance, and reference data. Additionally, the medical area is beginning to look at LANs and wide area nets to provide a means to simplify the billing process to insurance companies.

The future of the medical industry will be highly tuned into LANs and computer technology, as the technology matures, the applications for it will grow. LANs will be used to allow hospitals to monitor more patients more effectively using a variety of sensors and processing sites located in strategic locations in the hospital. Medical personnel will utilize computers in all aspects of their work and will share a large volume of information, increasing their ability to provide superb health care.

3.3   Educational

The educational sector of the population will also be driven to more computers, and utimately to utilizing LANs in order to provide more integrational sharing of information. Computers are found in just about every elementary school in the United States. It is only a matter of time before the schools realize that they can provide even more service to the student

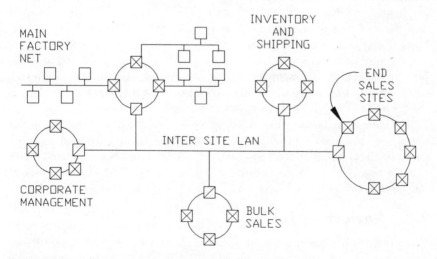

Figure 3.3   Integrated business LAN system.

population utilizing LANs. They can teach students about more integrated uses for computers, how to share information, and to communicate with others via computers.

Computers have found many more uses in the secondary educational level (high schools). High school systems teach computer usage (programming and operation) as a standard part of most curricula. In addition, many high schools have begun to introduce more up-to-date technology-oriented programs that deal with computers within the world of LANs. This tends to provide the young users with an appreciation of networking technology and its applications. Additionally, it produces users more attuned to the merits of this technology.

Where networks have really found a home is in the colleges. Most colleges in the United States have installed networks within their grounds to provide a means to link their collections of computing equipment together. The reason for the networking was to provide a means for the sharing of equipment between departmental users. Typical of such interconnections is that shown in Figure 3.4.

The major point to highlight within Figure 3.4 is the use of a ring to connect multiple sub-LANs together to form one total network. The ring could be a high-speed fiber optic link providing large block transfers with the global bus sub-LANs providing CSMA (contention-based) access to a variety of sub-elements. The mainframes provide major computing support for data processing, scientific computing, and simulation services. The minicomputers provide service to departments as either project machines or for management of student accounts. The PCs or workstations provide dedicated service to individual users (professors) for use in their applications. Finally, the concentrations provide the typical student with a view of the system. User terminals use these to acquire a system port and to interface to the computing elements within the system. University computing environments were some of the first to embrace LAN technology outside of the research and development communities.

The computer industry and university research and development components were the first to provide this technology. The first LAN came when these institutions developed the early systems, and then in an effort to provide test beds to look into future use for LANs. The previous section indicated a few uses for LANs, and I apologize if I left out your favorite.

3.4   Variety of LANs

The previous section illustrated some of the users who have been drawn into using LANs but did not stress where LANs have been found physically or the specific services provided by them. The following paragraphs will outline and describe these two issues in more detail. In particular, the

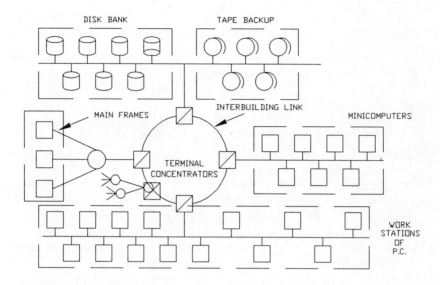

Figure 3.4   A university LAN.

coverage will indicate the breadth of environments where LANs are found followed by a discussion of services supplied by them.

3.4.1   Physical Use of LANs

Local area networks are not only for laboratories anymore. As has been seen by the drastic increase in the usage of LANs, they are appearing in just about every conceivable environment. For example, LANs have shown up in:

- Laboratories
- Offices
- Buildings
- Manufacturing sites
- Surface ships
- Subsurface ships
- Aircraft
- Spacecraft
- Oil drilling rigs
- Automobiles
- Homes
- Amusement parks

- Appliances
- Toys

These environments all exhibit some unique feature. Laboratories (computer-based) tend to be the simplest in which to install LANs. The raised computer floors exist, enabling cables to be easily run, and the distances are minimal—typically, only within a single room. LANs installed within offices tend to also be simple as a few machines are usually linked together via a simple cable-based LAN. The office LAN gets much more complicated when it must span space (i.e., rooms, floors, walls, etc.) The thrust, once this occurs, is to expand the LAN into the entire building. The easiest way to do this is when the building is being constructed. Existing structures present many complications. Cables must be fed through walls and ceilings and snaked throughout the building. If an inflexible design is chosen, growth may be impossible without more extensive cable laying.

Manufacturing sites require even more care. Due to the harsher environments found in manufacturing facitilities, LANs found in these environments require more structural engineering to protect the LAN cables from the environmental effects in place. The features found in these environments must be even more hardened for the military environments found in ships, planes, spacecraft, and land vehicles. These environments put excessive stress on components utilized in LANs and require special hard device equipment for connections and electronics.

Other environments into which LANs are finding their way include homes in the form of integrated control environments and cable TV links. LANs are even being found in appliances and toys to link multiple microprocessors together for the task being used. The emphasis on this list is to indicate the breadth of coverage LANs provide for information transfer. The differences in LANs from one application to another is in the complexity of the hardware and software and the volume of data transfer handled. They run the gamut from simple wires with simple access protocols to extensive collections of highly reliable, sophisticated hardware providing high-speed real-time interaction.

3.4.2   Services Supplied

The applications or services that LANs support are as diverse as the environments where LANs can be found. LANs basically provide one service, which is to reliably, quickly, and inexpensively transport information (no matter what the form) from one site to another site of use. The LAN provides a conduit for information to flow. The interpretation and use of this information provides the services that LAN users see and utilize.

There are basically four major classes of use that LANs have been applied to, namely:

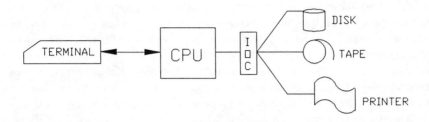

Figure 3.5   A typical central computer complex.

- Access to common resources
- Decentralized computing
- Information exchange
- Distributed control

3.4.3   Access to Common Resources

The model for describing a computer system that most people are familiar with is that of the central processing unit with a variety of I/O devices attached (Figure 3.5). This model is very limited and as computing needs have risen, so has the necessity to evolve this model. Early designers added special I/O controllers to provide more storage (disks, tapes), more printers for output, and concentrations to provide for user terminals to the CPU. The bottleneck was still the central architecture itself. To get more cycles, designers went to networking. This provided a means to put more computers at users demand. A user could, via resource-sharing protocols, log onto any machine on the network and use any peripheral device on the network. This type of architecture (Figure 3.6) is called a resource network. Typically, such networks are found in a company computing department to provide ready computing to all.

The main service provided by this class of LAN is access to remote computing power and devices. This class of service is useful for users who need a particularly expensive piece of equipment occasionally at many sites but due to the expense and usage levels cannot justify buying one for each computer and can easily justify it on an aggregate user population's needs. Another reason for a company to purchase a resource network is to provide more ready access to the computing power it already possesses. It is typical for many companies to possess multiple machines strewn about their organization for each department's needs. The problem is that one department will heavily use a machine whereas another only occasionally requires its machine's use. To better utilize the computing resources of the company,

a LAN is added to link them together. The service provided is a simple remote log-on/log-off type facility that allows a user from one site to log on to
another site and use the remote sites' computing cycles for their individual
use. This allows the users on the heavily utilized machine to offload some
of their work to the less utilized machine, thereby increasing the overall
productivity of the companies' computing assets. Resource networks tend
to be one of the most common forms of networking found in any company
with appreciable computing requirements.

3.4.4   Decentralized Computing

Once LANs had been accepted into the computing environment as an integral component, users began to find new uses for the technology. The
maturing of operating systems for distributed machines has led to another
use of distributed computers—distributed or decentralized computing. The
two terms have different meanings. In one case, the term refers to the ability
to perform one job broken up into multiple pieces on many machines simultaneously. This refers to distributed computing. Decentralized computing,
on the other hand, refers more to the ability to have multiple machines
doing their own jobs while exchanging information among one another in
support of their functions. In one case, there is tightly synchronized inter-
gration, whereas in the other there is a sharing of information; but only
through subrequests of user processes. The synchronization is performed
via checkpoints versus stop and wait-type protocols. True distributed computing, that is, the concept where thousands of machines perform one job, is
still out of the reach of present-day commercial technology. To realize such
power will require new programming languages, compilers, as well as basic
thought patterns on how to solve problems. There are many control issues
to be overcome before real distributed computing can be realized. Present-
day systems allow one to break up a job into subparts, but the breakdown
is multiple with loose synchronization between the subparts. The closest
approximation to the things to come can be found in distributed real-time
control environments.

3.4.5   Distributed Control

In distributed control systems, the concept is to have N disjointed computational sites that coordinate and converse with each other based on the
events they see over some time period. Typical systems utilizing LANs for
this technology are CAD/CAM systems for developing products, building
products, and monitoring their activities. Other applications of LANs to
real-time control include applications such as nuclear power plant control,
ship control, spacecraft control, and aircraft control platforms. LANs in
these environments are typically high speed, high data rate, and extremely

reliable. This is necessary in order for the total platform to meet its requirements for movement of data and reaction to events as they occur in the system. The job of the LAN in this environment is to provide the conduit for transfer of control and data to the disjointed computational and data entry points in the system.

3.4.6 Information Exchange

One of the most widely used applications for LANs is for information transfer. Information transfer can take many forms and can be applied in myriad ways. For example, LANs can be used to transfer video signals for use in video teleconferencing or for cable TV type applications. The can be used for transferring voice or textual information for use in a wide range of services from voice for teleconferencing, to wide distribution of video advertising. LANs in the typical office environment are used to transfer bulk files; such as sales, inventory, payroll, employee data, production, etc. from one department to the other for use in remote data computation. The information transfer can occur at varying levels of granularity based on the required endpoint computation requiring the information.

LANs provide the means to bring all elements of an enterprise logically together. The LAN is the integrating environment for the enterprise corporate information banks. It provides the elements in the system with the capability to access any piece of information known to the collection of connected components.

From this discussion, we can all see the benefits and uses that LANs provide to users. The real issue is not whether a LAN is useful, but what

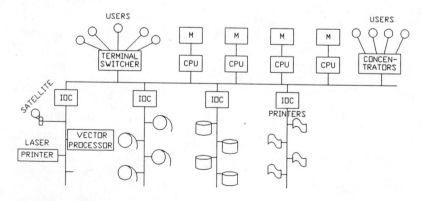

Figure 3.6   A resource network.

type of LAN and what class or classes of services do we need. These all fall under the category of LAN design or selection.

3.5 Summary

This chapter addressed the information industry and the users within it. In particular, the application of local area networking technology within this environment was addressed and clarified. The major users of local area networks were classified into six major areas:

- Governmental
- Industrial
- Educational
- Medical
- Financial
- Informational

The uses to which these users apply LANs were also broken down and were classified into four broad areas:

- Access to common resources
- Decentralized computing
- Information exchange
- Distributed control

The goal of this coverage was to provide a framework upon which we can get a better understanding of what a local area network is and how it can benefit users.

4. Designing Local Area Networks

4.1 Getting Started

Whether designing or selecting a LAN, the same steps must initially be taken:

- Determining a need
- Defining the functional requirements
- Defining acceptance tests
- Defining operational requirements

Each of these goals must be studied to determine the bounds upon which a LAN will either be selected from a set of existing plans or designed and built to more closely meet local requirements.

The major decision to make is determining if a LAN is required. Users must examine their computing needs to determine if adding another similar processor is more beneficial than putting in a larger computer. If the determination is to keep the software stable and add another like machine, a LAN is required. Once the decision to put in a LAN has been made, there must be a follow-on process to determine the physical and logical parameters it must meet.

Defining the functional requirements is comprised of three parts:

- Functional
- Performance
- Environmental

Function definition determines what the system is to do. This measure usually includes the definition of all the functions that the system must perform and their interrelationships. The interrelationships include data flow, control flow, communications, transformations, precedence, and priority. The level of detail required for these measures is dependent on whether this data is being collected for a new design or for use in selection of an existing system.

Performance requirements define how well the system must do its job. Performance measures at this level are used to define the rate or timing for a function to execute, its data processing capabilities, responsiveness to changes in conditions, precision requirements, and the accuracy limits acceptable. These measures can be directly correlated or attached to functional modules, their data, control, and interactions. Again, as in the previous discussion, the level of granularity is based on the need (i.e., whether this is for a design specification or for a selection specification.)

The final component of the functional requirements definition deals with environmental or physical constraints. Typically this phase of the functional requirements deals with the issues of what components are required for the functions (e.g., special purpose processors or peripherals or what hardware are we constrained to use. Additional factors include interfacing geographic environment, size, weight, power, etc.).

Once all these data items have been defined, a correlation and combination of the various parameters can be made to formulate the functional, performance, and environmental requirements that the LAN must support.

For example, from the data developed previously, information or aggregate data flows can be determined which can then, along with an allocation of functions to devices, yield a requirement for maximum LAN throughput requirements. The control flow transformations and communications patterns exhibited by the functions will provide the information to specify a class of protocol required (e.g., closed loop, broadcast, point to point, one too many, etc.). The type of cabling will be driven by response requirements as well as the environmental requirements previously defined. These will yield requirements for speed numbers and cable qualities to survive the environmental conditions.

The level of service necessary from users in terms of average volume of transfers and their timing requirements will provide data to specify the switching method required. For example, if there is not a need for highly reliable large transfers, maybe a datagram service would suffice. If devices need to lock onto each other for long periods of time to communicate with low delays, possibly a circuit-switching method could be used. Conversely, other arguments could be made to select packet switching or message switching to allow either many short messages to be interleaved with large ones or to have access locked out while a message is being transferred.

Each method can be directly correlated to the functional requirements previously derived.

Topology which refers to the mode of connection for the multiple devices in a network is easily derived from the environmental information or geographic dispersion of devices and their interaction requirements. For example, if one device or location is used as a clearinghouse to examine and perform some task on information, distribute this to the endpoints. Possibly a star configuration would serve the need better than a ring or bus. Likewise, a bus is typically well suited to demand-based communications in which access to the media based on my needs outweighs any fairness criteria. Rings, on the other hand, are well suited to general-purpose low-level information flow to a limited number of users.

The environmental constraints in place, such as size, weight, and power limitations, will drive the selection of components for the LAN and, therefore, also represent requirements levied on the LAN. To further refine the requirements for the LAN to be purchased or built, an organization must develop a set of operational requirements. These will typically break down into two categories—life cycle and allocated goals.

Life cycle goals typically look at long-term system qualities or attributes that must be achievable during the life of the system. These, in turn, tend to drive up the actual requirements for the LAN developed from the functional requirements. Some typical measures used here include reliability and fault tolerance, changeability, survivability, availability, maintainability, tunability, and growth. Availability, for example, refers to a measure of readiness for use that the system must exhibit based on some particular phase of operation. Accommodating such a requirement may cause the addition of excess capacity for the LAN so as to always have excess capacity available for use by periodic users.

Other measures, such as survivability and reliability, drive requirements in component count and connectivity. To increase the system's survival from hard failures or to enhance its ability to continue in the face of soft failures typically requires the addition of redundant paths (communications links), power supplies, communications hardware, and control protocol. Likewise, meeting some of the other requirements such as growth or changeability requires that the LANs components have excess addressing capacity, ports, intra-LAN communication devices, etc., which can provide the wanted effect of allowing growth and/or modification easily.

The second component of operational requirements deals with allocated goals. These tend to be more abstract measures that deal with overall system effectiveness criteria. For example, an allocated goal is that this new LAN must provide the capability to monitor and control all sensorized components in the factory and offices of a company. This often is only testable upon insertion of the device into the environment. The selecters or designers must use this goal.

The final step in developing the criteria for selecting or designing a LAN is the acceptance tests. In order to meet one's requirements, the set of disjointed measures must be brought together to formulate an acceptance test(s) to validate whether a LAN can meet the organizational needs today and in the future.

4.2   LAN Concepts

To better appreciate the need for this up-front effort requires an understanding of the makeup of LANs and how organizations view them. LANs are purchased to meet a need for communicating information among users. What makes this aspect important is what these users need the LAN for and how and where these users are distributed within their physical environments.

The concepts most important include the environment, the geographic considerations, user needs, and evolution. These concepts embrace the major reasons why LANs exist and prosper and why they will continue to be a more important piece of the future computing solutions and market.

4.2.1   The Environment

Something that drives the complexity of components for LANs is the environmental conditions that it will be exposed to. For example, if a LAN must be inserted in a space vehicle, its reliability must be extremely high, as must be its ability to withstand great pressures and extremes of temperature. Conversely, if the LAN is meant as a simple mailbox transfer media, its reliability and ruggedness can be much less stringent. The environments LANs can be found in are as varied as the LANs themselves. They have been installed in aircraft and spacecraft where reliability, tolerance to pressure, and accuracy are stringent. LANs have found their way into the ocean environment aboard ships, platforms, and just within the ocean environment. In these environments the LAN and its components must meet stringent tests to withstand temperature shifts, salinity, moisture, and differences in pressure, such as would be found from sea level down to the ocean floor.

LANs are being placed on land vehicles of all types such as cars, trucks, tanks, etc. These platforms require components that can withstand massive shock and vibration tests as well as humidity, wetness, dust, grime, dirt, and other land-based environmental conditions. This requires components well suited and designed for such conditions. This is definitely not your clean laboratory environment!

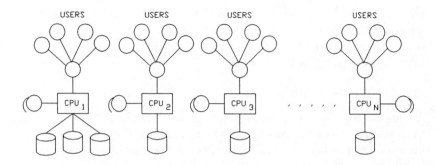

Figure 4.1   A typical data processing center.

Additionally, LANs provide interconnection of buildings which requires cable suited for installation and survival in exterior weather conditions. Finally, LANs are found within buildings, in laboratories, offices, showrooms, consumer sales, service, etc. These provide LANs with conditions a bit less stressful than the ones previously mentioned, though they nonetheless require components that can survive normal treatment.

4.2.2   Geographic

Similar to the previous discussion, geographic considerations also play an important part in the selection or design of a LAN. The media that is used is dependent on the distances involved and the location of the sites. For example, if a LAN is to be installed within one room (say a computer room), the geographic consideration is that the chosen LAN must be able to provide the wanted number of nodes and support the distances within the room. Conversely, if the LAN is over an entire complex of buildings dispersed over a few miles, the selection of LAN becomes much different. The major difference may be in media used, not in control or actual user software. The driver is the geographic dispersion combined with requirements for data transfer times that determines selection of one over the other.

As previously shown, geographically speaking, a LAN can be within some entity (a ship, plane, car, room) or between entities (rooms, in buildings, between buildings, between sites). The effect this has is on the media that can support the distance and timing requirements levied because of the geographic distances.

4.2.3   User Needs

One, if not the biggest, driver of all aspects of a LAN's requirements is the users' needs. Before we think about purchasing or building a LAN, there must be a need that can be broken down into a requirement for online information dispersal, resource sharing, distributed processing, or remote control of processes. These four classes of operations represent the major LAN job categorizations.

4.2.4   Resource Sharing

A common reason for organizations to migrate toward a LAN is to provide more resources to their data processing community. Typical data processing centers have banks of computers, which have small number of users connected to them (see Figure 4.1).

The problem is that with this configuration one computer may be heavily used and have very little reserve storage, and others may be practically idle with massive amounts of free storage. To rectify this situation, data processing centers, as well as others, have begun to migrate towards LANs and clustering (see Figure 4.2). The LAN used provides the conduit for all information to flow. Users log on to the system, acquire a computing device and any other peripherals necessary, and then perform their tasks. If necessary, they can off-load work to other machines while they continue work on this machine. This provides a means to better use all elements of an organization's data processing center. Additionally, it provides a means for the users who have large cumbersome, computationally bound jobs to

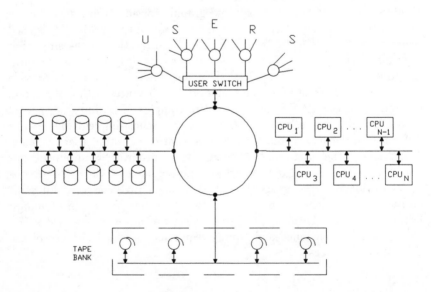

Figure 4.2   A resource network.

off-load these to other machines, providing these users with more resources so that they can do more work in the same time period.

4.2.5   Information Exchange

Organizations always have a need to exchange information within. To do this in the past required either written, typed, or electronic media that was physically carried from one place to another. This was adequate when businesses moved slowly, but it no longer holds true. To be more competitive requires the most up-to-date information. To get at information stored within a corporate data bank(s) dispersed over many sites, buildings, or areas of a building requires LANs. These LANs provided an inexpensive way to transfer information from site to site. The users of these LANs use the information exchange capabilities to send memoranda, notices, reports, sales, personnel, manufacturing, competition, and other types of information to any site on the network. This provides the organization with access to all information stored online within it.

4.2.6   Distributed Control

As computers have become more sophisticated and small, new uses have been developed. One use of computers is in controlling processes. Computers are being used more and more in the manufacturing and operations sides of industry instead of just in the office. Computers now routinely control robotic arms used in computer-aided manufacturing or in the monitoring and control of monotonous yet critical real-time control environments. Their purpose in these environments is to increase the productivity and operations of plants through automation. The problem is to provide to the operators the needed information to process and control interaction of the diverse control sites and units. The LAN provides a means to connect the various devices together, allowing them to continuously send status information to the user(s) of the system and to receive control information.

4.2.7   Distributed Processing

A final class of user requirement is to speed up overall the processing of a single job. This can be done by breaking up the job into smaller parts or stages that can be concurrently operated on. This concept provides for increasing overall job performance by shortening the elapsed time to complete. The problem before LANs came to be was that a job could not physically be broken up into pieces and peformed on other machines. The problem was one of synchronization and information transfer. LANs have provided the vehicle for researchers to begin to understand the algorithms, language, and computational aspects of distributed processing. There are many applications that naturally exhibit qualities that make them candidates for distributed processing. Applications that have many levels of iteration over some subprocess can be easily dispersed. Jobs that have related subparts that can be broken out and joined back together later on also call out for such processing.

The bottom line on all these is that, because of the users' perception of need based on one of these four classes of service, a LAN can be justified and beneficial.

4.2.8   Network Evolution

An important aspect in determining the need for a LAN and, therefore, the type of LAN to use is the perception the organization has of evolution. That is, is it important to this organization that the LAN selected have qualities that will make it easy to change, easy to add on to, or easy to interface with? These are deemed necessary so that the selected LAN can be used well into the future to service the company's projected growing needs.

4.3   Organizing a Network

Once the decision to procure or construct a LAN has been made, the organization must determine the type of LAN it wants along with specifics of its hardware and software structure.

4.3.1   Hardware Requirements

The major hardware issues to be addressed in the selection or construction of a LAN deal with the media to be used, the connector associated with the media, and interface devices to link the host machines or devices to the LAN.

4.3.2   Media

Media selection constitutes a very important aspect within the LAN development or selection process. If one chooses incorrectly, the LAN may not be able to support the offered loads or may have too many errors because of noise infusion. The proper selection of a media can limit many of these problems. The major media available are twisted pair, coaxial cable, and fiber optic. Each has its own features that make it desirable for one application over another.

4.3.3   Twisted Pair

Twisted pairs of wire represented one of the premier means to interconnect computers and other transmission devices for a long time. Twisted pair is

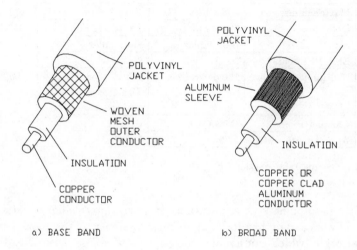

POLYVINYL
JACKET

POLYVINYL
JACKET

ALUMINUM
SLEEVE

WOVEN
MESH
OUTER
CONDUCTOR

INSULATION

INSULATION

COPPER OR
COPPER CLAD
ALUMINUM
CONDUCTOR

COPPER
CONDUCTOR

a) BASE BAND   b) BROAD BAND

Figure 4.3   Baseband and broadband cabling.

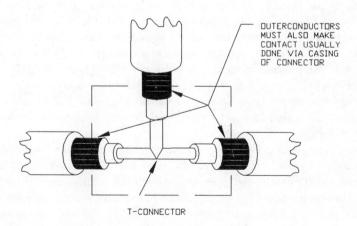

OUTERCONDUCTORS
MUST ALSO MAKE
CONTACT USUALLY
DONE VIA CASING
OF CONNECTOR

T-CONNECTOR

Figure 4.4   T-connector for coaxial cable.

	BASEBAND	BROADBAND
Maximum distance	2 km	10 to 15 km
Data rates	1 to 50 Mbps	100 to 140 Mbps
Mode	Half duplex	Full duplex
EMI/RFI imunity	50 dB	85 dB
Multidrop capability	100 devices max.	1500+ channels with 1 or more devices/channel
Channel access	CSMA/CD	FDM/FSK
Approximate cost/ft	$0.25	$0.35

Table 4.1   Coaxial cable physics.

useful in point-to-point type applications or where intermediary switches are used. Twisted pair has lost out in most systems to the more flexible coaxial cable, which can handle more signals with less noise. Readers interested in this technology should look into basic texts on transmission media.

4.3.4   Coaxial Cable

Coaxial cable has been around as a transport media for approximately 25 years. Coaxial ("coax") cable provides an inexpensive and flexible media that is usable in numerous applications and environments. Coax has shown that it can replace twisted pairs very easily and cheaply. A 1/2-inch diameter coax cable can provide the equivalent of 1500 twisted pair, providing the benefits of extensibility and growth to an organizations' LAN investment.

There are two major types of coaxial cable: baseband and broadband. Baseband is best suited to short hauls and broadband supports the long-haul connections.

The major physical difference between baseband and broadband cable is in the shielding and thickness of the core and insulations (see Table 4.1). Additionally, broadband provides better noise immunity and higher potential throughputs (see Figure 4.3). The connection to coax cables is accomplished using a passive T-connector. These simply cut and interconnect the inner conductors into a T (see Figure 4.4).

Broadband and baseband have major differences in the mode of use. Broadband coax cable operates as a set of unrelated channels. Each channel is assigned a frequency and can operate totally independent from the others. Devices all are connected to the same conduit and operate with their own protocols without concern from any requirements of others. The channels are encoded on their way in and are extracted on the receiver end using frequency division multiplexing mechanisms. Broadband systems are mostly used in point-to-point applications in which similar devices share the media. Examples are metropolitan networks connecting cable TV, information services, and future home computer resource-sharing devices.

Baseband, on the other hand, typically uses carrier sense, multiple-access techniques with collision detection to access the media. All devices on the LAN use the same protocol to access the media and use the media. The transmission is performed by frequency, amplitude, or phase modulation, and all recognize it.

The access scheme requires that all devices listen to the bus; when it is quiet, if one device has something to send, it sends it. While sending, it listens. If another device sent at the same time or within some collision period, it will hear the message garbled. This indicates a collision has occurred. The involved devices stop transmission and recompute a start time to begin accessing the link once more. These buses are limited because of the propagation delays and access rates. Networks of this class include the well-known Ethernet by Xerox Corporation, Hyper Channel from Network Systems Corporation, Net/One from Ungermann Bass, Inc., and Hyperbus also by Network Systems Corporation. All of these use the CSMA protocol and operate with between 64 to 250 users over distances from 0.4 to 1.5 km at speeds of 1 to 50 Mbps.

4.3.5   Fiber Optic Media

A very promising technology for the future is fiber optics. This media is immune to noise and can send information at remarkable speeds and densities. The concept is to send light waves over a glass media (see Figure 4.5).

Transmission using optical fiber cables is performed digitally. That is, the signals are converted from electrical pulses to light pulses. The light

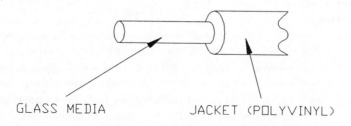

GLASS MEDIA   JACKET (POLYVINYL)

Figure 4.5   Fiber cable.

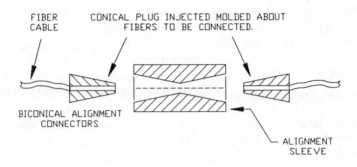

Figure 4.6   Biconical alignment connectors.

is pulsed as on and off or 1 and 0 state. This eliminates all the translations necessary in electrical cables that use frequency, amplitude, or phase modulation as the carrier. As such, it makes fiber cables look extremely attractive for digital transmission. There is a problem, though. Optical fibers do not as yet have the capability to be passively tapped into at any point. Because of this limitation, networks using fibers require either special cluster connections, passive stars, or active connections to provide a similar capability. The other option is to use optical cables in more point-to-point topologies such as a ring.

Another limitation or deficiency of optical systems at the present time is the connector losses associated with them. Optical fiber connections must be precise in order to minimize the loss of the light being transferred. This means that the connectors must align the fibers up to each other within very small tolerances and, once aligned, must keep them in place. The glass fibers must be kept clean and free of debris, or losses also will occur. Figure 4.6 illustrates an alignment scheme developed at Bell Laboratory that is referred to as a "biconical alignment"; it uses formed components to bring the fibers to the proper mating.

Even with these limitations, fiber optical cables and LANs are finding their way into industry. The reasons are their immunity to noise, small size, and high data rates. To better protect the fibers from environmental effects, the industry has gone to many types of cables and coatings using strengtheners, stiffeners, and cushioning to keep the transmission cables more stable. The major use of fiber cables will be in point-to-point environments until the time when suitable T-coupler-type devices exist to make fibers more versatile. Once this occurs, fiber will be the media of choice well into the future.

4.3.6   Installation

Whether fiber or wire is used, there are considerations for installation that must be examined before any LAN is chosen. The LAN cables must have suitable connectors for the environment being supported, as well as physical attributes for tolerance to conditions and path configurations. For example, a fiber cable that cannot tolerate sharp bends and curves may not be well suited for an environment in which this is a requirement.

Typical LAN installations are performed in buildings that already exist. This represents many problems to installers. A LAN that is being installed in this type of environment must have media that can easily be fished through walls, ceilings, floors, existing wire pathways, etc. Additionally, the LAN must have connectors that can be easily field installed with little trouble. If this is not the case, the chosen LAN may fall far short on its performance expectations.

In new construction, LANs can much more easily be installed in the same way as electrical wiring. The LAN wiring can be laid in conduits, installed in open walls using drills, and pulled through joists and other obstructions as is the case with regular wiring. This makes it much simpler to install a LAN in a large building. The ease of installation before the heavy floors and ceilings are installed makes the job much easier. Even in this environment, though, the LANs media must be able to withstand the stress of being pulled and bent as it is worked into the proper place.

4.3.7   Environment

A big concern during installation is where the LAN will be and what environmental stresses will be placed on it. The main four environments are air, sea, ground, and inside buildings. For air or spaceborn LANs, if any penetrations of the walls of the vehicle are necessary, the connectors used must have the proper characteristics to handle the pressures, heat, and moisture encountered there. The LAN itself must be constructed so as to easily lend itself to required spaces. For example, in a plane the requirement may be to use ribbon cables to keep the wires tight to the fuselage and keep the internal cabin free from devices. In a seaborne environment, the LAN must have immunity to salt, water, humidity, and extremes of temperature and pressure. For example, if the LAN is going on a deep submersible like Alvin, it must be compact, take little power, emit low heat, and have connections to the outside that can withstand extreme variations of temperature and pressure.

Another potential use of LANs is for placement on the ocean floor to link various test equipment or living environments together. Under deep sea exposure, the LANs media will be exposed to constant currents, fish,

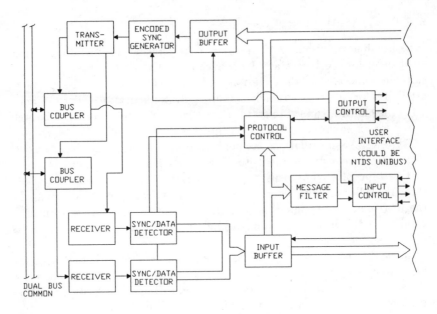

Figure 4.7   General network interface block diagram.

and other stray damaging occurrences. LANs in such an environment must exhibit much strength and integrity to survive such conditions. Land-based LANs require materials that can be buried in the earth, hung from poles, or strung through tunnels. These LANs typically are the metropolitan networks or interbuilding or site networks. The media here could easily be wire or fiber because of the typically nice straight runs. This environment, too, requires integrity from the media. LANs strung on poles must be able to withstand structural stress caused by wind, rain, hail, snow, and many other natural hazards. This requires a LAN with structural integrity that can be stretched, bent, heated, and cooled often without loss of transmission integrity. All these conditions must be taken into account when selecting or constructing a media for use in a LAN.

4.3.8   Interface Units (IUs)

The device that transforms the innate media into a usable, meaningful computer network is the interface unit. The interface unit provides the interface for the host devices to the network and vice versa. Pictorially, a generic interface unit is comprised of 11 major functional elements (see Figure 4.7). No matter what the type of interface unit, some level of each of these elements exists. The extent and complexity of each element is caused mainly by the media being acted upon and the protocols being implemented to control the network.

Some typical examples of IU hardware functional components and functions provided by IU elements follow. Interface unit basic components are:

- Bus coupler(s). IU to bus hardware connection (passive/active).
- Receiver(s). Electronic interface from bus to IU.
- Sync/data detector(s). Converts bus format to IU format; error detection.
- Input buffers (could have DMA-type properties). Signals protocol control of a message state; holding station of host's messages; signals message filter that a message has arrived.
- Message filter. Detects if message is addressed to this unit.
- Input control. Supplies needed control to transfer message(s) from IU to host.
- Protocol control. Determines if IU has bus control; requests bus control; handles timeouts; releases bus control; error detection.
- Output control (could have DMA-type properties). Tells protocol control a message is to be sent; holding tank for output messages.
- Encoder/Sync generator. Converts IU formatted data to bus formatted data; adds parity, CRC, etc.
- Transmitter. Electric interface from IU to bus; drives bus couplers.

Interface unit functions are:

- Initialization of bus. Start token passing, begin counting sequence.
- Maintenance. A monitoring function which allows all units to check the state of others.
- Enter. Allows a unit not on the bus to get into the sequence (some units, such as HXDP, will not have this capability).
- Exit. Inverse of enter.
- Receive. Procedure by which an interface unit can decide if a message is destined for it.
- Restart. From a warm position, restart the system (i.e., failure recovery).
- Transmit. Transmit procedure by which an interface unit will request transmission.
- Error control. ACK/NACK, status, parity, CR, ID, detection of duplication.
- Die. Will cause addressed unit to drop from ring.
- Buffer overflow handling. Procedure to handle this condition.
- Retry. On error or overflow, etc.
- Flow control. User allocation (central control), node allocation (decentralized control), special routines.

- Segmentation. Break up message, if too large, and control its transmission in some orderly fashion.
- Addressing. What (name device), where (address device), how (route).
- Security.
- Routing. (If desired by design.)

The trend today regarding interface units is to develop standards and then VLSI chips that will implement the standards. This simplifies the design and development of LANs immensely. First, cut chips are aimed at implementing the protocol controller with future devices being developed to handle more and more of the interfacing units task. Therefore, a network will develop into a collection of VLSI chips linked by a wire. Examples of such an evolution are the VLSI chips developed to the 802 standards:

- The National Semiconductor Corporation's DP8392 coaxial transceiver interface implements the IEEE 802.3 standard.
- The Motorola MC68824 chip implements the IEEE 802.4 MAC services.
- The Texas Instruments TMS380 LAN adapter chip set implements the IEEE 802.5 token ring standard.

These represent a fraction of the LAN chips now available. As time goes on and the standards mature, myrid vendors will supply all aspects of the network interface unit in VLSI format. This will enable the LAN designers and product designers to embed the required electronics into very small places such as in a wall socket or within a PC, thus making LANs even more accessible to all.

4.3.9   Software Requirements

As important, if not more important, than the hardware requirements are the software requirements. The software provides life and meaning to the innate hardware capability. It provides the view that the users see of the computer system. That is, the icons or textual input and output prompts that the user sees on the video screen are put there by the software. The main components of the control software that give this view are the operating system, the database management system, the network control protocol, error control and management software, reconfiguration and recovery software, and encryption and decryption software (hardware) if required.

4.3.10   Operating System

The operating system software provides the control and management of the components connected to the network. The class of service can be at the

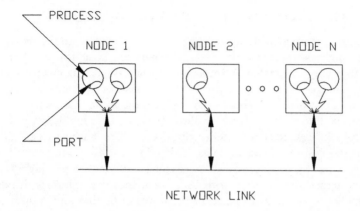

Figure 4.8   NOS parts and process linkages.

network only (send-receive) or at the upper levels for management of I/O devices, storage devices, computers, and the associated software processes operating on the system.

This choice for class of service is very important for the LAN designer or purchaser to consider as part of the total package. If the purchaser does not choose the proper services, the LAN may not perform the tasks initially envisioned for it. If we need tight control of diverse devices dispersed over a wide range, an integrated distributed operating system with services for synchronizing processes and providing distributed control is necessary. If our needs are only to have a network that provides simple services to send and receive messages, a simple network operating system will suffice. Such a network will provide control and management of ports on the network to allow processes to log onto the network, then send or receive messages from other process ports in the network (see Figure 4.8).

Such a simple operating system does provide us with the means to construct any type of synchronization and services we require. The issue is, does my company want to build its own services or buy someone else's that are already constructed? If we want the latter, a distributed operating system is what is wanted. The distributed operating system will provide an integrated set of services for users to build their applications software on. The user would have a set of computers to view and use as though they were one large uniprocessor. More details of operating systems can be found in Fortier [1986] or in Part 7 of this text.

4.3.11   Database Management System (DBMS)

The database management system provides the access to information strewn throughout the network. From the network layer this component can be either very integrated or act as an add-on. What this means is that the data manager for the system can either exist as a simple file server that provides protocols to access a remote local database, use its protocols, and access the information (transfer files), or it can be a highly integrated, cohesive set of software that provides global control and access to all information in the system. Most systems sold today use a remote-access-type capability. These systems provide a more consistent view by putting a layer of software across all sites that provides a consistent user interface, leaving underlying software layers to perform the location finding and translation to the remote database.

Of utmost importance for most LAN applications is information transfer. If the LAN you are looking at does not provide an information management system, it is not very useful. The users will be required to write their own information management packages to be able to use the network for correct and consistent information exchange.

The DBMS provides basic capabilities to store and retrieve information in a controlled environment. It protects itself from unauthorized users as well as from erroneous or conflicting updates. Database managers allow many users to use its services concurrently, thereby increasing the overall throughput of the system. For more information on distributed databases for LANs, see Fortier [1985], Sha [1985], and Date [1984].

4.3.12   Control Protocol

Control protocol represents the means and mechanisms by which users acquire use of the transport media. The basic types of control are contention, token passing, and polling. The variety of mechanisms based on the basic type are numerous and are explained in depth in previous texts [Fortier, 1985]. The following paragraphs will describe the three basic modes to clarify their meanings. Details of a few specific examples of these control protocols will be described in Chapter 4.

4.3.13   Polling

In polling, control is passed via the action of a requestor asking for use of the media by raising a signal or by the action of one device calculating the next poll address. In either case, once placed in action the operation is put in some order (in order, random, prediction, pattern, etc.) and the units are polled as to whether they wish to use the network or not. If they are asked and respond positively, they are given control of the media, are allowed to send their data, and then release the media. At this point the polling continues again. The polling can be centralized (initiated from a single site) or decentralized (issued from any site). An example of a polling-type system is HXDP (Honeywell's experimental distributed processing system). This system was developed in the 1970s and represents an important milestone in distributed systems protocol design. It operates as follows:

Each device (interface unit) has a counter and a 256-word register. The registers in each device are loaded with ones in the location of the count that this device requires. The action of comparing the count number (0, 255) with any corresponding location (0, 255) will yield whether a device has control or not (i.e., if it has a 1 in the location, it gets control; otherwise it does not). Once a device determines that it has this poll location, it can use the network to send data. Once completed, it sends out an increment poll code to all on the network. Each device increments its counter, which now shows the next location to examine. Through the proper selection of poll slots and number of nodes, a very tailored access scheme can be produced. Details of this and other polling schemes can be found in Fortier [1985].

4.3.14   Token Passing

Token passing protocols work logically and physically by passing a marker (token) from one site to an adjacent site in a particular direction. Typically this control protocol is seen in ring topologies (see Figure 4.9).

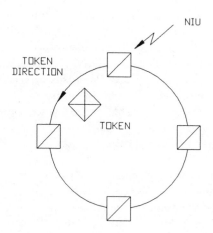

Figure 4.9   Token ring.

FLOW
DIRECTION

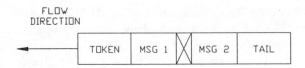

Figure 4.10   Token train scheme.

This topology naturally provides a unidirectional channel from point to point that ultimately connects all sites together into a ring. The protocol works through the interaction of the token flowing over the media and the network interface units that detect and act on this token. The process is as follows:

A token is placed on the media. The token flows from device 1 to device 2. When device 2 receives the token, it may append its message to the token to send its message. Once it does this, it sends the token back out with the message and a trailer (see Figure 4.10). This continues on from 1 to N until the token is received back at the start. Once my message returns to me, I check the status appended to it (received correct, errors, etc.), strip off my message, and do the whole process again. More details of this token scheme and other variations on it can be found in Fortier [1985] and in Part 4 of this text.

4.3.15   Contention

Contention-based control protocols cover a wide spectrum from simple CSMA (carrier sense multiple access) schemes to highly robust contention reservation schemes. This type of control protocol is found mostly within shaved media topologies such as a global bus or passive star topology. The basic concept of operation for protocols of this type is: (1) contend for the resource, (2) acquire or lose resource, (3) use or wait on resource, and (4) release resource; go back to 1. This process is the same whether the protocol is collision based or interrogation based. An example of this class of protocol is the simple Ethernet protocol which was decribed under "Coaxial Cable."

Another type of contention scheme is the contention reservation scheme. This protocol was described by Fortier [1985a, 1985b, 1986]. This protocol is based on a bus-style architecture with separate data and control parts that provide for increased performance. The concept is to cut up the transmission time on the media into chunks called frames. These chunks are contended for in order. The present slice was allocated based on a previous contention period. Such a control protocol operates as follows:

Users who wish to communicate in the next time frame contend for the media by contending on a bit-by-bit basis for the frame. Once the contention has yielded a winner, this user is given the right to send data in the next frame. The others will recontend on the next frame, and so on.

This protocol, when used with an intelligent pacing or interleaving mechanism, provides high user throughputs on the data media. Details of this and other contention-based protocols can be found in Fortier [1985].

4.3.16   Error Control

An important component of a LAN is the ability to respond to errors in transmissions. Error has two components, detection and correction. Detection of errors can be done either by hardware, software, or combined means. Hardware means typically use encryption or coding. This can be done in hardware through special-purpose devices that add the extra code bits for detection and correction and through reception hardware devices that decode and check the received bits to determine and correct errors. Other means include CRC checks and parity. The level of detail for hardware and software used for error control is dependent on how much a purchaser or designer is willing to pay for or require error-free communications.

More details on error management can be found in Part 2 and in Lin [1970] and Peterson [1971].

4.3.17   Reconfiguration and Recovery

Another important aspect of LANs, particularly real-time or critical-use LANs, is recovery and reconfiguration. Recovery deals with how to bring the LAN back to a consistent state after an error, and reconfiguration is the mechanism to restore operations after some failure. From a LAN viewpoint, the important aspects to look for in software for recovery are mechanisms to restore service or power glitches and to control token loss, bit errors, noise, and other minor faults in services.

Reconfiguration in a LAN typically looks at mechanisms to restore service upon loss of a link or interface unit. To reconfigure or recover from failures or faults requires the network to possess mechanisms to detect that an error or fault has occurred and to determine how to minimize the effect on the system's performance. Typical components include:

- Performance monitoring
- Fault location
- Network communication management
- System availability manager
- Configuration manager

These work in concert to detect errors, isolate them, determine their effect, assess how to fix them, and go to the recovery state. Details of operations and design for such components have been described in Fortier [1985, 1986].

4.4 Organizational Requirements

Beyond looking at a network's basic hardware and software elements, a prospective user or designer must examine and compare the organizational needs to truly assess if a network will meet their needs. For example, an organization must examine its needs for communications. If it has a large, centralized computer and must have remote sites communicate to it, a LAN may be necessary. If they only must communicate sporadically, modems may be more cost effective than a LAN. But if they communicate often, a LAN is probably a better choice.

Other considerations that an organization must consider in the purchase or design of a LAN include the distances that the LAN must cover, the number of user sites to be included, and the distribution of the user's hardware over the geographic area of interest.

Of major interest to the LAN specifier or designer is a definition for the range of devices that will be used on the LAN. The major classes of devices are real-time, resource, time-share, and interactive. Each levies a different class of requirements on the LAN. Real-time high-speed devices require contention-based access to the media with very high data rates available. Resource devices range from special-purpose processors to banks of secondary and backup storage. These require log-on and use-type protocols with speeds on LANs commensurate with their performance. Timesharing and interactive devices typically require sporadic use with small packets quickly and efficiently being shipped around the network.

To meet the needs today and into the future, the LAN designer or specifier must examine and know the organization's future plans for information processing and envisioned expansion needs. This information is necessary to develop criteria to evaluate a LAN's performance or in order to determine the best LAN for today and for later years.

The designer or specifier must prioritize the needs of the organization in terms of LAN support into three categories: primary, secondary, and future. The primary needs will define the basic architecture and capabilities required for the LAN to meet the organization's basic needs. The secondary need will be to define the "icing" that would be nice but is not essential, and the future describes capabilities that are needed to meet the projected life cycle needs of the organization.

The last component of network services that the organization must specify when acquiring a LAN is its needs for internetwork capability. This includes requirements for going from one LAN to another of the same type with bridges and to other nonsimilar LANs or metropolitan or wide area networks with gateways. Details of many of these topics will be addressed in the following chapters.

4.5   Summary

This chapter addressed the issues and considerations one must be cognizant of when designing or selecting a local area network. Included in this was an overview of the technical, managerial, and installation considerations.

4.6   References

Date, C. J., *Introduction to Database Systems*, Addison Wesley, 1984.

Fortier, P. J., "A Reliable Distributed Processing Environment for Real-Time Process Control," *Proceedings of HICSS-18*, January 1985a.

—, *Design and Analysis of Distributed Real-Time Systems*, McGraw-Hill, New York, 1985b.

—, *Design of Distributed Operating Systems: Concepts and Technology*, Intertext, Inc., McGraw-Hill, New York, 1986.

Lin, S., *An Introduction to Error-Correcting Codes*, Prentice Hall, Englewood Cliffs, NJ, 1970.

Peterson, W., *Error Correcting Codes*, MIT Press and John Wiley & Sons, Inc., New York, 1961.

Sha, L., "Modular Concurrency Control and Failure Recovery," Ph.D. dissertation, Department of Electrical Engineering, Carnegie-Mellon University, 1985.

PART TWO
Communications Technology

5. Digital Communication Technology

One of the most critical aspects of LAN technology is communications. Without the ability to efficiently and accurately transmit information between sites, LANs and their benefits could not be realized.

Communications in LANs is comprised of protocols (providing the means to encode and interpret the signals being transmitted) and signaling (which provides the basic means to transmit information along a media).

Chapter 4 of this book examined issues in protocols for LANs; therefore, this chapter will not address this aspect of communications technology. Instead, the emphasis of this chapter will be on basics of communciations, namely, communications signaling and error management.

5.1 Digital Communications

The transmission of digital signals across media is comprised of encoding (for recognition), interleaving (for multiple paths), and physical transmission (which is comprised of physical methods of transmission and media characteristics).

Communications on a signal line can be handled in many fashions. For example, it could be performed serially, in parallel, synchronously, asynchronously, half duplex, or full duplex. Typical of serial communications is a point-to-point link in which the data is serialized and sent simplex (one direction only) to the next site in the network. An example of such a link would be a fiber optic link connecting two hosts of a ring network. Flow is serial and in one direction only. This serial communications can be done synchronously or asynchronously. In synchronous communications

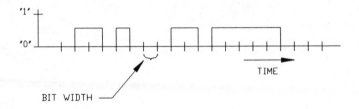

Figure 5.1   Digital signal for 0011010001101111.

the sender and receiver are synched up by a signal that is being sent continuously. When a message is to be sent, a pattern is sent to signal the beginning of the message and the message is sent. In asynchronous communications, the sender sends a sync signal or setup signal that sets up the receiver, which then can receive the message as it arrives. This type of communications typically uses half-duplex or full-duplex channels. A half-duplex channel provides a path in which data can flow in either direction but only one at a time, not simultaneously. Conversely, in full-duplex mode, the channel allows data to be sent simultaneously in both directions. To do this typically requires a higher bandwidth cable or multiple cables.

Given that we have these methods of sending and receiving signals, how do we interpret what is being sent? There basically are four major methods for sending and interpreting signals over transmission media. These are binary signaling, amplitude modulation, frequency modulation, and phase modulation.

Digital transmission uses the level transmissions to send 1s and 0s over the media. The advantage of having a media that can support straightforward digital transmissions is that no interpretation or encoding is required to receive or send the signal over the media (see Figure 5.1).

Figure 5.1 shows how a digital 16-bit word can be easily sent over the media. If a digital media is used, the memory, register, etc., where the word is stored simply gates the word out onto the transmission circuitry when commanded to do so. If some other technique is used, this digital word would have to be translated for carrying it over the media. The problem with most digital-type transmission services is that because of the physics of the media (other than fiber optics), digital transmission cannot provide long-distance service without assistance (boosting stations, etc.). To alleviate this, one of the analog modes of transmission can be used. Analog transmissions use various means to convert the digital signal into waveforms that can be sent over the electrical cables of the network. The basic types of analog signalling are amplitude modulation, frequency modulation, and

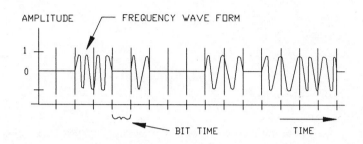

Figure 5.2   Amplitude modulation for 0011010001101111.

phase modulation. Each of these use a basic carrier signal (sine wave, etc.) and use augmentations of this basic wave as the encoding of digital 1s and 0s.

In amplitude modulation, a digital signal is transferred using analog waveforms in which the amplitude of the signal is adjusted to signal a 0 or 1 in the digital signal (see Figure 5.2).

Upon examining Figure 5.2, one will see that the detection of a 0 or 1 signal is based on sampling the amplitude of the waveform using the carrier frequency over the bit transition times for each bit location. This type of analog signaling is simple and requires fairly simple circuitry to realize.

Another form of analogy transmission used is frequency modulation. In frequency modulation, a set frequency or idle condition is sent continuously on the line. A 0 is detected as the carrier frequency and a 1 as an increased frequency (see Figure 5.3). This type of transmission service requires very accurate frequency detectors that can quickly (within less than a sample or bit time) determine that there has been a frequency change.

The final form of transmission modulation is phase modulation. This scheme for carrying digital signals down an analog circuit uses the concept of waveform phase changes (see Figure 5.4) to delineate the change from a 0 to a 1. The problem with this technique is that you need some form of

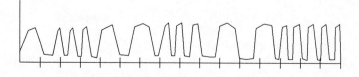

Figure 5.3   Frequency modulation of 0011010001101111.

PHASE CHANGES

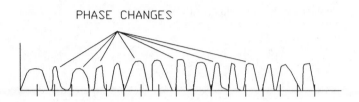

Figure 5.4   Phase modulation transmission of 0011010001101111.

carrier or marker to set up the receiver to receive and properly decode the message being sent.

Any of these techniques can be used to send computer information over a medium. The selection of one over the other is typically driven by the type of link and the service it provides to users. Typically, if one is using leased lines or phone lines, there is a requirement to send the signals in analog form. This usually will require a modem (modulator/demodulator) to convert the digital signal to analog and another modem on the receiving end to convert the signal from analog back to digital. This conversion takes time and adds another level of overhead to the communication process.

Digital transmission has distinct advantages over analog if it is available. Digital tansmission typically has a much lower error rate since it is not being manipulated as often. Digital transmissions provide a means to more efficiently use equipment. This is accomplished through the use of multiplexing mixed data types; voice, data, music, and video, for example. Additionally, because of the nature of digital transmission, one can operate at much higher data rates. This is possible because there is no need for extra hardware and processing to detect carriers or to detect changes with wide sample periods.

To effectively use channels or links in early networks, concepts were developed to interleave or share the medium (i.e., break it up into subchannels). The major type of services provided were multiplexing and concentration. Multiplexing provides a way to break up the channel into separate

Figure 5.5   Time division multiple access scheme.

subchannels, whereas concentration provides a way to put more channels or signals into one path to maximize the use of a more expensive media.

Two major schemes for multiplexing are time division multiple access (TDMA) and frequency division multiple access (FDMA). In TDMA the channel (link) is divided into N nonoverlapping time slots. Each of these time slots is singularly designated for a user. The user uses this time slot just as if it were a dedicated line (see Figure 5.5). If the link has fewer than N users, not all of the slots are used. If more than N users are seeking access, some will be denied service. The problem with this type of access is that the channel capacity may not be efficiently used unless all users send something during their slot. Users in such systems also have problems with the complexity of user synchronization.

Frequency division multiple access splits the channel up using varying frequencies. These provide N nonoverlapping frequency-based subchannels. Each of up to N users has a dedicated frequency channel. Again, as in TDMA, if there are less than N users, there are wasted capacities, but if there are more than N users, some are denied service. In this form of access, users cannot directly talk to each other and there is a potential for wasted capacity.

Concentration looks to answer one of these problems by providing a means for any user who wishes service to be granted service; capacity is more highly used. In terminal multiplexing this goal is realized. The input stream of 1 to N units is added together and given the available bandwidth. That is, the output rate is equal to the sum of the input rates. On the other hand, in concentrations the goal is to take N inputs and buffer them and forward multiplexed groups onto the link as available.

These early mechanisms for providing access to links proved inefficient as loads increased and the number of users increased. Therefore, more resilient schemes to access the media were necessary. These new schemes fall into three major categories: (1) circuit switching, (2) message switching, and (3) packet switching.

Circuit switching networks use single dedicated channels for communications between source and destination pairs which stay active and associated for the duration of a session (communications dialog). The mode of operation for circuit switched channels is as follows:

- The channel (path) is acquired (ready to send).
- The sink is queried to see if it is ready to accept.
- The message is sent.
- An end of transmission is sent.
- The channel is released.

This type of network is great for systems that have few users with long connect times and a lot of data to transfer. The penalty paid here is in setup time. Such a network will require some period of time to set up a path and ready the source and sink devices.

Message switching takes a different view. Instead of physically setting up a path from source to sink, the message in total is sent from one site to another until it ultimately reaches the destination. That is, a prearranged circuit does not exist for the message to traverse. It is sent from node to node using a routing scheme which will ultimately get it to its destination. This scheme requires the intermedaries to accept the message, store it, and forward it on once an avenue is determined. Such a scheme causes a wide variation in message delays through the network, but it provide a means to service more users in a given time frame.

The final form of transport technology found in the early networks was packet switching. This scheme is similar to message switching except the messages are broken up into smaller chunks called "packets." These packets are then sent independently to the destination node in a store and forward fashion. This provided a means to better use the parallelism (distribution) of the network and allowed a means to interleave the service of many users over the network. Later in this chapter we will look more closely at LANs and how these techniques have been applied to them.

5.2   Transmission Links

Transmission links or channels provide the connections between network devices. This connection provides the conduit for information flow. When looking for a link, the desired characteristics include:

- A fast rate of travel (propagation)
- A fast rate of signaling
- Low error rate or susceptability
- Maximum throughput (implying low overhead)
- Minimum cost

Each of these features is desirable, but it is almost impossible to have all of them in one link because of their conflicting realizations. For example, to guarantee a low error rate may require additional signaling or manufacturing quality. These, in turn, will drive up the cost of the medium. To deliver service, we must balance between the optimal of each and reach some accord.

The types of links found are varied, though four major ones come to mind:

- Ground
- Satellite

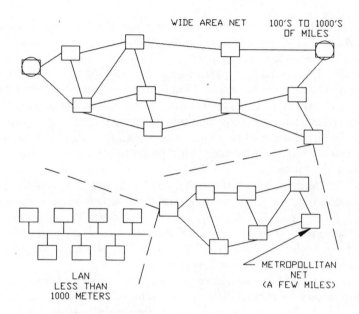

WIDE AREA NET   100'S TO 1000'S
OF MILES

METROPOLLITAN
NET
(A FEW MILES)

LAN
LESS THAN
1000 METERS

Figure 5.6   Hierarchy of networks.

- Radio
- Light guide

Ground wires are the typical wiring we see every day. These include telephone lines, cable television lines, leased trunk lines, and dedicated network wires such as coaxial cable. This type of cabling is typically used in one of two modes, either switched or dedicated service. Switched service provides users with only the level of service they need. When they log on and attempt to link up (dial) another user, they are switched in (connected, like a phone call) to the other device. In a dedicated service, a point-to-point link is set up between users.

The type of topologies we see in ground or terrestrial networks are hierarchical. That is, typically we have multiple network classes connected together using this technology. For example, the Arpanet is comprised of sites over a wide geographic area that talk to each other via leased or switched lines. This, in turn, is connected to metropolitan networks which link metropolitan districts into networks that, in turn, may have many LANs strung from it (see Figure 5.6).

The various classes of ground links used is based on the needs of the network. For example, the wide area network may wish to use switched lines because of short communications times, whereas the LAN and metropolitan networks are more heavily used and may wish to use dedicated lines to provide the necessary throughputs.

Satellite links provide a means to connect stations together over a wide area and in hostile environments. Messages are sent from an earth station to the satellite which, in turn, broadcasts this back down to an earth station. Networks using satellites provide transmission over very long distances with data rates around 50 Mbps. The problem or payment one must make in using satellites is the extremely high propagation delay, typically in the 1/4- to 1/2-s range.

Another form of link is the radio link. This link operates similarly to the satellite link. That is, one broadcasts to all others simultaneously. The biggest difference is that the users are close together. The advantage to the use of radio links is to provide communications to stations that cannot be easily or cost effectively serviced by ground links. A prime example of such a network is the Aloha net in Hawaii.

The final type of link to address is the optical carrier or fiber. This media provides a very high bandwidth, in the hundreds of megabytes per second range. Nice features of this media are its immunity to electromagnetic and radio interference and its extremely low error rates of 10-9. It additionally has a very small physical size with a wide range of operating conditions supported. Fiber optic cables have found their way into almost every facet of communications.

Before one link type can be selected over another, an analysis must be undertaken to address the issues that provide the transmission rates seen. Additionally, one must examine where the network is to be operated to select the proper set of characteristics that will meet these requirements.

The rate of transmission by which we wish to evaluate networks have many components that affect this performance. These include: topology, media, noise, propagation, and slew and spreading. Topology, which refers to the way the network is connected, affects transmission rates. For example, a shared global bus is limited to the links capacity minus the overhead associated with control. A ring topology is limited to the slowest component in the path, which is probably the interface units that take the data in, examine it, and send it back out. A mesh topology is limited by the slowest element in the path of the flow. A star topology is limited by the capacity of the central core switch.

Another driving factor in the capacity issue is the media's makeup. Based on the design of the media (as will be seen in the following section), there are limits to the volume of information that can be sent because of clocking rates the media can support. Additionally, this rate is driven by the media's resiliency to errors caused by noise. For example, a fiber optic cable will support a higher rate than a coax cable, which will support more than twisted pairs. This is because of the error rates or sensitivity of the media to outside noise from electrical or other sources. Another limiting factor in transfer rate is the propagation delay of a signal. Dependent on the media and the distances involved, this can become a significant factor. Two other considerations are a medium's susceptability to slew and the spreading of signals. This phenomenon could perturb the ability to correctly decode received signals.

5.3   Transmission Architecture

Local area networks provide a means to interconnect a diversity of devices into unified structures. The connection of these devices is physically performed by one of numerous interconnection media, with the most common being one of the following:

• Common carrier circuits
• Twisted pair
• Coaxial cable
• Cable TV
• Optical fiber
• Satellite
• Radio
• Value-added networks

Each of these technologies has its pros and cons.

Common carrier circuits (usually associated with dispersed networks) are readily available (Ma Bell), provide leased service, are maintained by the carrier, can be easily reconfigured to the customer's needs, are very practical economically over medium to long distances, and provide a variety of speeds based on cost.

Twisted pair has been around for a long time and provides an inexpensive medium with low speed for short distances. Additionally, with the use of modems, one can get moderate speeds over fairly long distances.

Coaxial cable has been in use for 20 or more years and is an inexpensive medium. It has been used to provide transmissions in the range of 10 Mbps. The medium uses either broadcast or point-to-point-type operations and provides fairly good noise immunity.

Cable TV provides the advantages of coaxial cable, but one can also capitalize on systems installed for video transmission.

Optical fiber is a fairly new contender in the market. It provides high bandwidth with low weight and size. It is immue to cross-talk and RFI and provides extremely low error rate in the order of 10-4 bit error rates. It is

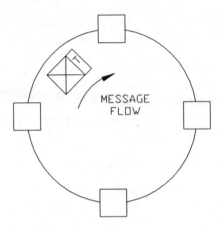

Figure 5.7   Single-cable ring.

increasingly being used, and its cost continues to drop as the technology matures.

Satellite links provide an extremely high bandwidth path at fairly low cost to users. There is a penalty though: it requires long delays to institute a transmission and it is a broadcast-only medium.

Radio networks again are based on broadcast technology. They provide good mobile data communications service and provide this at a fairly low cost. They are limited by their maximum service rates in data transfer.

Value-added networks are broadly available and provide to users flexible leased-based services. Usage-based charging is applied, leaving the user to pay for only what is used; maintenance and upgrading is provided by the carrier. Later in this chapter two of the most common media, coax and fiber, will be further discussed.

5.4   Media Design

As important as selecting the type of cable or transmission media to use is the design or configuration of the media. The number of links provided is based on a balance of price versus performance. If we desire to guarantee communications service under very hostile conditions, we may be willing to pay for additional lines and communications electronics. Additional reasons for wanting to pay more are based on speed requirements. If we must move large blocks of data over wide distances and within finite time, we may wish to possess additional output links to be able to send the information out over a much wider area more quickly. Basically, we are talking about

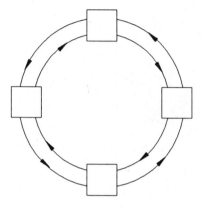

Figure 5.8   Dual-cable ring.

redundancy, single-cable networks over dual-cable networks, or multidrop cables. Using the differing cable numbers within a topology class will, in most cases, require changes in overall operations. For example, if we examine a basic ring, we see that with the single cable setup, we can only provide service to users in sequential order (see Figure 5.7). The time delay from one use of the bus to the next is based on the scan time plus usage delays on the way. The scan time is the time required for the control token to visit each node in order and return to its start point. To provide higher throughput, rings have been designed with dual cables (see Figure 5.8). This type of architecture provides an alternative path for signals to travel. By using both cables operating in opposite directions, we can improve the access time from scan time to half the scan time maximum. This provides a network with higher throughput and also with one that is fault tolerant. If one link fails, we can operate over the other. If pieces of each fail, we can reconfigure around both to maintain as much of the network as possible.

There are many issues associated with media design such as do we wish to use single medium or mixed media, a point-to-point or multipoint system, dedicated versus shared media, analog versus digital, and, as shown before, public or private media? The decisions to make within each set of variables affects all others. For instance, if we examine the issue of single medium (one type) versus mixed types, we have conflicting qualities that we must examine when deciding which to select for our needs.

Single media is simpler because it has only one type of interface, whereas mixed types require much more complex interfaces. Single media may not be adequate for mixed varieties and types of traffic, but mixed media could

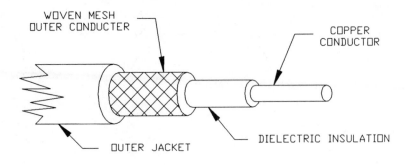

a) BASEBAND COAXIAL CABLE

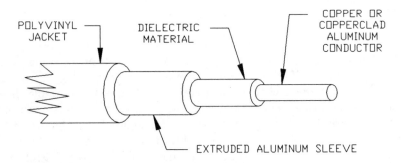

b) BROADBAND COAXIAL CABLE

Figure 5.9   Physical differences of coaxial cable.

provide more suitable factilities for varied types of traffic. Single media is good for traffic of one type but is vulnerable to failure and may limit growth in some environments, whereas mixed media networks provide good service for multiple media types, are less vulnerable to failures, and can provide some measure of growth.

Another media design issue is the selection of use of point-to-point links versus multipoint media. Point-to-point links tend to be more expensive than multipoint but are simpler and do not require arbitration for resources. Multipoint tends to provide less expensive communications overall because many people are sharing the media; but because of this sharing, we must suffer increased control delays and queuing problems. Related to this media design issue is the issue of dedicated or shared data paths. Dedicated

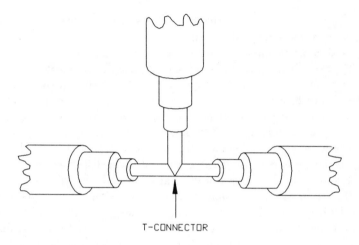

T-CONNECTOR

Figure 5.10 Coaxial cable T-connector.

paths provide for easier overall control with low delay but are expensive because of the limited amount of users; however, they are very simple. On the other hand, shared media will reduce the cost overall by amortizing it over many users. The problem is that shared media inevitably means increased hardware and controlled computation time. Shared media is very well suited to environment in which there is bursty traffic from users. The media is much better used under these conditions.

The selection of transmission signaling is mostly driven by distance requirements. If we are strictly a LAN, digital is preferred, but if we must cover greater distances, analog would be much more preferred. Analog transmission require modems to encode and decode signals, but it can use readily accessible transmission equipment such as telephone circuits. Digital transmission requires no modems, and it provides the LAN users with much more cost-effective service. The speed of transmission is very good and has excellent error characteristics.

Finally, there must be a decision on whether we use public or private links. Public links, like leased lines, etc., provide good service but not always at the designed rates. Private service provides tailored environments for the user.

5.5   Cable Design

Two of the most widely used cables today and for the future are coaxial and fiber optic cables. These cables, with their associated connections and services, provide for the majority of networks in service today and projected for local area networks in the future.

Coaxial cable technology as a transport media has been used for more than 25 years. It has proven its versatility as a communications media for digital transmission, as well as myriad others. It comes in two basic types: baseband and broadband. Baseband coaxial cable provides the means to transmit digital data without modulation. The drawback of digital transmission is that because of the digital transitions, one cannot extend for long distances without loss of signal strength. Because of this problem, baseband coaxial cable is typically used only for short distances, not more than a few kilometers. If greater distances are required, the broadband cable is used. This type of transmission requires modulation of the digital signal to one of the frequency carriers previously discussed. Broadband networks are used over distances in the tens of kilometers range. Networks of this type provide data rates of 100 to 150 Mbps with 1500+ channels per cable. The baseband networks provide data rates in the tens of megabit per second range. The baseband network will support up to 100 devices, whereas the broadband will support 1500 or more. The mechanisms to gain access to the baseband networks are typically carrier-sense multiple-access schemes in which all contend for use of the single channel. In the broadband case, each device pair is assigned a channel that is dedicated for its use. Physically, there is not much difference in their appearance. The baseband cable is composed of a center copper core conductor encased by a dielectric insulation. This is then surrounded by a woven copper mesh and finally an outer insulating jacket.

The broadband cable is comprised of a center core conductor of copper or aluminum enclosed in a dielectric jacket. This is then surrounded by a solid extruded aluminum sleeve. This is all encapsulated in an insulating jacket. The two types of cable are shown in Figure 5.9.

One of the most important aspects of coaxial cable systems is how they are used. All devices in the network are connected to the common cable via a simple T-connector. This connector pierces the outer jacket and makes contact with the inner conductors (see Figure 5.10). This type of connection makes this media very desirable in applications that require ease of adding devices anywhere in the network. The connectors required for this type of link are readily available from many sources. These devices are the same as those used by the TV cable companies for their taps and connectors.

Connecting into the wire and making it a network requires the use of an interface unit. An interface unit (NIU) provides the means for the user host device (mainframe, minicomputer, workstation, personal computer, etc.) to send and receive information over the computer network in some controlled way. For a broadband type of network there are basically three

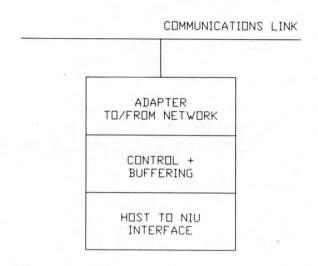

Figure 5.11 Components of a NIU.

major classifications of devices in the NIU; an adapter interface to the
network, a control section, and an adapter interface to the host device (see
Figure 5.11).

A more detailed block diagram will reveal that the adapter actually
is comprised of modulators and demodulators and their interfaces to the
control element. The control element is comprised of input/output and bus
control logic along with inputs and outputs to the associated interfaces.
The host-to-NIU interface provides the necessary logic to link the physical
host device to the network interface unit (see Figure 5.12).

The function of the particular elements follows: The modulator/demod-
ulator performs the task of encoding and decoding the digital signals into
the proper carrier format. The interface to the control section provides
buffering and logic to extract or insert information from or to the bus to
determine state or drive operations at the speed of the attached coaxial bus.
The control components provide for the orderly reception and transmission
of information from or to the bus under control of the bus controller. This
device implements the protocol corrections called for in the bus communications protocol specifications. This section of components also provides the
interface and control of the interaction of the host interface components.

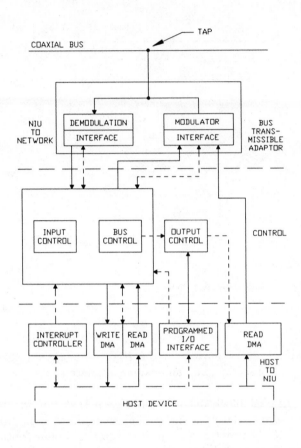

Figure 5.12 NIU block diagram.

The host to NIU devices provide the mechanisms for the host device to send and receive information from the bus.

This type of interface device is very typical in its representation of the block devices that one would find in most interface units for network interconnection.

5.6   Fiber Optics Link

Aside from the coaxial cable for LAN systems, one of the most important media for LANs in the foreseeable future is fiber optical cable. Fiber optical cable offers many advantages over coaxial. They are immune to outside interference, can be done totally in digital form, and can be used over long distances with the proper transmitters and receivers. Fiber optical cable is

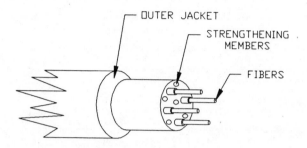

Figure 5.13 Fiber cable makeup.

lighter weight, consumes less space, and requires less power than its metal cousins. The promise of fiber optics as a replacement for coaxial will only be realized when an inexpensive means to produce a T-coupler for the bus exists. In point-to-point connections, fiber buses will easily outperform the metal coaxial cable, although the coaxial cables are still cheaper in today's market.

Fiber cables consist typically of a core of fiber transmission links coated with a jacket, surrounded by some form of stiffening, followed by an outside jacket (see Figure 5.13). Basically, a fiber optic cable is comprised of a fiber composed of a light-transmitting material like germanium borosilicate with a coating to protect the fiber. To transmit signals from one end of the fiber to the other requires a transmitter. The optical transmitter source is typically some form of light-emitting diode such as a galium aluminum arsenide diode. This device takes the TTL (transistor transition logic) digital signal and converts it to a comparable optical signal of 0s and 1s.

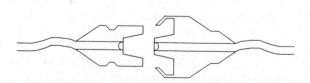

Figure 5.14 Fiber optic cable connector.

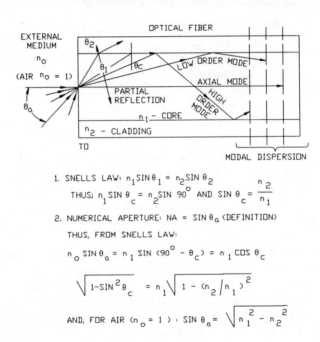

θ_a = ACCEPTANCE ANGLE

θ_1 = ANGLE OF INCIDENCE

θ_2 = ANGLE OF REFLECTION OR REFRACTION

n = INDEX OF REFRACTION

$n_1 > n_2$

1. SNELLS LAW: $n_1 \sin\theta_1 = n_2 \sin\theta_2$

   THUS: $n_1 \sin\theta_c = n_2 \sin 90^\circ$ AND $\sin\theta_c = \dfrac{n_2}{n_1}$

2. NUMERICAL APERTURE: NA = $\sin\theta_a$ (DEFINITION)

   THUS, FROM SNELLS LAW:

   $n_0 \sin\theta_a = n_1 \sin(90^\circ - \theta_c) = n_1 \cos\theta_c$

   $\sqrt{1 - \sin^2\theta_c} = n_1 \sqrt{1 - (n_2/n_1)^2}$

   AND, FOR AIR ($n_0 = 1$): $\sin\theta_a = \sqrt{n_1^2 - n_2^2}$

Figure 5.15 Light propagation in an optical fiber.

On the reception side, we need a PIN photo diode to convert binary optical signals to the comparable TTL digital signal levels.

The challenge in using and designing fiber optical cables for use in LANs is the connectors. Most loss in transmission strength is found in the connectors. Since we are sending light pulses down the line, we need precise, clean couplings to allow the signal to be properly received. The connections must be designed such that they will precisely mate the fiber ends together. If a fiber-to-fiber connection is made, the transmitter or receiver must be precisely matched with the fiber used. Various designs for connectors have been developed; one is a typical connector that uses a female- and male-type housing to bring the embedded cables to a tight fit (see Figure 5.14).

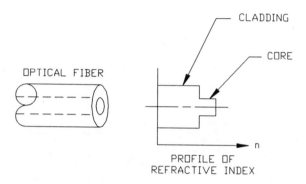

Figure 5.16   Step-index optical fiber.

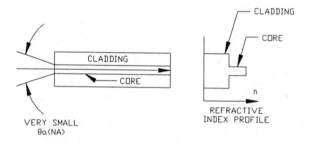

Figure 5.17   Single-mode step-index fibers.

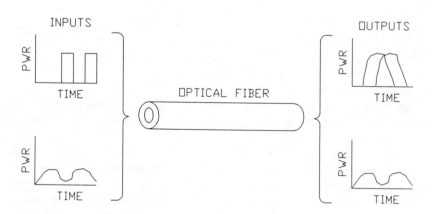

Figure 5.18   Multimode step-index fibers.

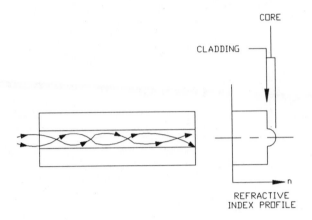

Figure 5.19   Graded index fiber profile.

Many variations of this basic design exist, and some will be shown on the accompanying data sheets.

5.6.1   Transmission Characteristics

Light travels through a conducting medium as a sinusoidal oscillation at constant frequency and wavelength. Within the electromagnetic spectrum, light is in a much higher frequency range, which is one reason for the higher data load capacity of light media.

The structural elements of an optical fiber are its cylindrical core and a concentric cladding. Both of these are conductors (transparent), but they have different indices of refraction (degree of refraction, bending of light). The index of the core is greater than that of the cladding. Total internal reflection occurs for all light rays where the critical angle of incidence (Θ_c) is exceeded (see Figure 5.15). This will be true for all light rays entering within an acceptance angle (Θ_a). This acceptance angle is thus an important parameter of an optical fiber and is generally given by the term "numerical aperture" (NA) where: $NA = Sin\Theta_a$.

Since fiber optic signal transmission involves light from a known controlled source, we can eliminate concern with any waves except those passing through the fiber axis. The central axial ray is a special case of this, and axially parallel rays would be equivalent. The remaining class, or "skew" waves, which do not pass through the fiber axis, are irrevelant.

The nonaxial waves, or "modes," illustrated in Figure 5.15 are identified as high or low order, which is a function of their entry angle within the acceptance angle (or NA). Obviously, the axial and lower-order modes will have less distance to travel in transmission. This results in the phenomenon of modal dispersion, wherein simultaneously launched rays become time-dispersed during transmission.

5.6.2   Fiber Index

A step-index fiber derives its name from profiling the refractive index for core and cladding as illustrated in Figure 5.16. The smaller the fiber core diameter, the smaller the acceptance angle (Θ_a) and NA. Therefore, fewer modes will be launched and propagated. There are two common categories of step-index fibers—multimode and single mode. A standard single-mode, step-index fiber has a core diameter of 2 to 8 micrometers (μm). This effec-

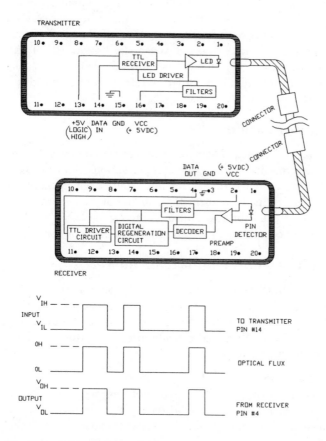

Figure 5.20 Fiber optic device structures.

tively eliminates modal dispersion, since virtually only one (axial) mode is transmitted. The single-mode, step-index fiber (see Figure 5.17) provides low dispersion and wide bandwidth ratings. These qualities makes them very efficient for high-speed, long-distance applications.

The larger and more common multimode class of step-index fibers gather light well with their large NAs, thus permitting a wider choice of light-emitter sources (see Figure 5.18). Core diameters are in the range of 125 to over 400 μm. Modal dispersion occurs for such fibers and is typically 15 to 30 nanoseconds per kilometer (ns/km).

A fiber may also be produced in such a way that the refractive index of the core reduces in value continuously as the distance from the axis increases. Such a fiber is a graded-index fiber and has a profile as shown in Figure 5.19. The graded-index fiber tends to equalize the transmission velocities of high- and low-order modes. This is because of the index gradation which imposes a gradual and continuous change in direction on the paths. The graded-index fibers increase the bandwidth of data rates or frequencies which can be reliably transmitted. Typical core diameters for graded-index fibers are on the order of 125 um and modal dispersions can be as low as 2 ns/km.

5.6.3   Attenuation

There are several principal sources of loss in signal power during transmission such as structural and chemical imperfections, which cause absorption and scattering, and curvature of the fiber routes, which causes loss of some of the modes originally launched. The major losses are because of the former. The attenuation losses also include some losses at the fiber ends, where the method and quality of termination are a factor.

5.6.4   Light Source and Transmitter

Either a light-emitting diode (LED) or injection laser diode (ILD) provides the light source for transmitter circuitry. A transmitter circuit translates the electronic signal input to the optical signal by modulating drive current to the emitter. Principal considerations determining the choice of a particular source emitter are:

- Output power
- Wavelength compatibility with fiber and detector
- Frequency response (modulation rate)
- Efficiency (percentage of light emitted which can be launched into the fiber core)
- Life expectancy and cost

Characteristic	LED	ILD
Power output	0.5 to 11.5 mW	3 to 10 mW
Spectral range	25 to 40nM	2 to 5 mW
Rise time (off to on)	3 to 20 ns	1 to 2 nsMode
Bias current range	50 to 150 mA	100 to 500 mA
Coupling efficiency	Medium	High

Table 5.1   LED and ILD characteristics.

Some of these factors are influenced by the emitter package construction. The current basic constructions that are of primary interest in fiber optics are shown in Figure 5.20. Note that pigtailed and ferruled emitters permanently incorporate a length of optical fiber. In these cases then, the emitter-to-fiber-optic interface is established at manufacture and the application involves fiber-to-fiber coupling only.

In Table 5.1 the important functional characteristics typical of LED and ILD emitters are compared.

5.6.5   Detector and Receiver

At the receiving end of the link, light must be detected, transduced, and amplified to yield an electrical signal representing the original input. Light detectors in fiber optics take one of the following forms, depending on characteristics required:

- PIN photodiodes. These are comparatively inexpensive, easy to apply, and have fast response times. Sensitivity is relatively low and there is no intrinsic gain.
- Avalanche photodiodes. Although more expensive, APDs are more sensitive than PINs and provide some gain in the detection stage. Furthermore, their response is even faster.
- Phototransistors.

A phototransistor, by definition, is an amplifying detector. Sensitivity and signal-to-noise ratios (SNR) are very good, but response times are slower than photodiodes. A phodarlington transistor is a two-stage chip with even better inherent gain. Phototransistors require receiver circuitry that is more complex than that for PIN photodiodes but less so than that for APDs.

The principal function characteristics typical of the common detector types are compared in Table 5.2.

Characteristic	PIN	APD	transistor	darlington
Responsivity	0.5 uA/uW	15 uA/uW	35 uA/uW	180 uA/uW
Rise time (off-to-on)	1 ns	2 ns	2 us	40 us
Required bias	10 V	100+ V	10 V	10 V

Table 5.2   Common detector types.

5.7   Components

The following text will review some typical components available off the shelf for use in LAN communications network design. This is only meant as a sampling; for more details of any of the components please refer to the appropriate manufacturer.

5.7.1   Coaxial Transceiver Interface

The National Semiconductor Corporation provides an IEEE 802.3 compatible Ethernet/Cheapernet local area network chip set (see Figure 5.21), the DP8392 Coaxial Transceiver Interface. It features the following:

- Integrates all transceiver electronics except signal and power isolation.
- Innovative design minimizes external component count.
- Jabber timer function integrated on chip.
- Externally selectable CD heartbeat for remote diagnosis.
- Precision circuitry implements receive mode collision detection.
- Squelch circuitry at all inputs rejects noise.
- Designed for rigorous reliability requirements of IEEE 802.3.

5.7.2   Token-passing Bus Controller

Motorola Corporation has developed a token-passing bus controller (TBC) MC68824. The MC68824 is an intelligent, 2 μm HCMOS, high-performance token-passing bus controller communications device that provides the media access control (MAC) function for an IEEE 802.4 LAN station. Interfaced with the appropriate physical layer, the TBC can support either carrierband or broadband physical layers of 1, 5, or 10 Mbps. The MC68824 provides the following:

- IEEE 802.4 MAC services
- MAC options suitable for real-time environments (Proway extensions

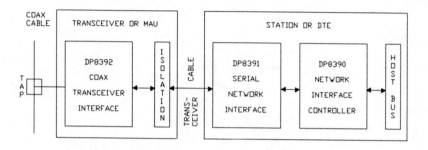

Figure 5.21   Ethernet/cheapernet chipset.

- Four receive and four transmit queues supporting four priority levels
- Immediate response mechanism
- Highly integrated M68000 family bus master/slave interface
- DMA transfer of data frames to and from memory using the 40-byte FIFO
- 32-bit address bus with virtual address capabilities
- Simple interface to other processor environments
- Byte-swapping capability for alternate memory structures
- 8- or 16-bit data bus
- On-board network monitoring and diagnostic aids
- Vectored interrupts and status reporting
- System clock rate up to 12.5 MHz
- Serial data rates up to 10 Mbps
- IEEE 802.4 recommended serial interface supports independent physical layer modulation techniques
- Simple interface to higher-level software by means of a powerful fully linked data structure

5.7.3   Fiber Optic Components

Codenoll Technology Corporation provides Codelink-20B, an asynchronous and synchronous 830-nm and 1300-nm wavelength optical data link. Features:

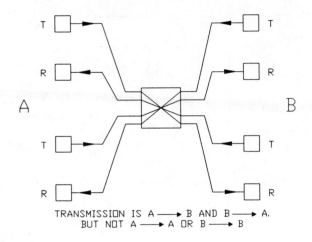

TRANSMISSION IS A ──→ B AND B ──→ A,
BUT NOT A ──→ A OR B ──→ B

Figure 5.22   Optical star coupler.

• Data rates: DC to 20 Mbps
• BER less than 10-9 for all data rates
• Distances greater than 5 km (830 nm) or 10 km (1300 nm option)
• Optional code data Manchester coding for synchronous transmission of data and clock
• Single +5-V supply
• Supply filtering built in
• TTL inputs and outputs
• PC card mountable miniature low-profile DIP
• Flexible optical pigtail for any fiber (from 50 um) or connector
• EMI shielded package
• Low power consumption

5.7.3.1   General Description

Codelink-20B is a dc-coupled fiber optic link that provides reliable transmission of arbitrary data formats at rates from dc to 20 Mbps. The link employs an LED transmitter and a PIN photodiode receiver. Using the standard link, with 830-nm LED and detector, transmission distances greater than 5 to 13 km without repeaters are possible. Greater distances of 10 to 13 km can be accommodated by using Codelink-20B with an option that uses a 1300-nm wavelength LED and detector. Codelink-20B links are TTL compatible and require a single +5-V supply.

The optical flux output from the dc-coupled Codelink-20BT transmitter is a replica of the input data pattern. The dc-coupled receiver, Codelink-

20BR, reconstructs logic levels from the transmitted optical flux pattern. As shown in the recommended operating conditions table, there are no restrictions on the input data bit pattern except that the minimum bit time is 50 ns. There are no restrictions on maximum bit time or duty cycle. Single-value bit streams of any length are acceptable. Synchronous transmission of data and clock signals from 250 kHz to 10 MHz is easily accomplished by using the optional built-in Codedata-10 Manchester encoder/decoder or the external Codedata-30. Codedata-10 Manchester encoder/decoder circuits are available as a built-in option in the Codelink-20B transmitter for use in duplex systems.

The dynamic range of the Codelink-20BR receiver is adequate for operation at any link length up to the rated maximum. There are no user adjustments required.

Complete power supply filtering is contained within the unit; no external capacitors or decoupling networks are required, the low-profile, dual-inline package mounts directly onto PC boards for wave or hand soldering. There is no need for lead bending (endangering glass-metal seals) or additional hardware. No heat sinking is required. Transmitter and receiver are completely enclosed in all metal packages for increased durability and complete immunity to EMI.

The package is furnished with an integral ruggedized fiber optic pigtail. The standard Codelink module is provided with an SMA-type optical connector, but it is available with an unterminated pigtail or with a connector of the customer's choice. The high-efficiency patent-pending Codelink pigtail permits optical cable connections to be made at the user's panel or bulkhead. The Codelink pigtail also facilitates the use of blind mate PC board/chassis connectors as in Codelink-2000 Optical Communications Systems.

5.7.4   Codestar Optical Star Couplers

These couplers are manufactured by Codenoll Technology Corporation. Features:

- Compatible with all broadcast networks including Codenet/Ethernet and serial bus coaxial systems
- Completely passive, transmissive design
- Bidirectional
- Fully connectorized
- Low coupling (insertion) loss
- Six configurations from 2 to 64 ports
- 50, 62.5-, 85-, or 100-μm graded index fiber
- Protective metal enclosure
- Suitable for rack mounting or as stand-alone modules

Codestar optical star couplers provide a simple means of implementing a fiber optic network for data communication through the interconnectio of 2, 4, 8 16, 32, or 64 nodes without the use of repeaters. Codestar couplers are entirely passive, transmissive devices, in which fibers are fused together to form optical mixers through the fused biconical taper technique.

Any light launched into one of the fibers on one side of the optical mixer will be equally divided among, and output through, all of the fibers on the opposite side of the mixer. This characteristic ideally suits Codestar couplers for use in any broadcast system, from the so-called serial bus coaxial cable systems to fiber optic Ethernet systems.

Networks larger than 64 nodes, up to several hundred nodes, may be constructed with multiple-cluster Codestar couplers and are interconnected to other stars in up to three layers. When going from one star to another, it is necessary to use a repeater, such as the Codenet 3037A.

A Codestar-implemented fiber optic network is a broadcast network, functionally and logically identical to any other broadcast medium, including coaxial cable. Consequently, any broadcast network may be implemented with Codestar fiber optic couplers.

5.7.4.1   General Description

The Codestar is an integral part of the Codenet fiber optic Ethernet physical layer, conforming to all aspects of the standard IEEE-802.3 CSMA/CD and Xerox, Digital Equipment Corporation, and Intel Ethernet networks. Since the Codestar is a completely passive device, its reliability is extremely high, giving the Codenet fiber optic Ethernet LAN system an unprecedented degree of reliability and performance.

Codestar fiber optic couplers are housed in rugged metal enclosures suitable for either stand-alone or rack-mounting applications. Units measure 19 x 10-3/4 x 1-7/8 in or 19 x 10-3/4 x 3-3/4 in. Standard coupler configurations are 2 x 2, 4 x 4, 8 x 8, 16 x 16, 32 x 32, and 64 x 64 ports. These couplers can be supplied with a choice of 50-, 62.5-, 85-, or 100-μm core-graded index fiber. All Codestars are sold fully connectorized with SMA-type connectors as standard. Codestar couplers having nonstandard dimensions, fiber, or connectors may be supplied on special order.

Physically, the Codestar is a fully connectorized, biconical tapered fiber optic star coupler. It is fabricated by assembling several optical fibers into a bundle. This bundle of fibers is heated, stretched, twisted, and fused together, forming an optical mixer. This configuration, generically known as a "fused biconical coupler," divides the fibers into two groups, with one group of fibers on either side of the fused optical mixer.

One side of the Codestar is arbitrarily declared an input-only side, and one side of the Codestar the output-only side. The network is interconnected by extending one of the input side fibers and one of the output side fibers to each node. Each node then has the capability of transmitting into the Codestar and of having its transmitted data received by all other nodes in the system. Similarly, each node has the ability to receive all the data that is transmitted by all other nodes on the network.

Any light coupled into any of the N ports designated T will be approximately equally divided among, and output through, each of the N R ports. The relationship between the input and output powers through the star coupler is expressed in terms of an effective coupler "loss" given by:

$$loss = 2C + E + 10 Log N$$

where

C is the connector loss (typically 1.5 dB)
E is the star coupler excess loss (typically 1 to 4 dB)
N is the number or optical ports

Cross-coupling between input (or output) ports is typically -40 dB.

5.7.5 Fiber Optic Switch by SIECOR

Features:

- Low insertion loss (typical 0.7 dB)
- Four-terminal bypass-type design
- Fast switching time
- Low switching variability
- High channel isolation
- Long mechanical life (more than 108 operations)
- Wide wavelength operating window
- Compact and lightweight package
- 50-, 62.5-, 85-, and 100-μm fiber versions

5.7.5.1 General Description

The Siecor fiber optic switch exchanges optical signals between two transmission paths with typical insertion loss of 0.7 dB. The switch is a bypass type, based on the fiber alignment principle. It passes stringent environmental testing for shock vibration and temperature extremes required in military applications. Maximum switching rate is 25 operations per second. The switch maintains a 0.1-dB repeatability over its mechanical life of over 108 operations.

In the operating position (ON), each optical input signal is channelled to a separate output fiber. The bypass position (OFF) causes one input

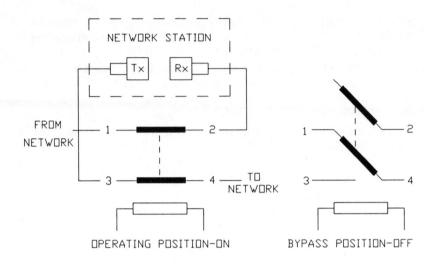

Figure 5.23 PIN diagram.

channel to be switched to the opposite output channel and disables the second input.

Siecor's optical switch is designed for fault-tolerant local area networks and for line switching between data communications paths. The low insertion loss substantially increases the possible number of nodes and distance between nodes in token-passing rings and other LANs.

5.7.6 AT&T ODL 200 Lightwave Data Link

Features:

• 100 kelvin ECL compatible
• Single 4.5-V power supply
• Ambient temperature 0 to 70 degrees centigrade
• Pulse width distortion less than 0.5 ns
• Rugged, connectorized 16-pin DIP
• High reliability

Description:

The ODL 200 Lightwave Data Link is a high-performance link designed for data rates from 40 to 220 Mbps (NRZ) at distances up to 3 km. The data modules typically provide a 15.5-dB power budget. An 11-dB power budget is predicted for worst case components over a 105-hour (h) service life. Microwave complementary bipolar integrated circuits (MCBIC) are used to achieve the high data rates. The transmitter and receiver are housed in connectorized 16-pin dual inline packages (DIPs). Each package has an integral lens-coupled optical connector that mates with the ST ferrule light guide cable connector. The ODL 200 link is designed to be used with 62.5/125-μm optical fiber, but is compatible with 50/125-μm fibers as well.

The AT&T 1252C transmitter consists of a long wavelength, high-speed LED, a silicon integrated circuit, and several discrete components.

The AT&T 1352C receiver is equipped with a PIN photodetector diode, and it includes components similar to those in the transmitter (see Figure 5.23). It requires a negative supply voltage. The 1352F receiver also uses similar components but requires a positive supply voltage. The ODL 200 is available in a models kit. Components include a 1252C transmitter, 1352C receiver, 50 ft of 62.5/125 μm connectorized cable, and an instruction manual.

5.7.7   Dynamic Measurements Corporation

This company supplies a 5651 transmitter and a 5652 receiver.

5.8   LAN Components–A Sampling

Local area networks come in many flavors. That is, they provide a rich mixing of media types and access mechanisms. As described in Chapters 5, 11, and 24, the major types of media found in LAN products include baseband coaxial cable, broadband coaxial cable, twisted pair, fiber optic cable, and twin ax. The major access schemes are token passing (802.4 global bus version, 802.5 ring version), carrier sense multiple access (collision detection and collision avoidance, 802.3), time division multiplexing, time slot allocation, and polling. When taken together, these provide a wide array of potential local area networks configurations and capabilities to meet most every user's needs. The listings below break down local area networks into categories based on the media first, then on the access mechanism used. These lists are included to indicate to readers the volume of LANs available on the market and is by no means complete. As such, we appologize for any ommisions.

Broadband	Token Passing	EM
"	"	LAN/I, LAN/II
"	"	Concord Data
"	"	Systems
"	"	Token/Net
"	"	Motorola
"	"	Map
"	"	Wang Labs

Broadband	Token Passing	Fastlan
"	CSMA/CD	Applitek Corp
"	"	UniLan
"	"	DEC
"	"	Ethernet
"	"	Kee Inc.
"	"	Kee Lan
"	"	Wang Labs
"	"	WangNet
"	"	Xyplex Inc.
"	"	Xyplex system
Baseband	Token Passing	Datapoint Corp.
"	"	Arc
"	"	Intercontinental
"	"	Micro
"	"	TurboLan
"	"	Magnolia
"	"	Microsystems
"	"	Magnet
"	"	Nestar Systems
"	"	Plan
"	"	Novell Inc.
"	"	NetWare/Arcnet
"	"	NetWare/ProNet
"	"	Phoenix
"	"	Digital Systems
"	"	OPTOnet
"	"	Proteon Inc.
"	"	ProNet-10/80
"	"	Stearns Comp.
"	"	Systems.
"	"	ViaNet
"	CSMA/CD	Asher Technologies
"	"	Quadnet
"	"	AST Research Inc.
"	"	PCnet
"	"	Codex Corp.
"	"	4000 series LAN
"	"	Communications
"	"	machinery
"	"	Ethernet
"	"	Corvus Systems

Baseband	CSMA/CD	Omninet
"	"	**Cyb Sys Inc.**
"	"	Unite
"	"	**Data General Corp.**
"	"	Ethernet
"	"	**Digital Equipment**
"	"	**Corp.**
"	"	Ethernet
"	"	**Exelan Inc.**
"	"	Exos
"	"	**Honeywell**
"	"	**Information**
"	"	**Systems**
"	"	Ethernet
"	"	**Ide Assoc.**
"	"	Ideanet
"	"	**MicomInterlan**
"	"	**Inc.**
"	"	Net/Plus
"	"	**Motorola**
"	"	Ethernet
"	"	**Novell, Inc.**
"	"	Netware/6net
"	"	**Tech, Inc.**
"	"	LTLAN
"	"	**Perkin Elmer**
"	"	**Corp.**
"	"	Pennet
"	"	**Siecor Corp.**
"	"	Ethernet
"	"	**Tienet Inc.**
"	"	Tienet
"	"	**Xerox Corp.**
"	"	XC22/24
"	"	**Xyplex Inc.**
"	"	Xyplex Sys
"	CSMA/CA	**Digital Equip.**
"	"	Ethernet
"	"	**NCR Corp.**
"	"	NRC PC2PC
"	"	**Xyplex Inc.**
"	"	Xyplex Sys

Baseband	Master/Slave Polling	**Digital Micro Systems**
"	"	Hinet
"	Dynamic Time Slot Allocation	**Gandalf Data Inc.**
"	"	PACXNET
Twisted Pair	Token Passing	**Asher Technologies**
"	"	Qnet IX
"	"	**Intercontinental Inc.**
"	"	Turbolan
"	"	**Magnolia Microsystems**
"	"	Magnet
"	"	**Novel Inc.**
"	"	Pronet
"	"	**Protron Inc.**
"	"	Pronet 10/80
"	CSMA/CD	**Apple Computer**
"	"	Apple Net
"	"	**Corvus Systems**
"	"	Omninet
"	"	**Cyb Systems**
"	"	Unite
"	"	**David Systems**
"	"	Ethernet
"	"	**Molecular Computer**
"	"	System 16/300
"	"	**PcLan Technologies**
"	"	LT LAN
"	"	**Tienet Inc.**
"	"	Tienet
"	CSMA/CA	**Complexx Systems**
"	"	XLAN
"	Time Division Mult	**Equinox Systems**
"	"	DataPBX
"	Dynamic Time Slot Allocation	**Gandalf Data, Inc.**
"	"	PACXNET
"	"	**Fox Research Inc.**
"	"	10NET

Twin-Ax	Token Passing	Prime Computer
"	"	PrimeNet
"	"	Quantum SW Systems
"	"	QWX OS
"	"	Datapoint Corp.
"	"	ARC
"	"	Novell Inc.
"	"	PRONET
"	"	Phoenix Digital
"	"	OPTONET
"	"	Prime Computer
"	"	Ringnet
"	"	Proteon Inc.
"	"	PRONET10
Twin-Ax	CSMA/CD	Siecor Corp.
"	"	Ethernet
"	"	Fibercom Inc.
"	"	Wispernet
Twin-Ax	Dynamic Time Allocation	Gandalf Inc. PAXCNET
Twin-Ax	Master/Slave Polling	Digital Microsys.
"	"	Hinet

5.9   LAN IC Chips

Chapter 24 describes a few of these networks and their protocols in further detail. The following listings describe LAN IC chips that exist to implement the IEEE 802.3, 802.4, and 802.5 LAN protocols. More details of the underlying standards can be found in Part 4.

802.3	CSMA/CD	Advanced Micro.	7996
			7990
"	"	EXAR	XRT82515
			XRT820516
"	"	Intel	82586
			82501
			82588
"	"	National Semi.	DP8790
			DP8341
			DP8342
"	"	Seeq Technology	8003
			8023

802.3	CSMA/CD	Thomson Mostec.	Mk 68590
			Mk 68591
"	"	Western Digit.	alWD83C510
802.4	Token Passing	Motorola	MC68184
			Bus MC68824
"	"	Signetics	NE5080
			NE5081
802.5	"	Texas Instruments	TMS38030
			TMS38010
			TMS38020
			TMS38020
			TMS38C51
			TMS39052

5.10   Summary

This chapter provided an overview of the basic technology applied to the transmission of information over a network. Covered were the basics of signal transmission for digital and analog signaling. This was followed by a discussion of the media used and the physical structure and operations of these media within a LAN. Also included was a sampling of a few LAN products that provide services like those described in this chapter.

6. Error Management

Errors occur in all media used in communications. In some cases these errors can be tolerated, such as in telephones or television, for which the loss of a few bits or one frame does not usually cause catastrophic disaster, unless of course this glitch causes you to miss an important word in your favorite soap opera or the loss of an important comment over the phone. In these situations, in which errors cannot be tolerated, error management is necessary. The sole purpose of error management is to ensure that errors do not occur or, if they do, that they can be compensated for. The goal is to have all information received correctly. The amount or sophistication of error management is dependent on the tolerance of the applications to errors. For example, if an application can, on its own, determine its message is in error and request a retransmission until it gets it right, there is not much need for error detection and correction at the low levels of communications. On the other hand, if the application is not designed to be fault tolerant, the communications media and its communications gear must be designed so that it provides the proper level of fault tolerance.

6.1 Causes of Errors

Errors occur for a variety of reasons in communications systems, though they can be characterized into one of four major classes: (1) failures, (2) distortion, (3) spikes, and (4) background conditions.

Errors induced via failures typically are represented by a lost transmission. The causes of this lost message, frame, etc., may be algorithm deficiencies, failed hardware, or failed software. This class of errors is best handled via timer interrupts that go off if a message does not indicate its success of transmission. This will usually result in multiple attempts to

113

retransmit the message. If this fails, the reconfiguration of the communications hardware, software, or algorithms may be undertaken to correct the condition. More will be said in the following sections about this correction.

The second cause of errors in communications systems is a phenomenon called "distortion," which is caused by statically generated frequency noise. This noise can be generated by just about any electrical circuit. Distortion is seen in about every device that we use. For example, radios experience this frequency-dependent interference. We all have had the experience of not being able to get a good signal because of this type of interference. Try to notice next time you experience this if you are near some major source of frequency-dependent signal source. For, if you travel Route 128, the beltway around Boston, you will encounter a point at which there is a major collection of transmitters for a variety of communications from air traffic control to television stations. All of these major sources of stray frequency components cause interference on your radio. This form of error is hard to easily characterize, and it affects various communications components differently.

Distortion will change the characteristic of the signals being sent over the media. Because of this change, it may become extremely difficult to properly decode the message being received. For example, if we are using frequency modulation as our carrier to indicate a 0 or 1 transmission, distortion of the signal may make it impossible to accurately determine what signal was actually sent.

The third souce of errors in local area network communications environments is called spike noise. This type of error is typically of short duration in the order of tens of milliseconds or less, and it causes the loss of data content during its occurrence. The causes of this type of error include lightning, relay arcing, surges in power lines, or static charges.

The fourth form of error over communications channels is called background noise. This form of interference is random and generated by many sources. Types of background noise include broadband spectrum noise produced by random traveling electrons in the wires. Also, low levels of radiation will generate interference of this type.

To deal with errors requires the use of techniques that provide extra information with the transmission to allow for detection of errors, correction of errors, or both. The major techniques used for error detection and correction are loop checking, error-correcting codes, error-detecting codes, or reconfiguration.

Loop checking is a technique for checking for errors which require the transmission of received messages back to the originator for error checking. The problem with this simple technique is that it wastes channel capacity to resend messages already sent, and it does not provide an easy way to

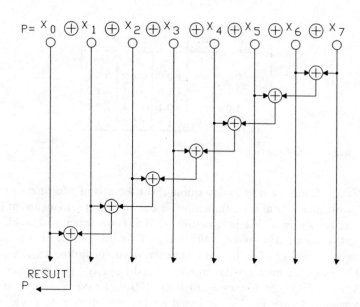

$$P = X_0 \oplus X_1 \oplus X_2 \oplus X_3 \oplus X_4 \oplus X_5 \oplus X_6 \oplus X_7$$

RESUIT
P

Figure 6.1   Modulo 2 addition.

determine if the error occurred in the initial transmission or on the way back.

Error-correcting codes use extra information embedded in the message to fix bits that have been transformed. Likewise, error detecting codes use extra information to detect the error in a message. Techniques such as sum checking have been used to determine if an error occurs. Sum checking is a technique that adds up the bits in a message and provides a total sum. If the sum at the receiver is the same as that computed by the sender, it is assumed that the message was received properly.

The final form of error correction is reconfiguration. This is the most drastic and is used only when failures in service occur. Reconfiguration is a method through which the physical ordering and actions of the system are changed to work around a failed item. Reconfiguration requires mechanisms to detect the failure, assess its impact on services, formulate alternative configurations, institute the fix, and resume regular services. More will be said on this topic later in the chapter.

6.2   Parity

One of the most common forms of error detection and correction involves the use of parity. Parity is a means for signaling the content of a word.

Valid Code	Errors		
	E_1	E_2	E_3
0 0 0	1 0 0	0 1 0	0 0 1
0 1 1	1 1 1	0 0 1	0 1 0
1 0 1	0 0 1	1 1 1	1 0 0
1 1 0	0 1 0	1 0 0	1 1 1

Table 6.1   Error detection.

That is, it provides a way to determine if the word is of odd or even weight. Each word in a digital communication is comprised of a sequence of 0s and 1s. The parity is added information that is associated with each word. This extra information is typically 1 bit. This bit (the parity) is selected so that the number of 1s in the computer word (including the parity bit) is either even for even parity or odd for odd parity. For example, if we have even parity, the binary word 00001100 will have a parity bit equal to 0 associated with it. This is based on the use of modulo 2 addition to compute the parity (see Figure 6.1).

To compute the parity for a word $X = X_0, X_1, X_2, X_3, X_4, X_5, X_6, X_7$ requires the modulo 2 addition of each bit in the word.

$$P = X_0 + X_1 + X_2 + X_3 + X_4 + X_5 + X_6 + X_7$$

This is shown pictorially in Figure 6.2. This type of computation can be easily performed by a simple hardware circuit that makes this computation very fast. Using the same circuit and technique on the receiving side provides the means to detect an error. The receiver recomputes the parity, compares this to the received parity, and, if they match, there are no errors.

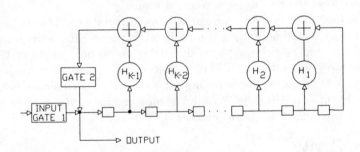

Figure 6.2   Parity computation.

If they do not match, there is an error. Even parity provides a means to detect odd numbers of errors.

6.2.1   Hamming Distance

The hamming distance of a code is defined as the number of digit positions by which two "valid" states differ from each other. As an example, we will look at a simple 2-bit word, $X = X_1, X_2$. With this word, there are only four valid signals possible, 00, 01, 10, 11. If we add parity to this, we get codes of 000, 011, 101, 110 as the valid codes with parity. The possible errors on these codes would be comprised of changes to any of the bits; they are enumerated in the Table 6.1.

Using Table 6.1 you can easily see how we could detect if an error occurred, though in all cases we cannot readily see which one of the valid codes it should be. This is because the code received, the error code, maps to more than one valid code. To be able to get more than detection requires more information.

6.2.2   Error Correcting

Hamming code can be used to detect errors if enough redundant information is introduced into the code to allow not only detection but also correction. The hamming distance is used as the measure. It provides a way to detect errors. In detection we require a hamming distance greater than $2e$ and to correct we need a distance of greater than $2e + l$, where e is equal to the number of errors. The correction is possible if we use the concept of maximum likelihood decoding. What this concept stresses is the notion that:

> One error is more likely than two.
> Two errors are more likely than three.
> Three errors are more likely than four, etc.

Using this notion, we can correct a single error by changing the error state to the nearest true one. For example, if we have two words, $W = 000, 111$, the hamming distance $d = (W_1, W_2) = 3$. For a single bit error on W_1, we have 001, 100, 010, and for W_2 we have 110, 101, 011, which will be transformed to 000 and 111, respectively. The notion used here is that if e errors occur, the error code word is still closer to the original true word than any other. Therefore, we can determine which word was actually sent. For example, if we have four valid codes of

$$0\ 0\ 0\ 0\ 0\ 0\ 0\ 0\ 0$$
$$1\ 1\ 1\ 1\ 1\ 0\ 0\ 0\ 0$$
$$0\ 0\ 0\ 0\ 0\ 1\ 1\ 1\ 1$$
$$1\ 1\ 1\ 1\ 1\ 1\ 1\ 1\ 1$$

by examination one can see that the valid code words differ by 5 bits; therefore they have a distance of 5 and can correct and detect 2 errors:

$$2e + 1 > 5 ===> e > 2$$

For example, if the code word received is

$$0\ 0\ 0\ 0\ 0\ 0\ 0\ 1\ 1\ 1$$

by inspection (comparison with the valid code word) it can be readily seen that the actual code word sent was

$$0\ 0\ 0\ 0\ 0\ 1\ 1\ 1\ 1\ 1$$

The actual algorithm that performs the task of detection and correction is based on the mixture of message and check bits and how they are computed.

6.2.3   Hamming Codes

There is an N-bit word, where N is equal to the number of message bits plus the number of check bits:

$$N = M + C$$

For the N-bit word, if errors are formed by single-bit invertings of bits and we systematically invert each of the N bits, we have $N + 1$ states possible for each good code word. Therefore, there are $2n$ possible codes overall but only $2^n/N + 1$ good codes. If 2^M represents the number of correct codes, 2^M is less than $2^n/N + 1$ which implies that $M + C + 1$ must be less than 2^M to provide for single-bit error correction. For example, if we have $M = 4$, $2^M = 8$, which implies that C is less than $8 - M + 1 = 8 - 5 = 3c = 3$. This number of check bits will provide us the capability to correct single-bit errors within the message words.

As an example, if we have code words with $N = 7$, $M = 4$ and we let the check bits be located in positions that are powers of 2(1, 2, 4, 8, ...), the following message format holds:

Message bits   Check bits

Message word

$$M_4,\ M_3,\ M_2,\ C_3,\ M_1,\ C_2,\ C_1$$

To compute C_1, C_2, and C_3, we require combinations of message bits that will provide for proper decoding. The following equations all use modulo 2 addition:

$$C_1 = M_1 + M_2 + M_4$$
$$C_2 = M_1 + M_3 + M_4$$
$$C_3 = M_2 + M_3 + M_4$$

Note that each C_1 has as its base at least two elements in common with each of the other check bit computations.

To determine if the message word arrived correctly requires that we compute the following terms:

$$C_1^1 = C_1 + M_4 + M_2 + M_1$$
$$C_2^1 = C_2 + M_4 + M_3 + M_1$$
$$C_3^1 = C_3 + M_4 + M_3 + M_2$$

Once they have been computed, we use these bits to determine the status of the word as follows:

C_1^1	C_2^1	C_3^1	Status
1	2	4	
0	0	0	No error
0	0	1	C_3; is wrong
0	1	0	C_2; is wrong
0	1	1	$2 + 4 = 6$; M_3 is wrong
1	0	0	C_1; is wrong
1	0	1	$1 + 4 = 5$; M_2 is wrong
1	1	0	$1 + 2 = 3$; M_1 is wrong
1	1	1	$1 + 2 + 4 = 7$; M_4 is wrong

6.3   Linear Block Codes

A block code is defined as the set of possible code words that can be generated from a set of message bits. For example, if we have K bits, there are 2^K possible messages implying that there are also 2^K possible code words generated from these messages. This set of possible code words is its block code.

To generate the code word requires a generator mechanism. Linear codes use the concept of a generator matrix to produce the code words from the message words. The code word is found by the relationship

$$MG$$

where G represents the generator matrix. For example, if we had:

$$G = \begin{matrix} & I & & & A & \\ 1 & 0 & 0 & 1 & 1 & 0 \\ 0 & 1 & 0 & 0 & 1 & 1 \\ 0 & 0 & 1 & 1 & 0 & 1 \end{matrix}$$

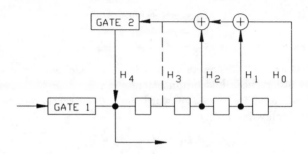

Figure 6.3   Generating k-stage shift encoding based on H(x).

Then we find the code for a message $M = (M_1 M_2 M_3)$ as MG, which is found as:

$$M_1 1 + M_2 0 + M_3 0 = U_1$$
$$M_1 0 + M_2 1 + M_3 0 = U_2$$
$$M_1 0 + M_2 0 + M_3 1 = U_3$$
$$M_1 1 + M_2 0 + M_3 1 = U_4$$
$$M_1 1 + M_2 1 + M_3 0 = U_5$$
$$M_1 0 + M_2 1 + M_3 1 = U_6$$

Each generator matrix has associated with it a $(n - k)$ by n parity check matrix. This matrix allows us to correct the errors in the received messages by computing the syndrome.

The parity check matrix is found by taking the identity matrix I and the A^T (A transpose) and switching them:

$$G[I \ A] ==> H[A^T \ I]$$

Using the previous generator matrix as the example yields parity check matrix as shown:

$$I \qquad A \qquad\qquad A^T$$

$$\begin{bmatrix} 100 & 110 \\ 010 & 011 \\ 001 & 101 \end{bmatrix} ==> \begin{bmatrix} 101 & 100 \\ 110 & 010 \\ 011 & 001 \end{bmatrix}$$

To construct, take the transpose of the A matrix, then add the identity matrix. The significance of this item will become more evident as we continue. The syndrome gives us a way to determine if there is an error in a code word and where it is. The syndrome is computed by:

$$S = (\text{received message})(\text{parity check matrix})$$

Coset Leader ===> Code Works 2^K							
000000	001101	010011	100110	011110	101011	110101	111000
000001	001100	010010	100111	011111	101010	110100	111001
000010	001111	010001	100100	011100	101001	110111	111010
000100	001001	010111	100010	011010	101111	110001	111100
001000	000101	011011	101110	010110	100011	111101	110000
010000	011101	000011	110110	001110	111011	100101	101000
100000	101101	110011	000110	111110	001011	010101	011000
001001	000100	011010	101111	010111	100010	111100	110001

Table 6.2   Standard array for the ((n,k) or (6,3)) code.

If the syndrome computes to all Os, there is no error. If not, we have an error in the code word.

For example, if we use the previous example with M message words where $M = 2^k$ and $k = 3$ as the size of matrix height, there are eight code words shown below:

Messages	Code vectors	Computed by
$M_1 = 000$	$V_1 = 000000$	$M_1 G$
$M_2 = 001$	$V_2 = 001101$	$M_2 G$
$M_3 = 010$	$V_3 = 010011$	$M_3 G$
$M_4 = 100$	$V_4 = 100110$	$M_4 G$
$M_5 = 011$	$V_5 = 011110$	$M_5 G$
$M_6 = 101$	$V_6 = 101011$	$M_6 G$
$M_7 = 110$	$V_7 = 110101$	$M_7 G$
$M_8 = 111$	$V_8 = 111000$	$M_8 G$

The code vectors for these messages are shown to their right, above. Using this information, we can generate a table referred to as the standard array. The standard array uses the code words and adds to them the error bits to generate an invalid code word. The leading element on the left of the Table 6.2 is referred to as the "coset leader."

From the standard array we can see that if errors occur in the positions seen in the coset leader column, we can determine the correct message transferred. Another interesting property is that any of the code words along the row of any coset leader will compute to the same syndrome pattern. Using this information provides us the means to correct the error as follows. The coset leaders are multiplied by the parity check matrices transposed to produce the syndrome (as below):

$$Syndrome = (CL)(H^T) \qquad Coset\ Leader$$

Syndrome = (CL)(H^T)	Coset Leader
000	000000
001	000001
010	000010
100	000100
110	001000
101	010000
011	100000
111	001001

To decode a code word to the proper code word, we do the following: The received code word is multiplied by the parity check matrices transposed to produce a syndrome pattern. This pattern is then used to look up the position in which the error occurred. The found coset leader is added to the received code word to produce to correct code word. For example, if we receive 001100, we multiply this by H^T:

$$S = \begin{bmatrix} 1 & 1 & 0 \\ 0 & 1 & 1 \\ 1 & 0 & 1 \\ 1 & 0 & 0 \\ 0 & 1 & 0 \\ 0 & 0 & 1 \end{bmatrix} \quad 001100 = 001$$

which indicates that there is an error, From the above mapping of syndrome to coset leader, we see that the error occurred in bit position 000001. To correct the received code word, we add the coset leader to it:

0	0	1	1	0	0
0	0	0	0	0	1
0	0	1	1	0	1

which is the correct word.

6.4   Cyclic Codes

Cyclic codes are represented by a code polynominal $g(x)$ of degree $n - k$ where $n + k$ came from the description of a (n, k) code:

$$g(x) = 1 + g_1 x + g_2 x^2 + \ldots + x^{n-k}$$

In coding all code words are multiples of g(x). G(x) is found from the factors of a polynominal $x^n + 1$ as:

$$x^n + 1 = g(x)h(x)$$

For example, if we have $x^n + 1$ set at $x^7 + 1$, its factors are $(1 + x + x^3)(1 + x + x^2 + x^4)$ and $1 + x + x^2 + x^4$ is equal to $(1 + x)(1 + x + x^3).g(x) = 1 + x + x^3$,

	Status		Register	
Step	G_1	G_2	Contents	Output
1	On	Off	1 x x x	1
2	On	Off	0 1 x x	0
3	On	Off	1 0 1 x	1
4	On	Off	0 1 0 1	0
5	Off	On	0 0 1 0	0
6	Off	On	1 0 0 1	1
7	Off	On	1 1 0 0	1

Table 6.3   Shifting the message bits.

which is the complete divisor of x^{n-1}. This is referred to as a cyclic $(7,4)$ code.

Using this generator polynominal, we can readily generate the code polynominals from the message. Messages in this $(7,4)$ code have the form

$$(M_1, M_2, M_3, M_4)$$

where $M_1 = 1, M_2 = x, M_3 = x^2, M_4 = x^3$. Then using this format, we can generate the code polynominals by

$$M(x)g(x) = V(x)$$

For example, if the message is

$$(1100) = 1 + x + 0x^2 + 0x^3$$

and $g(x) = 1 + x + x^3$, the code polynominal is equal to

$$(1 + x)(1 + x + x^3) = 1 + x^2 + x^3 + x^4$$

which equates to

1	0	1	1	1	0	0
1	x	x^2	x^3	x^4	x^5	x^6

$h(x)$, which is the parity check polynominal, is found by the following formula:

$$h(x) = (x^n - 1)/g(x)$$

For the (7,4) code used in the above example, this equates to

$$h(x) = x^7 - 1/1 + x + x^3 = 1 + x + x^2 + x^4$$

An important notion about the above descriptions is that the code poly-nominals represent shifts of the generator polynominal. Methods are de-scribed in Peterson [1970] and Lin [1970] to use this notion to construct circuits to encode and decode messages using shift registers whose elements are selected via the polynominals $H(x) + g(x)$.

If we are using $H(x)$ of degree k, a k-stage shift register circuit can be used to encode the signal. In the following example, the boxes represent shift registers, + represents an exclusive or, and x_i represents a connection when $x_i = 1$.

Using this, we constuct a k-stage shift register encoding circuit by build-ing a series of shifts and gates using the $H(x)$ polynominal of degree k. For the example we have been using, the (7, 4) code has $H(x) = 1 + x + x^2 + x^4$, k is 4; therefore, it is a four-stage circuit, implying four shift registers with connections at H_0, H_1, H_2, and H_k (see Figure 6.4).

The circuit operates by shifting in the message bits from right to left, leaving gate 2 off until the whole message word is in. The circuit continues for $n - k$. Additional shifts are made with gate 2 open to gate out the parity bits. For example, if we input $M = 0101$, the steps shown in Table 6.3 occur. Therefore, the code word sent out is 1100101.

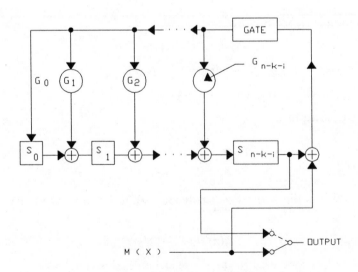

Figure 6.4   Encoding circuit for (7,4) code.

Transition	G	Registers	Output
1st	On	1 1 0	1
2nd	On	0 1 1	0
3rd	On	0 0 1	1
4th	On	1 1 0	0
5th	Off	0 1 1	0
6th	Off	0 0 1	1
7th	Off	0 0 0	1

Table 6.4   Contents of the shift registers.

A similar setup can be used to encode the output using the generator polynominal $G(X)$ (see Figure 6.5). In this case the general form uses $n - k$ stages.

The operation here is to input the message bits from right to left simultaneously, out the output and into the gate. Once the full message is input, the contents of the shift registers is the code words' parity. Using this technique, the previous example will look and operate as that in Table 6.4. The word that was output is 1100101, which is the same result as the previous example. Similarly, if we decode the incoming code and determine its syndrome, we can determine where the errors occurred, if any.

A very detailed analysis of error detection and correction codes can be found in Peterson [1970] and Lin [1970] and their associated references. The above descriptions highlighted some of the important aspects of codes and coding theory in use.

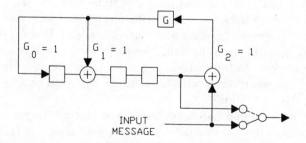

Figure 6.5   Encoding circuit for G(x) polynmomial.

6.5   Reconfiguration

Reconfiguration is an error management scheme that is used to work around major failures of network communications components. The process applied is to detect that an error condition has occurred that cannot be corrected by normal means. Determine what the error is, assess its impact on the network, formulate and implement a work around, and then continue operations as usual with the new configuration.

Error detection is performed via the use of normal mechanisms augmented by logging systems that keep track of failures over a period of time. This logged information is examined to determine if trends are occurring (e.g., to see if a component is continually causing errors to be inserted into the network or to sense the condition of a failed element by the monitoring system). Once the system knows that an error of significance that requires reconfiguration is occurring or has occurred, it must determine how this error or failure condition is affecting the network.

The component of the reconfiguration system that does this is typically referred to as the configuration assessment component. This element uses information about the present system configuration (connectivity, component placement, paths, flows, etc.) and maps information onto the failed component. This information is then analyzed to indicate how that particular failure or erroneous item is affecting the system and to isolate the major failed item. Once this assessment of what has failed and the determination of what is affected by this failure is determined, a solution must be worked out.

The solution can be from do nothing to reshuffling most of the operational processes to work around the error. The solution determination component must examine the configuration and the affected components (hardware or software), determine how to either move items around to bring the network back to an operational state or to indicate what must be shed because of the failure, and list items to be serviced. The determination of what to do is based on the criticality of keeping certain functions of the network operating and the resources available to do this. In some environments, nothing can be done because of device requirements or lack of extra resources. In these cases, the job of the solution component is to indicate to the servicing agent what must be corrected and to inform the users about the situation.

Once a work around has been determined, the reconfiguration system must implement the fix. In most cases this means rerouting transmissions, moving and restarting processes from failed devices, reinitializing a piece of software that has failed because of some intermittent error condition, or do nothing but tell all involved if the failure is not severe enough to force the payment of reconfiguring the system.

Details of techniques for these conditions is beyond the scope of this book; Fortier [1986] and more particularly Anderson and Lee [1981] cover the topic in much greater detail.

As networks find their way into many more facets of our everyday existence (banking, shopping, information transfer, etc.), the concepts of error detection, correction, fault detection, fault isolation, and reconfiguration will become much more important.

6.6 References

Anderson, T., and P. Lee, *Fault Tolerance Principles and Practice*, Prentice Hall International, Englewood Cliffs, NJ, 1981.

Fortier, P. J., *Design of Distributed Operating Systems: Theory and Concepts*, Intertext, Inc., McGraw-Hill, New York, 1986.

Lin, S., *An Introduction to Error-Correcting Codes*, Prentice Hall, Inc., Englewood Cliffs, NJ, 1970.

Peterson, W., *Error Correcting Codes*, MIT Press and John Wiley & Sons, Inc., New York, 1970.

PART THREE
Local Area Networks
Topology Considerations

7. LAN Topology:
Basic Concepts and Technology

As has been discussed in Chapters 1 and 2, LANs are required to overcome the fundamental limitation in processing capability inherent in single-
processor systems. The use of cooperating processors in LANs to overcome
this limitation introduces other issues with which a LAN designer must
cope. These appear in the form of network reliability, resource sharing,
load sharing, etc., which ultimately affect overall network cost. Just a few
of the issues associated with LAN design are listed below:

- Resource sharing
- Reduced duplication of effort
- Higher availability of resources
- Better reliability and maintainability
- Adaptable sharing of processing loads
- Access to unique resources
- Ease of incremental growth
- Graceful degradation of system in failures

A major determinant in how successfully these issues can be attacked
rests with the topology or interconnection structures of the LAN. The topology is a key element in a LAN's success or failure to perform its particular
task. For example, a LAN may be required so that a system can share a
number of costly processing resources. In such a system, the LAN designer,
for versatility's sake, might decide that a fully interconnected system is best,
in which each processor communicates with every other (see Figure 7.1).
The number of communication paths required is $N(N - 1)/2$ where N is

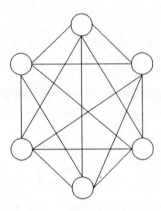

Figure 7.1   Fully connected network.

the number of processors in the LAN. As N becomes large, the cost of the interconnection network may quickly overcome the cost of the expensive resources themselves. Thus, the designer is faced with trade-offs which not only concern reducing the number of links to lower the cost but also the effects on throughput, response, etc., of the system.

In this chapter we will delve into some of the issues of LAN topology through the examination of the various options available to the LAN designer. We will also briefly discuss methods for designing LAN topologies and the information required to make intelligent choices about LANs.

7.1   Topologies

What do we mean be the term "topology"? In Clark [1981], it is defined simply as "a pattern of interconnection used among various nodes of the network." The number of different ways nodes can be interconnected presents a LAN designer with a bewildering array of choices, however. The most difficult problem facing a designer, in fact, is in the determination of what are the superficial differences and what are the important topological differences.

A designer has two basic choices that may be taken in selecting a LAN: (1) choose an existing LAN interconnection scheme that has been tested and meets the perspective requirements or (2) develop an interconnection scheme from scratch. Each approach has its own merits. In this section we will concentrate on the information required to implement the first approach, and in Part 3 we will concentrate on the latter.

What are some of the existing interconnection patterns that a LAN designer can currently choose from? There are rings, meshes, stars, buses, cubes, alpha networks, etc., to name just a few. None of these is best under every circumstance, and the designer must be careful to select one that maximizes his or her particular requirement, be it throughput, response, efficiency, or effectiveness. But how does the designer know which to choose to meet his or her requirements? To help answer this question, research into defining topology taxonomies has been undertaken for the past several years.

Because LANs represent evolutionary changes of smaller interprocessor communication systems, they are difficult to categorize. This is explicitly illustrated by the taxonomy work that has proceeded over the past dozen years. Early work in taxonomies, such as Chen [1974] and Siewirek [1974], were concerned with the interconnection schemes within or among processors used in distributed computing systems. (As noted in Thurber [1981], the differences between LANs, DCSs, and geographically distributed networks are more in type than in kind.) The taxonomy given in Chen concentrated on expanding how the classical method interconnections were classified within a single or multiprocessor system to include the linking of many of these systems [Jensen et al., 1976]. This can be seen below:

- Basic
  - Serial
    - Stars
    - Loops
  - Parallel
    - Trunk
    - Crosspoint
- Complex
  - Hierarchical
    - Trees
    - Others
  - Regular
    - Cubes
    - Others

About the same time, a taxonomy given in Siewirek took a different path. Here, instead of looking basically at the pattern of the interconnection, the communication aspects of the pattern were introduced as classification elements, as shown below. This addition is a necessary item for a designer to consider, even though it makes classification of LANs difficult. Should classification of LANs be based upon the pattern of the network structure, upon its communications rules, or both? And which aspect is more important?

- Topological characteristics
  Physical size
    Local
    Distributed
  Physical interconnection pattern
    Nonhomogeneous nodes
      Bipartite graph
    Homogeneous nodes
      Spanning tree
      Fully connected graph
- Communications characteristics
  Switch
    Centralized
    Decentralized
  Data paths
    Concurrent
    Serial
    Parallel
  Data discipline
    Circuit switched
    Message switched

The work done by Anderson [1975] tried to answer that question. In this classification scheme, the different types of LANs and the design decisions and system characteristics each type imposed on the designer were introduced. As illustrated in Figure 7.2, the classification of LANs was first made around the policy for communication and then around the resulting implementation pattern.

The highest, or strategic-level, decisions were concerned with how communication between nodes occurred. Transfer strategy then is concerned with transmission of messages from a source to a destination. An indirect path is one in which an intervening operation, defined as one or more switching entities that makes decisions on every message, is necessary.

The next level decision concerns the transfer control strategy. Direct paths have no requirement for transfer control since no operations are performed on the messages passed between system elements. However, in the indirect case, there are two possibilities defined. The message can be either centrally or decentrally routed. Central routing means that a single entity switches each message, while decentralized routing involves a number of intervening switches.

The next level, and the first that introduces implementation considerations, is whether the paths are to be dedicated or shared. A shared path is defined as one that is accessible from more than one point. Uni-

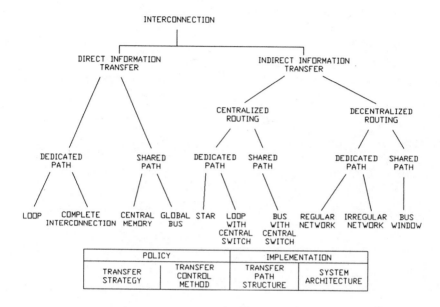

Figure 7.2   LAN classifications.

directional and bidirectional point-to-point paths are considered dedicated paths, while bidirectional paths which visit more than two points are considered as shared.

The final level of the taxonomy defines the actual types of LANs that reflect the design decision taken. Notice that different LAN patterns and implementations can represent the same design decisions.

One weakness in the above classification scheme is that usually a designer is trying to solve some particular problem and is looking for approaches that may help. A somewhat different classification approach was taken by Thurber [1981] to help in this area, as shown in Figure 7.3. LANs were considered as either solving some existing problem such as systems that were communication, I/O, or memory limited or solving some new one such as distributed processing. Notice that the pattern of the network is not considered very relevant and that there are many different implementation approaches to solving a particular problem.

Figures 7.2 and 7.3 illustrate the problem of LAN classification schemes. To be fully useful, some combination of the communication policy implementation approach and the problem trying to be solved approach seems necessary. It is beyond the scope of this book to define a taxonomy that can handle all three issues simultaneously, however, and we will leave it

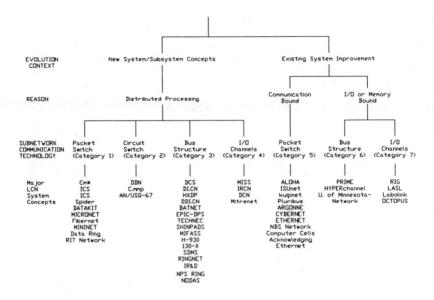

Figure 7.3   Another LAN classification scheme.

for some future time. We can, however, examine these issues in particular implementations, and so we have chosen to follow a simple classification scheme defined by Agrawal [1986]. This scheme concentrates on interconnection patterns and sees them constrained or unconstrained. Stars, rings, and buses are examples of the former, and meshes are examples of the latter. We will examine each of these in more detail in the next sections. Moreover, certain characteristics can be measured for each interconnection pattern to help classify them as to the particular problems they are trying to solve.

7.2   Types of Topologies

As was referred to earlier, there exists a wide range of topologies that support the interconnection of distributed computers. The following sections will describe some of the major interconnection schemes seen in local area networks: the mesh, star, ring, and bus.

7.2.1   Mesh Topologies

The mesh or irregular topology, as it has become known, is typically defined as a collection of computers connected in some point-to-point fashion. The lines used are source destination pairs such as are seen in the wide area

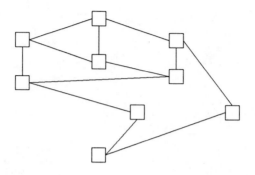

Figure 7.4   Simple interconnect.

networks. This type of topology can cover a wide range of complexity levels as well as topological variations. One of the simplest forms of irregular or mesh network would be comprised of a few links from each site, as in Figure 7.4, to a complete interconnect in which each site is connected to all others (Figure 7.5).

One can see that as N (the number of sites) increases, the attendant complexity (in terms of number of lines) increases at a rate which will quickly become intractable.

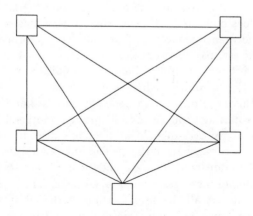

Figure 7.5   Complete interconnect.

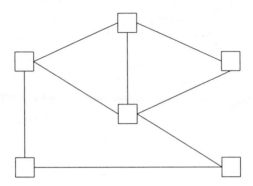

Figure 7.6   Partial interconnection.

7.2.1.1   Characteristics

This topology is one of the simplest to implement, requiring only physical
links and a controller capable of selecting one of $N - 1$ possible links for
message passing, although it raises many other issues. For example, the
addition of the Nth processor to a complete or fully interconnected network
requires the addition of $N-1$ links between it and the other processors in the
system. Also, the processors in the system must have the physical assets,
policies, and mechanisms in place to accept the new processing element as
a member of the LAN and a new source and destination of traffic. Thus,
this requires interfaces and software capable of accepting, as a minimum,
$M - 1$ parts where M represents the maximum limit the LAN was designed
for. But how does one select M? One can see that this represents a poor
cost-versus-performance trade-off. If we only have N processing elements,
we still, nonetheless, pay for the capability of $M - 1$ which is a very poor
design from a cost standpoint, although it supplies a desirable feature of
possessing growth possibilities, albeit limited ones.

Failures in this type of network topology can be handled fairly easily.
If a link fails, a message can be routed through another host to arrive at
the destination. If a processor fails, all links just discontinue service to the
failed host until it comes back on line. The link failure previously referred
to would require additional software and/or hardware to provide for the
dynamic rerouting of messages around failed links. This also would require
additional buffering at all the sites to support the additional traffic that
could come their way. This dynamic routing and buffer management is
expensive in terms of hardware and additional processing time required to
provide this service. Once we begin to look at the fully connected topology

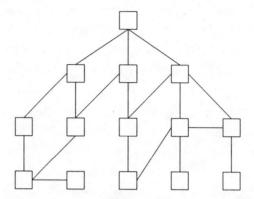

Figure 7.7   Hierarchical interconnect.

with failures, we now bring into play all the problems and issues seen in wide area networks such as Arpanet. We must be concerned with routing, flow control, addressing, link capacities, maximum path utilizations, and network utilization. What this really is looking at is the more general case of this topology in which not all processors are connected to each other. The interconnection can follow a variety of schemes in which the only similarity is that they are not fully connected or are in one of the three previously mentioned simple topologies (ring, bus, star).

For example, we may have a topology that exhibits many of the previous ones in that it connects to some number of the total but not to all (see Figure 7.6). Another variation would be a hierarchical interconnect as in Figure 7.7. In this structure there is a distinct hierarchy that can be seen though it need not be a classical tree structure. The major issues in these local area networks are those of throughput, complexity, and reliability.

The throughput of the network is determined or bounded by the capacity of the network. In reality, the throughput is determined by the overhead of the network and the actual offered traffic. These indicate the utilization of the network and, therefore, its actual throughput. To determine the overall throughput in messages per second, we can compute the overall network delay time average T. From this we can easily get the average throughput as $1/T$.

The average time delay is computed as the sum of the contribution of time delay for all links in the network. For example, if we had a network as in Figure 7.8, the average delay for this network would be found by applying the following formula:

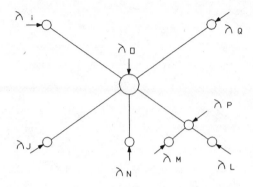

Figure 7.8   Network for example.

$$T = \sum_{i=1}^{N} \lambda_i t_i, \quad where \ t_i = \frac{1}{\mu_i c_i \lambda_i}$$

and where

$\mu =$ the service rate in bites per second
$ci =$ the capacity of the link and is the offered traffic rate

This can intuitively be seen as the sum of the delays divided by the total traffic rate. Details of this type of computation can be readily found in Kleinrock [1975].

The complexity of the network is derived from a collection of components, all of which are related to the selected topology. For example, as mentioned previously, if we have a totally interconnected network, there is no need for complex routing or flow control algorithms because of the simplicity of the connections. Conversely, in any other configuration, routing and flow control do become an issue since we do not have dedicated links for all source and destination paths. This gives rise to conflicts for assets. This conflict in turn drives the need for increased control of the network in order to maintain some suitable level of performance.

The control functions that must come into play include functions to establish the connections, control the flow once established, provide routing of messages in transit, monitor operations, provide maintenance and troubleshooting capabilities, and measure usage for cost accounting.

The connection establishment may be nothing more than providing an address for the network to use in sending your message; or it could be highly complex in which all links, buffers, and involved components are queried, set up, and readied for the communications to begin.

7.2.1.2 Flow Control

Flow control is a process in which the volume of traffic allowed over a link is either restricted or allowed to flow freely based on the capacity of the link and the source and destinations buffer capacities. The processes used are typically based on ordinary line control procedures. The flow control in the system has the responsiblity of controlling how much information is allowed to flow from a source to a destination in order to guarantee that there are sufficient resources to accept the sent message. Various strategies developed for wide area networks have found their way into LANs for the same purpose. For example, the use of choke packets to signal a source to slow up its transfer rate has been used in LANs, albeit in a different, simpler form. LANs, because of their increased speed and shorter distances, can afford to send more information between cooperative elements to better synchronize their actions. For example, LANs typically provide explicit acknowledgement of each packet (message) sent over the media. Using this capability, LANs can provide very effective flow control mechanisms. Another flow control scheme used is one that is referred to as a "reservation system." In this scheme, the sender must request the receiver to reserve space for the message that will be sent in the future. The receiver, if it has the reserve buffer assets for the sender, then sends a notification to the sender that it has reserved the required buffer assets for the message. Once this is done, the sender can send the message when it is ready. This type of scheme guarantees that messages will not be discarded because of insufficient buffer capacity. It requires more time to process a message because of the interaction and overhead associated with the flow control, but it provides more reliable message service. Typically in LANs, flow control is not as big an issue as it is in the wide area networks. Only in the mesh or irregular network is flow control required. The other LAN topologies that will be discussed provide for flow restriction through the control protocol in use, as will be seen later.

7.2.1.3 Routing Requirements

Another issue in the complexity of the mesh topology is the routing requirement. Routing is required in topologies in which the message can traverse more than one path (i.e., a decision must be made which way to go). In the best case the mesh topology with only two links per node must decide on one of two possible paths. In the worst case, it must decide on one of $N - 1$ paths. This need to decide where to go resulted in routing algorithms. If the network is a circuit-switched one (such as a multiway crossbar switched LAN), the routing is determined a priori and dedicated for a session (log in period). This setup can be handled by hardware as in the crossbar case or via software in the virtual case. Routing is not just the simple task of picking "a route" to the destination site; it encompasses selecting the route in some optimal fashion that does not degrade performance or cause unnecessarily long time delays in transmission. It can be seen that the complexity, in terms of the number of links, causes an increase in the overhead associated with the routing of messages in the network. A simple network such as a global bus does not suffer from these problems. Routing is relatively simple. It is a direct point-to-point link implemented by a single wire and unique addresses for nodes. This LAN topology is one of the few that requires routing to be instituted in order to provide adequate service to users of the network.

Routing in LANs of the irregular or mesh topologies has taken on similar characteristics of the routing schemes found in the wide area networks. For example, typical mechanisms used for routing include flooding, hot potato, and least cost.

Flooding uses a very simple technique for routing messages. The major idea behind this scheme is to take an incoming message and send it out over all other links except the receiving link. This technique guarantees that the minimum route will be found by the message. The problem is that because of the large amount of duplicates spread throughout the system at each site, a lot of the network's capacity is wasted. The redundancy consumes resources that could be used for other messages. Additionally, to keep messages from floating around forever and ultimately blocking use of the network, sites must be able to recognize messages they have previously seen.

Another scheme seen in mesh-based topologies is the hot-potato routing algorithm. This scheme takes incoming messages and places them on the first outgoing path whose queue can support it. The scheme is simple to implement though it does not guarantee a minimum path will be selected. It could either select the right path (optimal) by accident or choose the wrong path each time. This algorithm is simple but usually does not provide adequate service for a LAN environment.

A better candidate for a LAN is to keep routing tables at the sites. These supply the link address that will provide the optimal, or nearly so, service for the message being sent. Such a scheme requires a fast look-up algorithm to find the proper link, though in the long run it will provide fairly good service for routing messages in a quick fashion. The issue becomes one of whether the tables will be maintained statically (only changed on initiation or reboot) or will be dynamically maintained. Static maintenance provides optimal service on initiation, though as loads increase and bottlenecks or faults occur, it will degrade and fail at times to get messages through. The dynamic table requires overhead to update but provides adequate change resiliency, thereby providing better-built tolerance [Tanenbaum, 1976].

7.2.1.4   Monitoring and Maintenance

There are other issues to be examined beyond routing and flow control. The topology affects the monitoring and maintenance policies as well as the reliability of the system placed on top of the network. The topology selection drives the need for many other components, as we have already seen.

For example, to monitor the operations of a typical LAN with a simple topology may require only one monitor device to listen in on all traffic. This provides a means to easily assess the state of the network based on what occurred over some time period. In contrast, the mesh topology may force the need to have monitors at all sites in order to collect the needed usage statistics. Additionally, to provide a view of the system at any particular point would require the collection of the statistics from the multiple points into a single site, which would then construct a composite view of what the state is at this time.

This composite view is essential in order to be able to reconstruct the actions that have occurred in the network over some period of time. This is essential in order to run diagnostics and maintenance procedures to detect errors and/or check the state of components to schedule maintenance. The mesh topology and its derivatives require much more effort to collect and build the composite view. This topology also requires the institution of more detailed diagnostic and maintenance procedures in order to provide adequate isolation of problems and for better maintenance. From an overall reliability viewpoint, the mesh topology and its derivatives provide a more fault-tolerant architecture but not without its attendant increased costs. The mesh provides a more fail-safe system to the users. When a link fails, the messages can be routed around the failed link. Likewise, if a processor fails, routing of messages to other sites can be worked around the failed site. The price we pay for the increased reliability is the increased links and associated hardware along with the added support and control software.

7.2.1.5   Growth Capability

Another critical issue in selecting a topology is its growth capability. A topology is not very good if it cannot grow past its initial designed size. As we all know, whenever we put a computer system into use, we very quickly exceed the originally envisioned capacity. Therefore, a system that cannot grow quickly becomes obsolete and does not provide adequate service to the user community. This requires an expensive replacement of the entire network to bring the system back up to a useful level. The mesh topology and its derivatives do not provide expansion without much cost. In the worst case, to add a node requires $N - 1$ new links and hardware to support

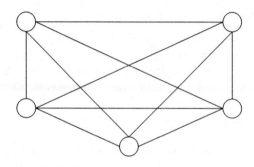

Figure 7.9   Fully connected topology.

them. In the minimal case, it would require the addition of a few links and adjustment of the routing mechanisms.

7.2.1.6   Technology

The technology employed in the mesh type of topologies can affect the reliability and fault tolerance of the network. Networks of this type typically require more hardware and processing assets to perform the switching function than do the networks that have simpler topologies. Typically, equipment performs the switching function if a circuit switch control is employed; equipment such as a switching station and concentrators are used if necessary.

Another aspect of the technology is the media used. Twisted pair, coaxial cable, or fiber optic transmission lines are usually found in local area networks. Each type of transmission media has intrinsic value and must be weighed by their cost versus performance ratio for the particular situation. The choice of which to use is based more on the required link speeds, the environment the lines will be exposed to, and the cost one is willing to

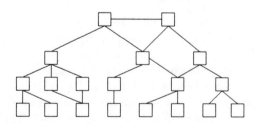

Figure 7.10   Hierarchical topology.

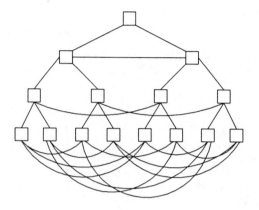

Figure 7.11 Hyper tree.

pay. Fiber is high-speed, lightweight, and relatively durable, but it is suited best for point-to-point links. It does not lend itself well to multipoint linkage because of the unavailability of an effective cost-effective T-connector. Twisted pair has been used for inexpensive links, but it does not lend itself to high speed. Coaxial cable is found in many LANs because of its value, durability, and communications qualities. A wide variety of connectors and controllers can be found for these medias.

7.2.1.7 Examples

A wide variety of networks is found in this classification, as we will show in this section. The classic topology within this classification is the fully con-

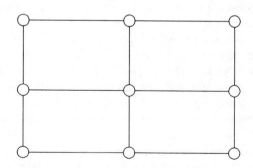

Figure 7.12 Regular topology.

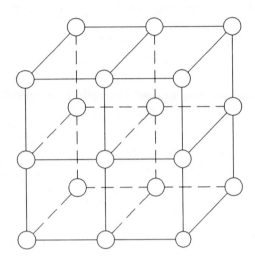

Figure 7.13 Cube structure.

nected topology (see Figure 7.9). This style of topology is used in situations in which high reliability is required and cost is not a consideration. This topology provides low delays for node-to-any-other-node communications.

A second example of topologies found under this classification is the hierarchical topology. This topology is recognized by an inverted tree-type structure with a single or multiple root having an increasing number of nodes on each level (see Figure 7.10). This topology is typically found in real-time control environments. The lower-level nodes represent the high-speed control elements. The next level represents the intermediary control and data reduction elements, and the upper levels are used as interactive control and process control elements.

Another example of a tree-type topology is the Hyper tree topology. This topology is characterized by a basic tree interconnection with side links to the other legs of the tree (see Figure 7.11). Variations on this structure have been developed and discussed in the literature. One variant is the multiple tree. In this variant N identical trees are interconnected through the linkage of the roots as leaves to elements in the other trees at the same level.

An interesting mesh topology is the regular mesh. This structure is typified by a regular lattice with each node having four internal links and the outside nodes having two links on the corners and three links on the external side nodes (see Figure 7.12).

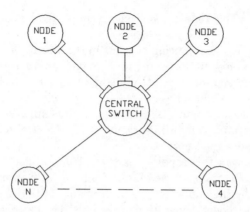

Figure 7.14 Star topology.

A variant, or extension to the regular network, is the cube and variants thereof (see Figure 7.13). The basic structure consists of nodes connected into a cube. Variants of this topology would add extra links to provide more paths to nodes and a more fault-tolerant system [Clark et al., 1981].

A more recent topology that can be classified as a mesh type of network is the Butterfly System of Bolt, Beranek, and Newman of Cambridge, Mass. This system is comprised of N computers linked via a collection of link segments with switches referred to as "butterfly" elements. The connection is made by the interpretation of the address supplied. The butterfly is a circuit-switched style of mesh topology, in which the paths are selected via the activation of the "switches" by the provided path address.

7.2.2 Star Topology

The star topology is best described as a collection of computers linked via an active hub controller. All messages are sent to the switching center for routing to the other nodes.

7.2.2.1 Characteristics

The star topology requires some form of active central hub which provides the switching (routing) function for all elements in the system (see Figure 7.14). The use of this central controller to perform all routing simplifies the structure for the host nodes, but at the expense of creating a complex routing station. For small simple networks, it provides a fairly good mapping of technology to a problem. The use of the central hub provides a means to put existing machines into a network without great changes to their structure. This topology provides a simple fix, but one that may only be temporary.

The central hub is a limiting element in the star network's growth. The central hub can only support some small maximum number of links. Therefore, it can only support a relatively small number of host computers. In order to be able to add a host to the network, the hub must have a spare port to plug the link into. This causes a problem if growth is essential to the organization's computing resources. The central hub blocks growth past the hub's designed port count.

Another issue in this topology is that of performance. The hub is involved in all interactions; therefore, it affects all communications. The delays caused by the hub affect the performance of the satellite hosts. This is caused by the mode of operation of the hub. The hub accepts requests for routing of messages to other hosts. The messages are queued in the hub's job file and acted on as resources are available. Depending on how the hub is designed, this queue is processed one at a time or in some parallel fashion. One can readily see that the hub represents a potential performance bottleneck and a reliability liability. The central hub must be a fairly powerful machine to handle the node taffic and must possess extra hardware to guarantee the reliability of the network. The increased complexity of the central hub may offset the benefit of the simple nodes.

For example, to guarantee a certain level of reliability may require that the central hub be designed with N level redundancy of all elements. This increases the control problem as well as the maintenance and diagnostics problem. The cost of the central hub host may outstrip the benefit of centralizing the communications function. Beyond the reliability issue, we also quickly discussed the performance issue. The central hub represents the point at which all communications must pass through; and, therefore, it represents a potential bottleneck for the network. If the hub is not of a sufficient power (much greater than the offered load), it will cause queuing delays that, in time, could build up to the point at which the network comes to a virtual halt, with queues loaded to the maximum and data flowing as fast as it can. The problem is that new offered information will not be accepted and could potentially be locked out indefinitely.

To rectify or try to fix this, some star-based networks have proposed using multiple star hubs in parallel. This provides a means to increase the throughput, but at an increased cost in terms of hardware and control protocol. The issue in control is how to determine which hub is the message to be routed through and when to switch from one to the other. We could select them randomly, which could work either very well or no better than a single source. For example, with the random choice method, we could always select the node that is least used, causing better overall performance.

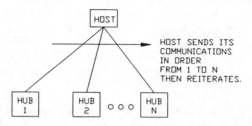

Figure 7.15 N-way hub controller.

The other side of the coin is that we could always choose the most heavily loaded host, causing the same problem we referred to earlier.

A better solution is to provide an algorithm that will select the hub of least cost based on its use. This would provide the node with its best performance available from the star network. The problem with this is getting this information. The information may be computed at the hubs and sent periodically to the user nodes. The issue here is that by doing this, we cause the user sites to perform a portion of the control function, which will affect their performance and cost because of the increased job they must perform. Other schemes could be envisioned that do not cause this, such as a simple daisy chain or polling scheme in which the sites use each hub controller in order and recirculate once they have gone to the first hub and so on (see Figure 7.15). This scheme spreads the use out across the hubs if all the hosts use the hubs in some fashion which does not put them all on the same hub at a time.

The issue in most of the above discussion is the bottleneck caused by centralized control. The fixes all began to migrate toward some form of distributed control. Though to keep within the intent of the star topology, we see that the fix only represents an increased cost for the hub controller and does not truly fix the problem of complexity, growth, or performance.

The hub controller scheme is a complex one from a hardware standpoint. The central switching node is itself a complex computing device, and it brings into the network a central point of failure. To work around the reliability problem requires increased hardware costs, as have been referred to, which often outweigh the benefits delivered to the network. Additionally, this topology has limited growth without going to some hybrid scheme.

7.2.2.2   Examples

There is not a wide collection of networks to discuss that fit this topology. Most that have been developed were built to interconnect a relatively small number of computing devices. Typically the linkage was performed

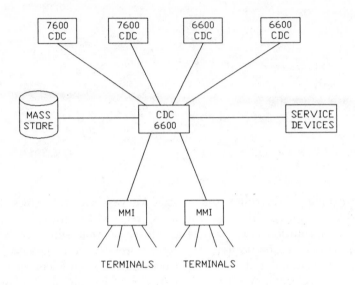

Figure 7.16 The hydra star.

to provide use of the laboratory or computing resources to researchers or engineers, not for end-user business types of applications.

We will examine five systems from a high level to see how they applied the star topology for use in network communications. The first example is NODAS [Shelly]. NODAS was designed as a data-acquisition system for medical and multilaboratory environments. It was developed at the University of Texas Health and Science Center in the late 1970s. The sytem consists of a large DEC System 10 time-sharing system as the central hub master with a relatively small number of PDP-11 minicomputers as the host machines. The central hub (DEC 10 System) performs the routing function for the peripheral hosts. The PDP-11s appear to the DEC 10 as intelligent, interactive terminals. The DEC 10 uses a service process to interpret requests and perform the routing and forwarding function. The maximum limit of remote hosts is dependent on the DEC 10's limit of terminals. Pictorially, the system appears much like that of Figure 7.14.

A second example of a star topology is the HYDRA [Christman, 1973] system. This star topology was built to provide for the interconnection of large computing resources into a single network. The goal was to provide a means to allow users access to all the laboratory computing resources. The system is comprised of a collection of CDC 7600 and 6600 computers

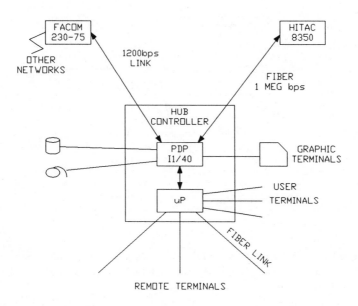

Figure 7.17 Labolink initial topology.

linked to each other and to service devices via a central hub controller, itself
a CDC 6600 computer (see Figure 7.16).

The central CDC computer provides the services needed to switch the
remote user requests and to link them up via message transfers to each
other. The central controller used tightly coupled slave processors to provide network interface services, data management services, peripheral device service management, and terminal interface management. These in

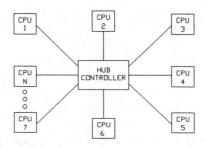

Figure 7.18 The distributed data network star topology.

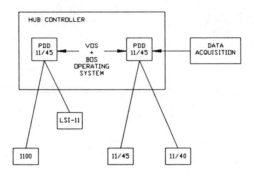

Figure 7.19 DCN star topology.

turn used the power of the CDC 6600 to provide the actual linkage and interaction betweeen the remote devices. Details of this system can be found in Christman [1973] and its references.

A third example of a star topology is the LABOLINK [Yajima] system. This star topology was developed at Kyoto University in Japan in the mid-1970s. It was developed to provide a network environment to support laboratory research and education. The central hub is comprised of a PDP-11/40 minicomputer and a microprocessor (see Figure 7.17).

The central hub controller coordinates the interaction of the user devices and computing resources in performing their computing jobs. The central hub coordinates the activity via the interaction of simple primitives. These primitives provide the necessary synchronization of the remote devices. Details of this example star topology and its applications can be found in Yajima [1977] and its references.

A fourth example of a star topology is the Distributed Data Network [Springer, 1978]. This network was developed at RCA Government Communication Systems for use in servicing high-volume real-time tasks. The system is comprised of a special-purpose central hub switching computer with N hosts attached (see Figure 7.18).

This system is controlled via a multiple-link space division switch which can accept up to 255 links. The central hub provides control for the establishment and breaking of the connections between user and devices. The controller (central hub) maintains status on all links and provides the services necessary to link the devices together. The hub is comprised of a circuit switching matrix which is controlled via two link controllers, one master, the other backup. Devices send requests for linkage to the central controller, which performs the function and sends a response back. Once

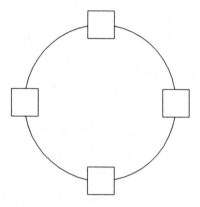

Figure 7.20   Ring topology.

a link is established, the controller assists in routing the message from the source to the destination via the internal switching and transmission facilities. Details of this system can be found in Springer [1978] and its references.

A final example of a star-based topology is found in the DCN [Mills, 1976]. The DCN was developed at the University of Maryland in the 1970s as a research tool for development and evaluation of resource allocation and management techniques for distributed systems. The processors are connected via their I/O channels and transmit information at relatively low rates. Data transmission occurs in a synchronous fashion. The system consisted of Sperry Univac 1100 series equipment and a number of DEC PDP-11 processors. The 1100 series machines are used mostly for background processing and user-code development. The PDP-11 machines were used as test beds and special-purpose development platforms.

The system concept was based around a virtual environment (hostel) which consisted of an abstraction of a virtual environment in which processes interact via a kernal operating system. The core consists of two hostels running a virtual operating system and a basic operating system (see Figure 7.19). Although this is not a rigorous adherance to the star philosophy, it does possess the main ingredients: central control points that provide the control of interaction with other machines in the network. Details of this architecture and topology can be found in Mills [1976] and its references.

7.2.3   Ring Topology

The basic philosophy of the ring topology is to have a number of processing elements or hosts strung together into a ring structure (see Figure 7.20). The elements are connected to two neighboring elements that terminate back at the start node. The flow of data in the network is typically in one direction, although some rings have been constructed to handle bidirectional transfers. In the ring topology one neighboring element of a host may be regarded as a source neighbor and another may be regarded as a destination neighbor. Messages circulate around the ring topology from source hosts to destination hosts, with immediate hosts acting as a relay or buffer unit. Ring topologies provide an environment in which many messages may simultaneously circulate within the network. To send a message from one host to another on the ring, the host (sender) places the message onto the media. The message then travels around the ring until it either reaches the destination host or is returned back to the sender. In most rings built, the sender removes the sent message when it comes back to it. Others have been developed in which the receiver removes it, although the former provides a means to acknowledge messages via changing the header or trailing information in the message. Conceptually, one can see how easily such a network can operate.

A loop configuration is very attractive for use in LANs for a variety of reasons:

- Routing problems become a thing of the past. All messages follow the same path. Logical addressing can be used allowing one to N users receiving a message.
- Addition is easily done by unplugging one connector, inserting the new node, and adding one additional link from the new host to the unplugged one.
- Information transfer is handled digitally and connections can be very simple since links are all point to point.
- The cost of loops is proportional to the number of nodes. For N nodes, we require N interface elements and N links.
- Throughputs can be fairly good since there is no contention for the resource. We are limited by the slowest element (i.e., the sender, receiver, or link speeds).
- The control is extremely simple, requiring little hardware or software to implement.

Many issues (pro and con) arise because of the loop topology. For example, what do we do when failure occurs? How do we maintain throughput as node count increases? The ring topology in its pure configuration is highly susceptible to failure of hosts or links. If a host fails and no means

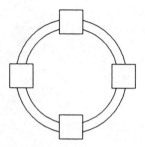

Figure 7.21 Dual ring topology.

to bypass it exists, the network is unusable. Likewise, if a link fails, we also see the network come to a halt. To correct these problems requires the network to possess redundant links and hardware to bypass failed nodes.

An additional issue to be addressed with the use of LANs is the transfer delay associated with data transfer. The ring topology that requires a source to send a message to its near neighbor, which is not in the proper direction, requires traversing $N - 2$ nodes and $N - 1$ links to arrive at its destination. This time delay could become excessive if the number of nodes in the network becomes large. The average time for transfer is $N + 1/2$,

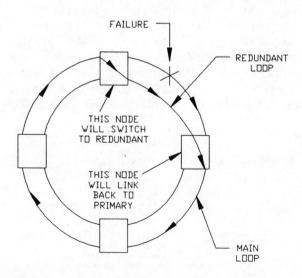

Figure 7.22 Redundant loop recovery.

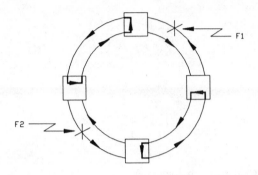

Figure 7.23   Dual loop failure.

which implies that on the average we will traverse half of the nodes to transfer messages.

An advantage of the ring is that interface units can be very simple, requiring transmit and receive circuitry with buffers for each. The technology developed in the wide area networks, stars, and mesh type networks can be used devoid of all their complexities.

7.2.3.1   Technology

Loop technologies are based on one of three basic types–the Newhall, Pierce, and delay insertion rings. The Newhall ring uses the concept of a control token that is passed around the loop in a round-robin fashion. The possession of the control token signals that this node is allowed to transmit its message onto the ring. When the node that possesses the token has completed its transmission, it sends the token back out onto the ring to the next unit on the ring. This simple scheme provides for interference-free

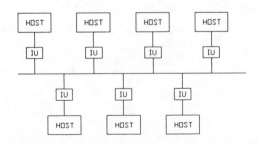

Figure 7.24   Global bus architecture.

transmission while not blocking the reception of messages down the line from the transmitting node.

The second style of ring is the Pierce ring. In this variation on the basic ring, the communications space is divided into some number of fixed-size slots. Messages can be inserted into the slots and removed based on the protocol implementation. The slots in the network have an indicator that signals whether the slot is empty or full. Interface units slice up their messages into packets (size of a slot) and examine the line until a free slot is found. The transmitter sets the indicator from empty to full and inserts the packet. Upon reception, the message packet is removed and the slot set back to empty.

The final category of ring found in this topology is the insertion ring. The insertion ring operates by providing mechanisms that delay incoming messages by some maximum amount of bit times to allow for the insertion of a message of the same delay time. To do this each interface unit is comprised of a size-N receiving buffer, a size-N sending buffer, and a switch to select delay, transmit, and run through for the interface unit.

From a purely performance view, it has been shown that the delay insertion loop provides better service than the Pierce or Newhall loops. Likewise, the Pierce loop provides better service than the Newhall loop. On the opposite extreme, the cost is inverse. The Newhall loop is the simplest followed by the Pierce loop, then the delay insertion loop.

Reliability is a big concern in these loops and must be addressed. As was previously mentioned, the loop configuration is vulnerable to errors and faults that can easily bring the network to a halt. A lost address or erroneous address causes a packet to be incorrectly delivered or to circulate indefinitely, both of which degrade performance. The failure of a ring interface causes loss of access to the ring and possibly failure of the entire network.

To work around these errors, monitors must exist to detect flawed messages and remove them. In the case of failures, bypass circuitry in the nodes must exist to isolate a node failure from the system. Additional equipment is necessary to handle the failed link case. The solution includes added links and switching to provide access to the redundant links. Two types of redundant link structures have been used: the spare link and reversed link methods. In both cases, the reliability is enchanced by the use of redundant data paths (see Figure 7.22).

In the first case, if a link fails, the interface unit simply switches to the redundant link that flows in the same direction (see Figure 7.23). In the case of the dual paths running in opposite directions, the interface units have the capability to loop back into the other ring to bring the loop back into operation. This topology causes longer paths, but it provides a way for the system to survive multiple failures, albeit in a stand-alone factored way (see Figure 7.23).

The loop with multipaths and different directions provides a way to maintain the loop in some working order. Upon 1 the network maintains its totality because of the multipath rerouting. The problem comes when more than one link fails as shown when F2 fails in Figure 7.23. When this occurs, the network partitions into two rings with two nodes in each. The system continues to function but has lost access to any information in the other sites.

7.2.3.2 Transmission Technology

Ring structures are well suited to the use of common carriers such as twisted pair and coaxial cable, though a more interesting and better technology is fiber optics. We saw in the previous chapters some of the qualities of fiber optics. One of its best is its ability to move digital data from one end to another quickly. This point-to-point nature of fiber optics makes it well suited to use in a ring topology as will be shown in later in the book and in this chapter. Systems have been developed and do use this technology.

7.2.3.3 Examples

To further enhance the presentation of the ring topology we will go through the examination of a sampling of ring topologies developed.

An example of the Newhall-style network is the Distributed Computer System (DCS) developed in 1972 at the University of California at Irvine [Farber and Larson, 1972]. The initial system consisted of five nodes with three Lockheed Sue minicomputers and two Varian 620/i minicomputers connected into a ring topology. The data ring operated at 2.3 Mbps. The interface for this early ring topology was complex and comprised of 140 ICs. This represents a fairly expensive interface unit, but it was corrected by the design of some custom chips. The DCS has some rather interesting features such as addressing messages to processes rather than locations. This complicates the network interface although it provides a much cleaner interface to users of the network. To use the ring network, a process must await the arrival of the token. Once the token is received, the host can send its message onto the network. Associated with the message are the destination process address (logical ID) and various control bits. The token has two formats: a connector and token. To use the bus, a node waits for the token. It turns the token into a connector, appends its message, then ships out a new token pattern behind it. The next node sees the connector and checks the address to see if it is addressed to any of its processes. If it is, it reads it; otherwise it continues to scan for the token. When it sees the token, it now is in control and can either transmit as before or simply let the token pass. To remove messages, the sender must remember what it sent and take it off as it comes around.

An example of the Pierce-style ring topology and control is Spider Net. This network was developed at Bell Laboratories by Fraser [1974]. Spider was an experimental packet-switched data communications system that multiplexes 64 full duplex channels, each with a maximum data rate of 500 kilobits per second (kbps) onto a single tie-line-type loop. The transmission line operates like a conveyor belt with time slots of fixed size passing along the length of the loop. Any device attached to the loop can send packets to the switches when they see a free time slot. Additionally, each packet is examined by all devices to see if it is addressed to them. As on the classical Pierce loop, when a packet is recognized, it is removed from the link and the spot is marked empty. More details on this loop topology and its design can be found in Farber and Larson [1972].

An example of the delay-insertion ring topology is the Distributed Double Loop Computer Network (DDLCN). This ring topology uses two rings to increase thoughput and reliability. The control DDLCN buffers incoming messages into an input buffer and outputs outgoing messages via the output buffer. Once the output is out, the input buffer begins to shift out the held message. A unique feature of this topology is the redundant buses. These buses can have traffic flowing on both, thereby increasing the overall throughput of the system. This implementation of the delay-insertion ring has the added fault tolerance gained by the redundancy of the links, while also gaining on performance by using the added link for traffic when all is well. Details of this topology and its control can be found in Wolf and Liu [1978].

7.2.4   Bus

The bus, as was the case in the ring, removes the need to have routing and the central node control mentality of the early nets. The global bus architecture is comprised of a number of processing hosts and interface units connected along a line segment (see Figure 7.24). The global bus is well suited to LAN use because of its low cost and distance limitations. The global bus topology uses low-cost coaxial cable and a wide range of controllers and connectors to supply a rich collection of LAN variations to users.

The main element that differentiates this topology from all the others is the global bus that interconnects the multitude of devices. Other than this, the global bus supports control protocols that exhibit features of the previously mentioned topologies as well as many new ones.

7.2.4.1 Bus Control Techniques

The global bus provides ways to supply both centralized and decentralized control. Three major classes can be quantified for both centralized and decentralized control. These are daisy chaining, polling, and request/grant.

In centralized implementations, the following schemes hold: daisy chaining, polling with global counters and local counters, and independent requests.

The daisy chaining control protocol operates as follows:

- Bus request is sensed by the central controller.
- A bus available indicator is issued by the controller.
- The bus available indication is propagated from the closest device to the controller to the furthest until it reaches the first requesting unit in the chain.
- The requesting unit receives the bus available indicator, thereby inhibiting the use of the bus by anyone else.
- The unit now has control of the transfer media. It performs its communications function on the bus.
- When it is finished, it drops all the held signals to a neutral state.
- The network is now in a ready state, waiting for the next request.

This scheme is simple to implement as well as easy to add to, and it can simplify the scheme by having control passed logically on the single bus instead of in strictly physical order. This would provide possibly a better use of the devices. The problem with the scheme is that a failure of the controller stops the system. A failure of the bus available signal, bus request, or bus busy indications disables the bus. A further problem is the control propagation; units furthest down the line (physical or logical) may be starved out and could possibly never get to use the media. Further schemes shown correct many of these problems.

Centralized polling schemes operate by providing fixed slots for the devices to use. This can be viewed as similar to the ring's token-passing scheme. The first class uses a central controller that puts out poll codes. The operation of this scheme flows as follows:

- The device requests the data bus.
- The controller begins to count on the polling line.
- When the count responds to the requesting deviced, it responds by indicating bus busy.
- The controller stops the poll count and gives control to the requesting unit pointed to by the poll code.
- The requesting unit performs its communications function.
- When finished, it releases the data bus.

- The control unit has two options; it can continue the polling from where it stopped (round robin), or it can reset and start initial count (prioritized).

This scheme can be adjusted by having the controller continuously rotate the poll count until it sees bus busy, which will give control to the unit being polled.

The second polling scheme uses fixed slots in the host interface units to divide the slots among the sites. The central controller is now dumb. It can be nothing more than an oscillator that goes off/on or is based on a control signal. This scheme operates as follows:

- The clock starts to send pulses.
- On each pulse, the units all increment their internal counters.
- Each unit examines its counter when it matches their slot code(s). They are now the bus master.
- The unit that wishes to use its slot signals the oscillator to stop counting to secure the bus.
- The unit that has control performs its operation.
- When finished, it releases the bus by allowing the counter to continue on.

This scheme is flexible and provides a means to tune the system to usage patterns. If we have fewer units than the number of codes, we could provide multiple codes to units requiring more service. The problem is that this is not dynamic, but static.

The next major form of centralized control of a global bus is the independent request scheme, which operates by having the N units possessing separate means to signal the central controller that they wish to use the data bus. The central controller must then, via some selection algorithm, decide which of the N requesters to give control of the data bus to. This scheme can easily implement any of the others very simply. The scheme conceptually provides shorter overhead in terms of bus control traffic and provides total control to the central bus master to decide how to manage the data bus asset.

Although the above schemes are effective in providing use of the bus, they do not use the topology as well as they could. The global bus topology is well suited to distributed control because of the ease of broadcasting information to all sites at once. As the following section will show, the previous three schemes can be applied to a distributed control scheme with good results.

In decentralized polling, we have two schemes by which to propagate control. The first scheme, based on requests,operates as follows:

- A device wishing control sends out a request signal (unless another device is already signaling).
- This signal is viewed as the bus available signal.
- This bus available signal propagates (bus transmission) until it reaches the requesting device.
- The requesting device stops the signal and then use the data bus.
- When finished, the signal is sent back out for others to use.

An example of such a control is the logical polling scheme described in Fortier [1986] and in Part 6. This scheme sends out a poll code that is incremented by the receiver (unit whose poll code was previously seen) and then sent out for the next unit to use.

The second polling scheme is a round-robin scheme in which the poll code is recomputed on each use and sent out for others to use. A significant example of this is a system in which each device has a set of poll codes known to it. These codes are unique within the system. To access the bus requires a device to have a code that matches its codes. Such a scheme is described below:

- A unit that just relinquished control sends out a poll code.
- If the code matches that of another device that wants the bus, that bus responds with an accept.
- The former controller drops the bus available indicators, signaling that another device has taken control.
- If the poll code matches no device (implying no unit wishes control), the unit under control now issues another poll code and so on until another unit picks up control.

This process can be viewed as a rotating bus master, which at any time controls the action of the bus.

A third class of distributed control in global buses is referred to as request/grant schemes. These have additionally been called contention-based systems. In a broad sense, the generic protocol for global bus control using request/grant contention schemes work as follows:

- Devices request the bus via some requesting mechanism.
- A requesting unit possesses some form of priority or recognition of itself in the network.
- Devices wishing to use the media control and win control based on how they interact with others wishing the same.
- All others, who do not win, back off and prepare to try again at a later time.
- The winner uses the bus and then releases it when finished.

7.2.4.2   Examples

The following pages introduce some sample bus topologies that provide the control previously described.

A well-known example of a global bus scheme is Ethernet. This scheme will be further described in Part 8; here we will only glance over its description. Ethernet was developed at the Xerox Research Center in Palo Alto, CA. The Ethernet system was designed to provide communications among computing stations dispersed over a close proximity (less than 1 to 1 km). The communications scheme uses a coaxial cable with a random access broadcast packet algorithm. A host in the Ethernet system connects to the passive coxial cable via a serial interface cable to a transceiver. When a host broadcasts a packet onto the cable, it listens to see if the packet goes out without problems. The broadcast is heard by all stations on the network and is copied in by the destination host. There is no routing of the packet, and control is totally distributed. In the case of multiple units wishing to transfer simultaneously, a collision (garbling of messages) may occur. If a collision is detected, the transmissions are aborted and rescheduled at a future time. This scheme is very simple and has been embraced as a standard, therefore making it widely available and used. Hardware and software for this system is readily available from many sources, which makes this topology and implementation attractive for use. The problem is that the control scheme is destructive and will only support low-use levels effectively.

Another well-known bus topology is the Hyper channel. This implementation provides high-speed data paths for user devices. This concept provides a scheme to connect high-speed devices together into a data-sharing network. This network incorporates a series of adapters. Each adapter contains channel interfaces to specific manufacturer's equipment, a data buffer, and trunk control for connection to the Hyper channel coaxial cables. All of the hardware is controlled via a microprocessor.

A third classic example of a global bus topology and control scheme is the Honeywell Experimental Distributed Processing System (HXDP). This system was developed as a vehicle for research in the science of engineering of processor interconnection, executive control, and user software design for distributed processing. Control of the global bus asset is performed by the incrementing of local control words which, when shifted to the proper sequence, give control of the media to the unit which perceives the match. This is an example of the distributed poll code described earlier.

The HXDP system can have a global bus of up to 1000 m in length and supports a data rate of 1.25 Mbps. The architecture of HXDP supports up to 64 loosely coupled devices connected over the bit serial global bus media.

An interesting global bus scheme was described in Fortier [1986] and its references. This scheme is referred to as a DOT OR. Devices wishing to access the global bus and send messages contend for use of data slots. The control is performed on a separate data line, providing more potential capacity for the data lines. The control operates by the devices wishing to send serially gating their node address and message priority onto the control bus beginning on a control frame start indication. As they send out their bits, they scan the line to see if what they see is what they sent. This is done on a bit-by-bit basis. If the sending bit does not match a device's, it drops out of contention. This utimately leaves only one device in control. This device is then allocated the next data frame, which it will use for sending one frame of data. All others contend again for the next packet and so on.

Many variations of this scheme have been proposed to get around problems of favoritism and blockout. Schemes such as spacing out messages over their maximum timeframes and message scheduling to provide adequate space for interleaving of high- and low-priority messages have been discussed in the literature. For details of this scheme look to Part 8 and to the references in Fortier [1986].

Further examples of these topologies will be found in Part 8. The topologies described are only a small portion of the total network. The network is comprised for a set of functions and hardware that provide the topology with its life and operational capabilities.

7.3   Summary

This chapter introduced the concept of topology. Topology refers to the interconnection scheme or network "map." The major types of topologies are the mesh, ring, bus, and star. These provide a rich selection of alternatives for LAN users to choose in configuring their network as was shown in the chapter. Additionally it was shown that these topologies provide a variety of access schemes as well as performance levels based on their interconnection structures.

7.4   References

Agrawal, D. P., et al., "Evaluating the Performance of Multicomputer Configurations," *Computer*, vol. 19, no. 5, May 1986.

Anderson, G., and E. D. Jensen, "Computer Interconnection Structure: Taxonomy, Characteristics and Examples," *Computing Surveys*, vol. 7, no. 4, Dec. 1975.

Chen, R., "Bus Communication Systems," *University Microfilms Dissertation*, 64-20493, 1974.

Christman, Ronald, *Development of the LASL Computer Network*, 1973, pp. 329-342.

Clark, D., et al., "An Introduction to Local Area Networks," in K. Thurber and H. Freeman (eds.), *Local Computer Networks*, 2d ed., IEEE, 1981.

Farber, David, and Kenneth Larson, "The System Architecture of the Distributed Computer System–the Communication System," *Symposium on Computer Communications Networks and Tele Traffic*, Polytechnic Institute of Brooklyn, April 4-6, 1972.

Fortier, P. J., *Design of Distributed Operating System: Theory and Concepts*, Intertext, Inc., McGraw-Hill, New York, 1986.

Fraser, A. G., "Spider–An Experimental Data Communications System," *International Conference on Communications*, 1974.

Jensen, E. D., et al., "A Review of Systematic Methods in Distributed Processor Interconnection," *IEEE International Conference on Communications*, June 14, 1976.

Kleinrock, L., *Queueing Systems, Vol I: Theory*, John Wiley & Sons, 1975.

—, *Queueing Systems, Vol II: Computer Applications*, John Wiley & Sons, 1975.

Mills, David, "An Overview of the Distributed Computer Network," *Proceedings of the National Computer Conference*, 1976, pp. 523-531.

Saffer, Shelly, J., et al., "NODAS–The Network Oriented Data Acquisition System for the Medical Environment," *Proceedings of the National Computer Conference*.

Siewirek, D., "Modularity and Multiprocessor Structures," *Proceedings of the Seventh Annual Workshop on Microprogramming*, October 1974, ACM.

Springer, Joseph, "The Distributed Data Network; Its Architecture and Operation," *Proceedings of Compcon 78*, Fall 1978, pp. 221-228.

Tanebaum, A., *Structured Computer Organization*, Prentice-Hall, 1976.

Thurber, K., and H. Freeman, "Architecture Considerations for Local Computer Networks," *Local Computer Networks*, IEEE, 1981.

Wolf, J., and M. Liu, "A Distributed Double Loop Computer Network (DDLCN)," *Proceedings of Seventh Texas Conference on Computing Systems*, pp. 6-19, 6-34, 1978.

Yajima, Shuzo, et al., "Labolink: An Optically Linked Laboratory Computer Network" *Computer*, IEEE, Nov. 1977, pp. 52-59.

8. Protocols for Interconnection Strategies

Protocols represent an agreement between two parties as to how they will react to some predefined situation. In the political world protocols represent how countries treat each other on a given set of issues. In networks they describe how information will be viewed and used in performing some end function. In the case of topologies (interconnections), protocols describe how the link is to be used and how to view the bits flowing over it. There are many levels of protocols in a network; we will only discuss them at a cursory level here and only as to how they relate to topology.

Development in local computer network (LCN) protocols have been proceeding in the direction of a hierarchical, multilayered, structural philosophy, as represented in Section 8.1. Basic architecture defines six layers of protocol in each processor-IU pair to be interconnected. Interaction between layers is defined to occur only between adjacent layers. Specific designs may add and/or delete various layers, or portions of layers, as the specific design warrants. The various characteristics of the layers are outlined in the list below.

Protocols have developed mainly to satisfy qualitative and quantitive requirements for process interaction. (Do designs meet requirements?) Qualitative requirements include (various layers require various requirements):

- Flexibility (to accommodate new uses and features)
- Completeness (to properly respond to all relevant network conditions)
- Deadlock avoidance and backout mechanisms (availability)
- Synchronization mechanisms (for interprocessor control)

- Error detection and recovery (what level and how done)
- Buffer overflow avoidance (processor-IU input/output)
- Message sequencing assurance (data received properly)
- Duplicate message detection and recovery
- Permeance (to implement the protocol uniformly throughout the local computer network)
- Priority mechanisms (various levels exist)
- Accounting mechanisms (monitoring functions)
- Security mechanisms
- Message delivery guarantees
- Data code and format transformations (between layers, nodes, and networks)
- Computer equipment featuring compatibility and interface
- Operating system featuring compatibility and interface
- Communication network featuring compatibility and interface
- Network transparency
- Usefulness (user applications, can network support them?)
- Application-oriented (extend commonality from system to system)
    File transfer
    Editor
    Compile
    Execute
    Debug
- Executive-oriented (extend operating system services one node to other)
- Command protocol (assign, print, time, date, status, etc.)
    Virtual scrolling, terminal protocol–remote device appears local
- Network-induced protocols
    Directory service
    Acccess authorization
    Endpoint declaration (global address queues)
    Transport control (node to node association)
    Interprocess synchronization
    Network system control ("built-in" maintenance and security check)
    Addressing (logical or physical)
    Flow control
    Routing
    Destination availability (buffering, scheduling, retry, timeout retry, interrupt, dataaccept, control and maintenance, etc.)

Quantitative requirements regarding speed of communications include:

- Delay (usually measured in average response time)
    - Components of delay
        - Transmission delay is proportional to message size/circuit rate
        - Processing delay
        - Queuing delay is proportional to system load
- Throughput (peak traffic level)
    - Components
        - Effective bandwidth of processing equipment
        - Effective bandwidth of transmission media
- Availability (measured as percent down-time)
- Response time
- Data integrity (bit error rate in the system)
- Queuing delay
- Security (the rate of message misdelivery)
- Utilization
- Message integrity (rate of message loss)
- Buffering requirements

8.1   Components of Physical Structure

As in geographically dispersed networks, LCNs are constructed using various IU and processor designs as well as a multitude of interconnection media, as illustrated in the following list:

- Common carrier circuit (usually associated with dispersed networks)
    - Readily available
    - Leased service
    - Maintenance by carrier
    - Easy reconfiguration
    - Practical over medium to large distances
    - Variety of speeds
- Twisted pair
    - Inexpensive media
    - Low speed and short distances require no modems
- Coaxial cable
    - Inexpensive medium
    - Can support multimegabit transmission, 1 to 10 Mbps
    - Broadcast or point-to-point operation
    - Relatively immune to noise

   May exist in building for CATV
- Cable TV
   Advantages of coaxial cable
   Capitalize on systems installed for video transmission
- Optical fiber
   High bandwidth
   Small diameter and weight
   No crosstalk
   No RFI
   Potential for low cost
   Very low error rates
- Satellite (dispersed networks)
   High bandwidth at low cost
   Large delay
   Distance independence
   Broadcast medium
   Low incremental cost
- Radio (dispersed networks)
   Broadcast medium
   Basis for mobile data communications
   Distance independence
   Potential for low cost
   Low incremental cost
- Value-added network
   Broad availability
   Flexible leased service
   Usage-based charges
   Distance independent charges
   Maintenance and upgrading charges

Communications along these paths can have various characteristics such
as synchronous or asynchronous transmission, either full or one-half duplex lines, and either bit, byte, or word-oriented message formats. Beyond
these, the communications can be performed using a wide array of available
switching methods as shown below:

- Circuit switch
   Dedicated physical path between communicating subscribers
   Telephone system, an example
   Inefficient for "bursty" traffic
   Path setup time traditionally on the order of seconds

No speed or code matching performed
No sharing of unused bandwidth
- Message switching
    Telex/TWX, Auto Din 1, Sita
    Message logical data unit
    Subscriber passes message to subnet
    Entry node stores message on disc
    Entry node forwards message to "next"node
    Process repeats
    Store-and-forward approach
    Network takes responsibility for delivery
    Attempt to optimize use of network lines
    Speed and code conversion possible
    Transit times usually on order of minutes
- Packet switching
    Logical outgrowth of message switching
    No use of secondary storage
    Message split into small units (packets)
    Packets routed independently, store-and-forward basis
    Packetizing allows "pipelining"
    Message delay typically fraction of a second
    Most dynamic switching technology
    Effective use of circuit bandwidth with sophisticated switches
    Example: Arpanet, Telenet, Cyclades, Datapac, Auto Din II

8.2   Interface Units

In geographically dispersed networks, the nodes are connected via common carrier, satellite, radio, or LAN media. The media interconnect or interface unit, which may or may not be embedded in the processor or host system, provides for the linking of the remote nodes via the media. These units tend to be very complex front-end processors or whole computers in design in order to perform the functions required in geographically dispersed networks (i.e., routing and flow control).

In LCNs, the interface units tend to be generally simple in design because of the processing requirements of the LCN. The interface units within any particular LCN are usually identical in design and construction, differing only at the device-to-IU interface. Network software, in most LCNs, tends to function identically, varying only in code for different types of processors interfaced to. Network software tends to be minimal (range of 10K bytes or less). Node-to-node hardware is usually simple because of the need to only interface to one or two channels. Messages are variable in length in most LCN designs, which is in contrast to ARPA-type messages that are of fixed size. Overhead involved tends to be less because of the simpler nature of internode communications software and hardware.

Some typical examples of IU hardware functional components and functions provided by IU elements are listed below:

Interface unit basic components:

- Bus coupler(s)
    IU to bus hardware connection (passive and active)
- Receiver(s)
    Electronic interface from bus to IU
- Sync and data detector(s)
    Converts bus format to IU format
    Error detection
- Input buffers (could have DMA-type properties)
    Signals protocol control of a message state
    Holding station for host's messages
    Signals message filter that a message has arrived
- Message filter
    Detects if message is addressed to this unit
- Input control
    Supplies needed control to transfer message(s) from IU to host
- Protocol control
    Determines if IU has bus control
    Requests bus control
    Handles timeouts
    Releases bus control
    Error detection
- Output control (could have DMA-type properties)
    Tells protocol control a message is to be sent
    Holding tank for output messages
- Encoder and sync generator
    Converts IU formatted data to bus formatted data
    Adds parity, CRC, etc.
- Transmitter
    Electric interface from IU to bus
    Drives bus couplers

Interface unit functions:

- Initialization of bus (i.e., start token passing, begin counting sequence)

- Maintenance, a monitoring function which allows all units to check the state of others
- Enter, allows a unit not on the bus to get into the sequence (some units will have have this capability: HXDP)
- Exit, inverse of enter
- Receive, procedure by which an interface unit can decide if a message is destined for it
- Restart, from a warm position, restart the system, (i.e., failure recovery)
- Transmit, transmit procedure by which an interface unit requests transmission
- Error control, ACK/NACK, status, parity, CRC, ID, detection of duplication
- Die, causes addressed unit to drop from ring
- Buffer overflow handling, procedure to handle this condition
- Retry, on error or overflow, etc.
- Flow control, user allocation (central control), node allocation (decentralized control), special routines
- Segmentation, break up message, if too large, and control its transmission in some orderly fashion
- Addressing, what (name device), where (address device), how (route)
- Security
- Routing (if desired by design)

Processors or hosts, as they have become known as, are part of both LCN and geographically dispersed networks. In both types of systems, processors used are usually of the commercial and military variety of microprocessor, minicomputer, or mainframe and have a word width of 8, 16, 32, or more bits per word.

Various details of the previous pages will be described in the following parts of the book:

- Part 2 covers more specifics of media design and use.
- Part 4 covers details of protocols.
- Part 5 addresses issues on security of networks and protocols.
- Part 7 addresses the management issues.
- Part 8 addresses examples of systems in use today.

8.3   Summary

This chapter was provided to convey the myriad aspects of protocols and mechanisms used in realizing these protocols in LANs. The details of the individual aspects will be addressed further.

9. Topology and Requirements

9.1 Matching Topology to Requirements

Knowing about the various local area network topologies and quantities is important, though not the only information necessary to select a LAN to fit your problems. One must look at the user needs, what the LAN is intended to be used for, how it will provide benefits, and what its limitations will be. One must examine why we perceive the need. Do we want a LAN because our competition has one and it is working for them, or do we see the LAN as a means to expand our present capabilities and perhaps foster new areas of involvement in our market domain? Where will the LAN be used? Will we simply connect up the corporate offices, the secretarial pool, or the entire operation to our LAN?

Typically, the major reason for a company's migration to LANs, or for that matter any network, is to provide more timely access to information and to access to a larger base of information and resources not economically available otherwise. Whatever the reason, in order to select a LAN that will provide the services we envision, we must match the LANs' qualities and capabilities to our present and projected requirements.

9.2 Introduction

Before we can speak simply of matching the given topologies and systems to our requirements, we must understand the underlying decisions and processes undertaken in designing a LAN in the first place. These will help us understand better how to apply our requirements to given LAN qualities and capabilities, thereby giving us a better method to match our requirements to give technologies.

There are many techniques available for the design of a network; they were discussed in Chapter 2. Before we look at specifics that drive the topology, let us look at some other generalizations for local area network selection and design.

In order to design a network, the community has provided us with many techniques. The two major ones are the top-down and the bottom-up approaches. the bottom-up approach takes the bare transmission facility and builds on top of this the required functionality. For example, we could add on host-to-host level control protocols, operating systems, data management processes, etc. The top-down approach works down from the intended end user requirements to a final physical implementation. Many approaches have been described in the literature for developing systems using these techniques; these will not be elaborated here. It suffices to accept the fact that systems have been designed from one or the other. The important points to be extracted are: 1.) in the top-down case the major stress is in developing a final product based on a need; 2.) in the bottom-up case the product is developed and made to fit as time goes on. An analogous view is that the top-down approach is driven by user needs whereas the bottom-up is driven by the engineers perception of need. In either case the result (hopefully) is a finished, working network.

The important aspects in selecting a LAN involve the environment, access, cabling and installation, expansion, support, management, and performance. The environment issue addresses the prospective user's site. Where will the nodes be (one per building, per floor, per office); how are they dispersed; what type of obstacles must be overcome, ceiling installation, duct installation, underground, in open air; what distances must be covered (a few feet or tens of thousands of feet); what extra precautions must be undertaken to properly locate active elements to facilitate servicing the LAN?

What type of access will the LAN be required to support; direct link access, contention access, remote dial in access? Based on these, what type of software services must be provided to support these (file transfer, data base management, security, etc.)?

A very important aspect, because of its representing one of the major costs of installing LAN, is the cabling and installation issue. Many papers addressing LAN issues tend to neglect the simple yet expensive issue of cabling. The cost of cable and installation can far outstrip the cost of other aspects of a LAN. Therefore, we must judiciously look at cabling as a major aspect of our LAN selection criteria. Some topologies will require more wiring and incur more cost. A consideration is to review what wiring one presently has in place and see how a topology, LAN protocols, and services can be mapped onto it. The consideration is whether the existing wiring will be able to support the ultimate capacity estimates of the LAN. Most existing twisted pair and coaxial cabling is limited to from a few magabits to possibly 10 megabits per second. Higher data rates may not be supported. Additional problems may be caused by the proximity of present installations to noise sources, and by run distances. These were adequate for low data rates and where noise could be tolerated; but in digital environments, noise and reflections cannot be tolerated.

One must consider the expansion planned or envisioned for the network. Expansion includes adding new nodes, expanding distance covered, linking to other LANs of differing types, linking to metropolitan and wide area networks. All these issues must be considered before we shop for a LAN that can meet our needs.

Another aspect of LAN selection is support. When you purchase your LAN and install it, does the vendor disappear from the face of the earth or is it always there when you need it? A vendor's ability to respond to users' service requests in a timely fashion is an extremely important component of the selection. If you cannot get service when you need it, you could be out of business. If you decide to go a route to save cost and buy hardware from one vendor and software from another, can you count on getting adequate service from both? This issue is many times not adequately addressed when one looks at a LAN purchase.

Who manages the network once we own it? Networks, just like computers, do not run on their own. They require operators, managers, and service personnel to maintain the operations. The manager and operators of the LAN have the same jobs as their computer center counterparts. They must monitor operations, provide service for adding, deleting, and servicing nodes in the network. They must be responsive to user requests for enhanced service as it arises as well as myriad other functions.

Last, but not least, is the issue of performance. How many users can a LAN effectively support, what are its true, running parameters (throughput, average delay, queue delays, priority service levels, reliability, fault tolerance, services offered such as logging, notification, backup, recovery, error management)?

The major issue to keep in mind in the selection process is what the LAN is to be applied to. This should drive all the other considerations but in the opposite direction. Once one has a realistic vision of the LAN's use and the users' needs, can we look at the other underlying issues with certainty? By following a sound process in selecting a LAN, an organization will reap the benefits many times over. Conversely, choosing incorrectly, or being sloppy about the choice, may necessitate the process being done many times, causing excessive costs.

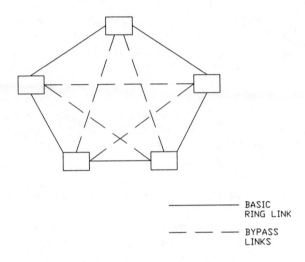

BASIC
RING LINK

BYPASS
LINKS

Figure 9.1   Ring topology with total bypass capability.

9.3   Distribution Patterns

The selection of topology by itself will not suffice. We need to examine and decide the distribution pattern we will have at the inception of the LAN and in the future. The distribution pattern could be simple: one of the basic four topologies—ring, bus, star, and mesh. The pattern would be the basic structure of the four, not a hybrid or extention of the basic structure. To determine the distribution pattern, we must examine the dispersion of the sites and the potential ways we could cable our system. For example, if the main computer assets are centrally located and we have a small number of peripheral sites we will be connecting, we may want to consider a star topology. This would be well suited to the task since the system is assumed to have many more communications from the central site to the peripherals and vice versa than between peripheral sites.

Another example of a distribution pattern is the global bus. The global bus pattern is well suited to installations in which many units must be linked together in a regular structure such as a collection of office personal computers. The ring topology or pattern lends itself to situations in which we have nodes strung over some distance and a shortest-round-trip algorithm can pick a path such that it minimizes the total path run. This is typically the case when we link multiple buildings within a cluster together. In any case, the selction of a distribution pattern or topology is weighted heavily by the dispersion of the sites and the potential installation paths that we must take.

The following section will examine a variety of patterns to look at the breadth of possibilities. As we saw in the previous sections the simplest distribution patterns are the ring, bus, and star (see Figures 7.20, 7.24 7.14), respectively. These represent topologies suited for limited numbers of nodes, less than 256 in most cases. To go beyond this or to meet some more difficult installation considerations may require us to look at hybrid topologies.

An example hybrid topology is the complete interconnection. This topology could actually be represented as a basic ring with bypasses for reliability (see Figure 9.1). This represents the worst case in which we require total redundancy to be able to bypass any failed element.

A ring variation we looked at previously was the double ring (see Figure 7.21). A variation to the ring and double ring because of site distribution requirements (i.e., two buildings that are well suited to rings but far enough apart to warrant separate ones) is the dual interconnected ring topology (see Figure 9.2).

The topological variation on this could be very different. The internetwork ring nodes could be the same instead of being interconnected over a line. In this case, the IU is called a bridge if the LANs are identical. One could, using this idea, connect a very large number of rings together. For example, we could have very high-speed rings on four computer nets and a medium to slow speed LAN as the LAN interconnect (see Figure 9.3). Many other variations are possible on the basic ring topology that allow it to fit many more potential situations than the simple ring could support.

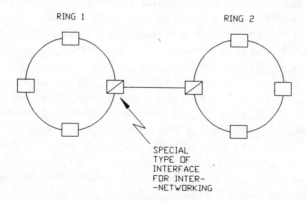

Figure 9.2   Dual interconnected ring.

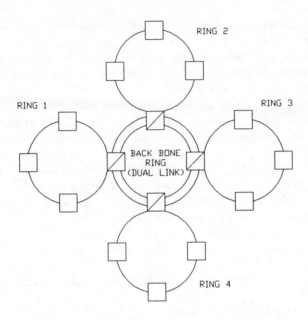

Figure 9.3   Multiring topology.

Another topology that has been widely used and adapted is the global bus. This topology has many variations over the basic single line show in Figure 7.24. For example, the global bus is typically limited to a relatively small distance, about 1 km. In many installations, because of building size and installation routing requirements, it must exceed these limits. To do this requires either use of repeaters to amplify and send on the signal or partitioning of the total LAN environment into multi-LANs that can function separately and converse with each other through gateways (interfaces to dissimilar LANs) or by bridges. Figure 9.4 shows some typical variations.

The third class of dispersion patterns to look at are those based on star or central control. The basic structure was shown in Figure 7.14. The star is best suited for applications in which a large mainframe must communicate with a collection of other computers on a regular basis, such as a large central data bank with peripheral data users. Variations on this topology have not been widely seen, though you could look at the wide area networks as examples of multistar interconnections. This is true if we look at the concentrations as the hub controllers. An example multistar topology is shown in Figure 9.5. Systems of this type would typically consist of a mainframe in each of three sites with personal computers or minicomputers

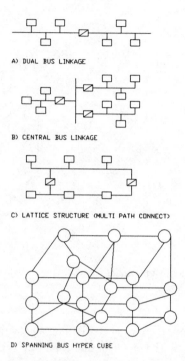

A) DUAL BUS LINKAGE

B) CENTRAL BUS LINKAGE

C) LATTICE STRUCTURE (MULTI PATH CONNECT)

D) SPANNING BUS HYPER CUBE

Figure 9.4   Examples of bus hybrids. (a) Dual bus linkage, (b) central bus linkage, (c) lattice structure (multipath connect), and (d) spanning bus hypercube.

strewn over the site. The mainframes would link together the three stars, providing a single larger star with three hubs of control.

Hybrid topologies are becoming more of a common occurrence. This has been brought on by the requirement of early LAN users to expand their systems beyond their designed parameters. Hybrid systems are comprised of pieces of various LANs. For example, a hybrid system may have a star as a central router with the outer computers replaced by buses with computers strung off them, or a hybrid may be a combination of ring, bus, and star. Figure 9.6 depicts a few hybrid topologies.

9.4   Dispersion of Sites

To aid in our prudent selection of a topology and protocol, we need to address the issue of where to place the hosts in our LAN or, based on where they already are, and how to route the LAN in an optimal way between them. To perform this requires that we know how the sites are dispersed

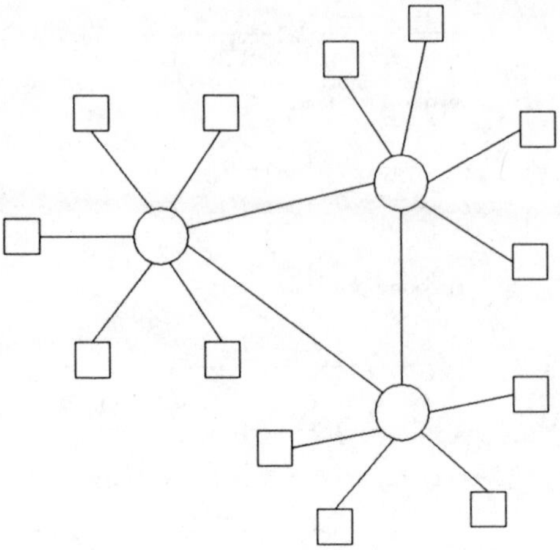

Figure 9.5   Multistar interconnect.

and be able to determine an average distance between them. This, in turn, can be used to examine the effect of one topology versus another. We wish to minimize the average distance to keep the nodes as close to each other as possible. This will provide better average throughput and service since all delays will be, on average, equal. Therefore, one of the important pieces of data we must collect is the locations of the various machines that will be connected to the network. We will see later how this information can be used to construct minimum-cost spanning trees and shortest-path routes, in essence generating the topology or at least the minimum distance routes between the nodes. The location of the sites could be widely dispersed. In this case, an optimal topology may be a central star with multiple links or connections to the periphery sites (see Figure 9.7).

Another example of disperson of nodes that can drive the topology is an office environment in which there is a personal computer or terminal in every office. We wish to connect these together in an intelligent fashion. With this piece of information (the dispersion) we can better select the topology. The office sites could be served nicely by either a global bus or a ring depending on the number of offices and the potential cabling options.

A related metric was described in *Computer Magazine* [1986]: the average distance. The average distance D is defined as the dispersion or the average between all nodes. This term is defined as (in terms of the number of links)

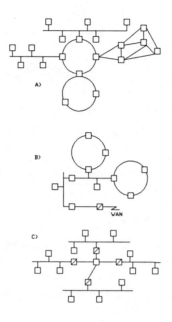

Figure 9.6   Sample hybrid topologies.

$$\overline{D} = \sum_{d=1}^{n} \frac{dN_d}{N-1}$$

where

N_d = the number of computers at a distance d links away

d = the diameter

N = the total number of computers

This can be seen as the weighted sum of the distances from a reference node, which can be any node.

When the topology is regular (i.e., each computer attaches to the same number of computers such as in a bus or ring), the average distance is a constant. For example, in the ring topology, the average distance is found as $(N+1)/4$, which says that on the average the distance between nodes is 1/4 times the number of nodes. This implies that as N becomes larger, the distance from one point to another may become unacceptably large.

The fully connected network, on the other hand, provides an average distance of 1. That is, each node is on the average one link from each other. The problem with this metric is that it does not take into account

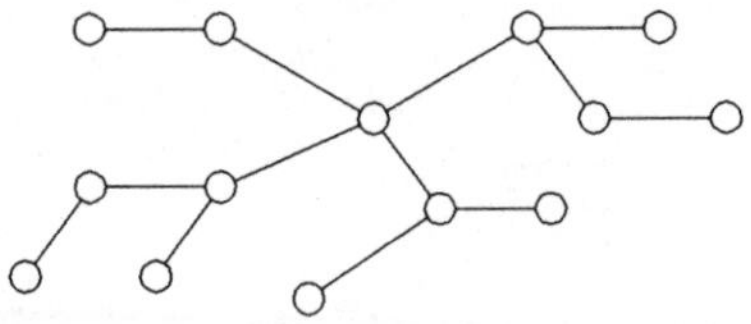

Figure 9.7   Potential star.

real distances. It is only another piece of information to use in weighing one design versus another.

9.5   Number of Sites

An important quantitative number is the number of sites we will have on the network. Knowing this provides us with a means to use the previously defined metric of average distance with some real numbers. The number of nodes will drive us away from some manufacturers that cannot support the number of sites we envision for our system. Another consideration we must examine when addressing the number of sites is the number of ports or interface unit links we are willing to pay for. In the fully connected case, we require $N - 1$ ports. In the global bus case, we require one port and in the ring topology, two ports. If N is of any significant size, say greater than 5, the cost of the fully connected network is only feasible if reliability is a must. We will instead look at the ring, or bus, with their lower cost in terms of ports. It will become more apparent in the analysis performed as to the importance of the number of nodes to the selection of a LAN topology, protocol, and software support.

9.6   Volume of Information Transfer

An aspect of the definition of an organization's LAN needs is the assessment of its informational needs. If an organization's informational needs are well defined, they can use this to assess the capabilities of a LAN to meet these requirements. Based on the known traffic flow between sites, one can perform an analysis to determine the best way to interconnect these nodes in such a way as to minimize the overall number of links or to minimize some other function. In Chapter 10 we will investigate some of these notions further.

In determining our LAN informational requirements, we not only look at our present computing needs but at potential future needs as well. A new or emerging concept is the mixing of various types of information over one LAN. For example, the mixing of video, textual graphics, voice, and other forms of information over the same media has become prevalent. Therefore, to better assess the needs of information transfer, we must examine all of our data requirements and look at how we transfer and use this information today and how this information is intended to be used in the future. The decision on what information we will transfer over the net and its volume will drive our media selection and even our topology considerations to some extent.

The volume of information we will need to move about will directly affect the protocol we select to use in controlling the network. For example, if we have requirements for transferring a large volume of information more or less continuously from site to site, a collision detection scheme may not be very well suited to our needs since this type of network will tend to virtually halt useful transfer of information above some threshold utilization. This topology would not be used in heavily used networks. A better choice may be a high-speed ring, or a bus with a reservation scheme such as described in Fortier [1986] would be much better suited to this use.

The important aspect emphasized in this section is to get a very clear picture of your user communities' information requirements before you invest in a LAN. The other side of the coin is that if we cannot get a very accurate picture of our needs, maybe making a reasonable engineering guess and adding some buffer to this to provide room for error would suffice. What has been seen in such situations is the use of safety margins far exceeding 100 percent of the proposed use. This was done to guarantee, it was hoped, that the network would meet its intended use adequately. The problem has been that, by the time all overhead is taken into account and we look at useful data throughput, it represents a fraction of the quoted capability. User communities typically quickly exceed the initial intended use, and this "safe margin" may only provide a minimal system capability.

9.7   Installation Considerations

As important as selecting a LAN is adequately planning for its installation. Once we have chosen the type of LAN we will use and the equipment associated with it, we must address the issue of actually physically running the cables to interconnect this equipment into a total LAN. The selection of a cable type is driven by the equipment needs and environmental factors.

Once one has selected the cable that can support the necessary equipment, information transfer rates, and distances, one must examine where this cable will be installed. Will the cable be strung indoors, outdoors, or both? Will it be buried, placed in duct work, risers, plenums, over aerial ways between buildings, or all of these? If it will run both inside and outside, we must be cognizant of the vulnerability to outside weather conditions such as wind, rain, ice, hail, wide fluctuations in temperature, and ultraviolet light damage. What about animals? If we bring cable under-ground or run it across rivers, lakes, etc., what types of natural phenomena do we need to address? For example, the telephone company in a very early article indicated that cables strung in the ocean were being attacked and chewed by sharks. The problem was caused by a tone given out by the electric power flowing in the cable. Another problem is burrowing ro-dents. This type of animal typically chews on cables, and if the cable is not adequately protected, it will not survive.

Once we have defined all the requirements in terms of where a cable will be placed and what it will be exposed to, we must prepare comprehensive drawings of an installation. This can be done by an installation firm or by the actual customer. These drawings or plans must define the cable types required for each environmental area. It must describe necessary connec-tors, conduits, electrical requirements, and all associated end mountings and connections. The proper performance of planning at this stage can save some very unpleasant and expensive surprises upon final installation. This step will help define any harsh requirements for the installation of the LAN.

The design planners must pay careful attention to how the cables will be pulled and placed to make sure that maximum bend radii are not exceeded. Exceeding this may cause the cables to operate improperly. That is, they could lose their connectivity, their ability to transfer information. If the cables are electrical instead of light-based (e.g., coax instead of fiber optic), we must be concerned with grounding on entry to buildings or any other area from the outside. This is to keep lightning and power ground loop currents from entering the building.

An additional issue is routing of cables. Once the feeder cable enters the building, we must place routing boxes to provide adequate spread for all connections. Again the type of connector panels and hardware will be based on the final chosen topology. Once the cable and components are chosen, the installation must be well planned out to assess the volume of components required.

The components for the LAN must be specified completely, as many vendors supply LAN components but standards do not yet exist in full force. With the IEEE 802 standards coming out, we hope to see more rigorous use of standard protocols and ultimately standards in the physical aspects of the components.

Installing a LAN has many aspects. For example, we must be careful to check out the cable specifications in terms of fire retardant characteristics and, more importantly, its toxicity. This issue of toxicity has become more of an issue with today's air-tight buildings, and as such we must select a LAN cabling that meets the emerging new codes. Building installations are subject to local and national code requirements, although most cable constructed today would be allowed for conduits. Cable for risers and air plenums require special characteristics. All cables found in risers must be encased with a fire retardent jacket. Cable used in plenum installations must pass UL tests.

Cable installation beyond the consideration for cable qualities requires the physical placement of cable in new construction. This is done as is any other wiring. The problem comes when a LAN is being put into an existing environment. We must take into account the bending ability of the cable and the pulling tension that the cable can sustain. All these considerations must be made to ensure that the laying of the cable provides a good basis for the LAN. Additionally, during installation we may wish to have extra cable for expansion installed in walls and ceilings since the cost after will be more than during the initial installation. This will save the organization money in the long run.

9.8   Servicing the LAN

What about after we have spent lots of money to have a local area network installed throughout our organization: Who keeps it running? What does it take? Will I have to hire and train a full operations staff? These questions must be answered for the organization to know what they are really getting. If we do not know how the LAN will be maintained, we may be primed for failure. The ideal LAN is one in which the seller remains around and is responsive to all problems of the purchaser in a way similar to IBM's philosophy to provide excellent service to their products once they leave the factory and throughout their life. The ideal LAN vendor is able to provide high-quality, single-source responsibility for all levels of service from initial planning, installation, into life cycle maintenance and servicing. In reality, most vendors come somewhere in between. They provide some service but typically not comprehensively. Thus, once we select a LAN, we must find a service contract which will provide adequate coverage to guarantee our uptime and performance. This service contract, or a vendor's ability to provide one, is as important an item as any other in the LAN. Acquiring a service contract is like buying insurance; you buy it just in case, hoping you will not need it. The cost of this service may run 10 percent or more of the base hardware costs.

A more important aspect is what services are offered. We need services that will keep the downtime to a minimum. Downtime is not cheap. Downtime experienced by large financial data networks can amount to tens of thousands of dollars per hour. Systems such as banks, airlines, hotel reservation services, stock exchanges, etc., experience much fustration and lost revenues if their LANs fail at inopportune times. To address this, LAN designers have built in much redundancy and backup. This still, though, only will increase reliability if we can easily and quickly detect and isolate faults. Once isolated, we must still service and repair the failed item to bring back the reliability measure of the LAN. The job of the service organization is to keep the LAN products running and in good repair.

Servicing of LANs is expensive as we said earlier. It requires people with a variety of skills such as analog and digital technicians, communications protocol experts, software and firmware experts, as well as a variety of monitoring devices specialized to the job of troubleshooting networks. The service equipment for LANs is improving and with it the mean time to repair will come down. Therefore, we must be careful when selecting a LAN that we not only look at its technical merits, but also at its life cycle costs and the vendor's ability to support the product adequately with service and upgrades throughout its useful life.

9.9   Routing Variables

This section, as well as the next one, looks more at the up-front analysis issues in LAN design. The examination of routing variables and topological design will be addressed.

The major function of routing is the directing of how to send a message from one site to another in the network. A routing scheme must be simple, reliable, stable, adaptable, and globally optimum while being fair. All these are features we would like to possess from a routing scheme, although they appear at first glance to be contradictory. Simplicity refers to a routing scheme's structure and operation. We expect a good routing scheme to be simple to implement, that is, to require as few as possible assets from the system to perform. As was described earlier, there are many routing schemes for the mesh-style network, but how do these apply to the other styles of networks? We will see later that in all systems built and operated, the topologies are typically of a hybrid variety, and therefore some routing is necessary.

Reliability refers to the ability of a routing scheme to continue operation even in the event of a failure. If the scheme is reliable, it will not crash because of the loss of one or many sites; it will merely adjust to the change.

If a routing algorithm is stable, it will provide good service to all. It will not oscillate between blocked and free. That is, the algorithm must be such that it will operate properly and with nearly the same performance for all potential loading scenarios.

A good routing scheme can adapt to change. If links fail or links become overly congested, the scheme should be robust enough to work around the failure or block and continue to provide service. The scheme should provide for the lowest delay path as possible so as to provide the users with good performance; it should also be fair. That is, it should utilize all links as equally as possible to keep overall system throughput at an optimum level. In most local area networks, routing is not a major problem. It is determined by the topology and leaves no variations. The ring and bus topologies are such examples. The issue in routing for LANs comes up when we look at hybrid topologies, that is, topologies in which we have multirings, multibuses, or other combinations of structures. In these cases we must look back at the work done in the wide area networks and use their notions for routing of messages between LANs. Once inside a LAN the local environment will take care of it. The issue is how to route to the other links.

Most LANs use a routing-table-type scheme in which the operating system, user, data manager, etc., provide to the LAN environment an address (logical or physical) that the LAN uses to perform its routing. Typically, the routing is a table look-up that indicates this address is in domain N, where domain N represents a LAN within the total collation of LANs in a configuration. The routing can be adaptive or nonadaptive as was previously discussed. The adaptive algorithms will provide a way for the LAN operating system to control where things are loaded after initialization, whereas the nonadaptive version will tend to block any dynamic movement of process sites of operation because of its inability to adjust its operation to changes in the system mappings. If hybrid systems are to be used, one needs to further address this issue as part of the prepurchase work in planning for a LAN.

9.10   Summary

This chapter addressed the topology issues relating user needs to local area network performance parameters. Introduced were metrics one can use in specifying a network for purchase or for developing requirement specifications for the construction of a LAN.

9.11   References

Computer Magazine, April 1986.

Fortier, P. J., Design of Distributed Operating System: Concepts and Technology, Intertext, Inc., McGraw-Hill, New York, 1986.

10. Automated Topology Generation and Analysis

10.1 Automated Topology Generation

Of theoretical interest and as a learning tool, automated topology generation can lead to insight into topological nuances. Though typically simulation would be used over graph theory and analytical techniques, in reality not much of this type of work is really done. Topological design still tends to follow the path of the art rather than the science in real-world applications.

The brunt of the work done in this area was performed by the people doing work on the wide area network connectivities. Therefore, this will be described somewhat in Sections 10.2 and 10.4. In Section 10.3, tools that have been developed to aid in topological design decision for LANs will be addressed.

10.2 Graph Theory

If we look back to work done on topology for wide area networks, we find that what was used were concepts found in graph theory. Aspects of the minimum flow algorithms and minimum spanning tree problems have been used for topology generation from a site. The general problem addressed was typically centralized network design in which there was a central computer and some number of terminals (see Figure 10.1). A typical problem is given below; it is usually aimed at one of three conditions:

1. How many concentrations are there and where should they go?

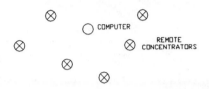

Figure 10.1 Sample design.

2. Given a set of concentrations, what terminals should be connected to a particular concentration?
3. How should terminals be connected?

This example will focus on the last two:

1. How should concentrations be hooked up to the CPU?
2. How should terminals be hooked up to concentrations?

They will be used to address the terminal layout problem. In this problem we wish to minimize the cost of lining up all devices with the constraints of maximum time delays we can have and a minimum reliability.

Reliability in the above network can be realized by a few simple techniques. For instance, we can insist on having two connections to all sites (i.e., redundancy). Another option is to provide a mechanism where, if a link fails, the number of discounted terminals is less than some small design number. This again implies some level of redundancy. Designing around time delay is a much more difficult problem. An approach is to assume maximum flow for each link, which implies a maximum link delay (a worst case).

To formulate the following problem solutions, we need the following inputs:

1. $N-1$ terminal nodes labeled i equal 1, 2, 3,..., n.
2. Cost matrix C_{ij} is a cost to link i to j.
3. Traffic flow for each peripheral device ai equals traffic from peripheral i.
4. Capacity of links.
5. Maximum number of terminals allowed to be disconnected because of link failure.

The first solution will attempt to simplify the problem by dropping constraints 4 and 5. We will look at the use of Krushal's minimum cost-spanning tree algorithm for solving the problem of finding a network of minimum cost, which connects all nodes. Krushal's algorithm works by

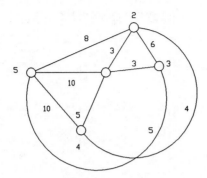

Figure 10.2 A sample graph.

connecting least-cost links one at a time, starting with the lowest-cost link. The algorithm then selects the lowest-cost edge (link) and brings it into the solution set. This is done with the restriction that the new node to be brought in cannot form a closed circuit. If it does, remove this link from consideration. Do this process until all the nodes are connected.

Another way to construct an optimal spanning tree is the branch and bound technique. The principle is to partition the set of feasible solutions into k subsets $S, \ldots, S_k$. With these, calculate the lower bounds for costs of each subset. Let L_i be the lower bound for S_i:

$$(S_1 - L_1, \ldots, S_k - L_k)$$

On the next step, pick S_J, which has the minimum lower bound L_J. If there exists a feasible solution in S_J with a cost of L_J, it must be optimal. If not, partition S_J into two or more subsets. This requires calculating new lower bounds. Once completed, repeat the above.

Another good algorithm to apply is one called Prims. The basic notion of this algorithm is to connect the nodes closest to the center first and work out from there. The algorithm operates as follows:

1. Construct a cost matrix $T = [T_{ij}]$ in which

$$T_{ij} \Leftarrow \quad for \ i = l, \ J = 1, 2, \ldots, n$$

$$T_{ij} \Leftarrow C_{ij} \ for \ J = 1, \ldots, n$$

2. Find the minimum T_{ij}.
3. Check if constraints are violated by inclusion of $(_{ij} J)$ or if a loop is formed. If yes, set this $T_{ij} \Leftarrow$ and go to step 2.

a)

	1	2	3	4	5
1		③	3	5	10
2			∝	∝	∝
3				∝	∝
4					∝
5					-

B)

	1	2	3	4	5
1		-	③	5	10
2			6	4	8
3				∝	∝
4					∝
5					-

C)

	1	2	3	4	5
1		-	-	5	10
2			6	4	8
3				③	5
4					∝
5					-

D)

	1	2	3	4	5
1		-	-	5	10
2			6	4	⑧
3				-	5
4					10
5					-

Figure 10.3   Sample cost matrices.

4. Add link $(_{ij} J)$, set $T_{jk} \Leftarrow C_{jk}$ for all nodes R not connected to network, and go to step 1.

To illustrate the algorithm, an example will be worked. We have a graph G which illustrates the network and potential links (see Figure 10.2). On the first iteration of Prims algorithm, we begin with the cost matrix from one set, as in Figure 10.3a. On the first iteration we select link (1,2) as the minimum cost to our set S.

We will then select (1,3), as shown in Figure 10.3b. On the third pass we select minimum cost link (3,4) of cost 3, as shown in Figure 10.3c. On the fourth pass we select (2,4), then (1,4), then (3,5), then (2,3), all of which are found to violate constraints of forming loops. We choose (2,5) ultimately as the next lowest-cost link that does not form a loop. The final network is shown in Figure 10.4.

In network design we ask questions such as how many concentrations to use and where to locate them. We have shown some algorithms that can be applied to the solution of network topology design, but there is more.

Exact solutions are based on exhaustive enumeration and branch and bound procedures. These tend to be computationally expensive and, therefore, are not used for large problems. To address this problem many heuristic solutions have been developed such as the add algorithm, the drop algorithm, and the Bahl and Tang algorithm. The add algorithm operates as follows (see Figure 10.5):

- We start with all peripherals connected to S_o (all concentrators closed).
- Open concentrations one at a time to give maximum decrease in cost.

- Continue until opening another concentration does not decrease cost.

First test S and find that S improves the connection at $T1$, $T2$, and $T3$. The algorithm will continue to scan the other links until no more gain is found. This algorithm has a fairly good run time. With N nodes it will require in the order of N^2 time to run this algorithm versus the exponential $2N$ for an exhaustive search. Details of this and other techniques can be found in references Kleinrock [1975], Tanenbaum [1976], and Fortier [1975].

10.3   Simulation Techniques

Simulations have found a home as an evaluation tool for LAN developers and purchasers. In the last few years we have seen an improvement in the quality and availability of tools for evaluating LANs that use simulation. Simulation provides a means to study alternative architectures, topologies, and designs without the expense of building test systems or running tests on systems in operation.

A network evaluation tool, to be truly useful to a wide range of users, must provide a way to allow general input and tailored definition of the intended topologies and systems to be studied. The tool must have a means to input realistic data flows and must provide a means to map this onto a real system. The system should provide a way to map any type of software partitioning on the system in order to study a variety of placements.

The design of the connectivity (topology) should also be easy to implement, adjust, and test. If a tool existed that could provide these capabilities along with real component performance characteristics, we would have a means to select LANs with fairly good confidence.

A fairly generalized simulation tool was partially described in Fortier [1985]. This tool provides a means to tailor simulation to a topology and system that the user wishes to study. The model is constructed as a collection of software packages wrapped around the GASP IV simulation language. You are allowed to describe your topology in terms of connectivity of nodes together and their distances. For example, to define a bus topology you would call the topology definition package, which allows you to call up each node in order (number of nodes is unlimited). With each node you can specify the links to other nodes that exist and the distance associated with it. For the bus you would describe the topology as a connection to each site with the distances derived by the proximity to the other nodes. Once the topology is defined, this tool provides a means to specify the protocols in place for the topology. Presently the tool provides 36 canned protocols (similar to those defined throughout this book). Additionally, it provides templates with which users can define their own protocols and insert them

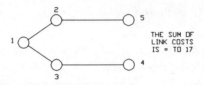

THE SUM OF
LINK COSTS
IS = TO 17

Figure 10.4 Example cost matrices.

into the model. The model allows simulation at varying levels. For example, you can model at the bit level or at the message level or node level only. Each provides a useful metric.

The bit level modeling provides a means to study low-level bus tranactions, though because of this modeling level you can only examine very small real-time periods of time because of capacity overhead. Whereas you can examine a longer period if you look at the word, message, or node level only. Each will provide you with some useful information upon which to decide your network needs. This tool is in working order and now should be available as a product. Again, details of this tool can be found in Fortier [1985] and its references.

Simulations of this type provide an environment in which to study a wide range of topologies and protocols for our problem in a fairly cost-effective way. Simulations have and will play a more important part in the selection of LANs as this technology matures.

10.4   Analysis of Topology

The previous sections outlined some of the important issues in LAN topology design and selection. To clarify some of the issues and highlight important aspects, the following sections will address specific issues as they relate to the four major topologies addressed. Specifically, the sections will

EXAMPLE

ti \ SJ	S0	S1	S2	S3
T1	2	1	2	4
T2	1	0	1	2
T3	4	1	2	2
t4	1	2	1	2
T5	2	3	2	0
T6	4	4	3	2

INITIALLY ALL
CONCENTRATORS S_1 - S_3
CLOSED AND S0 OPEN,
WE USE S_0
COLUMN ONLY TO
BEGIN
CONSTRANT e = 3
CONCENTRATORS COSTS
R_1 = R_2 = R_3 = 2

Figure 10.5 Prims algorithm MCST.

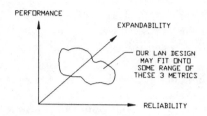

Figure 10.6 LAN metrics selection.

address how these topologies map to each other in reliability, availability, capacity, performance, recoverability, and expansion capability. The examinations are more qualitative than quantitative (see Figure 10.6).

10.4.1   Reliability

Reliability from a topological viewpoint addresses the issue of a network's ability to continue operations in the face of failures. A reliable network can continue operations even if it is degraded when a failure causes the loss of some critical element. An example is a network in which if we lose a link, there is a way to continue service around the failure. Another example is a network that will not come down to its knees if a node fails. This notion is embodied in the term "fault tolerance"; a fault-tolerant system can take faults and handle them in a way that does not cause catastrophic failure. In terms of the topologies of intent, it can be said that:

The mesh topology provides good reliability in terms of continued service because of link failures. The loss of a link or multiple links will not bring this topology down to its knees.

The loss of a single or multiple node will not cause the system to halt. It will only cause the loss of communication to the failed nodes and rerouting of messages to the others that had used these failed nodes.

The cost we pay for this is a large volume of redundant communication links that will typically be underutilized. We also pay for a substantially larger volume of software for providing control of the added links.

The star topology is a different case and has characteristics that are slightly different. In terms of reliability because of link failures, the star provides fairly good reliability. The loss of a link will cause loss of communications to that site, but it will not affect the operation of other nodes. The problem with the reliability of this topology is caused by the central hub. If the central hub has a fault or failure, the entire network is affected. This piece is the weak link of this topology. Conversely, the loss of a peripheral node will only cause loss of service to the failed node. This is the same as loss of a link. Overall, the reliability of the star topology is driven by the reliability of the central hub.

The third topology is the ring. In its basic form, it provides poor reliability to both node and link failures. The simple ring uses link segments to connect adjacent nodes together. Additionally, the nodes are actively involved in the transmission in the basic configuration. Because of these conditions, the basic ring lacks the ability to continue operation upon failure. For example, the loss of a link anywhere in the ring will halt all operations within the LAN; no unit will be able to communicate with another one. Additionally, the loss of a link node will also bring the network to a halt. Because of these basic anomolies of the ring topology, it has extremely poor reliability aspects. To rectify this situation and make the ring a truly useful topology requires additional components to provide adequate work arounds to the failure nodes. These work arounds include redundant links and bypass circuitry to provide the reliability required. We could go to extremes and provide work arounds to all failures. This would lessen the cost effectiveness of the ring topology, although the reliability would improve.

The fourth topology is the bus. This topology provides poor reliability to link failures in its basic format. If the link fails, the entire network is useless. On the brighter side, if we lose a node, the network will not fail. To work around this and increase the reliability and fault tolerance of the global bus we must provide redundant links. The redundant links are used when one bus fails or a interface or node causes the bus to become inoperable.

10.4.2   Availability

Availability is a measure of local area network performance dealing with a LAN's ability to service all users who wish to access it. A network that is highly available provides services immediately to users who access it, whereas a network that is not available provides low access to the system.

The mesh topology provides, in the best case, total interconnectivity, which implies that the network is always available to service any user who wishes to communicate to any other users. On the average, the mesh topology provides good availability of communication services to users.

The star topology can only support what its central hub can handle. In any case, it can only service one user at a time and could, because of heavy loading, starve out others from getting services. Because of this, the star rates low on availability. To rectify this requires additional assets at the hub to provide parallel service to the peripheral nodes.

The ring topology, in the basic form, provides a fair-to-low availability number. This is because of the operational characteristics of the topology. The ring operates by circulating a token around the ring. If you just missed it, you must wait until it comes around again. Other ring topologies, with different operational characteristics, provide higher availability. The insertion ring and the slotted ring provide such improvements.

The global bus topology provides a fair-to-good availability measure. This depends on the protocol in place and the offered traffic load. In the global bus topology, if the bus is free and a device wishes to send, it can. Under a CSMA protocol with low loading, it will be able to send the majority of the time.

The key to all the above topologies is their ability to be available for users to access the topology.

10.4.3 Capacity

Capacity is a measure of the volume of information that a network can transfer. This typically is a maximum number and in reality is some number less than the maximum rating.

In the mesh topology the capacity is based on the number of links in the network and their rated link capacities. For example, if we have 10 links each with a capacity C, the total capacity of the network is $10C$. In reality this number will be lessened by many factors such as the nodes' ability to send and accept messages from more than one channel at once or the links' overhead that will lessen the actual real data throughput.

The capacity of the star topology is limited more by the hub than by the link capacities. In the best case, the central hub circuit switches the links together and provides full potential link capacities. This yields a potential network capacity of some number less that NC, where N is the number of nodes and C is the capacity of the links. In most star networks, though, the capacity of the network is limited by the capacity of the central hub switches.

The capacity of the ring topology is limited to the volume of bits that it can hold in its full distance. For example, if a slotted ring has N slots each with capacity C, our total capacity is NC. In the insertion ring and token ring the capacity is simply C, the rated capacity of the entire ring. Advertized ring networks are in the tens of megabit range for performance with this increasing up to 100 Mb for fiber rings.

The bus topology is the simplest to evaluate. The global bus supports one message at a time, and with only one link the capacity of this topology is simply its rated speed C. In LANs use, this is in the range of 1 to 50 Mbps.

The capacity of a LAN is meant as a gross measure of its ability to transmit information. Before putting much faith into these numbers, one should look at actual installations of a LAN and compare the actual capacity to the theoretically capacity.

10.4.4   Performance

Performance is defined as a collection of metrics which encompass the aspects of a network's ability to transfer information. Typical metrics applied to the performance include bandwidth, response time, scan time, and error rates. In all cases the bandwidth, response time, and error rates are very dependent on the media selected as well as on the control hardware. These data items should be determined based on the selected topology and hardware. An item that we can look at without knowing the media is the scan time. Scan time is a measure to describe the time it takes for control to pass through all nodes and return back to the originator.

In the mesh topology, control is performed at each site. The time it takes for one to get control of the media is only held back by waiting for the immediate user to give it up. This is on the order of one use or $0(1)$ in big "0" notation. This implies a very low scan time, which implies, as we saw previously, a very available network.

The star topology provides performance on scan time based on the control protocol in place in the hub. In the best case it provides a scheme to give control to the first contending unit. In the worst case it is a polling-based scheme. The performance is between $0(1)$ and $0(N)$, implying either you can immmediately get control or you must wait until all others are served. This topology therefore allows a way to tailor the scan time. One need only select a control protocol that will give the wanted performance.

The ring topology is more rigorous. The basic token ring provides a scan time of $0(\frac{N+1}{2})$. This is because on the average we must wait one-half of the total number of nodes to see the token. The ring, though, can be better. The insertion ring can approach a scan time of $0(1)$. This is because when it wants to send, it can by initiating its sending and holding up any receiving messages until it has finished sending. This can continue with each message until the node buffers are full; then it must send out the received messages.

The bus topology is another interesting scheme. It can have a scan time from $0(1)$ to $0(N)$. That is, we can have a contention-based scheme with low utilization that will allow all nodes to get in when they want to. Conversely, we could have a priority scheme that will, on the average, make the unit wait until all others are done before it can get onto the network.

Performance is a measure that provides an important point to weigh against other aspects of the system in selecting a LAN.

10.4.5   Recoverability

Related to reliability is recoverability. This measure embraces many aspects of a topology and its services. Basically, this is a measure of topology services and includes:

- Detection
- Diagnosis
- Isolation
- Recovery
- Repair

What this measure applies to is the services the network vendor supplies to make the basic network more workable. From a strictly topological sense, the measure is the same as reliability. That is, if the topology can survive failures, we can use recovery to bring it back to full service. The mesh provides good recoverability. The star, ring, and bus have single points of failure and, with redundancy, can have good recoverability. A discussion of the terms that make up this measure are beyond this chapter and will be addressed in Part 7 under Systems Management.

10.4.6   Expansion Capability

This metric is a measure of the ability of a topology to grow. Other terms that have been used to describe this metric include extensibility, modularity, expandability, flexibility, and adaptability. What these all look at is the ability of a topology to be modified and grow. Is this easy or hard to do? Is it expensive or relatively inexpensive? These become the metrics to look at for these terms.

The mesh topology has a varied weight for this measure. The fully connected version is extremely expensive to add nodes to. Therefore, it has a low measure for extensibility. The mesh style, such as in Arpanet-type topology, requires the addition of one node and some number N of links. Also, this addition will cause changes in other sites for routing, etc. Therefore this version has low-to-medium expansion costs.

The star topology has low extensibility because of the limiting nature of the central hub. Once we have reached the maximum node count on the hub, we cannot grow without replacing the hub. Because of this limit this topology has a very low extensibility measure.

The ring topology provides good extensibility. To add a node requires the addition of the node and one new link. The impact on the rest of the network is minimal as we do not make a connection to them. We will lengthen the scan time and add a new destination, but this can be easily rectified by signaling all nodes that a new one has entered and supplying its address (logical name).

The bus topology provides for easy expansion. To add a new node requires the tapping of the bus and the linking of the new node to the tap. To make it operable, we must signal all others of the new node. The limiting factor in this topology appears to be the addressing limit and loading limit for the nodes and bus, respectively.

10.4.7   Complexity

Complexity is a network measure that takes into acount the impact the topology has on all aspects of the LAN. This complexity is measured in terms of how much extra hardware or volume of hardware is required to provide the service.

The mesh topology has a high complexity measure. This is because of its requirement for multiple links and multiple sets of hardware to control these links or all nodes. Additionally, the mesh topology requires extensive software support to provide the communications services. This extra software is required because of the topology to support routing, flow control, link control, and overall end-to-end message transfer.

The star topology has medium complexity overall; the peripheral nodes have low complexity, while the central hub has high complexity. This is because the peripheral nodes only have one link to worry about and have very simple protocol. They request service and respond to requests from others. The central hub, on the other hand, must service N links along with processing potentially complex algorithms for linking nodes together logically and performing the message transfer job.

The ring topology has low complexity. This is because of the extremely simple topology and control associated with it. The ring topology requires that each node has the ability to support two links and has a control mechanism which only needs to read the passing data stream, recognize addresses, and have a token sequence. This, it turns out, requires little hardware and software to perform.

The bus topology is a fairly low-complexity topology. The bus topology requires each node to be able to support one link physically and, similarly to the ring, have hardware to discern data from control signals. The logical (software) complexity of the bus can be low to very high. This is dependent on the type of control and extent of control we want nodes to have.

The global bus can support a simple CSMA protocol in which all the nodes need to do is possess the ability to send a message and listen. It must be able to compare what is sent to that received and determine if they are different. If different, the nodes must process a simple algorithm to pick a future period to try again. On the other extreme, we could have a complex scheme that requires each node to process some control information, compute many parameters, and from this determine who has control. Because of this topology, it has a low to low-medium complexity measure overall.

10.5 Summary

We have seen the aspects of topology that must be considered in selecting a LAN. Before we discuss these, let's summarize and review some important aspects. In the early sections of the chapter we looked at the basics of the topologies. What was covered were the aspects of the physical interconnects, their number and types of links required by the topology, as well as how selecting one topology over another will affect the control software that we must examine and select. These, taken together, provide the realization of the LAN and its services. Beyond the basic discussions of the mesh, star, ring, and bus, we looked at some of the issues associated with designing and selecting a LAN. In particular in selecting a LAN we must remember the major steps:

1. Define what we are trying to do
2. Collect all requirements
   a. Information transfer
   b. Building topography
   c. Potential linkages
   d. Growth requirements
   e. Internet linkages (planned or first phase)
3. Define the site plan
4. Examine alternatives that will meet requirements
5. Select a LAN
   a. Select topology
   b. Select components
   c. Select media
6. Plan installation
   a. Refine installation plan
   b. Order components
7. Install LAN

Each of these steps have issues to examine and topology plays a part in many of them.

Beyond this discussion, the chapter examined some of the qualitative and quantitative issues we need to be cognizant of in selecting a topology. These metrics are often conflicting, and we must determine the extent of each that we wish to have in our LAN. For example, performance, expandability, and reliability are often on different planes (see Figure 10.6).

The determination of a performance level may affect the expandability and reliability of the LAN. If we require a highly reliable network, we may drive down our performance because of increased overhead. The increased reliability could also lessen the expandability of a LAN. If we have added hardware because of the reliability requirement, we increase the cost of expansion. The bottom line on the discussion of these different metrics is to examine them closely against the needs of the organization and develop a weighing for each based on the needs of the organization. This can then be used to provide a crude measure for weighing various LANs against.

For example, if because of our requirements we can say we need reliability over expansion and performance but still require a good level of overall capacity, we could place weighings on these items. Reliability may be given a weight of 0.5 while performance is given 0.3 and expandability 0.2. These can then be used to provide a means to calibrate the selection process toward our requirements. The most important aspect of all these discussions is to develop requirements, weigh proposals against them, and select the LAN that best meets your requirements.

10.6   References

Fortier, P. J., *Design and Analysis of Distributed Real-Time Systems*, McGraw-Hill, New York, 1985.

Kleinrock, L., *Queueing Systems, Vol I: Theory*, John Wiley & Sons, 1975.

—, *Queueing Systems, Vol II: Computer Applications*, John Wiley & Sons, 1975.

Tanenbaum, A., *Computer Networks*, Prentice-Hall, 1976.

PART FOUR
Local Area Networks
Control and Standards

11. Local Area
Network Control

11.1 Introduction

The topology of local area networks is structured such that, other than the star net, it is not immediately apparent how it is determined which node may transmit data and when. The mechanisms of control determine these issues. The problem in controlling access to the media is that it is a shared resource, and therefore it must be allocated in a way which will provide "fair" service to all, fair referring to a system quality of service based on the operational needs of the particular LAN and its associated applications.

Network control, within the LAN, is associated with various functions, not all immediately obvious. It consists of media access (How do I get on?), addressing and routing (How do I know where to send messages, and how do I send them?), and flow control (control access to keep a system availability level).

Media access is concerned with the question of how to allocate the bus to those connected users and when to do this. Typically this is accomplished by one of three methods: contention based, reservation based, or sequential (round robin) based.

Contention-based schemes rely on the competitive interaction of devices wishing to use the communications media. This competition can take many forms from simple collision techniques such as used in Aloha [Metcalfe, 1976] to much more elaborate contention resolution schemes as seen in DSDB [Fortier, 1983]. In either case the main mode of operation is to send out the message (data control or both) and either wait until collision occurs (sense and stop) or until a nack arrives (no response or explicit), indicating a problem. If no problem is sensed or indicated, assume all is well and continue on.

Reservation-based systems use some form of predefined allocation of time slots to be used by the nodes on the system. When a device's time slot arrives (either explicitly or via some signaling mechanism [Jensen, 1978]), it now has control of the media. It is allowed to send an item over the LAN and then release control for others to use.

Sequential-based schemes operate in a round-robin fashion (logical or physical). They allocate the media in a set sequence that does not change with time. That is, the sequencing occurs based on the structuring of the system. Each device (node) receives control once during a scan cycle. A good example of this type of control is shown in ring networks [Willett, 1987]. The ring structure operates by the circulation of some control mechanism. The control is allocated to the holder of the circulating mechanism (token, typically). When its use is completed, the token is issued to the next sequential unit on the string.

A second major component of control mechanisms is addressing and associated issues of routing and flow control. Addressing in local area networks has the problem of defining and maintaining the names of entities within the network. The issues in this include the use of logical versus physical designations for entities, the use of unique names, hierarchies of names, flat addresses, or hierarchical addresses to provide the mapping for process-to-process communications.

Another aspect of this is routing. In LANs, as in wide area networks, routing affects the performance of the LAN. If a poor route is chosen (longer distance to traverse), unnecessary delays will be caused. In LANs, particularly hierarchical or tiered connections of multiple LANs, routing becomes very important to the performance. Techniques for routing include embedding within the address the routes or using some elaborate algorithms or table look-ups. Associated with this is the issue of flow control. To provide some level of service to the user community at large, we must provide for the controlled use of the assets. That is, we cannot allow for the saturation of the data links, which would lock out others.

Each of the above issues affects the control and performance of a LAN and will be covered in greater detail in the coming section. As important as this description is, it is overshadowed by the issue of standardization. Standardization is coming on strongly. This one thing will provide for aggressive growth of devices for LANS. As such the second section of this chapter will address some of the major standardization activities: the ISO/OSI reference model, the 802 LAN standards, the IBM SNA Standards, and DEC's DNA.

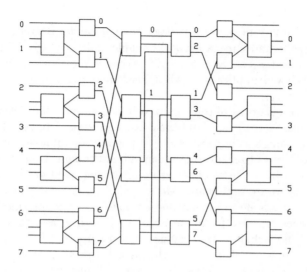

Figure 11.1 Sample circuit-switch network.

11.1.1 Control Protocols

As was indicated earlier, control protocols deal with the controlling of the access to the LAN media. Part of this is the concept of switching strategy, how the data is physically sent over the media in a protocol sense. The major classes of strategy found in LANs and wide area networks are circuit switching, message switching, packet switching, and broadcast.

Circuit switching in the basic form consists of the setting up of a dedicated channel between the source and destination nodes for the duration of their session (interaction). In terms of local area networks, it is becoming more viable as interconnection switches become easier to build and operate

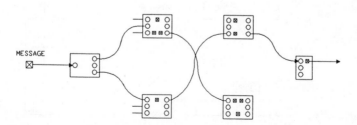

Figure 11.2 Message-switched network.

(VLSI). Examples of such technology include BBN's Butterfly network or the Hypercube and Omega networks shuffle and exchange. These types of circuit-switched networks can provide a viable means to interconnect devices for tailored applications when hard links are required in situations (see Figure 11.1).

Typical of networks of the circuit-switched class include mechanisms to prepare links (setup), send information, and release links. The prepare links can be simple commands sent to precondition all nodes in between or physical addresses to nodes that set up a link through the addressed nodes.

Message-switched networks have no prearrangement or allocation of circuits. Messages are sent from node to node in a store and forward fashion from the source node to the destination node via some intermediary nodes. The messages traverse from one node to the other, and they are queued up at each node before transmission (see Figure 11.2). There is a wide variation in message delays through this network because of the store and forward process of sending the messages and queuing them up along the way.

Packet-switched networks provide a similar form of service. That is, they take messages and send them in a store and forward fashion through the network. The major variant is that the messages are broken up into segments called packets. These packets are then sent independently through the network to the sink node. Like message switching, packet-store buffers are required at each node to hold the packets when in transit. Additionally, since the entire message is not sent as a whole, this scheme requires that we have mechanisms to break up the messages and reassemble them properly at the destination.

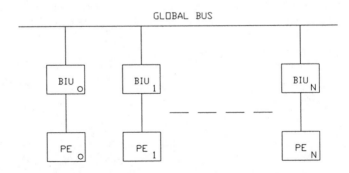

Figure 11.3   HXDP system configuration.

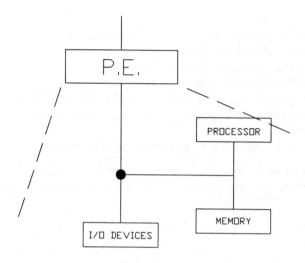

Figure 11.4 Processing element components.

From a comparison basis, packet switching is faster (more parallelism) than message-switched systems, and, likewise, message switched is better than circuit switched. This assumes that the circuit-switched system must search a path, set it up, and then use it. If this does not hold, the circuit switch may be quicker.

Broadcast systems take a different approach to control. They use a single channel with all nodes on it able to see all traffic flowing. The control is effected by the agreed-upon way to view the traffic being seen. That is, they have a policy in place by which they each "see" the information in the proper light for control. For example, in "pure" contention-based systems, all stations having something to send do so; if more than one is sending, a collision occurs, destroying all messages. This scheme works, though, it is only good for low-use systems (less than 18 percent).

The following section will describe in greater detail the three major LAN control schemes: contention, reservation, and sequential.

11.1.2   LAN Introduction

Local area networks or LANs continue to be a driving force in computer technology and computing growth. They have characteristics that differentiate them from the wide area networks (WANs of the past). For example, the LAN typically exhibits some of the following:

- Single shared media
- Owned by or operated by single organization
- Mixture of hosts, workstations, and terminals
- Very high-speed data rates (1 to 100 Mbps)
- Bounded by a few miles of cable
- Low propagation delay (relative to their WAN cousins)
- Communication is peer to peer, not via intermediaries as with WANs
- Ability to support a large number of connections

Local area networks have evolved to meet goals in interconnecting computing devices. For example, reliability is a reason to use a LAN over some

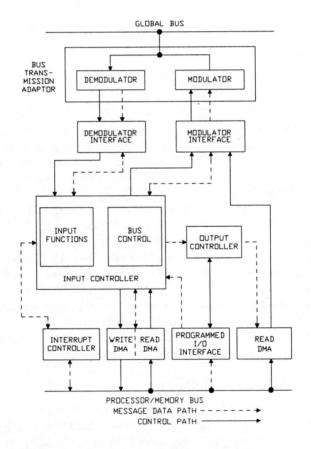

Figure 11.5   Block diagram of a bus interface unit (BIU).

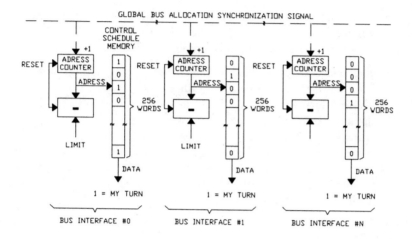

Figure 11.6   Time-slot vectors.

other means. LANs have no central point of failure. They provide a means to interconnect even inexpensive devices at competitive rates while supplying higher-speed data paths and communication rates. They have allowed the growth of distributed computing and more unified environments for users to come into being (see Part 7 for details).

11.1.3   LAN Control

Since the medium of most LANs is shared (star excluded) and not all devices can converse simultaneously, there needs to be means to govern who goes and when. This is the job of the media access protocol or the control protocol. As indicated earlier, there are three basic classifications of media access protocol; contention, reservation, and sequential based. Each of these mechanisms offers a different type of service to the underlying physical media and treats the media and its signals differently. Additionally, the use of one mechanism over the other affects the level of service provided to the upper layers. For instance, the use of reservation-based mechanisms provides a means to tune systems to fixed periodic service, whereas the contention-based service is much better tuned to the bursty environment (aperiodic).

11.1.3.1   Reservation

In reservation-based control schemes the "system" maintains some time division breakup of its assets among the user nodes. This breakup can be tuned and adjusted based on needs, but in the pure sense it is fixed for the network's present setup. Variations exist, as will be seen, but in the purest sense, this control mechanism does not change its fixed asset distributed during run time. The basic node operates as follows:

- The network bus communications assets are broken up into some fixed number of slots or time frames.
- These frames are then allocated in some fashion to the nodes on the system based on needs.
- During run time the system cycles through these frames, allocating them to the proper assigned nodes on each cycle.
- Users use their allocated cycle and then wait until their next slot; no matter how badly they need the assets, they are forced to wait until the next "owned" slot.

Examples of this type of system control are exhibited by the HXDP, IR+D, and DSDB communications systems.

The HXDP system [Jensen, 1978] provides a nice example of this type of control protocol. The system is comprised of N bus interface units and process unit pairs connected together on a global bus (see Figure 11.3). Each of the processing elements is comprised of a processor, memory, and I/O devices (see Figure 11.4). These provide the local user environment in which applications programs reside and operate.

The bus interface units consist of a bus transmission adapter, input controller, and DMA and programmed I/O interfaces (see Figure 11.5) The bus transmission adaptor provides the means to send and receive bit streams to or from the global bus. These are implemented via modulator/demodulator hardware. The input controller provides the means for the specific host to sense messages for it and determine when control is to be taken over by this device. The remaining circuits provide the interface to the processor, memory, and I/O devices in the host.

HXDP is designed to provide space for up to 256 devices. In reality it will be configured with much less than this to provide more slots to each device. The control scheme in HXDP is based on a time slot reservation scheme. It operates in a distributed fashion with each device making a decision on its time slot based on its knowledge of the present state. To perform this determination, the individual bus interface units perform an operation on a 256-word slot reservation memory to determine if their turn has come up. The operation is done by a counter (256 words long) that is bumped up one space at a time upon the reception of a bus allocation synchronization signal. This counter then points to one of the 256 locations in its slot reservation memory. If the location a device is pointing to has a 1, it has the coming time slot; otherwise it waits for the next (bus allocation/synchronization) signal to try again. Figure 11.6 depicts this

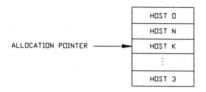

Figure 11.7 Control table.

operation. In this figure, bus interface unit 0 will get control of the media since it has a 1 in the corresponding addressed location. The other units will not send any data since their pointers reveal 0s in this location.

The issue in this scheme is how to determine the setup of the N units so that there is a fair allocation of slots based on the various nodes needs. With systems that have well-known needs, this protocol provides adequate service, although it is inflexible to changes during run time.

The IR+D system is again a global bus structure, but instead of an update signal as used in HXDP, this system sends an explicit message to the next unit (in this nodes view) that will get control. Using this scheme, we can construct a sequence of control allocations that will provide adequate service to the host nodes. Each of the nodes maintains a list of what node

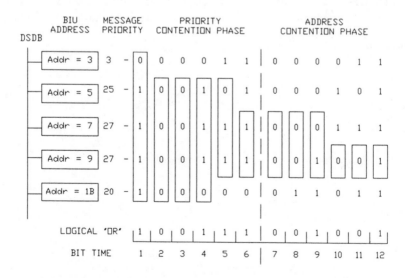

Figure 11.8 DSDB distributed reservation contention resolution.

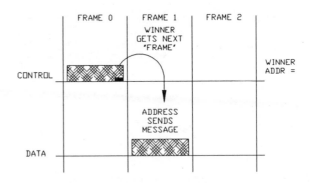

Figure 11.9 Timing of reservation procedure.

is next within its control cycle (see Figure 11.7). The operation is to cycle through this list in a round-robin fashion, allocating control next to the node being pointed to by the allocation pointer.

Through the judicious setup of each node's table, we can construct a wide range of scan styles and rates for the nodes in the system. Again, as in the previous case, the versatility is limited to the architect's ability to "guess" at optimal allocations of the time slots.

The DSB is a more robust reservation scheme that as shown in Fortier [1983]. This scheme uses a mechanism referred to as a "DOT OR" to resolve control allocation for users wishing to use the media in the future. The allocation is determined in the following fashion: Devices wishing to

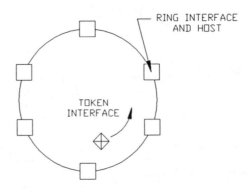

Figure 11.10 Ring topology.

DIRECTION
OF FLOW

Figure 11.11 Message stream.

use the next future time frame send out, over the control bus, their message priority and physical address. This is sent in a bit-by-bit fashion, with each unit sending a bit and comparing what is seen to what was sent. If the received bit is different from what a unit sent, it drops out of reservation contention for the remainder of the frame. If the received bit matches, the unit goes on to the next bit and so on until the entire message priority has been sent. If a tie still exists, the unit continues through the address (physical) contention phase in which, based on allocated physical address, only one of the remaining devices will win. This process is depicted in Figure 11.8. The winner of this reservation contention phase is given the control of the data bus for the next future time frame (see Figure 11.9).

On each time frame all users on the bus that wish to send vie for use by this protocol. This continues for each frame. By the use of priorities, the system can guarantee some level of service to each major class of message. That is, high priority will win most often; therefore these should be saved for critical system functions. Lower priorities will get use occasionally and therefore should only be allocated to messages of little importance or of background importance. Details of this scheme can be found in Fortier [1983, 1985, 1986].

11.1.3.2   Sequential Based

The class of sequential-based control protocols is highlighted by the token ring protocol. In general, protocols of this type allocate control to the communications media in a strict round-robin fashion, with each unit receiving only one chance at use per scan cycle. (Scan cycle refers to the time to sequence through all units once.) The control is round robin, although

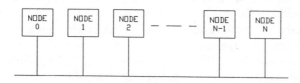

Figure 11.12 Token bus used in example.

the connectivity can be almost by any topology as long as the round-robin control pattern is adhered to.

11.1.3.3   Sequential Control

The classic form of sequential control is seen in the token ring. In this topology we have each device connected to two other devices formed into a ring (see Figure 11.10). Control in such a topology is effected by the circulation of the control token in one direction from unit to unit in the ring. When the token arrives at my unit, I can change it to a connector, send my message out, then reissue a token upon completion of my transmission (see Figure 11.11).

The next unit down the line will review the message; if it is addressed to it, the node will read the message. If not, it will continue to scan the message. When the token is seen, if it has something to send, it will turn the token into a connector, add its message, and then put a new token at the end. In this way, trains of messages can be circulating in the network, although only one unit at a time, and in a controlled fashion, can add a message to the train.

This scheme is very resilient, with loop-around and bypass techniques, to a variety of failures. It also provides a very nice level of performance to the connected devices. The critical parameter to examine in determining the token ring performance is the scan time (mean time interval between token arrivals at a given station).

A second version of the sequential control scheme is the token bus. In this scheme, control is allocated in a logical ring fashion. That is, during each scan cycle each of the devices is accessed once with a control token message from another source. Typically this works by having each device have a predecessor and successor address known by which it converses in the logical ring version. An example operation of this scheme will help to illustrate the mechanisms (see Figure 11.12). Node 0 has as its predecessor node n on the bus, and node 1 as its successor. Control flows via explicit addressed messages from node 0 to node 1, from 1 to 2, and so on until control returns back to node 0 from node n. The method used to signal control is to send a token with an address into the global bus; since it is a broadcast medium, all will hear the signal. The node with the matching address will take control and send out its message in the next cycle. This continues on until all have received control once. At this point the cycle begins again. In this way, the token bus will supply the same control sequence as though the units were connected in a physical ring. The difference is that the global bus will allow the units to send their messages and have them received in the same frame instead of waiting for it to circulate around the physical ring.

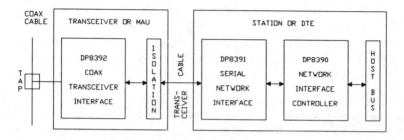

Figure 11.13 IEEE 802.3 compatible Ethernet/Cheapernet LAN chip set.

A final example of a sequential control scheme is the delay insertion ring. In this sequential access technique, control is allocated by the individual devices based on resource availability. Each of the devices on the ring operates in the following fashion. If a device has something to send and there is currently no message flowing past its interface unit, it begins sending its message out. If while it is sending its message another begins to arrive at the unit, it will store the incoming message (delay it) until it has finished sending. It then sends out the buffered message from the other source. If the media is busy, it will wait until an end-of-message marker and then insert its message. This scheme provides a way to more fully use the rings' capacity, thereby increasing throughput.

11.1.3.4   Contention Based

The third classification of control protocols is the contention-based scheme. These are represented by the mechanism of contending for the medium and winning or losing. The contention is a destructive one in which if multiple units contend on the media simultaneously, there will be a collision (garbling of the messages). This in turn must be detected and resolved to allow units to ultimately get control.

The basic modes of contention are classified as carrier-sense multiple access schemes. The major protocols in this classification are l-persistent, nonpersistent, P-persistent, and Ethernet. Each of these has qualities worth mentioning; therefore, we will briefly describe each in the following paragraphs.

11.1.3.5   l-persistent CSMA

The l-persistent CSMA protocol is devised in order to (presumably) achieve acceptable throughput by never letting the channel go idle if some ready terminal is available. More precisely, a ready terminal senses the channel and operates as follows:

1. If the channel is sensed idle, it transmits the packet with
   probability = 1.
2. If the channel is sensed busy, it waits until the channel goes idle
   (i.e., persisting on transmitting) and only then transmits the
   packet.

A slotted version of the l-persistent CSMA can be considered in which
the time axis is slotted and the slot size is t seconds (the propagation delay).
All terminals are synchronized and are forced to start transmission only at
the beginning of a slot. When a packet arrival occurs during a slot, the
terminal senses the channel at the beginning of the next slot and operates
according to the protocol described above.

11.1.3.6   Nonpersistent CSMA

While the previous protocol was meant to make "full" use of the channel,
the idea here is to limit the interference among packets by always rescheduling a packet which finds the channel busy upon arrival. On the other hand,
this scheme may introduce idle periods between two consecutive nonoverlapped transmissions. More precisely, a ready terminal senses the channel
and operates as follows:

1. If the channel is sensed idle, it transmits the packet.
2. If the channel is sensed busy, the terminal schedules the
   retransmission of the packet to some later time according to the
   retransmission delay distribution. At this new point, it senses the
   channel and repeats the algorithm described.

A slotted version of this nonpersistent CSMA can also be considered
by slotting the time axis and synchronizing the transmission of packets in
much the same way as for the previous protocol.

11.1.3.7   P-persistent CSMA

The two previous protocols differ by the probability (1 or 0) of not
rescheduling a packet which upon arrival finds the channel busy. In the
case of a l-persistent CSMA, we note that whenever two or more terminals
become ready during a transmission period, they wait for the channel to
become idle (at the end of that transmission), and then they all transmit
with probability 1. A conflict will also occur with probability 1! The idea
of randomizing the starting times of transmission of packets accumulating
at the end of a transmission period suggests itself for interference reduction
and throughput improvement. The scheme consists of including an additional parameter p, the probability that a ready packet persists ($1 - p$ being
the probability of delaying transmission by t seconds). The parameter p
is chosen so as to reduce the level of interference while keeping the idle

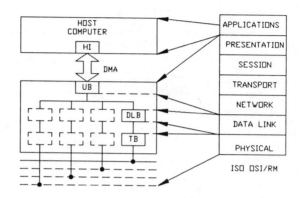

HI - HOST INTERFACE
UB - USER BOARD
DLB - DATA LINK BOARD
TB - TRANCEIVER BOARD

Figure 11.14 E-BUS II interface.

periods between any two consecutive nonoverlapped transmissions as small as possible.

More precisely, the protocol consists of the following: The time axis is slotted, where the slot size is t seconds. For simplicity of analysis, we consider the system to be synchronized so that all packets begin their transmission at the beginning of a slot. For example, consider a ready terminal:

1. If the channel is sensed idle, with probability p, the terminal transmits the packet. With probability $1 - p$, the terminal delays the transmission of the packet by t seconds (i.e., one slot).

2. If at this new point, the channel is still detected idle, the same process is repeated; otherwise, some packet must have started transmission, and our terminal schedules the retransmission of the packet according to the retransmission delay distribution (i.e., acts as if it had conflicted and learned about the conflict).

3. If the ready terminal senses that the channel busy, it waits until it becomes idle (at the end of the current transmission) and then operates as above.

11.1.3.8   Ethernet

Ethernet was developed at Xerox Parc by Metcalfe and Boggs in 1976. The basis is a global bus architecture formed from a coaxial cable. All

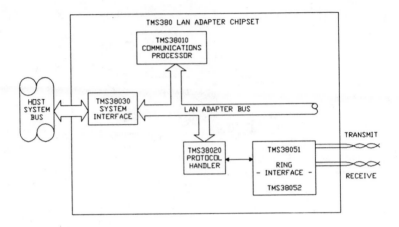

Figure 11.15 TI ring chip set.

stations on the network monitor the cable (the ether) during their own transmissions. If a station has something to send, it first listens to the media. If the media is free, it defers a set idle time (9.6 ms); if it is still free, it begins to transmit and listen. If it senses a collision (garbled message), transmission is immediately halted. If there is no collision, the message is sent, and an idle period follows.

If a collision had been detected, the colliding units would each send out a jam signal indicating to all that a collision occurred. Once this is accomplished, the colliding units determine a future time to attempt a retransmission of their messages. This time period is chosen in a random fashion by each involved station, using a back-off algorithm. This back-off algorithm is referred to as "truncated binary exponential back-off." The delay, in time units (1 unit = 51.2 users) before nth attempt is a uniformly distributed random number from 0 to $2^n - 1$ for $0 < N \leq 10$. In this way on each successive collision we will choose a random number from a larger pool, thereby increasing our chances of an ultimate success. This protocol has been accepted as one of the IEEE 802 standards (802.3; see Figure 11.4). A variety of vendors now supply parts for this media access protocol.

11.2   Example Protocol Devices

The following data sheets represent some examples of chips and chip sets available to provide these protocols in a standard form.

11.2.1   DP8392 Coaxial Transceiver Interface

The features of this interface (Figure 11.13) are:

- Integrates all transceiver electronics except signal and power isolation
- Innovative design to minimize external component count
- Jabber-timer function integrated on chip
- Externally selectable CD heartbeat for remote diagnosis
- Precision circuitry to implements receive mode collision detection
- Squelch circuitry at all inputs to reject noise
- Designed for rigorous reliability requirement of IEEE 802.3

11.2.2   E-BUS Interface

The E-BUS interface unit (Figure 11.14) provides a connection to the E-BUS local area network for a variety of host computers. When used in conjunction with appropriate host software, it becomes an integral port of a seven-layer protocol based on the ISO Open System Interconnect Reference Model. The following functions are provided by the interface unit:

- Reliable transmission of packets to destination node
- Error detection and retransmission using CRC
- Individual and group address recognition (up to 8K recognizable addresses per interface)
- P-CSMA/CD media-access mechanism (prioritized carrier-sense multiple-access with collision detection)
- IEEE 802.3 compatible
- Tack-On-Ack (hardware acknowledgement)
- Automatic cable rerouting upon error detection
- Systemwide flow control
- Process location independence
- Collection of over 250 statistics
- Test functions (including local and remote loop-back)

11.2.3   TMS 380 LAN Adaptor Chip Set

The convenience and efficiency of an industry standard, token ring local area network (Figure 11.15) was once available only for the business office. Today, Texas Instruments brings this technological advantage to the stringent and demanding real-time control environment. Based on An/IEEE 802.5, the TI LAN can now be designed for a wide array of equipment. Through the use of a redundant path, token-ring method of station-to-station interface, the TI LAN offers a simple, reliable, more efficient method of communications than that previously available to real-time control users.

Reliable uninterrupted communications in the real-time environment are not only important, they are a necessity for successful mission accomplishment. The TI LAN offers the advantage of a network with no single point of failure, a network in which communication can continue in spite of a down station or a reconfiguration of the interface network. Because of this advantage, the TI LAN is the only network to offer the flexibility so necessary in such environments. Its features are:

- Deterministic performance token-passing architecture (IEEE 802.5)
- Dual-path network with no single point of failure
- Fiber optic or wire media
- Graceful network degradation under multiple failures
- High levels of integration for host and peripheral embedment
- Single card data bus interface module embeds in subsystem
- No physical determination required for bus breaks
- Off-loads low-level communication tasks from host processor

11.3   Summary

This chapter provided an overview of the major classes of control protocols available to control the transsmission of information over local area networks. The intent was to quantify the major categories and provide examples thereof.

11.4   References

IEEE Computer Magazine, June 1987.

Fortier, P. J., "Generalized Simulation Model for the Evaluation of Local Computer Networks," Proceedings of HICSS-16, January 1983.

—, "A Reliable Distributed Processing Environment for Real-Time Process Control," Proceedings of HICSS-18, January 1985.

—, Design of Distributed Operating Systems: Theory and Concepts, Intertext, Inc., McGraw-Hill, New York, 1986.

Jensen, E. D., "The Honeywell Experimental Distributed Processing System: An Overview," Computer, Vol.11, No.1, January 1978.

Metcalfe, R. M. & Boggs, D. R., "Ethernet: Distributed Packet Switching for Local Computer Networks," Communications of the ACM, Vol. 19, No. 7, July 1976.

Willett, M., "Token Ring Local Area Networks—An Introduction," IEEE Network, Vol. 1, No. 1, January 1987.

12. Local Area Network Routing and Addressing

Addressing and routing in local area networks are both critical aspects of performance within the network. That is, without robust addressing schemes, the LAN may not be able to provide for future growth nor will it guarantee adequate user volume or uniqueness. Without this the LAN may limit the organization's use of the LAN's potential power for information sharing and resource sharing. Likewise if the scheme for routing is not adequate, performance will suffer. For example, if a poor scheme for routing is used, the time associated with file transfers and other forms of communications may become so excessive as to render the network useless.

To alleviate these and other problems, local area network developers and vendors have constructed policies and mechanisms for providing robust addressing and routing for LANs. The analogy for addressing a process in a LAN is that of addressing mail for an employee of company x. The address typically consists of the employee's name, office number, department name, building number, the building street location, possibly the industrial park the building lies in, the town or city, the state, and ultimately the country. Likewise in a network environment, we would address a computer process as a name (process identifier), a host node, a host LAN, possibly a wide area network that the LAN resides on, and so on. This representation is referred to as a hierarchical addressing scheme and will be discussed further in this chapter.

To send a document or other correspondence to the aforementioned employee would require the use of one of many alternatives, such as an employee courier, the U.S. mail system, or one of the commercial carrier services such as Federal Express. These organizations, in turn, would use their internal structure policies and mechanisms to facilitate the transfer of the document from the source to the destination. In a network we have the same occurrence; the source process indicates it wishes to send a message or document to a destination process. The built-in addressing capabilities of the LAN will determine a physical location. This is then used by the routing and flow control elements to determine a "best" path through the network that will minimize the time associated with the transfer. This is the same procedure that a company like Federal Express would use in determining what planes and trucks to use to best route a package in order that it positively will be delivered overnight.

This chapter will examine the major schemes for addressing and routing in local area networks. In addition, it will look at how the various schemes aid or hinder the operation of various LAN architectures.

12.1   Addressing

Addressing in local area networks typically follows one of the two well-known schemes [Shoch, 1978]: hierarchical and nonhierarchical. Each of these provides a mechanism for establishing unique naming conventions for the LAN.

In the nonhierarchical, or flat addressing, scheme, names have no particular relationship to geography (host location) or any other hierarchy. The names (addresses) must be guaranteed unique within one single (flat) address space. This, therefore, implies a more complex distributed number generator mechanism for generating the addresses in a centrally controlled facility. This method of address allocation is inherently difficult for dynamically created processes at various hosts. There are no known simple ways to accomplish this task without excessive interaction and delay at the hosts.

Hierarchical addressing schemes use a hierarchy of addresses that when taken together provide a unique systemwide address. Each process in such a scheme could at the individual local level have the same local identifier, but the global address will differ because of the incorporation of additional address information for the host or network. This type of scheme is analogous to the telephone network numbering system. For example, the number 1 401 792 2701 represents a unique address in the telephone company; 1 indicates country (United States and Canada), 401 is the area code (Rhode Island), 792 is the telephone office (North Kingstown), and the last number is the subscriber address (the Computer Science Department at the University of Rhode Island). Likewise in a distributed collection of computers forming a local area network or networks, we could have addresses defined as follows:

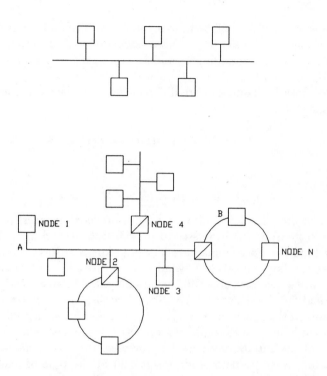

Figure 12.1 a.) Simple LAN topology (top) and b.) complex LAN topology (bottom).

$$< Network\_ID >< Host\_ID >< Local\_ID >$$

where $Network\_ID$ indicates which local area network we are addressing, $Host\_ID$ is the specific processor that the wanted process resides on, and $Local\_ID$ is the specific, unique local identifier assigned to this process at its creation. Using this hierarchy, we can guarantee the uniqueness of each and every process (static or dynamic) within the system under question. Hierarchical addressing has advantages over nonhierarchical for routing and growth.

Other considerations for addressing in local area networks deal with the use of ports, or clusters of processes. It is typical in LANs to group resource servers and other systems service processes or user processes and to associate these with a single port address. This type of association allows a single manager process or one of the cooperating processes to access the port to get the enclosed information. This provides a level of protection or information hiding in the system simplifying the use of the environment. A

similar construct is the mailbox in many systems. The mailbox is a repository for messages addressed to processes associated with the given mailbox.
Again, this provides the hiding of underlying details or the protection of
the underlying processes from direct access.

In either case the addresses are different; users in the system access via
addresses such as:

$$< Network\_Id >< Host\_ID >< Port\_ID >$$

or

$$< Network\_ID >< Host\_ID >< Mailbox\_ID >$$

It then becomes the job of either a port or mailbox manager (part of the
operating system) or the processes to provide policies and mechanisms to
map and bind the port or mailbox names (addresses) to the unique user
or process names (addresses). Beyond these basics, the LAN environment
must provide a means to map or bind user "logical" names to the unique
system identifiers used in the LAN. To accomplish this requires protocols
or mechanisms that perform at various levels based on the actual run-time
conditions at hand. For example, if a process is loaded and put into service
and will not instantiate any new subprocesses, the logical names can be
fixed via mappings (table or code insertions) at the time of loading into
the active state. Alternatively if the process involves other processes at run
time, we need a means to provide dynamic binding at run time. That is,
there must be a mechanism (operating system service) that can provide a
unique name upon demand. Typical of this is the create process command
in process-based systems.

12.2   Routing

Routing is concerned with defining and maintaining a "path" through the
network for messages to flow. This idea of path is important in the context
of routing. The path can be a fixed physical path held for the duration or
a variable logical path set up and adjusted as situations warrant.

Part of the routing protocol is that of service provided. If a virtual circuit
is required, we have additional conditions levied on the routing scheme,
whereas if a datagram service is used, the router is left up to its own
judgment as to how to send each of the single units of communication.

Virtual circuits represent dedicated paths that are set up between both
ends of a communication and that exist for the duration of the ascribed
interaction. Such a service requires the routing algorithm to be responsive
to the needs of delivering packets in order and to interact with error control
procedures to guarantee correct reception. With the datagram the packets

or messages are accepted and transmission is attempted to the remote unit; there is no error control or network interaction to guarantee correctness or order. This typically is the type of service seen in most local area network environments.

12.2.1   Routing Techniques

Routing in local area networks tends not to be as big an issue as it is in wide area networks, the reason being that typically LAN topologies are simple, and store and forwarding is not necessary. It does, however, become an issue when LANs are connected together and, as such, techniques are included for completeness of presentation and to make users and designers are aware of its need and operations.

For example, if we assume a simple LAN topology as in Figure 12.1a, the routing algorithm is simply "broadcast" to all. All listen and the one it is addressed to will hear it and strip it off. Alternatively, the LAN of Figure 12.1b is more complex and will require some form of routing algorithm to effect the transmission of a message from a unit on one sub-LAN to that on another. The possibilities range from fixed routing tables indicating host names and routes from sources and to destinations to simple flooding of all sub-LANs to an adaptive scheme which takes into account variability and change of conditions in the network.

12.2.2   Flooding

In this algorithm for routing, each node that receives a packet or message first determines if it has seen it before, and, if it has, it discards it; if not, it forwards it out to all the neighbors except the one(s) it arrived from. In the case in Figure 12.1b, if node 1 wishes to send a message to node n, it would ship the message out ("broadcast") onto the global bus it is connected to. In turn this message would be received by all the nodes on this bus who would then, based on how they are connected, forward this on. In this case nodes 2, 3, and 4 would forward the message onto their connected subnetworks; ultimately the message would get to the destination node n.

This form of routing is extremely robust; that is, it will always work under all conditions. Additionally, it is guaranteed to find the optimal path from any source to any destination. The problem is that because of this robustness, we have added message loading that otherwise is unneeded. For example, again using Figure 12.1b, if we assume the same scenario as above, we are forcing the two uninvolved subnets to also be burdened with the extra message from node 1 to node n even though they do not need it. This is okay if we have low utilizations on the networks, but as traffic increases, all subnets will feel the impact.

12.2.3   Static Routing

A second form of routing referred to earlier is static routing, also known as directory routing. This form of routing requires that a predefined routing table be specified and exist for each source-destination pair in the network. Additionally this static table does not adjust to changing conditions within the network.

In the previous example, to send a message from node 1 to node n would require looking up a predefined route through the networks. In this case, broadcast on network A to node 3 will then send a message around the ring to node n. The table for this entry may look like this:

$$\textit{Sourcenode} \quad \textit{Destinationnode}$$
$$1 \ldots n$$
$$1 \qquad 1 - 2 - 3 \ldots 3$$

This shows what node to send to in order to ultimately get to n. Node 3, in turn, would have an entry of source 3 and destination n to send directly to n.

12.2.4   Adaptive Routing

The third major class of routing algorithms is referred to as adaptive strategies. These strategies can change and adjust according to the traffic flow and availability conditions in the LAN. These types of schemes would be beneficial in applications in which reliability is put ahead of cost and timing. That is, to perform the dynamic schemes will cost more in terms of design, maintenance, etc.

There are basically three basic types of routing:

- Centralized
- Isolated
- Distributed

Centralized adaptive routing uses a central routing control center which takes in the system's status information (failures, traffic, etc.) and computes new routes for each node. These new routes are downloaded to the sites and used as their new routing tables. The issue becomes one of how often to do this and by what parameters the new routes are decided upon.

Isolated routing is a scheme by which each node uses its own knowledge to base routing decisions upon. An example of an algorithm of this class is the hot potato algorithm. This algorithm operates by taking incoming messages and outputting them as fast as it can on another link, preferably the lowest used or shortest queued up one.

Distributed routing is a form of routing in which each node exchanges information with its neighbors (in the case of a global bus LAN, this may be all the nodes on the bus). This information is then used to calculate optimal routes. In the LAN environment, this may mean that each node tells all others who it is connected to. This in turn can be sent to the other nodes so that they can build a view of the topology and a routing table from it.

12.3   Flow and Congestion Control

Flow and congestion control are needed in networks in which excessive message loading causes loss of messages and degraded performance. Congestion is the "malady," and flow control is a preventative means to halt congestion. Congestion is the problem of more messages arriving at a node than it can hold. This is a node-to-node phenomenon. The problem with congestion in a LAN or other network is that it will degrade performance (transmission delays will increase) and reduce throughput and can lead to deadlock in the system. It is caused mainly by four conditions:

- Network interface units are too slow to perform their tasks (queuing buffer, table update).
- Input rates exceed output rate (queuing phenomenon).
- Insufficient buffers in interface units.
- Unusually high error rates (retransmissions, etc.).

The problem is that if one condition exists, the others will ultimately also occur. To alleviate these problems requires the use of congestion control procedures. This is the fix-once-it-happens type of control. The main techniques used in wide area networks and in LANs are preallocation of buffers, packet discarding, and choke packets.

Preallocation of buffers means exactly what its name implies. That is, the sending node issues a request to the receiving node to reserve buffer space for the incoming packet(s). This type of mechanism is being currently used; an example is found in the DSDB design [Fortier, 1983]. In this scheme a control bus is used to preallocate space for high-priority messages to guarantee assets will be available for their use. Other LANs have also adopted this scheme for high-interest items.

Packet discarding is a very simple method of congestion control. It operates by merely discarding any messages it does not have room for. This will work as long as the network is not too heavily loaded, and the retry mechanisms on messages are constructed such that they do not feed the congestion but help to alleviate it. An example of this type scheme would be a LAN that discarded messages when it was full, and a retry algorithm that would perform some form of binary backoff to not cause further congestion.

The final form of congestion control is choke packets. This scheme uses explicit protocol message interaction between the interfacing nodes to control congestion. It operates as follows: If a node reaches its allowable threshold from a source, it will send a reduction message to the source, commanding it to reduce its load by some percentage. Likewise, if it has spare capacity, it may tell the source to increase its flow. This is an adaptive scheme that works well, though it adds additional traffic in terms of control messages onto the network, which in themselves can cause further congestion.

Flow control, on the other hand, deals with the prevention of congestion via the fixing of it once it occurs. Flow control is a networkwide end-to-end phenomenon. It has two major classes of solutions: centralized and distributed.

The centralized technique deals with the collection of statistics in terms of buffer availability message throughput and arrival rates. These are then used to compute message flow assignments for each node in the network. This in turn is used by each node as part of its routing tables (address maps) to control the volume of information allowable from source to sinks in the network.

Distributed flow control, on the other hand, comes in more flavors and deals with solving a different form of the problem. The major types of schemes are adaptive routing, isarithmic flow control, and end-to-end flow control; each addresses a different aspect of the condition.

In adaptive routing each node selects the adjacent forwarding node that will minimize delay. In a LAN with a shared media, this technique cannot be applied as we only have one way to send out the information.

Isarithmic flow control, on the other hand, is a means by which we fix the allowable number of messages or packets that can be in the network in a period of time. In a LAN this can be accomplished by allocating the LAN assets as slices of time and allowing a single user at a time to use the slice. This will provide a means to limit how much data is flowing totally in the network(s) in a period of time. Other means exist to perform this, such as capability access in which a node must acquire a network capability token before it can attempt to send a message. This will cause possible excessive delays if the capabilities are not managed fairly.

End-to-end flow control looks at the problem as a sender-receiver problem. This scheme puts the burden of control on the sender and receiver to limit their message interactions over the network. A means to do this is to regulate the window size (allowable number of packets that can be sent) to some agreeable value which will not cause the sender or receiver to choke up. This is a scheme found in many systems to regulate the volume of information flowing between cooperating devices in LANs today and in their wide area network predecessors.

12.4   Summary

This chapter covered the issues of addressing, routing, and flow control as they relate to local area networks. Covered were the aspects associated with hierarchical and static addressing of processes in LANs. Additionally, the aspects of routing in a local area network were addressed in terms of policies for routing and mechanisms to realize them. This was followed by an examination of flow control concepts and how they relate to and effect LAN performance.

12.5   References

Fortier, P. J., "Generalized Simulation Model for the Evaluation of Local Computer Networks," *Proceedings of HICSS-16*, January 1983.

Shoch, J. F., "Inter-network Naming, Addressing and Routing," *Proceedings of the IEEE Compcon*, Fall 1978.

13. Local Area Network Interconnection Standards

A degree of standardization is always necessary for any industry or product line to be economically and technically feasible. Within the standardization framework, there are many different conceptual and physical levels at which standardization models can be constructed. A physical-level model specifies such things as cable type, connector size, and so on. On the conceptual level, models define logical correspondences and overall organizational details that are not evident from a physical examination of a product or system.

This section deals mainly with conceptual-level models for local area networks. "Mainly" is used because many of the standards also adopt physical implementation characteristics that are sometimes difficult to separate from the conceptual operation of a particular local area network.

Just as the automobile industry is split into different camps, each claiming to have the best product to meet the perceived customer needs, so is the LAN industry. Many different standards for protocol, interconnection, and user support have been specified. This, however, is quite natural and results in a number of successful, long-lived standards that will each find its own application niche. One of the problems with this type of industry evolution, however, is that it is often difficult to perform comparative analyses of the various implementations. Also, some standards are quite broad and do not describe any particular technology, whereas others actually describe whole product lines. A partial solution, however, lies in the adoption of a standard from which the particular LAN can be implemented, thereby providing a framework to compare similar designs.

At some point in any discussion of standards, the distinction between what constitutes a "standard" versus a "specification" is blurred. Before we continue, let us establish their definitions. For the purposes of this chapter, a standard will be defined as a collection of criteria, principles, and guidelines that together form a model to be used as a basis for constructing and comparing systems. A specification, on the other hand, enumerates the specifics of a given implementation. Thus, a specification may be based upon a given standard, and two or more specifications that claim adherence to the same standard may actually be incompatible.

The definitions given above are quite strict and typical standards have flavors of both, although there are exceptions. For example, the Open Systems Interconnect Standard (OSI) is relatively "pure" in that it does not attempt to provide any implementation details. The physical layers of the IEEE 802 families, on the other hand, provide specific details that enable standard-adhering implementations to be fairly compatible. Thus, groups of standards fall into general categories according to their generic level. One standard may even claim compliance to another while setting forth more specific guidelines (this often happens with LAN standards). All of these guidelines, specifications, and models can make the study of LAN standards confusing indeed, especially when each standard-generating organization has its own particular standard format, vocabulary, and purpose. The following discussions provide a background upon which more serious LAN standards study may be based. The intent here is not to judge the various standards but rather to provide a technical description and assessment of their particulars.

There are a number of sources of standards in the LAN community, all of which can be classified as either de jure or de facto. The de jure, or official, standards are the products of such organizations as the Institute for Electrical and Electronic Engineers (IEEE), the International Standards Organization (ISO), and the American National Standards Institute (ANSI). The products of these groups are motivated by a desire to establish some order within an industry so that the particular products and technology of that industry may advance without the hindrance of having to constantly build a better mousetrap. With this approach, vendors are encouraged to adopt one or several standards and to build supporting and complementary products rather than another basic capability as provided by the standard product. Also, standard product suppliers can design to mature standards and ensure a level of compatibility with other available equipment.

The second source of LAN standards, the de facto group, consists mainly of large corporations whose products, by virtue of their widespread use, force the development of company-standard interconnection and structuring. Corporations such as International Business Machines (IBM) and Digital Equipment Corporation (DEC) have provided de facto standards that are accepted and adhered to by other industry sources. The motivations for developing a company standard that may become de facto are several.

In several cases, the lack of mature standards upon which to base new products has forced the evolution of standards or parts of standards. Often these efforts make the transition into industry standards because of the large installed equipment base and the desire to offer alternate sources for compatible equipment. Another motivation derives from a conscious decision to secure a particular portion of the consumer market by introducing a product or product line with a unique communication environment. Finally, the development of a new standard may be necessary to meet changing system needs or consumer demands. In these cases, the use of a LAN is not discretionary, and the mandating authority wishes to establish a model for future work; hence a new, specific standard is developed. Each of the above motivations have led to the establishment of successful and not-so-successful LAN standards.

Unless you are part of the military establishment and must follow the directives of a higher authority when developing a new product, the choice of which standard, if any, to use is discretionary. The end result of this reality is that standard adherence is voluntary, and that standards are subject to public approval by virtue of their popularity. Thus, each standard-producing organization proposes standards, whether de jure or de facto, for industry acceptance. For instance, ISO's reference model, called Open System Interconnect (OSI), and IBM's System Network Architecture (SNA) offer different views on the "correct" layering of functions in a network environment. As mentioned earlier, however, proposed standards are not always conflicting, as in the case of the IEEE's 802 family of standards that are designed to complement the ISO model. In any case, a discussion of some of the major efforts in this area is necessary in order to logically place the current deluge of LAN information. The discussion below is by no means comprehensive; much greater depth would be required than is possible in a book of this size. Rather, what follows is a presentation of the most influential and current standards. We will discuss OSI, the IEEE 802 family, SNA, DECNET, and other efforts by ANSI and the Society of Automotive Engineers (SAE).

13.1   Open Systems Interconnect (OSI)

Without question, the most influential and widely referenced standard for local area networks is the ISO model for Open System Interconnect (OSI). Work on the OSI standard was initiated by ISO and the Comite Consultatif Internationale de Telegraphique et Telephone (CCITT) in the late 1970s in an attempt to formalize the various levels of interaction within

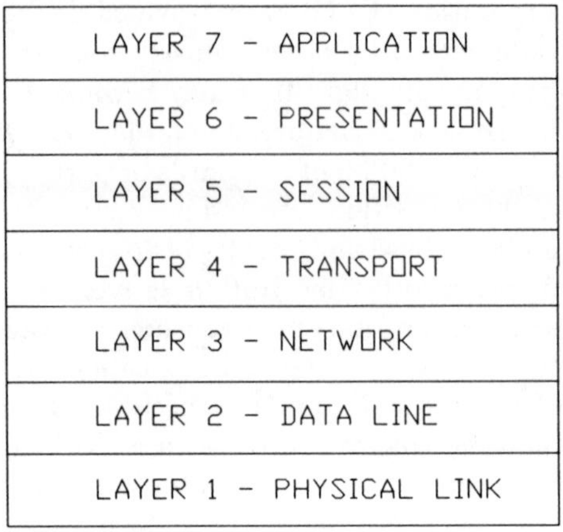

LAYER 7 - APPLICATION
LAYER 6 - PRESENTATION
LAYER 5 - SESSION
LAYER 4 - TRANSPORT
LAYER 3 - NETWORK
LAYER 2 - DATA LINE
LAYER 1 - PHYSICAL LINK

Figure 13.1   The ISO model for OSI.

intercomputer connection networks. The major outcome of this effort was the reference model for OSI, which is a logical framework defining the various protocol levels that are possible in a network implementation. The OSI model is an official standard. Figure 13.1 shows the overall organization of the model.

The reference model consists of several layers that range from the bit level to the application level of detail. Each level defines the capabilities that the technology used to implement that level should possess, without actually specifying the implementation strategy. As mentioned earlier, the model for OSI is a "pure" standard in that it is deliberately and carefully devoid of implementation hints. The specifics for each level are filled in by subsequent standards (e.g., IEEE 802, CCITT X.25). Before discussing the function of the layers in the model, we will first examine the layering concepts that pervade the OSI standard.

The structure of the OSI model is layered in that the higher-numbered layers build upon and utilize the services of the lower layers. This does not imply that all layers must be represented in every LAN implementation that follows the OSI model; some layers may be absent or "null." Within the standard are defined the following entities: application processes that exist within the system and communicate through it; connections that form conduits for information passing between application processes; and system, which is a set of elements that cooperatively process information. A system is logically decomposed into a collection of subsystems that perform the functions of a layer. Thus, subsystems that are all at the same layer and

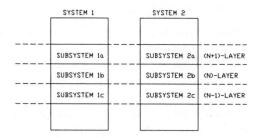

Figure 13.2 Layering concepts for OSI.

that are parts of different systems form what is known as an (N)-layer. Using the layering principle, an (N)-layer uses the services provided by an $(N-1)$-layer and provides services to an $(N+1)$-layer. Figure 13.2 illustrates the layering concept for two systems.

Between the stacked layers are interfaces, called service access points, where an (N)-layer can use the services of an $(N-1)$-layer and provide services to an $(N+1)$-layer. When we have a null (N)-layer, the service access points extend between the $(N-1)$ and $(N+1)$-layers. Among adjacent (N)-layers in different systems, cooperation is governed by protocols. A protocol is a defined set of communications that may occur between entities in peer-level (N)-layers. The (N)-layer protocols form the mechanisms by which data is transferred through the collection of systems. In keeping with the layering concept, each (N)-layer protocol uses the services of the $(N-1)$-layer to accomplish data transfers. The $(N-1)$-layer in turn uses the $(N-2)$-layer to support the $(N-1)$-layer protocol and so on to the lowest layer, where the layer protocol is physically implemented. The layering concept ensures, however, that the (N)-layer protocol user is not aware of the number of kinds of $(N-1)$ and lower-layer interactions but instead sees a peer-to-peer communication session.

The above concepts, layering, (N)-layer to $(N-1)$ and $(N+1)$-layer service access points, and (N)-layer peer protocols form the basis for the establishment of more detailed model parameters. In particular, models exist within this structure for mapping addresses to service access points, entities between systems, controlling (N)-layer protocols, specifying data units for transfer, providing different classes of service, handling error conditions, sequencing messages, identifying connections, and otherwise managing the operation of an open system. Further details on the ISO terminology, standard organization, and the basic OSI model are contained in ISO [1984c]. These additional details are not provided here; the basic information provided above is sufficient to understand the remainder of the model.

Let us now return to a discussion of each of the seven layers shown in Figure 13.1. Starting at the bottom (bit) layer and working up (to the application layer), one first encounters the physical link layer. This lowest layer of communication must supply and control the physical communication medium for the transfer of information and control bits. Thus, the physical link layer is an (N) layer, without an $(N-1)$ layer, whose (N)-layer protocols interact directly with other physical link (N) layers. Connection at the physical layer may be serial (1 bit at a time) or parallel (n bits at a time) and a single physical connection may be either duplex (allows simultaneous transfer in both directions) or half duplex (allows transfer in both directions but not simultaneously). It must also provide a means of directing the transferred bits through the link and to their appropriate destination or destinations by the use of unique identifiers for the attached entities. It is assumed that the bits arrive in the same order as they were transmitted and that fault conditions can be detected and reported. The physical link layer is also responsible for establishing connections between higher-level (data link) layers. A connection is defined here as an association between two or more $(N+1)$-layer entities, which is implemented using (N)-layer capabilities. Thus, the data link $(N+1)$ layer uses the physical (N) layer to form its connection. Specifications that deal with physical-level issues typically contain topics such as connector types, voltages and waveforms for data transmission and detection, and cabling medium. An example of this level of specification is the CCITT X.21 definition, which describes the interface and logical operation of a low-level eight-line interface. Another example is the RS-232 serial specification (also known as V.24).

Layer 2 of the OSI model, the data-link layer, provides facilities for the transmission of blocks of data words between two network stations. A station is defined as a collection of subsystems belonging to the same system that implements all or part of the seven-layer model (in Figure 13.2, each column labeled "system" is also a station). This layer performs the detection of errors at the physical level and also provides an error recovery scheme such as retransmission or network reconfiguration. The data-link layer also may control the rate at which it receives packets from a data-link connection (as defined in the previous paragraph). In general, the control of the physical layer is continued in the data-link layer so that an error-free interface is provided to the network layer. Implementations of layer 2 functions typically concentrate on the mechanisms used to detect and recover from error conditions (e.g., acknowledgement schemes) and to activate and deactivate data-link-level connections for the purpose of packet exchange.

The third OSI model level is called the "network layer." It provides two basic types of services to the transport layer, underlying network transparency and a known transmission cost. Network transparency refers to the situation in which the communication services provided to the transport layer are identical (except for transmission cost) regardless of the actual implementation of layers 1 (physical) through 3 (network). This characteristic is important when several subnetworks of varying quality and services are concatenated to form the network connection. The definition of the services that are provided by the network layer to the transport layer includes the general quality of the link in terms of error rate, link availability, throughput, and delay; an addressing capability that allows transport entities to uniquely identify and communicate with other transport entities; the sequencing of data units over the connection; flow control for the metering of data transfer; and termination services for closing a network connection. All of the above services are provided to the transport layer at a cost that is predetermined so that the desired level of service can be requested at the transport layer. Cost is not explicitly defined in the OSI standard; therefore they allow LAN developers to develop their own cost models based upon the criteria that are judged important for the particular application (e.g., delay, volume, connection time, etc.).

As indicated earlier, the network layer must establish and maintain network connections for use by the transport layer. There are, however, a number of other functions that the network layer must be capable of in order to support the services outlined earlier. To support transport-level addressing, the network layer must provide routing and switching functions that enable a connection to a specific address to be established. This function may not be necessary for networks that have broadcast-type transmission since every station receives every transmission. If the use of data-link-layer connections is to be minimized, the network layer may serve to multiplex every network connection over a single data-link connection. Another area that is tied to the quality of service provided to the transport layer involves the detection of and recovery from error conditions at the data-link layer. Finally, the network layer provides the mechanisms for resetting it and the lower layers by a higher level. This action causes the lower layers to reinitialize to a known state from which network setup and communication can begin.

A typical example of a network-layer implementation is the CCITT X.25 standard for a packet-switching exchange. In general, the network layer should provide a common interface to the higher levels of the model in spite of the configuration of the lower levels.

Next in the OSI model is the transport layer. This layer serves as an end-level "quality checker" of the network layer. The definition of the layer is, at best, noncommittal; but the basic idea of the transport layer function is to somehow remedy or optimize the service and quality problems associated with the lower levels. A range of possible transport-level facilities is given in Deasington [1985] and includes the following classes of service:

Class 0: Add extra addressing capabilities and perform message segmentation into smaller units for transmission

Class 1: Add sequence numbers to all messages so that major network failures (e.g., disconnect) can be corrected by retransmission

Class 2: Multiplex several transport layers onto a single network layer without class 1 error recovery

Class 3: A combination of classes 1 and 2

Class 4: A combination of class 3 and a checksum capability to detect individual message errors and enable retransmission

Users of transport-layer services are identified only by a transport address, but the details of routing, switching, and establishing the proper network connections for that address are of no concern at the transport layer. Specifically, the transport layer provides session-layer users with the controls and mechanisms that are required to establish two-way communication links of a desired quality.

In operation, the transport layer uses three phases to effect data communications. These are labeled the establishment, data transfer, and termination phases. In the establishment phase, a transport connection is created between two transport users. This action involves a number of considerations that arise from the quality, type, and availability of the underlying layers. In particular, a given service class is chosen, the size of protocol data units is set, the network layer is manipulated to form a network connection or to use existing network connections, and the transport connection address is established for the transfer. In the data-transfer phase, the network connections that were set up during the establishment phase are used to move data between the transport entities. Here, transport-level-specific messages can be combined into single blocks of transport-layer data, several blocks of transport-layer data may be concatenated into a single network-layer data unit, larger transport-layer-specific messages may be segmented into smaller network-layer data units, the decision to share a network connection with another transport entity is made, and transport-level error detection and recovery is performed. During the termination phase, the transport-level connection is de-established. This action may free resources for other transport connections and record termination conditions for error monitoring purposes.

The session layer represents a break between the activities associated with the physical message transmission and the logically higher-level processes that use the message transmission facilities. The primary purpose of this layer is to control application process communication in terms of synchronization and medium access and to maintain continuity of service to the upper layers. Each session-level connection is mapped into, and uses the services of, a single transport connection. The services provided by this layer include normal data exchange and associated flow control and a capability called "quarantine service" that forces a receiving session entity to queue messages until authorized to release the data to the presentation layer or to delete it. In addition, three classes of interaction are defined: two-way simultaneous, in which entities may concurrently send and receive; two-way alternate, in which entities may take turns sending and receiving; and monologue, or one-way, communication.

The synchronization of presentation-layer entities at the session layer provides the capability to recognize and record given synchronization points and to reset the session-level connection and establish the next synchronization point at both ends of the session connection. As with the other layers in the OSI model, the session layer also identifies functions for error detection and recovery, flow control, and general connection management.

The presentation-layer's name implies its function, which is to appropriately format or translate incoming and outgoing message data for presentation to the application or session layer. These are several syntax types that may exist for data transfer within any LAN environment. A syntax type is defined here as the collection of transformations and formats that are applied to data during the traversal of the OSI layers, particularly the presentation layer. Mainly, syntax types exist in three places, originating syntax at the message source, a transfer syntax between the two involved presentation entities, and a receiver syntax at the message destination. The two instances of application-level syntax, at the origin and destination, are specified by the application and must be understood by the presentation layer. The transfer syntax between presentation entities is agreed upon by the involved presentation layers. It may be chosen based upon ease of translation to and from application entities or based upon lower-layer network characteristics.

Presentation-layer entities are matched with session connections on a one-to-one basis; no multiplexing is provided. Thus, session and presentation access points may share the same addresses if desired. Examples of presentation-layer function would be the translation of ASCII to EBCDIC data formats or the encryption and decryption of message data.

At the top of the OSI layered stack lies the application layer. Its primary function is to provide the mechanisms and interfaces that enable an end user to communicate within the network environment. This layer is the only direct interface between the end user and the rest of the communications system. As such, it must be responsive to user-specific application

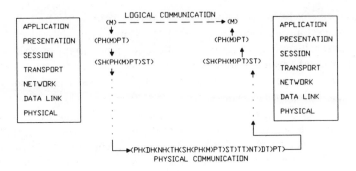

Figure 13.3   Peer-to-peer communication through the OSI layers.

requirements in terms of network use. This layer's actual composition, then, depends greatly upon the end user's requirements and may even be intertwined with actual end-user applications. The ISO standard, however, identifies a number of the types of services that one might expect to find in an application-layer interface. These include facilities for identifying and addressing other users within the network and for determining the availability and quality of the communication system for the end user, allocation of the network resources necessary to hold a communication session, end-to-end synchronization and error recovery, establishment of application-layer syntax, and, finally, message transfer. In essence, the application layer must provide all of the extra "glue" that makes actual end-to-end communication possible.

The seven layers outlined above each work at peer level among stations in the system. That is, a message originating at the application layer is successively "wrapped" for transmission by each layer in the model. On the receiving end, each layer recognizes and "unwraps" the appropriate package and interprets the peer-level information that is contained within that layer of wrapping. In addition, messages may originate and terminate at any layer within the protocol stack. These peer-level messages are treated no differently at lower layers; they are wrapped and unwrapped just as an end-to-end message is. This type of communication, however, is recognized and interpreted at the appropriate layer rather than percolating to the uppermost layer. Figure 13.3 illustrates peer communication at the application level. All of the overhead that is added to each message in the figure may seem excessive and, in certain instances, may not be necessary. As mentioned earlier, entire layers of the OSI model may be left out of an actual implementation if the functions provided by those layers are not needed. Also, the model provides for what is called "expedited service" at almost all layers. This mechanism allows the definition and implementations of less functional, but more efficient, paths through the OSI hierarchy. These paths may also co-exist with more encompassing services at the various levels, with the choice of which path to choose through a layer being deferred until connection or message transmission time.

In addition to the basic reference model for the open systems interconnect just described, there are a host of additional ISO standards that deal with other related and important communication network concepts. For example, several standards deal with the specification of transfer protocols for different layers within the model [ISO, 1984a, 1984b]. These specifications offer guidelines for the implementation of layer protocols. Also, standards exist to further define the services provided by each layer of the model and to establish the terminology used to describe the various protocols and services (e.g., ISO [1986]).

13.2   IBM System Network Architecture (SNA)

A second model for the construction and operation of computer network systems is the Systems Network Architecture (SNA). Developed by IBM during the early 1970s, this de facto standard is referred to as "an operating system for the loosely coupled, multiple computer systems formed by the interconnection of the diverse IBM products that support SNA" [Kuo, 1981]. As such, it provides, like the OSI model, a framework within which you fit the various elements that enable effective interprocessor communication. SNA is defined here as a six-layer hierarchy, the lowest layer being dedicated to the physical link and the highest to boundary and application interface functions. The middle ground is divided into functions which allow the configuration of various SNA nodes of differing capabilities. Although SNA is not the standard of any international organization, it is nonetheless a de facto standard for the significant number of IBM-compatible equipment manufacturers and users. SNA, then, by the sheer influence of IBM in the marketplace, deserves discussion.

Although SNA was originally designed to support communication between intelligent devices (i.e., computers), it was also configured to support the connection of nonintelligent peripherals with intelligent hosts. The basic SNA architecture uses the layered concept to define three major functional areas: application, function management, and transmission management [McFadyen, 1976]. Figure 13.4 shows the position of these layers, along with a more detailed breakdown, which will be discussed later.

In terms of functionality, the transmission management layer performs generic data movement and control operations to effect communication between nodes. Within this layer, all of the protocol functions, data buffering, physical connections, and intermediate node functions are implemented.

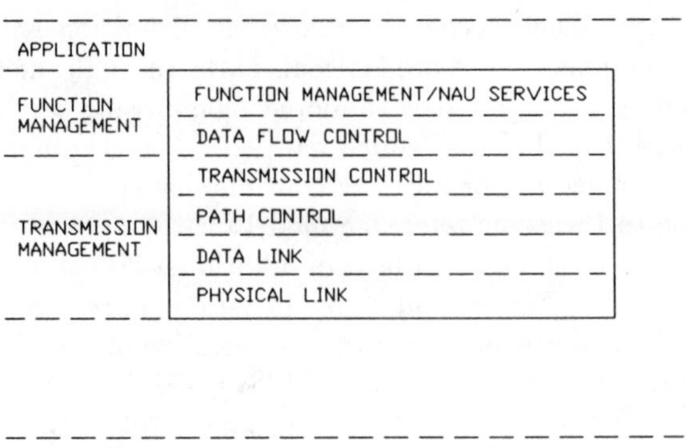

```
 _ _ _ _ _ _ _ _ _ _ _ _ _ _ _ _ _ _
 APPLICATION
 _ _ _ _ _ _ _____
 FUNCTION    | FUNCTION MANAGEMENT/NAU SERVICES |
 MANAGEMENT  |_____|
             | DATA FLOW CONTROL               |
 _ _ _ _ _   |_____|
             | TRANSMISSION CONTROL            |
             |_____|
 TRANSMISSION| PATH CONTROL                    |
 MANAGEMENT  |_____|
             | DATA LINK                       |
             |_____|
             | PHYSICAL LINK                   |
 _ _ _ _     |_____|

 _ _ _ _ _ _ _ _ _ _ _ _ _ _ _ _ _ _
```

Figure 13.4   IBM's SNA architecture.

The main service of this layer is to provide a transparent network interface at which raw data units are exchanged.

The function management layer serves as the network interface and controller for the application layer. Primarily, the function layer converts data to and from the application-required format and provides a degree of control over the higher-level exchange protocols (e.g., duplex mode, application data rate control, etc.).

The application layer contains user programs, peripheral equipment, or operators at terminal equipment. These are the end users of the communication system and the interaction at this level consists of logical connections over which user-level data is passed.

As with the OSI model, there are two types of communication that occur within SNA. The first is the physical communication between adjacent layers and over the actual network. The second, logical peer-level communication, is built using the physical services. Thus, in theory, the SNA architecture supports changes in network configuration at one layer without disturbing the operations at the other layers, provided the interlayer interfaces remain constant.

The following paragraphs describe a more specific implementation of SNA in a local area network environment. The layers on the right of Figure 13.4 show the individual functions that are performed in a network node. This information is based upon the general SNA architecture but is tailored to a LAN environment. Strole [1983] illustrates this architecture in the context of a token ring network. The following information is based upon that work and upon IBM.

At the bottom level of the SNA architecture is the physical link layer; its function corresponds to that of the ISO model physical link layer. The next layer, data-link control, is again similar in function to the ISO data-link level. An example of an SNA data communication protocol is called Synchronous Data Link Control (SDLC). It is a bit-oriented protocol that allows variable data frame lengths and uses special bit patterns to denote control information. Bit stuffing is used to guard against the random occurrence of a control pattern in a noncontrol data stream. The SNA architecture definition specifies that each SNA node must contain two data-link control elements which connect to adjacent SNA nodes. In many SNA products, SDLC is used to implement this data-link control.

Path control in SNA is concerned with data routing and network efficiency. The path control function also supports hierarchical addressing, which allows communication between groups of hosts or processes. Thus, intergroup message traffic can be bundled into a single larger message, thereby increasing network efficiency. The flow of network data, in terms of system load contributed by individual nodes, is also controlled at this layer.

The transmission control layer defines and controls what are called "sessions" and "half sessions." A session denotes a two-way communication operation which has as components two half sessions, one for incoming data and one for outgoing data. SNA sessions do not correspond exactly with the ISO-defined session layer. Rather, an SNA session is an extension of the ISO session definition to include both lower-level functions (i.e., ISO transport) and higher-level functions (i.e., ISO presentation). As such, the transmission control layer may perform some of the multiplexing functions found in the ISO transport layer. Additional transmission control services include pacing (the practice of spreading out data transmissions to avoid impulse loading conditions), session sequence control (handling the setup of logical session links), and data formatting (encryption and decryption).

SNA level 5 is called the data flow control layer and it also operates on sessions (and half sessions). The primary function here is to provide access control to the lower-level SNA functions. Examples of access protocols defined in this layer are full duplex (in which half sessions must share a common data path).

The function management and network access unit (NAU) services level provides software interfaces that allow user processes to communicate over the network. NAUs are logically split into what are called "service managers," of which there are three types: logical unit (LU), physical unit (PU), and system services control point (SSCP). A LU-type service allows communication with user processes active on the network at an NAU site. For each node in the network, there is a PU service manager which allows information about the status of the node's communication hardware and software to be communicated to the SSCP. Additionally, PUs respond

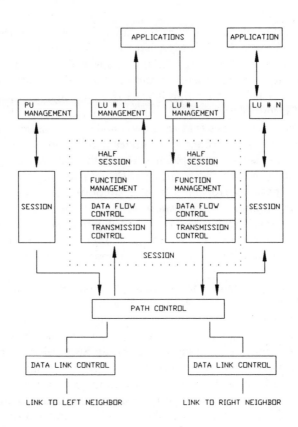

Figure 13.5 SNA node (noncontrol type).

to SSCP commands to control certain network functions (e.g., change path control routing tables to match new system load characteristics). The above function implies that the SSCP is responsible for overseeing network operation. To accomplish this, communicating nodes are grouped into domains, each domain having a single SSCP responsible for that domain's operation. The SSCP, then, is responsible for maintaining domain status and issuing control commands through communications with the various PUs in the domain. The size or configuration of a domain is not rigidly defined, and it can be changed to accommodate geographical and network usage conditions. Function management is present at this level in a form similar to the ISO presentation layer.

The three top layers in the SNA architecture (functional management, data flow control, and transmission control) define a session in SNA termi-

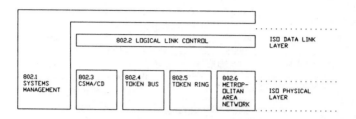

| 802.2 LOGICAL LINK CONTROL | ISO DATA LINK LAYER |

| 802.1 SYSTEMS MANAGEMENT | 802.3 CSMA/CD | 802.4 TOKEN BUS | 802.5 TOKEN RING | 802.6 METROPOLITAN AREA NETWORK | ISO PHYSICAL LAYER |

Figure 13.6   The IEEE 802 standard.

nology. Thus these three layers cooperate in controlling session operation and maintaining session control information.

Above the function management and NAU layer are the various interfaces to user applications and system functions. A node, in SNA terms, encompasses the functions of all of the services mentioned above. Figure 13.5 illustrates the noncontroller SNA node type.

13.3   IEEE 802 Standards

In a continuing effort to bring cohesion into the electronics and computer industry, the IEEE formulates and supports many standards efforts in a wide range of topic areas. One such effort, the 802 Standard Committee, is developing local area network standards in conjunction with industry and other standards bodies. The IEEE 802 standard is not a single unifying structure; rather, it is a family of related and complementary works for various levels of communication.

The basic IEEE 802 standard family for local area networks was approved in mid-1983 and established a baseline for standardization of several different network access protocols. Since that time, the standard has undergone refinements to arrive at its current state of specification. Basically, the 802 standard deals with the physical and data-link levels of the ISO reference model. It consists of three major portions, the specification of physical and lower-level data-link control characteristics for different access protocols, a description of logical link control (i.e., the remainder of a data-link layer), and systems management. Figure 13.6 shows the relationships of the various portions of the 802 standard with reference to the ISO model.

The lower levels of the 802 standard deal with different types of physical-level protocols. These are the carrier sense multiple access with collision detection (CSMA/CD) bus, the token-passing bus, the token-passing ring, and a metropolitan area network. The operation of each is discussed below.

The IEEE 802.3 standard establishes the criteria for a 10-Mbps broadcast communication bus using the CSMA/CD protocol. The initial development

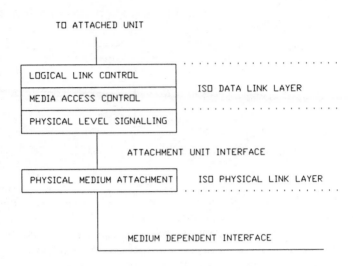

Figure 13.7   IEEE 802 protocol specification structure.

work on CSMA/CD was done at the Xerox Corporation and integrated into the ALTO computer communication hardware. Figure 13.7 illustrates the 802.3 specified configuration and shows the approximate correspondence to the ISO reference model. The items of interest in the illustration are the media access control and the physical components. Note that the figure applies to the 802.4, 802.5, and 802.6 standards as well, and that the media access control and physical link components are specified in each standard.

Because Figure 13.7 applies to all of the physical-level specifications of the IEEE 802 standard, the following discussion applies to all. The media access control-level interface to the logical link control level in the 802 standard performs three basic services. These are data request, data confirm, and data indication. The data request service actually defines the message destination address, the data unit to be transmitted, and the quality of service (i.e., acceptable error rate) desired for this message. The data confirm service provides an indication of message success or failure to the logical link control layer. Upon arrival of a message at the media access control level, a data indicator service is performed which transfers the message data up to the logical link control layer. In addition to the interface services described above, the media access control level implements the protocol specified in the appropriate 802 standard. Basically, the media access control layer is responsible for data encapsulation into message packets and reassembly on the receiving end and also for attaching packet header and trailer information. Message address generation and recognition, synchronization of medium access, error detection, and error resolution are also media access control layer responsibilities.

Returning to our discussion of the 802.3 protocol, the physical link-level portion of the standard specifies everything from connector hardware to voltage waveforms to algorithms for carrier sensing. An in-depth discussion of this information is beyond the scope of this book, so suffice it to say that a person wishing to build an 802.3 interface can certainly find all of the design information in the standard.

As mentioned earlier, the 802.3 standard specifies the use of the CSMA/CD protocol. This is a broadcast-type protocol in which all nodes are connected to a common communication medium and all nodes "hear" every transmission. The protocol itself is relatively simple and, therefore, attractive for many in the local area network business. The following is a simplified version of the CSMA/CD protocol algorithm for media access and control.

To transmit:

1. A node wishing to communicate senses (listens to) the medium for a specified period of time to determine if any other node is currently transmitting. This is the carrier sense portion of the protocol.
2. If bus traffic is detected, wait for a random interval of time (controlled by a back-off function) and try step 1 again.
3. If no traffic was detected in step 1, commence transmission of the message on to the medium.
4. Simultaneous with step 3 (message transmission), listen for possible interference from other transmissions. This is the collision detection portion.
5. If a collision is detected, send a jamming signal to ensure all nodes recognize the collision, wait for a random interval as in step 2, and return to step 1.

To receive:

1. Listen for the specific synchronization pattern indicating the start of a message frame.
2. Receive and decode the message header information and decide if the message address matches the node address.
3. If a match was found in step 2, continue to receive the message data until the end of the message is detected. If no match was found in step 2, stop receiving message data and return to step 1.

The second component, 802.4, of the physical link level in the 802 standard is a specification for a token-passing bus. Simplistically, a token bus is a logically ordered group of communicating nodes which access the medium in a round-robin fashion. This type of medium control implements a broadcast communication method with access control implemented through the passing of a special control sequence called the "token." As in the 802.3 standard, the medium access control layer (see Figure 13.7) implements the basic interface services to the logical link layer. These are identical in function to those for the 802.3 standard and are not described here.

The functional responsibility of the media access control layer in the token-passing bus includes the management of the order of access to the bus (through control of the token). This management allows for the addition and deletion of nodes in the logical token sequence and for the handling of faults which may disrupt the normal token generation and passing process. The passage of a token among stations in effect creates a logical access ring structure, which is controlled by the possession of the token at any particular node. This implies that there must be only one active token in the network at any one time; a condition other than this will lead to an error requiring reinitialization of the token-passing mechanism. All stations in a token bus scheme are connected to a common bus. Each node listens for the token and accepts it when its destination address matches the node address. The token, therefore, can be thought of as a special message that, when in a node's possession, gives that node transmission access to the bus. A brief algorithm for the control of the token mechanism in the 802.4 standard follows.

To transmit:

1. Listen to the medium to detect the synchronization pattern defining the start of a bus frame, and monitor the bus for the special token pattern.
2. Decode the address in the token and decide if it matches the node address.
3. If the token matches the node address, then message transmission is allowed. Note that a node may not actually have a message to transmit and, in that case, does nothing in this step. If the token does not match, return to step 1.
4. If the node is last in the logical sequence of nodes, reinitialize the token address and transmit it onto the bus. If it is not the last node in the logical sequence, set token address to next node and transmit it onto the bus.

To receive:

1. Monitor the medium for frame synchronization and message header information. If a token is detected, go to step 2 of the transmit portion.

2. Decode the message address and determine if it matches the node address. If there is a match, receive the message; if not, return to step 1.

As with the 802.3 standard, the 802.4 standard provides all of the essential physical-level details such as cable impedance and voltage waveforms.

The third portion, 802.5, of the physical-level specification in the 802 standard is for a token-passing ring. The feature that characterizes most ring-type architectures is the presence at each node of data receiver-repeater pairs through which all network traffic must pass. The ring architecture, then, is a store and forward type of system. The amount of storage that is allowed at each node depends on the network design. Physically, each node in the network is connected to two other nodes, a left neighbor and a right neighbor. Message traffic always flows in one direction, say from the left to the right neighbor, and never in the opposite direction. Access to the medium in the 802.5 ring is metered by the passage of a token whose function is not unlike that of the 802.4 token. There are some notable exceptions, however. One of these is that the next logical node in sequence is, by the very nature of the ring architecture, the next physical neighbor in the data flow direction. Thus, the physical structure of the ring actually forces a logical media access sequence among the nodes. It should be noted that the above is the simplest case of token control in a ring architecture. There are provisions in the 802.5 standard for multiple node classes and token priorities so that the logical control sequence may actually skip over some nodes in the physical sequence. It is still true, however, that control must "flow" around the network in the same direction as the data flow and that two nodes of equal priority will receive access based on their relative physical locations.

Some token rings allow segmentation, which enables two or more stations to transmit simultaneously, provided the data paths share no common links. This is possible because of the store and forward characteristic of the ring architecture. The 802.5 standard, however, does not allow segmentation and therefore supports only one message in transmission at a time. In this way, the removal of spent messages can be done by the originating node instead of the receiving node as in the segmented case. Also, routing of the message back to the sender allows the receiver to append completion status bits to the end of the message (sometimes called piggybacking) and to allow round trip error detection. As with the 802.4 bus, the token consists of a special data pattern that is recognized when it appears at a node. A node wishing to receive the token simply alters the token bits as they pass through the store and forward circuitry. Unlike the token bus, however, a ring token need not have an address associated with it since the next logical node is determined by the physical positions of the ring nodes. As with the 802.3 and 802.4 standards, the 802.5 standard provides the three interface services to the logical link control level. A simple version of the ring protocol algorithm follows.

To transmit:

1. Monitor the ring for the token bit pattern and decide if the token priority is less than or equal to the node priority.
2. If the node has data to send, alter the token sequence as it passes through the store and forward buffer so that subsequent nodes cannot recognize it. If node has no data to send, let the token pass unaltered.
3. If token was altered, transmit message onto ring and remove the message from the ring as it comes back around.
4. When done transmitting, reissue the token with appropriate priority and/or node class.

To receive:

1. Monitor the ring for the start of a message and decode message address information.
2. If message address matches node address, copy message data to a node buffer as it passes through the store and forward buffer. If message address does not match node address, go back to step 1.
3. When finished receiving the message, append the message completion status bits onto the message in the appropriate bit slots and return to step 1.

In addition to the above algorithm, the 802.5 standard describes various mechanisms for error recovery in the case of a lost token as well as node addition and deletion circumstances.

The last low-level IEEE standard, 802.6, specifies the protocol and access mechanisms for a metropolitan area network. This network will be wider, in terms of geographic coverage, than the others just discussed; but it will retain upper-level compatibility with the other 802 standards. At the time of this writing, however, sufficient information on 802.6 was not available for detailed discussions.

Sitting on top of the physical layer protocols (802.3, 802.4, 802.5, and 805.6) is the logical link control specification, 802.2. Its major function is to provide a clean, virtual interface to the lower layers while performing error checking and recovery. In actuality, the logical link control level should enable the interchange of lower-level protocols with little or no impact on higher-level functions. The 802.2 specification, then, discusses the methods used for "disguising" the lower-level protocols with a commmon interface.

The logical link control (LLC) sublayer is actually composed of three portions: network layer interface functions, MAC sublayer interface functions, and LLC sublayer management. The topic of sublayer management in LLC is not elaborated upon in the 802.2 standard, although it is identified as an area that requires investigation. From an operational standpoint, the network and MAC-layer interfaces give the basic mechanisms by which data is passed to and from the attached network and host.

At the network layer interface, the LLC standard specifies the types of data transfer services that provided for the next-higher layer (the network layer of the OSI model). There are two basic types of service specified here, unacknowledged connectionless and connection oriented. In unacknowledged connectionless service, the network entity passes a data unit (packet) to the LLC layer for transmission to another network entity or group or for broadcast onto the network. The LLC acknowledges to the network layer, the local receipt of the data unit to be transferred. The data is then transferred according to a priority provided along with the transmission request. Note that no acknowledgement is expected or given by the receiving station; the network entity can only be certain that the data unit was successfully passed to the local LLC and no more.

The other type of LLC service that is provided to network entities is connection-oriented service. Here, a data-link-level connection is established and maintained until disconnected, and error detection and recovery mechanisms are supported. The connection-oriented service provides the following primitives at the interface to the network layer. The connection establishment service is used to request that a data-link-level connection be formed between LLCs and to report the status of the attempt. Also, a connection request from a remote node may be passed through this service up to the network layer. Associated commands allow a network entity to disconnect or reset a connection. Data transfer over the connection uses the connection-oriented data transfer service to send and receive data units and to receive status on the last transmitted message. In order to prevent the overloading of the communication medium or reception buffer storage, a flow control service exists that allows one network entity to request a given data flow level of another entity across the network.

The LLC-to-MAC sublayer interface reflects the low-level nature of the data transfer at this point. There are three basic interactions possible at this interface: data transfer request, data reception indication, and confirmation of the transmission status of the last data transfer. The transfer and reception interactions carry with them a data unit containing message information.

The existence of the two LLC service classes for use by the network layer implies that different inter-LLC protocols must exist in order to perform

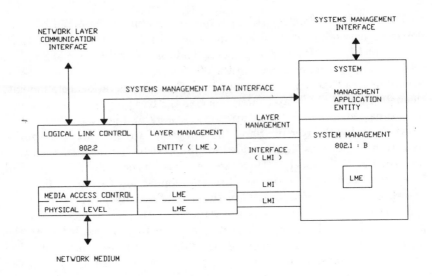

Figure 13.8 Systems management architecture.

the described functions. The 802.2 standard describes two basic LLC types, one to handle unacknowledged connectionless service and one that supports both unacknowledged connectionless and connection-oriented service. The support of unacknowledged connectionless service is rather trivial and consists mainly of a path from the network layer, through the LLC sublayer, and to the MAC sublayer. It allows basic data communication, the exchange of basic LLC control information (e.g., LLC type, data format, and data unit size) and the testing of an LLC-to-LLC connection via the timely exchange of fixed data units over the connection.

A connection-oriented-type LLC contains procedures (in addition to those necessary to support unacknowledged connectionless transfer) that establish acknowledged data exchange protocols. The essential component of this LLC type is the operational commands for asynchronous balanced mode data exchange. Basically, asynchronous balanced mode data exchange causes the necessary data exchanges that allow errors to be detected and LLC conditions to be monitored and communicated. The standard defines a number of state transition diagrams and protocol data units that identify the proper procedures and information to accomplish communication.

At the top level of the 802 group of standards lies the 802.1 standard. The 802.1 standard actually consists of three parts: 802.1:A, 802.1:B, and 802.1:C. The 802.1:A section provides details on how the 802 family of standards fit in with the OSI model standards described earlier. It is not discussed here. The 802.1:C section addresses internetworking issues and is not yet suitably defined for discussion. The third section, 802.1:B, forms the heart of this standard and will receive our attention in the following paragraphs.

So far, the 802 standards that we have discussed have concentrated on the transmission and control of message data in the network. There is, however, another major function that must be performed in order to initialize and keep the network running smoothly. This is the job of systems (or network) management and is the topic of the 802.1:B standard. This document prescribes a management architecture for the other 802 standards which roughly correspond to the bottom two layers of the OSI model.

The basic architecture for systems management, shown in Figure 13.8, calls for layer managers in each 802-specified layer, an overall system manager that uses the individual layer managers to accomplish its tasks, and a set of layer management interfaces over which management and control pass. The basic components of the architecture are described below.

Within each protocol layer in the 802 standards architecture, there resides a managing entity that is used to set up and control the operations of that layer. This function is implemented via a layer management entity (LME) within each 802-specified layer. The functions the LME provides to the systems management function are dependent upon the layer that the particular LME resides in. For example, the LME associated with the media access control portion of one of the lower-level standards might control such functions as protocol initialization or error replacing. Associated with each LME is a corresponding layer management interface (LMI) that provides the conduit for management information between the layer and the system manager (the term "station" manager is also used in the standards, but it is taken to be equivalent to systems management). The structure of each LMI in the system is identical in that the same types of commands for interchanging information are the same for all layers. The attachment of an LMI to a particular LME, however, specifies the kinds of information that may be passed via the LMI commands.

On the right-hand side of Figure 13.8 is the basic systems management configuration of the IEEE 802.1:B document. The bottom box, labeled systems management application entity, contains all of the specific functions that are required to manage local and remote stations. These functions are not specified in the standard, only the architecture that supports their implementation for specific networks. Notice that the systems management section contains its own LME so that it may be managed itself by higher-layer entities. At the top of the systems management box is the systems management entity, which supplies the interface to the higher-level

DNA   OSI

USER	APPLICATION
NETWORK MANAGEMENT	
NETWORK APPLICATION	PRESENTATION
SESSION CONTROL	SESSION
END-TO-END COMMUNICATIONS	TRANSPORT
ROUTING	NETWORK
DATA LINK	DATA LINK
PHYSICAL LINK	PHYSICAL

Figure 13.9   Correspondence of DNA and the OSI model.

management entities (via the systems management interface) and also to the lower levels of the protocol stack. This interface, labeled the systems management data interface, is used to allow systems management to send and receive management information over the network using the same data transfer protocols as for data messages. Implied in this interface is a mapping function that identifies management data units as they percolate up through the protocol stack. The systems management interface provides the window for upper-level functions that specify the management policies to access the implementation mechanisms contained in the systems management application entity.

In total, the family of IEEE 802 standards provides the architecture for constructing, using, and managing the lower levels of local area networks. The standards themselves are promulgated as a family, although subsets of the total set may be used in different combinations to create custom or subset implementations. Additional details on the IEEE-802 family can be found in IEEE [1985a, 1985b, 1985c, 1985d, 1986].

13.4   DEC Digital Network Architecture (DNA)

The Digital Network Architecture (DNA) is the Digital Equipment Corporation (DEC) framework for all of its networking products. Based upon the OSI model structure, DNA consists of eight layers and is shown in correspondence to the OSI model in Figure 13.9. Each layer is discussed briefly below.

As with the OSI standard, DNA distinguishes between interlayer and peer-to-peer communication. Interlayer communication within a node takes place via interfaces whereas peer-to-peer exchanges between different nodes are accomplished with protocols. In the following descriptions of the DNA layers, the protocols that are used for each layer are stated where appropriate. The interfaces are assumed and are not discussed except to say that they remain constant and thereby facilitate the changing of individual protocols without having effects on other layers.

The lowest layer in DNA is the physical layer. Its function corresponds to that of the OSI physical layer. The network architecture supports several physical link implementations including Ethernet, X.25, point-to-point, and multipoint connections.

The data-link layer, as in OSI, establishes and maintains low-level connections between nodes over the physical medium. The protocols employed by DNA include Digital data communication message protocol (DDCMP), X.25, or Ethernet. DDCMP, a character-oriented protocol, is used for point-to-point multipoint installations. The X.25 protocol is similar to the IBM high-level data-link control (HDLC) protocol, and it uses a bit-stuffing mechanism to maintain data transparency [Tanenbaum, 1981]. The Ethernet protocol is carrier sense multiple access with collision detection (CSMA/CD).

The DNA routing layer is capable of performing adaptive routing (where applicable) to control network congestion and flow. The DNA protocol that supports this function is a Transport protocol, and its functionalilty is determined by the type of underlying network.

The end-to-end layer uses a network service protocol to handle program-to-program-level operations that create and control logical communication links which are provided as network access points to the upper layers.

Session control in DNA handles the particular actions that command the end-to-end layer to manipulate logical communication links. Also, message transfer over the logical links is managed here. A session control protocol is used in this layer to accomplish the aforementioned functions.

The data access protocol is used by the network application layer to perform file transfers, loop-back testing, and general communication of remote commands and virtual terminal data. Network management, through the network information and control exchange protocol, allows user tasks to transfer raw data, acquire remote program code, and perform network testing.

At the user level, user-generated programs perform application-specific tasks that use the lower layers for user-level peer communication.

In actual DNA implementations, several of the specified layer functions and protocols are lumped together into cohesive entities that provide a

DNA	LOGICAL GROUPING
USER	
NETWORK MANAGEMENT	NETWORK USER GROUP
NETWORK APPLICATION	
SESSION CONTROL	COMMUNICATION CONTROL GROUP
END-TO-END COMMUNICATION	
ROUTING	ROUTING
DATA LINK	MESSAGE TRANSMISSION GROUP
PHYSICAL LINK	

Figure 13.10 Logical grouping of DNA layers for implementation.

range of services. Figure 13.10 shows one such grouping of the layers into larger entities. At the top, the network user group of functions contain end-user and application-oriented capabilities. In specific system implementations, the facilities for these functions are provided by special-purpose software coupled with command-level and operating system services.

The communication control function group provides the management of the network facilities that are used to carry out the network user group requests.

Routing remains as it was, a facility for controlling flow and access patterns to the network.

The message transmission group encompasses the physical and low-level access protocols that are required for the different network implementations.

From the above discussion, we can see that although DNA is specified so that individual layers may be replaced without affecting the others, the practice of bundling layers into integrated products may make this difficult. This is not abnormal, however, and is often necessary in order to gain the necessary performance.

13.5   Summary

In this section, we have presented four standards that are currently the most influential in the LAN marketplace. These standards have generated much interest in organizations that are trying to develop standards more suited to their own needs as well as in the compatible equipment industry. Several other groups, other than those discussed herein, are promulgating LAN standards of varying scope and depth. Several examples are: The American National Standards Institute's (ANSI) fiber distributed data interface (FDDI), a high-speed token ring standard (see Part 8 for more detail); the Society of Automotive Engineers (SAE) parallel efforts on linear and token-passing buses; the Manufacturing Automation Protocol (MAP) and Technical Office Protocol (TOP) effort to standardize on LAN implementations on the factory floor and in the office environment (see Part 8); and the U.S. Navy's Shipboard Advanced Fiber Optic Network (SAFENET) effort to define military LAN standards. Each of these standards is being developed to address the needs of a specific user community. Also, each standard indicates, to some level, what an individual vendor must do in order to maintain compatibility with the standard intended. Thus, the standardization of local area networks allows a wider variety of standard compatible products to be interconnected and operated than could ever be possible with a plethora of vendor-specific LANs.

13.6   References

Deasington, F. J., *X.25 Explained: Protocols for Packet Switching Networks*, Ellis Horwell Limited, New York, 1985.

IBM Corporation, *Systems Network Architecture: Concepts and Products*, Order No. GC30-3072, IBM.

IEEE, ANSI/IEEE Std. 892.2, *IEEE Standards for Local Area Networks: Logical Link Control*, IEEE, 1984.

IEEE, ANSI/IEEE Std. 802.3, *IEEE Standards for Local Area Networks: Carrier Sense Multiple Access with Collision Detection (CSMA/CD) Access Method and Physical Layer Specifications*, IEEE, 1985.

IEEE, ANSI/IEEE Std. 802.4, *IEEE Standards for Local Area Networks: Token Passing Bus Access Method and Physical Layer Specification*, IEEE, 1985.

IEEE, ANSI/IEEE Std. 802.2, *IEEE Standards for Local Area Networks: Token Ring Access Method and Physical Layer Specification*, IEEE, 1985.

IEEE, Draft Standard 802.1:B, *Systems Management*, IEEE, 1986.

ISO, *Information Processing Systems - Open Systems Interconnection-Connection Oriented Transport Protocol Specification*, ISO 8073, February 7, 1984a.

ISO, *Information Processing Systems - Open Systems Interconnection - Basic Connection Oriented Session Protocol Specification*, ISO 8327, September 1984b.

ISO, *Information Processing Systems - Open System Interconnection - Basic Reference Model*, ISO 7498, October 15, 1984c.

ISO, *Draft Proposal of Management Information Service Definition - Part 2: Common Management Information Service Definition*, ISO SC21, September 10, 1986.

Kuo, F. F. ed., *Protocols and Techniques for Data Communication Networks*, Prentice-Hall, Englewood Cliffs, NJ, 1981.

McFadyen, J. H., "Systems Network Architecture: An Overview," *IBM Systems Journal*, no. 1, 1976.

Strole, N. J., "A Local Communications Network Based on Interconnected Token Rings: A Tutorial," *IBM Journal of Research and Development*, September 1983.

Tanenbaum, A. S., *Computer Networks*, Prentice-Hall, Englewood Cliffs, NJ, 1981.

PART FIVE
Local Area Network Security

14. Local Area Network Security–An Overview

14.1 Introduction

The design of any security system should start with an assessment of potential threats in the order of their significance. The significance of threats has to be defined by the security system designer and has to include careful analysis of the specifics of the operating environment to be protected.

According to Seltzer and Schroeder [1975], the design of the security system should be based on the following principles:

1. Cost effectiveness of the system.
2. Acceptability of the user interface.
3. Security not based on the secrecy of the design (secrecy of the design may be required by some organizations but it should not be the only protection of the system).
4. Sufficient and necessary privilege; every part should have only the rights absolutely necessary to perform its function.
5. Monitoring of every access to every part of the system.
6. Every two parts of the system share as little as possible (to minimize the potential of information leaks).
7. Privilege partition. Execution of partitioned privilege requires cooperation of more than one part.

These general concepts, originally formulated for computer systems, remain valid in the case of computer networks and local area networks in particular.

Damage to a system can be caused by malignant or nonmalignant activities. In most cases the security measures applied to minimize the potential of malignant damage will prevent or at least to some extent minimize the potential of nonmalignant damage with the exception of natural hazards such as fire or flooding. Attacks (malignant activities) on a system can be aimed at hardware and information storage media or at information. The first class of attacks is subject to the physical security measures which will be discussed later.

The second class will require much more attention. All attacks on information have to be performed through legitimate or illegitimate hardware interfaces attached to the network or to the communication system utilized by this network. The potential of attacks through illegitimate hardware interfaces can be reduced by the choice of LAN technology. For example, twisted pair has the level of emission sufficient to read the transmitted information using a sensitive detector placed next to the wires. This type of tap is almost impossible to detect. Broadband and baseband coaxial cables have to be physically tapped. Fiber optics, because of their lack of emissions, are very difficult to tap and therefore should be used in applications where high security is required, but adequate physical protection of the cable run is impossible.

Limiting access to legitimate interfaces through physical security measures in general increases security of information but does not solve all of the problems. The following two cases address the need for other than physical security measures:

1. Physical security can be enforced over the whole installation (owner has administrative and physical control of the whole network and communication system) but a legitimate user is an attacker.

2. Physical security cannot be fully enforced because the communication system is under control of some other party (i.e., the telephone system) or communication media is generally accessible (i.e., satellite communication).

The problem of an attack by a legitimate user is very serious and cannot be solved completely. Every legitimate user has some privileges in the system. Users need these privileges to perform their jobs. Their activity can be monitored to prevent access to unauthorized information; but it is impossible to stop users who have legitimate access to information from, for example, memorizing it and then passing it to a person without such access rights. The probability of this type of information theft can be minimized by appropriate personnel policies enforced by the system owner.

The second case involves information passing the border of the area controlled by the information's owner and being entrusted to a second party. In consequence, the information is subject to misuse by this party or an intruder acting as a result of weak security policies. Types of misuse of information can be classified as:

Information disclosure: Attacker only reads the information.

Information modification: Attacker changes the information.

Service denial: Attacker postpones or prevents the information from being delivered.

Information disclosure can be prevented by use of encryption. Unfortunately, no measures prevent message modification or service denial. The existing security measures allow the message owner to detect the activity of an attacker, but no more than that. To detect message modification, various encryption techniques combined with redundancy checks are used. To detect service denial attacks, encryption is used together with either time stamps or message numbering. Techniques involving encryption will be discussed in more detail later in this chapter.

In every communication it is essential to identify communicating parties. This opens a new class of potential threats; namely, an intruder pretending to be a legitimate user or a user pretending to be some other user. The subject of identity authentication will be discussed in Chapter 15.

14.2   Physical Security

Physical security is the most elementary security measure and should be included as part of the protection mechanism of any system. The physical security cannot be supplied by the system vendor and thus becomes the responsibility of the owner. In most cases a LAN is controlled by one party and, therefore, consistent implementation of physical security based on rules defined by the network owner is highly visible.

Physical security measures should be applied to all components of a LAN: workstations, communication devices, and wiring. Physical security measures can be divided into the following categories:

1. Site access control. Site access control deals with the physical management of entry to the general area where the LAN is located such as a building or plant. Control is accomplished by:

   a. Channeling traffic through control points.

   b. Protecting (by locks or blocking) all other entrances to the site, such as windows, loading docks, vents, etc.

   c. Monitoring by guards control points and the site area.

  d. Requiring badges with pictures carried in a visible place by each person for all personnel allowed to enter the site during any visit to the site.

  e. Making available to all security personnel at all times the updated plans of the LAN layout (cables, communication equipment, data processing equipment) and site layout plans.

  f. Maintaining an entry and exit log for each entrance to the site with the name of the person, company, and time of entry and exit. If there is more than one entrance to the site, the logs have to be compared for matching entries on regular basis, at least once a day. A search for persons who entered the site and did not leave should be performed.

  g. Assigning escorts to persons without appropriate clearances like visitors, maintenance, and delivery persons.

2. Hardware security. The goal of hardware security is to control and prevent unauthorized direct access to network hardware including the cable run and network information storage media. Implementation of extensive hardware security measures is very important, especially in LAN installations that have no site access control. The basic security measures in this area are:

  a. Limit the number of personnel having access to the network devices. Lock network equipment in separate rooms that have access either by key or magnetic card. Place locks that are accessed by either key or magnetic card on the network devices.

  b. Place terminals so that the screens face walls without windows (this also applies to printers or plotters; the printout should not face the windows).

  c. Place cables and wires in such a way that uncontrolled access to them is difficult (for example, cables should not be laid through maintenance closets.) This requirement is difficult to fulfill.

  d. Closely monitor the activities of maintenance persons (the use of power tools that generate a strong magnetic field can damage information on magnetic storage media or in memory).

  e. Shred or burn computer printouts containing sensitive information.

  f. Completely erase magnetic storage media prior to moving them to a lower-security area of the system.

  g. Attach small devices to tables, floors, or walls to prevent their damage or theft.

3. Organizational policies. In many organizations there is a substantial increase in the number of employees using computer equipment. These employees should be carefully screened and

trained for their jobs. In particular, organizations using local area networks where sensitive information can be potentially accessed from many locations should introduce clear security regulations and personnel training. The organization should provide the following:

a. Clear definition of security policies and security-related responsibilities of the personnel.

b. Clear distinction between sensitive and nonsensitive information.

c. Information on how to use and protect the equipment.

d. Reporting procedures of security violations.

e. Password, badge, magnetic strip card protection (how to use them and how to protect them).

f. Appropriate security training program for new employees plus up-date sessions for all personnel.

g. Separations of duties (two or more persons have to cooperate to perform sensitive operation).

h. Record keeping for all security violations.

i. Procedures for backups of all information essential for continuous operation and other important data.

h. Appropriate background checking for personnel (very expensive, performed almost exclusively for government agencies).

i. Collection of badges and cards and deletion of access rights for all persons dismissed or moved to other jobs not requiring these rights.

j. Giving the user no more privileges than absolutely necessary to perform the job.

k. Adequate security monitoring procedures.

4. Hazard protection. The goal here is to protect the system from hazardous conditions. This is accomplished through the design of the facility holding the LAN. The facility must protect the equipment from water damage and power surge. This is accomplished through the application of adequate building codes and measures. For instance, if the water damage is a serious threat, the organization should consider equipment certified for the water conditions they expect. This would be the case if the LAN was being installed on a ship or in close proximity to where spray can effect the wires and other hardware components. An overlooked hazard in our age of air-tight offices and buildings is that of fire, not in the traditional sense, but in the sense of smoke from burning cables. For some time, Underwriter Laboratories

have been examining the toxicity of smoke emitted from wire and fiber cables. They have shown that many of the materials used today will burn quickly and emit large volumes of toxic smoke. Therefore, of concern when we are installing a LAN is the rate at which a piece of wire will burn and the amount of smoke it will emit. This is more critical in vertical installations than in horizontal ones. The last issue in physical hazard protection is power controls. The network equipment should be protected from surges resulting from a lightning bolt striking the power grid or building. The LAN designer, or purchaser, should be aware of this and provide adequate surge protection.

14.3   Encryption

Encryption deals with pairs of transformations (E, D) operating on strings of symbols. Transformations E, D have the property that $D[E(s)] = s$ where s represents a string of symbols. The only pairs of (E, D) that are of practical importance are those for which it is computationally very difficult to derive s from $E(s)$ and at the same time implementations of E and D are relatively simple (fast). E is called an "encryption transformation" and D is the corresponding "decryption transformation." The following terms will be used in this section:

Cipher. A cipher is a transformation mostly involving secret parameters of data, called plaintext, to a scrambled form, called ciphertext.

Encryption (encipherment). Encryption is a process of transformation of a plaintext to a ciphertext.

Decryption (decipherment). Decryption is a process of transformation of a ciphertext to a plaintext.

The strength of a cipher can be based on the secrecy of the enciphering algorithm or the secrecy of the algorithm's parameters. The security of a cipher should not rely on the secrecy of the algorithm alone, even though modern technology allows encapsulation of algorithm implementations in integrated circuits that resist reverse engineering attacks. Security should involve secret parameters called "keys." In most applications, except military or secret government communications, the algorithms are public knowledge and the security of the cipher is based exclusively on the secrecy of keys. The encipherment and decipherment can involve the same key; such a cipher is called symmetric. When encipherment and decipherment keys are different, the cipher is called asymmetric. Asymmetric ciphers are often called public key ciphers because there is no reason for keeping both keys secret. The encryption key can be made public and the decryption key is known only to its owner. This opens a one-way secure channel of communication to the owner of the secret decryption key from anyone with the knowledge of the public key. The concept of public cryptography was introduced by Diffie and Hellman in 1976. In symmetric ciphers, where the key is known only to the sender and the receiver (we assume that the key was not compromised), the message enciphered under this key identifies the sender as an author of the message. Public key cipher systems do not have this property. Problems associated with message origin authentication will be discussed later. Symmetric ciphers are based on substitution and transposition of elements of plaintext. The known public key ciphers are based on operations of finite arithmetic. The following notation will be used in our discussion of encryption:

$E^k(p)$: Ciphertext resulting from encrypting plaintext p with key k.
$D^k(c)$: Plaintext resulting from decrypting ciphertext c with key k.

The corresponding graphical notation is given below.

$$
\begin{array}{ccccccccc}
k & & & & & k & & & \\
\Downarrow & & & & & \Downarrow & & & \\
p & \rightarrow & E & \rightarrow & c\ldots\ldots c & \rightarrow & D & \rightarrow & p
\end{array}
$$

There are three classes of attacks on ciphers where an attack on a cipher, called "cryptoanalysis," is understood as an attempt to either determine the plaintext of a known ciphertext or to determine the secret parameters (keys) of the cipher. The case in which keys are obtained by theft is of no concern in this discussion.

The most difficult is an attack in situations when only ciphertext is available. In this case statistical properties of the language of the plaintext, such as the frequency of letters and groups of letters, possibly together with attempts to guess the most probable words of the plaintext, have to be used to break the cipher. In the second group of attacks, both the plaintext and the corresponding ciphertext are available. The third class assumes the knowledge of the ciphertext of a chosen plaintext and gives the attacker an opportunity to obtain the material most suitable for cryptoanalysis.

14.3.1   Data Encryption Standard (DES)

United States Government agencies have used encipherment for many years. Increased use of communication devices and computers intensified the demand for data security and created an increasing need for encipherment for commercial use. For example, the banking community started using encipherment to protect the electronic transfer of funds from bank to bank and to protect any important information transfers, such as user account balances, passwords, background credit check information, etc. To meet this

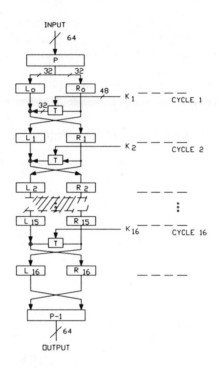

Figure 14.1 Logical diagram of DES.

general growing need and to provide standardized equipment, in 1972 the United States National Bureau of Standards (NBS) began the search for an appropriate encipherment algorithm. The requirements established by NBS included (among others): security not based on the secrecy of the algorithm, and, if visible, in terms of current technology, fast and inexpensive hardware implementation. In 1976 an algorithm based on IBM's LUCIFER cipher was adopted as a Federal standard and became mandatory on July 15, 1977 [NBS, 1977, 1981; Smid, 1981; ANSI, 1981].

Since its introduction, DES has been implemented in various communication devices by many vendors. The information about data encryption equipment and security requirements for equipment using DES can be found in Abbruscato [1984], Gait [1977], and FTSC [1981].

Data Encryption Standard is a symmetric block cipher with a block size of 64 bits and key size of 56 bits. Encipherment and decipherment are performed in 16 cycles, each involving a different subkey, where the

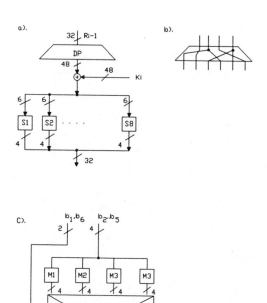

Figure 14.2 (a) Logic diagram of transformation T of DES, (b) example of a duplicating permutation with four inputs and six outputs, and (c) structure of an S-box.

subkey consists of 48 bits of the original key. The logical diagram of DES is presented on Figure 14.1.

The 64 bits of the plaintext block are transposed by permutation P, divided into two groups of 32 bits, and stored in registers L and R. The encipherment process from this moment involves combining the contents of register R, using transformation T, with the 48-bit subkey. The result of this transformation is added modulo 2 to the contents of register L and then stored in register R. The original contents of register R are swapped to register L. This cycle is repeated 16 times. The contents of registers L and R in cycle $i = 1, 2, \ldots, 16$ are as follows:

$$L_i = R_{i-1}$$
$$R_i = L_{i-1} + T(R_{i-1}, K_i)$$

At the end of the sixteenth cycle, the contents of the register R are taken as more significant bits and the contents of L as less significant bits of a

INPUT	OUTPUT
0000	1110
0001	0100
0010	1101
0011	0001
0100	0010
0101	1111
0110	1011
0111	1000
1000	0011
1001	1010
1010	0110
1011	1100
1100	0101
1101	1001
1110	0000
1111	0111

Table 14.1   Table of mapping M_1 of S-box S_1.

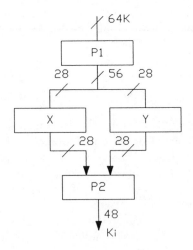

Figure 14.3   DES subkey generation.

CYCLE NO.	ENCRYPTION LEFT SHIFTS	DECRYPTION RIGHT SHIFTS
1	1	0
2	1	1
3	2	2
4	2	2
5	2	2
6	2	2
7	2	2
8	2	2
9	1	1
10	2	2
11	2	2
12	2	2
13	2	2
14	2	2
15	2	2
16	1	1

Table 14.2   Number of shifts in the DES cycles.

block that is subject to the transposition by the inverse permutation P^{-1}. Transformation T combining 48 bits of the subkey with 32 bits of register R is illustrated in Figure 14.2a.

Transformation T introduces nonlinearity to DES. First the 32 bits of register R are transposed, and 16 of them are duplicated, resulting in a 48-bit output of duplicating permutation DP (an example of a duplicating permutation with four inputs and six outputs is given in Figure 14.2b). These 48 bits are added modulo 2 to 48 bits of the appropriate subkey. The result is split into eight groups of 6 bits, and each of these groups is input into one of the "S-boxes."

The structure of an "S-box" is shown in Figure 14.2c. The least and the most significant bits are used to select the result of one of the mappings M performed on the remaining 4 bits. Each mapping M is a permutation of 4 bits. The table of mapping M_1 of S-box S_1 is shown in Table 14.1. All M mappings in all S-boxes are unique.

To complete the description of DES, the method of generating subkeys $K_1, K_2, \ldots, K_{16}$ from the original key will be discussed. The key string in DES consists of 64 bits with 1 bit of each octet being a parity bit, which reduces the size of the actual key to 56 bits. In the first step $P1$, (see the

1F	1F	1F	1F	0E	0E	0E	0E
E0	E0	E0	E0	F1	F1	F1	F1
01	01	01	01	01	01	01	01
FE	FE	FE	FE	FE	FE	FE	FE

Table 14.3   Weak keys of DES (hexadecimal).

01	1F	01	1F	01	0E	01	0E,| 1F	01	1F	01	0E	01	0E	01
01	E0	01	E0	01	F1	01	F1,| E0	01	E0	01	F1	01	F1	01
01	FE	01	FE	01	FE	01	FE,| FE	01	FE	01	FE	01	FE	01
1F	E0	1F	E0	0E	F1	E0	F1,| E0	1F	E0	1F	F1	0E	F1	0E
1F	FE	1F	FE	0E	FE	E0	FE,| FE	1F	FE	1F	FE	0E	FE	0E
0E	FE	E0	FE	F1	FE	F1	FE,| FE	E0	FE	E0	FE	F1	FE	F1

Table 14.4   Semiweak keys of DES (hexadecimal).

diagram in Figure 14.3) strips the key string of parity bits and transposes the remaining 56 bits. The result is split into two 28-bit parts and loaded to registers X and Y. These registers are shifted left in the encipherment mode and right in the decipherment mode. The numbers of shifts in all cycles are shown in Table 14.2. After the registers are shifted, the subkey is generated by transposition of 48 bits selected out of the total of 56 bits of X and Y. This operation is performed by $P2$.

Encryption and decryption in DES are performed using the same algorithm with subkeys applied in the opposite order. The subkey used in encryption mode in cycle i will be used in decryption mode in cycle $17 - i$, where $i = 1, 2, \ldots, 16$.

As the result of the way subkeys $K_1, \ldots, K_{16}$ are generated in DES, there are keys K such that all corresponding subkeys are identical. This is a serious weakness and the use of those keys (shown in Table 14.3), called weak keys, should be avoided. There is another group of six pairs of keys (k, k') such that for corresponding sequences $k_1, k_2, \ldots, k16$ and $k'_1, k'_2, \ldots, k'_{16}$ of subkeys

$$K_i = K'_{17-i} \ for \ each \ i = 1, 2, \ldots, 16$$

In consequence

$$E^{k'}[E^k(p)] = E^k[E^{k'}(p)]$$

This does not present a threat as serious as the encryption with weak keys. Pairs of semiweak keys are shown in Table 14.4.

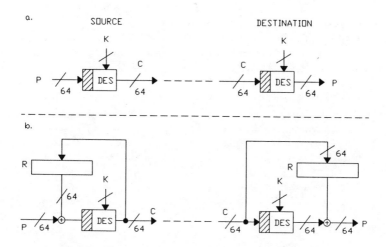

Figure 14.4 Modes of DES operation: (a) electronic codebook, (b) cipher block chaining.

The DES algorithm can be used in the following four modes [NBS, 1980; ANSI, 1983a]:

- Electronic codebook
- Cipher feedback
- Cipher blockchaining
- Output feedback

The selection of the appropriate mode depends on the application. Most encryption devices using the DES algorithm offer more than one mode of operation. When purchasing a DES encryption device, one should make sure the device operates in the desired mode.

The basic mode of DES operation is called an electronic codebook. In this mode (Figure 14.4a) 64-bit blocks are enciphered independently of each other. This is the major weakness of the codebook mode because communication protocols are very repetitive in terms of message formats, packet headers, and padding bits. Such regularities can result in an easy guess of the contents of specific blocks or parts of the ciphertext because every two identical blocks of plaintext will correspond to identical blocks of ciphertext. With DES working in the electronic codebook mode, deletion of blocks, switching block order, or the substitution of a block from some other message encrypted with the same key is not difficult and cannot be detected without additional security measures. The electronic codebook

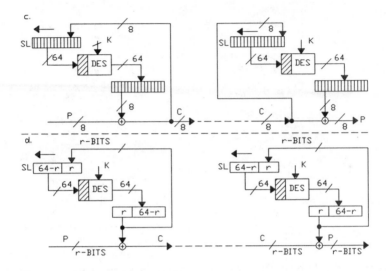

Figure 14.5   Modes of DES operation: (c) cipher feedback, and (d) output feedback.

mode is suitable for short messages not exceeding one block. The repetitions should be avoided and blocks should be padded with random numbers or some other variable parameter like a message number or time stamps. The use of time stamps or message numbering will also prevent playback attacks. In general this mode of operation is of little practical importance.

In cipher block chaining (see Figure 14.4b) the ciphertext of block B_i (the ith block of the message) is a function of the plaintext of B_i and all blocks of the message encrypted before B_i. To start the process of encipherment, register R has to be loaded with some value. If R contains all 0 bits, the first block is encrypted in the same way as in the electronic codebook mode. This is unacceptable especially when the first block of messages tends to be repetitive and regular in structure, for example, containing headers of the protocols. Thus, encryption in addition to the key should involve one more parameter, the initial value of register R denoted by IV. It is essential that both communicating parties have the same key and the same initial value in register R. Value IV can be kept secret, but its secrecy does not add any strength to this mode of operation. The safety of the method can be increased by frequent changes of IV. The problem with frequent changes of IV is that both the sender and the receiver have to change it at the same time. One possible solution involves the use of the message number as IV.

If no messages are lost, both communicating parties should have the same count of messages.

Cipher block chaining requires that the size of each message be equal to a multiple of 64 bits. To satisfy this requirement, the last block of the message may have to include padding bits. The best results are obtained by padding the last block with random numbers, with the last byte containing the count of padding bits. An error in the ciphertext of the block B_i will result not only in the scrambling of the plaintext of B_i but also of B_{i+1} because the faulty value of the ciphertext of block B_i will be added modulo 2 to the result of the decryption of the ciphertext of B_{i+1}. This mode of operation is of great practical importance, especially for transmission of long messages. Its major disadvantage is its lack of self-synchronization. Insertion or deletion of even 1 bit of the ciphertext will cause the loss of synchronization of the cipher, and all the blocks of plaintext starting from that point will be garbled. Cipher block chaining mode has to be used with the addition of synchronization mechanism.

In the cipher feedback mode, the ciphertext is generated 8 bits at a time. It starts with some initial value in shift register SL. The contents of SL are encrypted, and the most significant 8 bits of the ciphertext are added modulo 2 to 8 bits of plaintext p, forming enciphered octet c. At this point register SL is shifted left 8 bits and c is loaded into the 8 least significant bits of SL. Because only 8 bits are enciphered at a time, this method of encryption is much slower then electronic codebook or cipher feedback. The major difference between cipher feedback and the former mode is that the plaintext stream is not processed directly by the DES algorithm. In the case of an error occurring in the ciphertext, the octet containing the error and eight following octets of the plaintext will be garbled. This occurs because the faulty octet of the ciphertext will remain in register SL during the decryption of the next eight octets.

In cipher block chaining, both communicating parties have to start with the same value IV in register R. A similar requirement is in force in the case of cipher feedback mode. This time, initial synchronization of communicating parties can be accomplished by sending at the beginning of each message at least 8 bytes of random numbers. These bytes, after encipherment, will be fed into SL registers on both sides of the connection. Thus the sender and receiver will start with the same value in registers SL. The cipher feedback mode can be used with blocks of any size smaller then 64. In practice, it is used in communication involving blocks of small-size, for example, characters.

In the output feedback mode the DES algorithm is used to generate a key stream which is added modulo 2 to the data stream. The data stream does not pass through DES. Starting with some initial value in register SL, whose value has to be the same in the sender's and receiver's SL registers, DES encrypts the contents of this register. The r most significant bits of the generated cipherblock are added modulo 2 to the first r bits of the plaintext. The same bits are loaded into the r least significant bits of the SL register, which in the meantime was shifted r bits left. The cycle repeats until the whole message is encrypted. Because no external information enters the key generating cycle involving DES, the key stream will be cyclic. The cycle can be very long, but at some point there will be a repetition of the key. This forms the major weakness of this mode of DES operation. Similarly to the cipher feedback mode, output feedback is not self-synchronizing. Insertion or deletion of even 1 bit of the ciphertext will result in the scrambling of all bits which follow.

14.3.2   Public Key Cryptography

In an asymmetric cipher the encryption key is different from the decryption key. In consequence it is not necessary to keep the encryption key secret. The public encryption key allows for secure one-way communication from a node with access to the encryption key to the node with access to the secret decryption key.

To have two-way communication between n nodes, n pairs of keys are necessary in which for each node A the encryption key p^A is public knowledge and decryption key s^A is known only to A. This method gives a substantial reduction of the number of keys required to connect n nodes and compares favorably with symmetric ciphers in which the number of keys required for direct communication between any two of all n nodes is $\frac{1}{2}n(n-1)$. The major disadvantage of public key cryptography in its basic form is the lack of authentication of the sender. The public nature of the encryption key p^A does not allow A to identify the message originator. The message sender, on the other hand, knows that the message can be decrypted by the owner of the public key only. The issues involving key management and authentication in public key cryptography will be discussed in later in the chapter.

There are several public key ciphers; most of them are based on operations of finite arithmetic. A short description of one of them follows.

The best-known algorithm was created by Riveset, Shamir, and Adleman (the RSA cipher) and is based on the power function in modulo m arithmetic [Riveset, 1978]. The process of generating a pair of keys starts with a selection of two very large prime numbers, b_1 and b_2. This process of generating large prime numbers requires substantial computational resources. The suggestion of buying large prime numbers from a vendor specializing in their computation is not viable because the security of the RSA algorithm is based on the secrecy of these numbers. Users of RSA would have

to trust the vendor in terms of the security of the vendor's number production and distribution procedures as well as the vendor's honesty. After
prime numbers b_1 and b_2 are selected, all further steps are computationally
simple.

Two additional numbers, m and p, are created, where

$$m = b_1 b_2 \ and \ p = (b_1 - 1)(b_2 - 1)$$

Then numbers d, e are selected from the range $3, 4, \ldots, p$ in such a way that

$$de = 1 \ (modulo \ m)$$

Pairs of numbers (e, m) and (d, m) form the encipherment and decipherment
keys, respectively. Encipherment and decipherment are performed using
power functions in mod m arithmetic. Thus,

$$ciphertext \ = \ (plaintext)^e \ (mod \ m)$$

$$plaintext \ = \ (ciphertext)^d \ (mod \ m)$$

In this method the plaintext block is treated as a binary number. The
size of the block is limited by number m and cannot exceed n bits, where
$2^n < m$.

The next well-known public key cipher, called the trapdoor knapsack
cipher, is based on the knapsack problem. This cipher requires long public
keys (thousands of bits) and suffers from substantial text expansion. The
ciphertext is between 30 and 100 percent larger then the plaintext. The
strong side of this cipher is its speed. Its encryption and decryption compared to RSA cipher are much simpler and therefore faster. Decryption in
knapsack problem ciphers is 4 times slower then encryption. RSA ciphers
are slower but requires shorter public keys (a range of 1 k bits). The security of knapsack cipher is not well researched. No commercial hardware
implementation of this algorithm was known to the author at the time this
was written. There are hardware implementations of the RSA algorithm.

A comparison of the speed of hardware implementations of public key
ciphers with DES is:

Cipher	Range, bits/s
DES	$50M$
RSA	$50k$
Knapsack	$20M$

Public cryptography is not widespread because of the deficiencies of the
known public key ciphers. Public key cryptography is much younger than
traditional cryptography. It was first suggested by Diffie and Hellman in
1976.

14.3.3   Role of Encryption in Network Security

The discussion in this chapter up to this point concerned basic concepts and differences between symmetric and asymmetric ciphers with no reference to the implementation of encryption within LAN structures. This section is concerned with issues essential in understanding the role of encryption in LAN security systems.

There are two basic types of encryption in computer networks: link encryption and end-to-end encryption. The distinction between them results from different functionality and placement within the network layers.

Link encryption involves one key per each line connecting two network nodes. If nodes A, B and B, C are connected by lines with corresponding keys k_{AB} and k_{BC}, each message sent from A to C will be first encrypted with k_{AB} in A, sent to B, decrypted with k_{AB} and encrypted with k_{BC} in B, sent to C, and finally decrypted with k_{BC} in C.

The major advantage of link encryption is that it is implemented in the lowest network layers and therefore allows encryption of not only the message contents but also protocol headers giving protection from potential traffic analysis attacks.

The key management in link encryption is simple because key changes involve only two nodes sharing the key. Link encryption is attractive if the number of links in the network is small. In most cases, the encryption hardware operates at line speed causing no noticeable degradation of transmission performance.

Link encryption is transparent to the user (performed without the user's interaction), and it has to be implemented on all links of the network. The upgrade of network interface units with encryption capabilities is not exceedingly expensive, especially if it is done at the stage of network design.

Link encryption offers protection from attacks performed through line tapping. As mentioned, both data and routing information (protocol headers) are encrypted, and therefore no message disclosure or information about the message destination can be obtained by line tapping without the knowledge of the encryption key.

Unfortunately link encryption offers no protection from attacks performed through network terminals. The messages are available in plaintext in all higher layers. In consequence there is no separation of processes or users resulting from link encryption.

End-to-end encryption involves encipherment of messages at the level of communicating processes. In this case the messages are not available in plaintext at the lower layers shared by different processes. A meaningful end-to-end encryption is possible in layers no lower than the transport layer. Implementation of encryption in the transport layer has an advantage of potential recovery but offers no selective protection. Mostly, end-to-end encryption is implemented in the presentation layer where the selective protection is possible.

In end-to-end encryption the headers of the protocols are not encrypted (encryption takes place in layer above the layers in which these protocols are used), and therefore this kind of encryption offers no protection against traffic analysis because each layer adds more routing information that is transmitted in plaintext form.

The end-to-end encryption has an advantage over link encryption by protecting the information between and within the network modes. Key management in end-to-end encryption is usually more complex.

End-to-end encryption can be implemented as a nontransparent or semi-transparent service. In nontransparent implementations the user can choose the encryption mode and will be asked to submit the encryption key. The semitransparent implementation may involve keys loaded into secure areas in the terminal from the card carried by the user. The process of session key acquisition will be performed without user intervention.

In link encryption every node has to have cryptographic devices, but with end-to-end encryption cryptographic capabilities have to be available only in these nodes that originate and receive encrypted messages.

The advantages of end-to-end and link encryption are complementary. The first offers protection of information within the nodes; the second offers protection against traffic analysis. If both types of protection are required, both types of encryption should be used (this solution may carry a significant expense and be cost effective only in high-security applications). In many commercial applications traffic flow security is not important, and end-to-end encryption is sufficient.

14.4   References

Abbruscato, C., "Data Encryption Equipment," *IEEE Comm. Magazine*, vol. 22, no. 9, 1984, pp. 15-21.

American National Standards Institute, *Data Encryption Algorithm*, ANSI Standard X3.91, 1981.

—, *Modes of Operations for the Data Encryption Algorithm*, ANSI Standard X3.106, 1983a.

—, *DataLink Encryption*, ANSI Standard X3.105, 1983b.

Davies, D., "Some Regular Properties of the 'Data Encryption Standard' Algorithm," *Advances in Cryptology*, Proc. Crypto '82, 1982, p. 39.

Diffie, W., and Hellman, M., *New Directions in Cryptography*, IEEE Trans. Inf. Theory, vol. 22, no. 6, 1976, pp. 644-654.

Federal Telecommunications Standards Committee, *General Security Requirements for Equipment Using the Data Encryption Standard*, Federal Standard 1027, 1981.

—, *Interoperability and Security Requirements for Use of the Data Encryption Standard in the Physical Layer of Data Communications*, Federal Standard 1026, 1983.

Gait, J., "Validating the Correctness of Hardware Implementation of the NBS Data Encryption Standard," *National Buerau of Standards Special Publication*, pp. 500-20, 1977.

National Bureau of Standard, *Data Encryption Standard*, Fed. Info. Processing Standard Publication 46, 1977.

—, *DES Modes of Operation*, Fed. Info. Processing Standard Publication 81, 1980.

—, *Guidelines for Implementing and Using the NBS Encryption Standard*, Fed. Info Processing Standards Publication 74, 1981.

Rivest, R., Shamir, A., and Adleman, L., "A Method for Obtaining Digital Signatures and Public Key Cryptosystems," *Comm. ACM*, vol. 21, no. 2, 1978, pp. 120-126.

Seltzer, J., and Schroeder, M., "The Protection of Information in Computer Systems," *Proc. IEEE*, vol. 63, no. 9, 1975, pp. 1278-1308.

Smid, M., "Integrating the Data Encryption Standard into Computer Networks," IEEE, *Trans. on Comm.*, vol. 29, no. 6, 1981, pp. 762-772.

Tardo, J., "Standardizing Cryptographic Services at OSI Higher Layers," *IEEE Comm. Magazine*, vol. 23, no. 7, 1985, pp. 25-29.

Zimmermann, P., "A Proposed Standard Format for RSA Cryptosystems," *IEEE Computer*, vol. 19, no. 9, 1986, pp. 21-34.

15. Authentication and Key Management

15.1 Introduction

This chapter is devoted to two major groups of issues of computer security, both of which have to be addressed in the design of any network security system. The first of these groups results from the special role of keys in computer communications systems. The security measures used to protect keys are discussed in the first part of the chapter devoted to key management. The second group concerns mechanisms of checking the integrity of principals, data, and parameters of communication and will be discussed in length in the section devoted to authentication.

15.2 Key Management

Security of any cipher system is based on the secrecy and authenticity of the keys. The distinct role of keys in cryptography requires special security measures to prevent key disclosure or misuse.

The key management system structure should be determined, taking into consideration factors such as type of cipher (symmetric versus asymmetric), size of the network in terms of the number of keys required, and the required level of security.

The major key management functions can be divided in three groups:

• Key generating
• Key distribution
• Key storage

These functions will be discussed separately for symmetric and asymmetric ciphers. This approach is a consequence of the major differences in the key characteristics of symmetric and asymmetric ciphers resulting in different key management requirements.

The question of centralized versus distributed key management will be addressed. In general, a fully distributed solution requires that all key management functions should be performed by each node of the network, which usually results in high costs. Certain key management functions, especially those related to key authentication and key certification, are very difficult, if not impossible, to implement in a fully distributed manner. The known implementations are based on a central, trusted, and highly protected server performing these functions.

In centralized key management systems, key generation and distribution are performed by a central server. The role of network nodes is reduced to storing one key, called the terminal key, which will be used for safe communication between the node and the server in the session key acquisition protocol. The choice between centralized and decentralized implementation of key management functions should be based on the nature of the function, the cipher, the required security level, and cost and performance criteria.

Key distribution in symmetric cipher systems can be either automatic or manual. A secure manual key distribution takes place by means of a tamper-free key loader. The automatic key distribution takes place through secure communication channels. These channels cannot be established without manual delivery of at least one key to one of the communicating parties by the other party who generated or acquired the key. Delivery of further keys can take place using a manually delivered key. In asymmetric cipher systems, the distribution of keys (public keys), in general, does not require secure channels. Even though protection of public keys is of no concern, their authentication is of the highest importance.

15.3   Key Management in Public Key Systems

Public key systems will require one pair of keys for each node of the network. For a node A its decryption key s^A should be kept secret and its encryption key p^A should be made known to all nodes of the network.

The public key systems have an interesting property. Their security is based on secrecy of one group of keys and wide publicity and authentication of the other group of keys. This two-fold nature of public key systems suggests a different treatment of both groups of keys. Because the decryption key should be known only to the key owner and because the encryption and decryption keys have to be generated together as a pair, the key generating process should be decentralized and performed in each node. Thus every node of the network has to contain a key generating facility unless pairs of keys will be generated by an entrusted party with secret keys delivered to their owners through secure channels.

To ensure high protection of the decryption key, it is desired that this key be generated and remain permanently in the tamper-free module. This approach requires enclosing the decryption hardware in the same module. The encryption and decryption keys are generated together from the same seed. The encryption key leaves the module and is made available to all nodes of the network. The decryption key is stored in the module.

Because one of the keys of the pair is public and both keys are certainly related, it has to be ensured that it is extremely difficult to derive the secret key from the public key of the pair. From our discussion of public key ciphers, it is known that the process of the generating key is much more complex for asymmetric ciphers then for symmetric ciphers. In the context of the requirement that each node has its own key generating facility, the complexity of the key generating process forms a drawback of public key cryptography. On the other hand, the fact that the keys are generated by their owners and the secret key is not transported makes the key distribution process much easier. The key distribution process reduces to distribution of public keys only. The distribution of public keys does not require secrecy; on the contrary, every node of the network should have an access to updated copies of public keys of all other nodes.

In our discussion of public key ciphers, it was indicated that public keys for the known ciphers are very long—in the range of thousands of bits. In large networks, each node will need a substantial amount of memory to store the public keys of all network nodes. In addition, if each node stores its own list of public keys, the change of a key of any node requires an update of lists in all network nodes. Each node, after generating a new pair of keys, would have to communicate with all nodes in the network to announce the new public key. The overhead of the communication used for the key management would be unacceptable.

The solution to this problem is in centralizing the public key management. The public key center (PKC) implemented in one of the nodes of the network will be responsible for storage, delivery, and maintenance of updated copies of all public keys in the network. Node A, in order to communicate with node B, will have to acquire the public key of B from PKC. The protocols of communication between all nodes of the network and PKC involve the public and secret keys of PKC. These keys are not going to be used to ensure the secrecy of information transferred but as a key authentication mechanism.

The protocol of key acquisition is demonstrated below using notation SENDER → RECEIVER : MESSAGE.

$$A \rightarrow PKC \quad : \quad A, B$$

$$PKC \rightarrow A \quad : \quad E^{s^{PKC}}(B, p^B, t), \quad E^{s^{PKC}}(A, p^A, t)$$

$$A \rightarrow B \quad : \quad E^{s^{PKC}}(A, p^A, t)$$

In the above protocol s^{PKC} represents the secret key of the public key center; p^A and p^B are the public keys of nodes A and B, and t represents the time stamp (the clock reading at the time when the message was formed). The use of time stamps in key distribution protocols in described in Denning [1981].

The secret key s^{PKC} is known only to the public key center, where all nodes have the updated copy of its public key p^{PKC}. A message $E^{s^{PKC}}(B, p^B, t)$ can be decrypted by any node as follows:

$$D^{p^{PKC}} E^{s^{PKC}}(B, p^B, t) = B, p^B, T$$

In this case the public key center uses a digital signature to authenticate public keys. (The concept of digital signatures is explained in the part of this chapter devoted to authentication.) It has to be noted that this method of key authentication works only if the used cipher has the following property:

$$E^p D^s(x) = D^s E^p(x) = x$$

where p and s indicate the public and secret keys, respectively (for example, the RSA cipher).

A compromise of the secret key of the public key center (s^{PKC}) has very serious consequences. With the knowledge of s^{PKC}, the attacker can masquerade as the public key center and deliver to node A, which is requesting the public key of B, the attacker's own public key. In this situation A receives

$$E^{s^{PKC}}(B, p^{AT}, t), E^{s^{PKC}}(A, p^{AT}, t)$$

and sends the second part of the message to B. In consequence, A and B will exchange messages encrypted with key p^{AT}; these messages can be decrypted by the attacker using the corresponding key s^{AT}. Because the attacker can easily obtain public keys of nodes A and B (from PKC), it can masquerade as these nodes in their communication with each other.

In addition to the space savings obtained by maintaining just one list of all public keys in the network and the simplification of key updating procedure (a node changing its key has to notify only the public key center instead of communicating the change to all network nodes), the centralization of public key distribution in PKC offers a mechanism for public key authentication. This property is essential in the case of disputes between nodes about validity of public keys. The above-presented protocol includes time stamps, and, thus, the node which acquired a public key P encrypted by the public key center with its secret key s^{PKC} can present the message $E^{s^{PKC}}(B, p^B, t)$ as evidence that p^B at time t was registered with PKC as a valid public key of B. Each node is responsible for registering its public key with PKC. The registration should take place immediately after a new pair of keys is generated. At registration PKC can issue to node A a receipt in the form:

$$E^{s^{PKC}}(A, p^A, t)$$

The major advantage of public key systems over symmetric ciphers is the simplicity of the key management. In symmetric ciphers keys have to be distributed through secure channels, and in public key systems the only concern is the public key authentication.

15.4 Key Management in Symmetric Cipher Systems

The more often a key is used for encryption of data transported through an insecure area, the higher the probability of key compromise. Therefore, the keys used for encryption of large amounts of data should be changed very frequently. Manual delivery of encryption keys, if performed too often, will be annoying or sometimes unmanageable. The other option, automatic key distribution, will require special mechanisms to ensure the security of transported keys (see ANSI [1985], Balenson [1985], Bauer [1983], Greenlee [1985]). Delivery of the new key encrypted with the old key is strongly discouraged because the compromise of one key will be inherited by all its successors. The problem can be solved by using two types of keys—data encryption keys and key encryption keys. This defines a hierarchical key system in which the keys of each level are protected by encryption using keys of the next higher level. Keys of higher levels are used less frequently than keys of lower levels; therefore, their lifetime can be longer. The top-level key (most likely there will be just one key of this type), called the master key, should be stored permanently in a tamper-free hardware module. This key should be entered manually and all operations involving it should be restricted to the module.

On the lowest level in this hierarchy there are keys used for data transmission between network nodes. These keys should be changed very frequently. In the extreme case, the lifetime of a key will be restricted to one session. This approach requires a large supply of keys. First, let us consider a situation in which each node has the ability to generate a new session key and then send it to its partner in the prolog part of the communication protocol of the session. This solution has a major drawback that results from safety requirements for transmission of session keys. The session key would have to be encrypted with a key of a higher level known to the destination node. (Encryption of the session key using the old session key is strongly discouraged.) This means that each node should store one higher-level key for each node in the network. The above approach "solves" the key distribution problem in the lower level by moving the problem to the higher level.

Instead of storing in each node higher-level keys of all nodes in the network, one can introduce a centralized key service implemented as a server in one of the nodes. It is called the key management center (KMC). The KMC will generate session keys and deliver them to the network nodes using a second-level key. One such second-level key is required for each network node. This key is known to both the node and the KMC and is used exclusively for communication between these two parties to request or pass the session keys. The second-level keys have to be delivered to the nodes through a secure channel, most likely in a manual fashion.

The storage required for all the key encrypting keys can be substantial. It would be difficult to design a separate tamper-free memory module to store them; therefore, the keys encrypted with the master key m will be stored on a disk. The tamper-free module will have to protect only the master key. As mentioned, the master key never leaves the tamper-free module. Session keys are generated in the module, then the appropriate encrypted second-level key is read from the disk and entered into the module. This key, after being decrypted with master key, is used to encrypt the session key. The protocols used for session key delivery are discussed below.

Protocol

$$A \;\to\; KMC \;\; : \; A, B$$

$$KMC \;\to\; A \;\;\;\;\;\; : \; E^{k^A}[s, E^{k^B}(s, A)]$$

$$A \;\to\; B \;\;\;\;\;\;\;\; : \; E^{k^B}(s, A)$$

The request for a session key can be sent to the KMC in a cleartext (as above) unless traffic analysis should be prevented. In this case the message from A requesting a session key for communication with B would contain the name of A in the plaintext and the name of B encrypted with k^A.

KMC after receiving the key request, generates a session key s and fetches $E^{k^{KMC}}(k^A)$ and $E^{k^{KMC}}(k^B)$ from the disk, where $k^K MC$ denotes the master key. After $E^{k^{KMC}}(k^A)$ and $E^{k^{KMC}}(k^B)$ enter the tamper-free hardware module containing k^{KMC}, they are decrypted, giving k^A and k^B. First k^B is used to generate $E^{k^B}(s, A)$ and then k^A is used to produce $E^{k^A}[s, E^{k^B}(s, A)]$. This message is sent by KMC to A, where it is decrypted with k^A giving s and $E^{k^B}(s, a)$. In the next step A can send to B a request for a session $E^{k^B}(s, a)$.

If node A is allowed to have more than one session key request pending, the response of KMC has to include a request identifier, for example, taking a form of $E^{k^A}[s, B, E^{k^B}(s, A)]$.

KMC is not involved in the delivery of the session key s to node B because the synchronization of key delivery to B with the initialization of communication performed by A would be very difficult. The solution, where A delivers the session key to B in the prolog of the communication session, is much more natural and easy to implement. In addition, this solution allows for an authentication of the caller because the delivered session key is sealed by KMC together with an identifier of the caller $E^{k^B}(s, A)$.

The security of the described system depends on the security of the KMC and the secrecy of all key-encrypting keys. Special physical security measures at the node implementing KMC are required. If a file of keys is destroyed on the disk, the whole network may be paralyzed. Communication can be restored by loading the backup file. It is important to update the backup file if a change of any second-level key or master key takes place. The change of a second-level key also involves delivery of this key to the node. Methods of key transportation will be discussed later. If KMC is implemented in software (for example, as part of the operating system), the security is in general much lower than in the implementation with tamper-free hardware modules.

The key delivery process is a very sensitive operation and should be protected from various types of attacks. In the hierarchical key system, the compromise of a key of a higher level is inherited by all keys of lower levels related to the compromised key. In the case of a master key compromise, all keys are compromised. If the second-level key k^A is compromised, an attacker can masquerade as A, acquiring session keys from KMC and then prolonging the attack to the communication with any mode in the network. The rights of an attacker will be limited only by the rights of A that are associated with the possession of key k^A. Because of that, special care should be taken of key-encrypting keys both in storage and in transportation.

Another form of attack can be performed by tricking a node to use an old compromised session key. This type of attack can take place at the session key acquisition stage between A and KMC or during the key defining process taking place between A and B. In the first case, an attacker has to install an active wiretap between A and KMC. When A sends a request, A, B to KMC, an attacker intercepts the response of KMC that is carrying the session key and replays to A a recorded response containing the old compromised session key $\hat{s}$:

$$E^{k^A}[\hat{s}, E^{k^B}(\hat{s}, A)]$$

Node A will accept key s and send

$$E^{k^B}(\hat{s}, A)$$

to B. The intruder with another active wiretap on the line between A and B, and knowledge of $\hat{s}$, can perform an active or passive attack on communication between A and B during this session.

In the second case, an attacker replays to B a recorded message $E^{k^B}(\hat{s}, A)$ containing the compromised key $\hat{s}$. From now on the attacker can masquerade as A in the communication session with B.

The potential of both of these types of attacks is a serious threat for the security of the system described above. The security measures used to prevent these attacks include exchange of random numbers and time stamps.

To prevent the first type of attack the protocol of key acquisition is modified in the following way:

	Use of random numbers	*Use of time stamps*
$A \rightarrow KMC$	A, B, n	A, B
$KMC \rightarrow A$	$E^{k^A}[s, n, E^{k^B}(s, A)]$	$E^{k^A}[s, t, E^{k^B}(s, A)]$

where n is a random number generated by A for each key request and t is a time stamp applied by KMC. The attacker cannot trick A into using the old compromised session key any longer. Node A compares the number received from KMC with its own value of n and rejects the key if the numbers are not equal. Using time stamps, the node compares the time when the request for the key was sent to KMC with the time stamp of the response. If the time stamp is smaller than the request time, the key is rejected. In the case when time stamps are used, clock synchronization between KMC and all network nodes is required.

Prevention of the second type of attack involves a global handshake with the exchange of time stamps. The modified protocol is described below:

$$A \to B \quad E^{k^B}(s, A)$$
$$B \to A \quad E^s(t_1)$$
$$A \to B \quad E^s(t_2)$$

To explain the protocol, let us assume that t_0 is the time when A sends $E^{k^B}(s, A)$ to B. Node A will terminate the session if $t_0 > t_1$, which indicates that the response was generated prior to the current key delivery. Node B will terminate the connection if $t_1 > t_2$, which means that the response to the $Es(t_1)$ challenge was generated earlier than the challenge.

The process of generating key-encryption keys takes place in the KMC. Key generating for symmetric ciphers is not a complicated process. Almost any random string of bits can be used as a key. Some of these strings may be more vulnerable to attacks than others; therefore, they should be avoided. An example is weak keys in DES. The process of generating key-encryption keys should take place in the tamper-free hardware module. In this solution, the keys of the second level as well as the session keys will not be available in cleartext outside of the secure module. The transportation and loading of the second-level keys to terminals takes place by means of a portable tamper-free key loader. This type of secure loader is produced by many vendors together with encryption hardware. The keys are transferred to the loader through the interface that is used to attach the loader to the encryption device. The process of transferring the key to the terminal's hardware encryption module will take place through the same type of interface.

The keys are transferred to the key loader together with parameters indicating their destination. These parameters are used by the loader to identify the terminal prior to the transfer of the key. This method is used to protect the keys from being deposited to wrong devices, possibly devices under control of an attacker. In the case of a parameter mismatch, the loader destroys corresponding keys. This prevents tampering with the key loader. The specifics of the key loader design and the interface used for loading and depositing keys depend on the vendor.

15.5 Authentication of Data Integrity

Operations on information such as entry, storage, retrieval, or transmission involve the risk of intentional and unintentional changes introduced to the manipulated data. In certain applications, data integrity is much more important than data secrecy. For example in banking transactions, where messages contain amounts of deposits or withdrawals, the authentication of message integrity is of the top importance. Protection from unintentional errors is not our concern here. The methods such as error detecting codes, error correcting codes, or checksums used successfully for this class of errors cannot be used in their basic form to detect attacks on data integrity.

There are no effective methods to prevent attacks on data integrity. The only defense is based on physical security and selection of LAN technology. There are security measures to detect changes deliberately introduced to the data. These measures of data integrity authentication will be our major interest.

It is very difficult to imagine any authentication of data integrity without encryption. To check the integrity of a message, the receiver has to apply to the message appropriate tests and then interpret the results to determine the validity of data. To interpret test results, the receiver has to be furnished with the results of the identical tests performed by the sender on original data. These results are called an authenticator. Because the tests performed on data to validate its integrity are usually public knowledge, a potential intruder could change the data and corresponding authenticator and, in consequence, trick the receiver into accepting false information. The application of encryption, which hides the message content, helps to solve the problem.

If the receiver has some special knowledge about the contents of the message, this knowledge can be used to evaluate validity of data after decryption. This applies, for example, to text messages. Depending on the type of encryption algorithm used, it can be very difficult for an attacker to modify the ciphertext in such a way that the corresponding cleartext makes sense. This statement assumes that the encrypting key was not compromised. Thus, encryption by itself can be used in some situations as an authentication mechanism. The fact that a message decrypts with the appropriate key into a readable text is taken as a proof of the message integrity. This method of authentication is very weak and should not be used in applications in which authentication of message integrity is important. In addition, in situations in which the receiver does not have sufficient knowledge about the expected contents of a message (for example, messages containing numbers with an unspecified range), no authentication is possible without an authenticator generated by the message originator and delivered with the data.

Authenticator a is generated from the plaintext p according to an algorithm implementing function f, where $a = f(p)$. Function f is chosen in such a way that knowing f and a, it is very difficult to calculate the value p when $f(p) = a$. This type of function is called a one-way function. For practical reasons, f is also not a one-to-one function, which means that the same authenticator may correspond to more then one plaintext. This weakness is the result of a compromise. For a one-to-one function the number of bits of an authenticator would equal the number of bits of the plaintext. If function f is publicly known, it is easy to generate an authenticator for any message. In this situation one can introduce a secret parameter s, known only to the communicating parties and used with authenticating function f, where $a = f(p, s)$. In consequence only the user with knowledge of s could produce a valid authenticator.

The discussion of specific methods of authenticator generating is beyond the scope of this chapter.

15.6   Authentication of Time Integrity of the Connection

Time integrity of the connection is preserved if all messages are delivered in real time. In consequence, the only delays allowed result from technical characteristics of the network and the network load.

The time integrity of the connection can be violated either by a delay in message delivery or a replay of an old message. The second type of attack, known as playback attack, also violates the integrity of the stream of messages discussed in the next paragraph.

To detect playback attacks the communicating parties can use time stamps, message numbering, or a full handshake with an exchange of random numbers. In systems based on time stamps the sender, prior to encryption, supplements the message with the current time stamp. The receiver, after decrypting the message, compares the time stamp with the time of its own clock. If the difference exceeds the defined threshold value, the message is rejected. The use of time stamps requires synchronization of the clocks of the communicating parties. Time stamps are also useful in the detection of message delays. Message numbering, discussed in the next paragraph, does not have this property. An example of the full handshake with an exchange of random numbers is given in Section 15.8, which is devoted to identity authentication.

15.7   Authentication of Message Stream Integrity

The security measures used to detect an attack in which an intruder changes the order of messages in the stream or deletes a message or inserts a new message into the stream include time stamps and message numbering.

Time stamps can be used to detect switching the order of messages or insertion of a message. They are of no use to detect message deletion. In systems using message numbering, both the sender and the receiver keeps the count of messages. The value of the counter is sent with each message and then the counter is incremented. The receiver increments its counter after accepting a message; thus when the message arrives, the value of the receiver's counter has to be equal to the value of the sender's counter sent with the message. This method allows for detection of message switching, deletion, and insertion.

If the combination (message number encryption key) is kept unique, which means that the lifetime of the key should not be longer than the cycle of the counter; message numbering can be used as a powerful countermeasure against undetected attacks on message stream integrity. If an authenticator is used together with message numbering or time stamps, the numbers or time stamps should be added to the message before the authenticator is determined. In this way the authenticator protects also the message number or the time stamp.

15.8   Identity Authentication

Identity authentication is concerned with verifying the identity of communicating parties and the identity of principals requesting access to protected resources. The accurate mutual identification of communicating parties and the accurate identification of the resource user is essential for the security of the network. The importance of identity authentication results from the fact that the rights one can exercise in the environment depend on the particular principal (node or user). Reliable identity verification is a necessary condition of access control.

The identity authentication can be either implicit or explicit. An implicit identity authentication is a side effect of security measures introduced for reasons other than authentication. For example, in symmetric cipher systems the knowledge of a key authenticates the identity of communicating parties assuming that the key was not compromised. This type of authentication does not involve any expenses, but it does not offer much protection either. In applications where identity verification is important, explicit measures of authentication of principals should be implemented.

The identity authentication can be implemented in a distributed or centralized manner. The distributed approach requires that each node has a template with sufficient information to identify all other nodes of the network. Depending on the type of authentication parameters used, the distributed solution may involve extensive storage requirements and special measures of updating the templates stored in all of the network nodes. There are situations in which the template is trivial and takes a form of a dynamically generated challenge exchanged between communicating parties. The following protocol used by nodes A and B for mutual identity verification is an example of an explicit, distributed identity authentication method for communicating parties. In this protocol, A and B exchange random numbers to verify each other's identity.

$$A \rightarrow B \quad E^{p^B}(n)$$

$$B \rightarrow A \quad E^{p^A}(n, m)$$

$$A \rightarrow B \quad E^{p^B}(m)$$

Node A generates a random number m and sends it to B encrypted with public key p^B of B. Node B decrypts the message, extracts number n, generates its own random number m, encrypts both with the public key, and sends them to A. A decrypts the message with its secret key and checks to see if n is equal to the original. Equality indicates a positive identification of B. To complete the process, A encrypts m with p^B and sends it to B. After decrypting the message, B has an opportunity to compare the received m with the original. If they are equal, a positive identification of nodes to each other is completed. An attack on this protocol would require the knowledge of secret keys of A or B. Possession of a secret key of either node allows an attacker to extract the random number, which can be then be returned encrypted with the public key. In this case a masquerade of the node with the compromised secret key takes place. In addition to authenticating the identity of communicating parties, the exchange of random numbers authenticates the time integrity of the connection (provides proof that the communication takes place in real time).

An explicit centralized identity authentication can be implemented on one of the network nodes as a service available to all network principals (nodes, users). In further discussion, the name authentication center (AC) will be used for this server. The authentication process between any two principals, A and B, takes place through the AC; therefore, specific measures have to be established for authentication and secure communication between each network node and AC.

The AC stores all the information required to authenticate all network principals. This information consists of values of all identity attributes for each principal as well as requirements for identity attributes and their threshold values for authentication of partners submitted by each principal. This results from the fact that the authentication information to be checked by the AC may be a function of a principal, its partner, and possibly some other parameters indicating the level of sensitivity of the operation specified by one or both parties. This diversity, if required, can be incorporated in AC much easier than in a distributed system. The process of authentication takes place as follows.

Principal A identifies itself to the AC, indicating the partner B and the type of operation. The AC checks the credentials of A against the requirements of B in terms of the indicated operation. In the case of a positive result of the check, the AC issues a certificate c^{AB} which is sent to A via a secure channel. Principal A delivers c^{AB} to B. Principal B can either recognize and accept c^{AB} as a proof of A's identity or check authenticity of c^{AB} in the AC before accepting it. Principal B can perform the check of the authenticity of c^{AB} by itself in the case in which a digital signature is used by the AC to certify c^{AB}.

For example, centralized explicit identity authentication is a side effect of the key management based on the KMC in a symmetric cipher system. The KMC in response to the request for a session key from principal A for communication with B, sends to A the message $E^{k^A}[s, E^{k^B}(A, s)]$. Principal A, after extracting $E^{k^B}(A, s)$, sends it to B. This message received by B delivers the session key, but it also authenticates A by its identifier sealed with k^B by the KMC. According to the protocols used, and assuming that the keys were not compromised, only A could extract $E^{k^B}(A, s)$ from $E^{k^A}[s, E^{k^B}(A, s)]$, which is generated by the KMC. In the next step, B extracts key s from $E^{k^B}(A, s)$. From now on knowledge of s implicitly authenticates A and B to each other.

Our previous discussion concerned an environment in which the message originator and recipient trust each other and cooperate to enhance the security of communication. This assumption is not valid in many applications. One of the following can happen:

1. Sender denies authorship of the message.
2. Receiver claims that no message arrived.
3. Receiver claims that the message arrived too late.
4. Receiver claims different message contents from the original (sender's copy).

In general, the message recipient is in a much better position than the originator. Methods of authentication discussed earlier give the recipient a certain level of guarantee of the origin and content integrity of the message. This type of guarantee is not available to the originator, who has to depend on an acknowledgement from the receiver. The methods discussed earlier are not adequate in the case of disputes between communicating parties. Different measures have to be applied to give both parties evidence to support their cases, which are judged by an independent arbitrator.

A method known as digital signature solves problems 1 and 4. The digital signature will be explained using the public key cryptography. There are also methods of digital signature based on symmetric ciphers. The concepts of digital signature is illustrated in Figure 15.1.

Sender A signs message p by applying its secret key s^A. Then A encrypts the token indicating its identity together with the signed message using key k. The layer of encryption using key k, known only to A and B, is used exclusively to ensure the secrecy of message contents. Node B, after receiving $E^k[A, E^{s^A}(p)]$, decrypts the message and obtains A and $E^{s^A}(p)$.

Figure 15.1 Digital signature concept.

Token A can be used to select public key p^A corresponding to A which will be used to decrypt $E^{s^A}(p)$. As evidence of the received message, B should save $E^{s^A}(p)$ and p^A. The correctness of this method is based on authenticity of public key p^A where p^A can be ensured by registering public keys in a public key center (PKC). The public key center can certify validity of the public key p^A by applying its own signature $E^{s^{PKC}}(p^A, t)$ and using a time stamp t. The message $E^{s^{PKC}}(p^A, t, A)$ together with p^{PKC}, which is public knowledge, forms evidence of the validity of p^A as a public key of A at time t. In this method it is very important that signed message $E^{s^A}(p)$ depends in a nontrivial way on all bits of p; otherwise B could change certain bits in p without changing the signature, in consequence performing a successful attack of the type 4. The layer of encryption applied to ensure the data secrecy can be either using a symmetric or an asymmetric cipher. The case of public key encipherment is shown in Figure 15.2.

There are other methods of digital signature. Some employ symmetric ciphers. It has to be noted that not all public key ciphers are suitable for digital signature. Only those in which encryption and decryption are commutative (for example, the RSA cipher) can be used for that purpose without modification. The discussion of other methods of digital signature is beyond the scope of this chapter. Problems associated with the receiver claiming that a message sent by the originator did not arrive, or arrived too late, are complex and can be approached by including certified acknowledgements with time stamps in the communication protocols.

15.9   Identity Verification

Verification of a user's identity is essential in enhancing the physical security by control of the physical access to computer hardware and then, when this type of access is granted, to control a user's access to computer system resources.

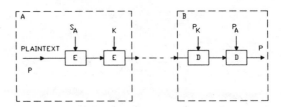

Figure 15.2 Digital signature with public key encipherment.

Identity verification of users can be based on their personal characteristics or on tokens in their possession. Methods based on personal characteristics include fingerprint, hand geometry, retinal patterns, voiceprint, and signature. Methods involving tokens include magnetic strip cards, smart tokens, keys, and passwords. The major differences between these two groups of methods include:

• Methods based on personal characteristics are relatively new in their computer applications and require sophisticated methods of measurement. In consequence they tend to be more expensive.

• Methods based on personal characteristics have higher margins of error because the measured characteristics depend on the physical and mental condition of an individual.

• Methods based on personal characteristics are more difficult for users to accept, especially if direct contact of the sensor with parts of the human body is required.

• Tokens can be stolen, but forgery of the personal characteristic is very difficult—for some characteristics, almost impossible.

• In methods based on personal characteristics the verification process involves comparison of the measurement with a threshold value stored in the system. This results in two types of errors: legitimate user is rejected and illegitimate user is accepted.

Lowering threshold values increases the number of errors of the first type, and an increase of the threshold values increases the number of the second type of errors. Acceptance of illegitimate users is a security violation. Rejection of legitimate users creates a nuisance and encourages users to bypass the security system. Fine tuning of threshold values is very important and depends on the security requirements of the specific application. The error margin in this group of methods ranges from a few percent to practically zero percent in the method based on retinal patterns.

In all methods of this group the introduction of the user to the system takes place by taking several measurements of the characteristics and transforming them into representation of user's identity stored by the system and used in future identification attempts. Characteristics measured depend on the method. For example, in identity verification based on a fingerprint, the configuration of lines such as loops, arches, whorls, and ending and splitting lines is taken into consideration. In methods based on signature static and dynamic characteristics are measured. Static characteristics reflect the shape of the signature; dynamic ones reflect the speed and pressure applied to the pen.

In applications requiring high throughput, the time of a single user identification is an important parameter. The time required for a single user identification for systems currently available on the market vary, but most of them are in the range of seconds.

15.10   Summary

The implementation of certain key management functions as a centralized service requires special security measures applied at the node of service implementation. The attack on any communication channel in the network can usually be performed by an attack on a central service. Therefore, all network users have to be satisfied with the security of centralized services. One way of increasing the security of centralized services is by creating more than one server, each with limited responsibility. In this solution, each server contains only partial information, that is, just enough to perform part of the service function. The user has to apply to all servers of the system to receive a complete service. This solution is, in general, more expensive, but it prevents an attack in which an intruder masquerades as a centralized service without users' knowledge. With the split responsibilities the probability of all subservers, implemented on different nodes with separate security systems, being taken over by an attacker is very low. This approach applied to the key management functions will result in the implementation of a few key servers in which the user receives one communication key from each server and combines all the keys (for example, by addition modulo 2) to generate the key to be used during the session with a desired node. An attack on some of the servers cannot result in the use of a key known to the attacker. To succeed, the attacker would have to be in control of all servers.

15.11   References

American National Standards Institute, *Financial Institution Message Authentication*, ANSI Standard X9.9, 1982.

—, *Financial Institution Key Management*, ANSI Standard x9.17, 1985.

Balenson, D., "Automated Distribution of Cryptographic Keys Using the Financial Institution Key Management Standard," *IEEE Comm. Magazine*, vol. 23, no. 9, 1985, pp. 41-46.

Bauer, R., Berson, T., and Feiertag, R., "A Key Distribution Protocol Using Event Markers." *ACM Trans. Comp. Syst*, vol. 1, no. 3, 1983, pp. 249-255.

Brocklehurst, E., "Computer Methods of Signature Verification," *Nat. Physical Lab. Rep. DITC*, 1984, pp. 41-84.

Davies, D., and Price, W., "The Application of Digital Signature Based on Public Key," *Cryptosystems. Proc. 5th ICCC*, 1980, pp. 525-530.

Denning, D., and Sacco, G., "Timestamps in Key Distribution Protocols," *Comm. ACM*, vol. 24, no. 8, 1981 pp. 533-536.

Greenlee, B., "Requirements for Key Management Protocols in the Wholesale Financial Services Industry," *IEEE Comm. Magazine*, vol. 23, no. 9, 1985, pp. 22-28.

Israel, J., and Linden, T., "Authentication in Office System Internetworks," *ACM Trans. Office Info. Syst.*, vol. 1, no. 3, 1982, pp. 193-210.

Jueneman, R., Metyas, S., and Meyer, C., "Message Authentication," *IEEE Comm. Magazine*, vol. 23, no. 9, 1985, pp. 29-40.

Meijer, H., and Akl, S., "Digital Signature Schemes for Computer Communication Networks," *Seventh Data Comm. Symp.*, 1981, pp. 37-41.

PART SIX
Modeling and Analysis of Local Area Networks

16. The Modeling Problem

As system complexity is increasing with advancement in technology and as system design incorporates multiple processors networked together, the performance of these networks is becoming more important to the overall system development. One of the major advantages to multiple processor system architectures is expandability.

The heart of this concept is the network. As workloads increase, components can be added or replaced with higher-speed technology to accommodate the increase in workload with minimum impact on the other components in the system. That is with the exception of the network. In spite of concepts of layering and standard interfaces such as ISO OSI model, implementations to date do not provide the clean layer concepts that allow levels of protocol to be replaced without affecting the other layers.

With these considerations, it is obvious that when a system is being developed, it is of utmost importance that the network selected be capable of meeting the performance requirements of the system. The system engineer must consider and predict system workloads for the network for the expected life of the system. From these predictions, evaluation of candidate network protocols must be made early in the system's conceptual stages. Evaluations of the network must continue throughout the life of the system.

Performance prediction and evaluation of a network may call for varying methods depending on the system, the system's state of development, and the objective of the analysis being performed. This chapter presents three methods and how they may be applied to meet the needs of the system engineer in evaluating and selecting the network to be used in the system being developed or evaluated.

16.1   Network Performance Evaluation

Modeling has been shown to be a useful tool which adds a quantitative factor to the design process for any network. Additionally, modeling also provides a qualitative function by verifying intuitive notions of actual system performance. Through modeling, proposed system designs can be analyzed and unacceptable design approaches can be eliminated. Also, various modeling techniques provide the facility whereby the sensitivity of selected architectures to changing design parameters or requirements can be evaluated. Hence, these techniques can be applied throughout the various stages of design.

Distributed systems require new components and constraints to be considered in the modeling process. One component, the interconnecting structure, allows cooperating programs or processes executing in different computers to communicate and exchange information via messages in the performance of the overall system operations. Again, the additional time delay inherent in this operation complicates process synchronization and data management. Consequently, modeling techniques must have the mechanisms to evaluate various interconnection structures and the associated implications (such as the execution of cooperating, asynchronous processes).

In general, there are several techniques which may be used in performance evaluation of network systems. The primary catagories are:

1. Analytical
2. Simulation
3. Empirical

These approaches are listed in increasing order of detail, complexity, and cost. In theory, these techniques are used sequentially by increasing the level of detail until the desired confidence in the design is achieved. In practice, however, modeling requires a trade-off between realism and cost.

Historically, analytical and simulation techniques have been the most commonly used methods in developing system models. Although some feel that these techniques are inadequate to model distributed systems, others appear to use these methods with success. In empirical methods the model would be a prototype of the network being evaluated or the actual system itself. The development of prototypes to investigate various architectures and designs is, under normal circumstances, prohibitively expensive. However, the techniques used may be applied to the final network during actual operation. Consequently, these three primary methods will be examined in greater detail.

As system designs become more complex through the distribution of functions among processors connected via networks, more and more implementation alternatives are made available to system developers. Networks are perhaps the primary component of these systems and the overall effectiveness of these systems is primarily dependent on the performance of their networks. This chapter will address the performance evaluation considerations of LANs.

The performance of a LAN can be characterized by quantitative values obtained through the three primary methods:

1. Analytical modeling
2. Simulation modeling
3. Empirical methods

The modeler of a network system must have a performance profile of the system for each method. A profile of a system is to be considered a view of the system from a specific perspective, hence the term "profile." Any system may have a number of profiles developed for it depending on the various views required of the system. Examples of various profiles may be inventory, size, cost, etc. Each profile will consist of its own matrix of information to describe the system from its specific view. We will define in this chapter a matrix of performance parameters which may be used to develop a "performance profile" of a LAN system.

All three methods can extract common quantitative parameters. However, the values of these parameters may vary from one method to the other unless the evaluators take great care in assuring that their perspective of the network system remains constant throughout its development and as their approach moves from one evaluation method to another. Too often, modeling efforts are done independently of one another for a given system and also independently of the system test design. Each evaluator and test developer may have a different interpretation of the system performance requirements and develops his or her own performance profile as shown in Figure 16.1. This results in different sets of performance values that appear to have common terms, but their results grossly differ because of the different perspectives in extracting the performance information from the different performance profiles. To avoid this result, the evaluators must develop a common performance profile from the system definition from which all evaluation approaches are to be implemented.

The performance profile consists of three major models:

1. Workload model. Specifies the characteristics of the resource demands on various equipments in the system.
2. Configuration or system structure model. Specifies the hardware characteristics of the system.
3. Scheduling model. Specifies the scheduling algorithms whereby resources are allocated.

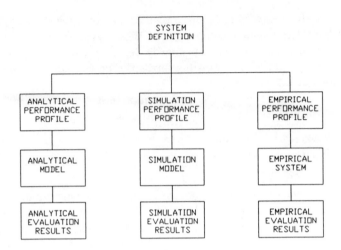

Figure 16.1   Common performance evaluation approach.

Assuming that the different evaluators all perform evaluations on a common performance profile, the results from the different models should be within acceptable proximity of one another. This assumes not only that the configuration model, the scheduling model, and the workload model are all identical but also that the evaluation criteria are the same. The evaluation criteria consists of what information is extracted from the model and where it is extracted.

A common base which explains the various methods is evaluated for the examples given in this chapter. However, the performance profiles were developed independently of one another. This is to allow you to evaluate how a common network can be viewed from different perspectives and how well the results track given this approach.

16.2   Analytical Modeling

Advances in modeling techniques are making analytic models more capable of representing sophisticated network systems. Consequently, these techniques have been growing in popularity.

One method commonly used in network design is queuing models. These models are more precise than other analytical techniques which predict performance based on average values. One reason is that queuing models allow greater detail to be used in describing network systems and hence to capture the more important features of the system.

Queuing models can be categorized as either deterministic or stochastic in nature. If the design parameters to the model are known from prior experience or measurements, a deterministic analysis of the system may be carried out. Conversely, if the design parameters are not known, a stochastic analysis using various probability distributions is normally required.

Typical design parameters would include such items as:

1. The interarrival rate of events
2. Service times of these events
3. Number of servers being modeled
4. System capacity (i.e., number of events currently being processed and in queues)
5. Queuing discipline employed (i.e., FIFO, first-in, first- out; LIFO, last in, first-out, etc.)

Normally, queuing models provide some of the following performance attributes:

1. Average queue lengths
2. Average waiting time in queues
3. Utilization statistics
4. Average response times

Although queuing models have one overriding advantage in that they are cheap to use, there are a number of significant limitations to this method:

1. Because these models assume the system has reached a steady state or equilibrium, peak or transient conditions are not modeled.
2. These models are limited to the complexity of the problems that can be solved. As problems become more complex or additional details required, other methods must be used to model the systems.
3. Without actually measuring various design parameters, it is difficult to determine whether the characteristics of the data used will represent the system under investigation.

16.3   Simulation Modeling

As queuing models or other analytical techniques become more detailed, they will eventually become too complex to analyze. Discrete simulation techniques can be used to model this increased complexity. Thus, simulation modeling is often viewed as the next logical step in system modeling.

Techniques used in discrete simulation models are well known and well established. Because simulation techniques represent systems more faithfully than analytical methods, simulation models are more common in practice. Furthermore, this area has been the subject of considerable research for several years. Numerous computer languages (such as GPSS, GASP, SIMSCRIPT, etc.) have been developed, tested, used, and enhanced in order to facilitate the development of simulation models. Modeling tools for the specific applications of networks and computer systems are starting to evolve (such as Network II.5). Thus, this area could be characterized as being mature.

Simulation models provide designers with numerous options. The degree of realism incorporated into the model directly reflects the level of detail it incorporates. Depending upon the detail and complexity required, a wide range of models can be developed. Consequently, it is the prerogative and decision of the designers to determine the required model complexity.

In addition to handling varying levels of complexity, simulation models overcome other limitations of analytic techniques; namely, peak loads and transient behavior can be investigated. Also by varying design parameters, sources of performance fluctuations can be identified. Finally, the time compression capability of simulation models allows designers to examine the performance modeled system for differing intervals of time.

Despite the numerous advantages of simulation models, a number of limitations inherent with this type of approach do exist:

1. Despite the fact that simulation is less expensive (in terms of actual costs) than emulation or prototype development, simulation is more expensive then analytical techniques. Apart from understanding, analyzing, and developing a network system model, computer simulation software must also be designed, developed, tested, and verified.

2. As in the case of analytical techniques, it is difficult to ensure (a) that the simulation model is approximately equivalent to the real system and (b) that (in the absence of performance measurements) the input design parameters actually characterize the network system with respect to workload, configuration, and scheduling models.

3. Often, the results of simulation models are difficult to interpret.

16.4   Empirical Methods

Empirical methods are the most accurate performance determination approaches for network systems because they evaluate measured data extracted from running hardware. The evaluation may be done both dynamically, where performance parameters are determined and provided to the evaluator while the network system is running, or statically, where the network is monitored and raw data is extracted while running but the evaluation of the data is performed after the monitoring period. Dynamic evaluation is a more specific method in that the parameters of interest must be predetermined to the specific case in order to minimize the impact of data collection and evaluation on the running system. This method is useful in performance monitoring of running network systems to determine in-use workload effects. The static method is perhaps the most useful for performance determination and prediction requirements. The raw data is collected during a test run in which the workload is controlled to determine the performance of the network, given specific workload requirements. The static method will be examined in this chapter since it can demonstrate the data extraction and evaluation methods for both approaches. However, the dynamic method would be a subset of the static approach tailored to a specific application.

The empirical methods may be applied to the actual network system being developed or a prototype designed for evaluation. Again the method of data extraction and evaluation for each would be identical. However, the best method for minimizing monitoring and data evaluation processes is by using passive hardware. But this method is costly, in that it requires a complete system to perform the performance evaluation processes beyond that of the network system in question. The advantage of using a prototype would be that the hardware and software would be specifically designed for evaluation purposes. This would help minimize the impact of system monitoring and data extraction components on the system. A prototype may be designed to perform at a scaled-down speed, which makes the monitoring time to execution time ratio smaller than on the actual network system. Then, as part of the data evaluation process, the ratio factor can be brought into the equation to scale the performance back up to the speed of the actual network.

Empirical methods provide distinct advantages over analytical and simulation modeling methods. They are:

1. The evaluation is performed on an actual running network system.
2. There is no need to validate the system configuration of actual network implementations. (However, prototype implementations must be verified or validated the same as analytical and simulation models.)

Empirical methods also have disadvantages, which include:

1. The cost of developing a prototype is normally beyond the budget of most programs.
2. By the time the actual network system is implemented, the financial and time investments are too great to make any major design changes.

3. Performance monitoring and evaluation processes normally affect the performance of the system, which in turn alters the results of the evaluation.
4. Passive monitoring and evaluation approaches normally are impractical because of expanded cost and the size of monitoring equipments.

16.5   Summary

In practice, analytic, simulation, and prototyping empirical methods provide the designers with useful information to evaluate various hardware and software architectures. However, the strength and value of these approaches lies in the synergistic relationship between them. These three approaches have one overriding weakness: it is difficult to verify that the models accurately represent a proposed system in the absence of a real system. Clearly, designers must establish some confidence in these models if design decisions are to be based on the results obtained from these models.

The most obvious technique used in such situations is to verify the queuing model, the simulation model, and the prototype model against one another. Although this is not a rigorous validation of the models, few additional options exist when no actual system exists in which real and predicted measures can be compared. In this manner, designers can establish some level of confidence in the models they employ.

As the development of the actual network system evolves, the level of detail in all three models should also evolve, which in turn would ehance the confidence level in their respective results. Once the actual system has been developed, the models may be stringently validated by comparison with the evaluation results of the actual system. From this point on, modeling can provide a useful method for the evaluation of the impact that alterations, enhancements, varying workload, etc., may have on the network system.

17. Analytical Modeling

17.1 What Is Being Tested?

Before we can look at technologies used in evaluating network performance, we must determine what is being evaluated and what its importance is overall. Typically, in the past networks were evaluated mainly on capacity of links and saturation of the network. LANs, on the other hand, because of shared channels and diverse collections of protocols and devices, must be evaluated across a wider range of parameters. In particular, LANs must be evaluated as to their communicator's capacity, protocol efficiency, component limitations, bottleneck analysis, fault tolerance, and sensitivity. Each of these measures relates to some specific aspect of the system's architecture such as topology, switching method, communications method, interface unit design, media physics, etc.

17.1.1 Communications Capacity

Capacity, in the raw sense, is the rate of flow of bits or transitions that a media can support. Capacity in real terms must be broken down to the underlying physical realizations including clocking speed (data transitions), propagation delay, and carrier sensing time.

The clocking speed sets the rate in bits per second that the media will support (this speed includes the transmitter and receiver rates with the media rate). Propagation delay takes into account the time necessary to send a single bit or transition from point A to point B. The propagation delay is driven by the media being used and is based on the physical characteristics of the media, such as its ability to transmit electrons or light

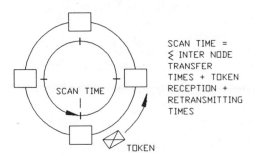

Figure 17.1 Token ring scan time.

waves and at what speed per second. This basic property of the media yields a propagation delay based on the distance. Therefore, in designing or evaluating a LAN, it is important to take into account the total distance that the LAN must cover. The last component is the sensing time. This represents the time it takes for the electronics on the receiver end to determine a logic value for a received signal or to set up its electronics to begin reception. When all these are taken into account, a capacity for the link can be established.

17.1.2   Protocol Efficiency

This measure of LAN performance deals with the overhead associated with control protocols. The measure examines the time associated with acquisition of the media to transfer information and the volume of information allowed to be transferred upon acquisition. A typical measurement taken to determine protocol efficiency is the scan time. Scan time generally defines the time associated with acquiring control of the media. For example, in a token ring the scan time with no messages to send is the round-trip token transition time around the ring (Figure 17.1).

In a reservation bus scheme, as in HXDP, the scan time is viewed differently. It is composed of the time on a node-to-node basis from the slot I am on now until my next reserved slot (see Figure 17.2). If a comparitor result is true, I have control or else I must wait for the increment counter and try the next location.

In other schemes, the protocol efficiency level is harder to determine; for example, in a contention reservation system the scan time depends on my contention, priority, and precedence in the system. This could turn out to be a single slot or infinity. Because of this, measuring the protocol efficiency of this class of system is very load dependent and is based on what

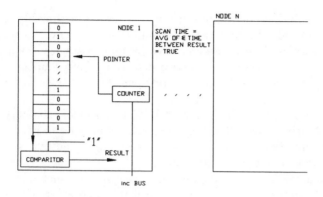

Figure 17.2 Reservation slot scheme.

perspective the efficiency is being measured from. The topology also affects the protocol efficiency measure. If the control is performed on the same media that the data is being transferred on, this will drop the efficiency measure. If separate data and control lines are used, the protocol may operate more effectively. An important part of protocol efficiency is the fairness or normal distribution of users on the bus. What this means is that a good protocol will provide some level of service to all users rather than biasing a few. This measure is derivable via statisical averages.

17.1.3 Network Stability

The stability of a LAN determines the measure of its effectiveness during abnormalities of operation. A LAN with a high mark for stability will not degrade or drop the level of service in the face of peaks and valleys of loading or in error situations. These measures take into account the topology of the network, the error correction and detection in place, the protocol's resiliency, the capacity of the links, and the protocol's stability. This measure is best derived via testing, simulation, or worst-case analytical modeling.

17.1.4 Network Reliability

Reliability is a metric often looked to as a measure of a system's quality. As a term, reliability can be defined as the range of acceptable versus unacceptable behavior of the system and its components. Reliability has often been viewed as a measure of user satisfaction with the system operations. If the users view the system as totally performing their functions as desired, it is providing reliable service. As a measure in reality, reliability is viewed as the interval between failure in a system or mean time between failure (MTBF). In order to meet these reliability metrics, a system such as a local area network must possess features for fault tolerance. Typically these features include mechanisms for error detections, fault confinement and assessment, error recoverability, and treatment of conditions that caused the failure.

Therefore, if we are looking at a LAN in terms of reliability, we must determine how it does all of the above actions in order to have a clear picture of reliability. Typically LANs use redundancy and bypassing as main methods in realizing reliability values. One of these values is performance-monitoring hardware or software combined with fault detention and isolation hardware or software. These, when taken together with the proper control hardware or software, provide a means to detect errors, determine their effect, set a plan in motion to restore service, execute this plan to bring the network back to an acceptance level, and perform diagnostics to determine how to fix the problem if necessary.

The LAN designer or purchaser must examine how reliability is met in each of these component areas to determine the true service range for the LAN. In particular, reliability measures are placed on the media (links) between nodes, the interface units to the network, and the associated software used to provide network services.

17.1.5   Component Limitations

The goal of performance assessment for this measure is to determine the boundary levels of operations for the components associated with the LAN. For example, what are the operating parameters for the links, the connections, the interface unit, the component of the interface unit, and the software associated with the components? The metrics used will be average performance and worst-case performance. This is done to get the range upon which the devices will operate as specified.

17.1.6   Bottleneck Analysis

This form of performance assessment seeks to define which areas of the LAN will limit the overall performance. It is typical for systems to operate at the maximum speed of the slowest component. Analysis of systems for such conditions will bring out these deficiencies. Some are critical, while others are not. The major conditions that are measured for are throughput and response time of the devices in the LAN to see their limitations. These, in turn, are analyzed as to their effect on total system performance. Typical means of testing for such conditions include analytical and simulation techniques.

17.1.7   Fault Tolerance

A very important analysis of a LAN or any device is its fault tolerance. Fault tolerance refers to the ability of a device to continue service in the face of faults or errors. The level of continued service (fault tolerance of the system) depends on the requirements levied on the system to maintain user operations. In some cases there is not a stringent need for survivability under error conditions; in others it is essential. Performance assessment of LANs for this metric typically consist of insertion of error conditions and examination of the effect on the enviroment based on these conditions. The best means to do this include simulation or run-time evaluation. Analytical models typically are not very useful to examine slight deviations or glitches in performance caused by faults but can be used to evaluate hard failures in some cases.

In all of the above cases, the overall goal is to determine how this LAN will perform with my applications' limitations in mind. As varied as applications are, so are LANs' performance. LANs were designed for varying conditions; therefore, they possess varying performance characteristics. For example, we probably would not wish to pay the price of using a LAN developed for a space station to link with our office personal computers. The cost associated with the space-based LAN's fault tolerance, reliability, and stability far outweigh the needs of the office LAN in most situations. Conversely, we would not use a simple office LAN in such a hostile environment.

17.2   Analytical Models and Analysis

The use of mathematical rigor to evaluate and predict performance of systems has been around for hundreds of years. The application for evaluating computer systems has only been rigorously applied for 20 to 30 years. The basic mathmatical techniques used are probability concepts and queuing theory. Classic works on the topic include Leonord Kleinrock's two volumes on queuing systems theory and computer applications. Other noteworthy contributions are Kobayashi [1984], Trivedi [1982], and Lavenberg [1981]. These texts rigorously examine the theory and applications of queueing theory to computer system performance evaluations. The goal of this section will be to highlight some of the important issues and show a representative example of applying queuing theory to the evaluation of a LAN.

17.2.1   Probability Concepts

To appreciate probability and its application to computer systems, some basic principles of probability will be examined. Probability provides a measure of the likelihood of occurrence for random phenomena. To understand this measure, one must have some basic elements to describe this measure, namely, sample space and events. Sample space represents the set of possible outcomes for an experiment. The notation used is typically S. For example, the toss of a coin in sample space terminology is $S = \{H, T\}$, indicating that the sample space has two possible outcomes: either heads or tails. An event is a subset of the sample space. In the previous example, H is an event within S. Some important properties of probability include the seven axioms of algebra sets (events):

1. $A + B = B + A$ *communicatative* $(A + B = A$ *and* $B)$
2. $A + (B + C) = (A + B) + C$ *associative* $(AB = A$ *intersect* $B)$
3. $A(B + C) = AB + AC$ *distributive* $(\bar{A} = A$ *complement*$)$
4. $(\bar{\bar{A}}) = A$
5. $\overline{AB} = \bar{A} + \bar{B}$
6. $A\bar{A} = 0$ *null set*
7. $AS = A$

and the three axioms of probability:

1. $P(A) >= 0$ *for any event* A
2. $P(S) = 1$ *The sum of all probabilities in a set equals* 1.
3. $P(A + B) = P(A) + P(B)$ *if* $AB = 0$

An important probability relation, conditional probability, defines the probability of an event A given event B shown as:

$$P(A/B) = P(AB)/P(B)$$

Many other derivations can be drawn from this basic formulation and the ones above.

Without going into much detail, but for the sake of completeness, another major element of probability required by queuing theory is random variables and their associated properties.

A random variable X within sample S is a function or mapping that assigns some real number $X(s)$ to each sample point $s \epsilon S$. The distribution function is an important measure in probability theory. Given a probability measure of an event $\{X \leq x\}$, where X is the random variable and x is a real number, one defines a distribution function as

$$F_X(x) \triangleq P\{X \leq x\}, \quad -\infty < x < \infty$$

and $F_X(x)$ monotonically increases, bounded between 0 and 1 by the second axiom of probability, where

$$F_X(-\infty) = 0, \; F_X(\infty) = 1$$

and

$$P\{x_1 < X \le x_2\} = F_x(x_2) - F_x(x_1)$$

There exists a probability density function (pdf) such that

$$P\{x_1 < X \le x_2\} P_X(x)\Delta x; \; \Delta x = x_2 - x_1$$

From these basic notions one can determine others; namely, the basic properties of pdf:

$$1) \; P_X(x) \ge 0$$

$$2) \; \int_{-\infty}^{\infty} P_x(x)dx = 1$$

$$3) \; \int_{-\infty}^{\infty} P_x(z)dz = F_X(x)$$

$$4) \; \int_{x_1}^{x_2} P_x(x)dx = P\{x_1 < X \le x_2\}$$

which yield important measures for first and second moments and the standard deviation for the random variables:

$$E = \text{Expectation}$$

$$M_n = E\{X^n\} \triangleq \begin{cases} \int_{-\infty}^{\infty} x^n P(x)dx \; \text{continuous} \\ \sum_{i=-\infty}^{\infty} x_i^n P(x_i) \; \text{discrete} \end{cases}$$

$$\text{Mean} = \text{1st moment}$$

$$N_x = M_1 = E\{X\}$$

$$\text{Variance} = \textit{2nd} \text{ moment}$$

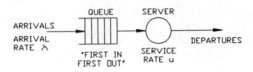

Figure 17.3   Basic queue model.

$$Var\{X\} = E\{(X - N_x)^2\} = \int\limits_{-\infty}^{\infty} (x - N_x)^2 P(x)dx = E\{x^2\} - N_x^2 = \overline{x^2} - \bar{x}^2$$

Standard deviation

$$\sigma_x \overset{\Delta}{=} \sqrt{VAR\{x\}}$$

17.2.2   Queuing

Queuing theory is a branch of mathematics that studies the phenomenon associated with the waiting line. This queue, or waiting line, is derived via the existence of a limited service capacity versus the arrival rate of the system. In regular life we see the phenomenon every day; for example, on the way to work, how many times have we gotten stuck in a traffic jam caused by the road's inability to support the given traffic or had to wait at a toll station because everyone must slow down to be serviced by the toll taker? From a computer system's viewpoint, especially a LAN, queuing is seen in the message queue buffer lengths, transmission delays, protocol service time, resource utilization, etc.

The queue is comprised of three major elements: arrivals, queues, and service (see Figure 17.3). This basic queue is known as the $M/M/1$ queue, where M denotes Markov or Poisson arrivals, the second M denotes Markov or exponential service, and 1 denotes the number of servers. Where a Poisson arrival implies

$$P_k(t) = \frac{e^{-\lambda t}(\lambda t)^k}{k!}$$

an exponential service implies (Figure 17.4)

$$P_\mu(t) = \mu e^{\mu t}$$

Other important notations are queue length equals number of customers waiting in the queue and time in queue equals total time spent waiting in queue. Performance in queuing system is measured by L^q = *mean* queue length, T^q = *mean* time in queue and the steady state *pdf* of the queue length.

In queuing analysis most analysis is done at steady state. That is when the queue has reached some equilibrium conditions. For the $M/M/1$ queue the steady state formulations flow as follows. Let $P_k(t)$ equal probability that k messages are in service or waiting for service at time t. Then we have probability of 0 in queue with no arrival as

$$P_0(t + \Delta t) = P_0(t)(1 - \lambda \Delta t)+$$

and probability of 1 in queue with no arrival and 1 deportive as

$$P_1(t)(1 - \lambda \Delta t)\mu \Delta t$$

which is approximately

$$\approx P_0(t) - \lambda \Delta t P_0(t) + \mu \Delta t P_1(t)$$

and continuing, $k - 1$ queued, 1 arrival, no departure:

$$P_k(t + \Delta t) = P_{k-1}(t)\lambda \Delta t(1 - \mu \Delta t)$$

$+k$ in queue, no arrival, no departure:

$$P_k(t)(1 - \lambda \Delta t)(1 - \mu \Delta t)$$

$+K + 1$ in queue, no arrival, 1 departure:

$$P_{k+1}(t)(1 - \lambda \Delta t)(\mu \Delta t)$$

$$\approx \lambda \Delta t P_{k-1}(t) + [1 - \lambda \Delta t - \mu \Delta t]P_k(t) - \mu \Delta t P_{k+1}(t)$$

which after some algebra and simplification for steady state yields the equilibrium equations for $M/M/1$ queues:

$$1)\ \lambda P_0 = \mu P_1$$

$$2)\ (\lambda + \mu)P_k = \lambda P_{k-1} + \mu P_{k+1};\ k > 0$$

We next define another term referred to as traffic intensity e, which is equal to the mean service time of a single arrival $\frac{1}{\mu}$ divided by the average interarrival time $\frac{1}{\lambda}$ or

$$e = \frac{\frac{1}{\mu}}{\frac{1}{\lambda}} = \frac{\lambda}{\mu}$$

Using this formulation in the equilibrium equations yields

$$P_1 = \left(\frac{\lambda}{\mu}\right) P_0 = eP_0, \ k = 0$$

$$\mu P_2 = (\lambda + \mu)P_1 - \lambda P_0, \ k = 1$$

$$P_2 = (1 + e)P_1 - eP_0 = (1 + e)eP_0 - eP_0 = e^2 P_0$$

$$P_3 = e^3 P_0; \ k = 2$$

Thus,

$$P_p k = e^k P_0$$

and since

$$\sum_{k=0}^{\infty} P_k = 1$$

which yields

$$P_0 \sum_{k=1}^{\infty} e^k = 1$$

then

$$P_0 = \left(\sum_{k=0}^{\infty} e^k\right)^{-1} = \left(\frac{1}{1-e}\right)^{-1} = 1 - e$$

and, substituting, yields

$$P_k = (1 - e)e^k$$

Using these basic formulations provides us the means to solve for some additional performance parameters, one is the mean queue length (L_Q).

$$l_Q = E[K] = \sum_{k=0}^{\infty} KP_k$$

$$= \sum_{k=0}^{\infty} K(1 - e)e^k$$

$$= (1 - e) \sum_{k=0}^{\infty} K e^k$$

$$= (1 - e)(e + 2e^2 + 3e^3 + \ldots)$$

$$= (1 - e)e \underbrace{(1 + 2e + 3e^2 + \ldots)}_{\frac{1}{(1-e)^2}}$$

$$= (1 - e)e \frac{1}{(1 - e)^2}$$

$$= \frac{e}{(1 - e)}$$

Another important measure as previously indicated is mean time in queue. A formulation called Little's equation provides an easy way to find this quanity:

$$l_Q = \lambda T_Q$$

Therefore,

$$T_Q = \frac{l_Q}{\lambda} = \frac{e}{1 - e} \frac{1}{\lambda} = \frac{\frac{\lambda}{\mu}}{\lambda(1 - e)} = \frac{\frac{1}{\mu}}{1 - e}$$

and time in service

$$T_s = T_Q(1 - e) = \left(\frac{\frac{1}{\mu}}{(1 - e)} \right)(1 - e) = \frac{1}{\mu} = \text{ mean service time}$$

From these we can easily get the mean waiting time

$$T_W = T_Q - T_S = \frac{e}{1 - e} T_S$$

With those basic formulas and theory many variants can be derived. For an example for an $M/M/m$ queue, see Figure 17.5.

The following holds. If we let K be the number of customers either waiting for service or in service and $K \leq M$, all K customers would be simultaneously serviced. Whereas, if $K > M$, queue of K customers is equal to M customers simultaneously being served with a queue of $K - M$ waiting for service. Therefore,

$$\lambda_K = \lambda \text{ and } \mu_k = \begin{cases} k\mu; & \text{if } k < m \\ m\mu; & \text{if } k > m \end{cases}$$

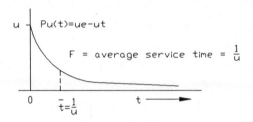

Figure 17.4 Exponential service time distribution.

Then server utilization

$$e = \frac{\frac{\lambda}{m}}{\mu} = \frac{\lambda}{m\mu}$$

$$\sum_{K=m}^{\infty} e^K = \frac{e^m}{1 - e}$$

Therefore, the probability of K customers in the queue is found from

$$P_K = \overbrace{\left(\sum_{K=0}^{m-1} \frac{(me)^K}{K!} + \frac{(me)^m}{m!(1-e)} \right)}^{S} \left[\frac{\lambda_0 \lambda_1 \ldots \lambda_{k-1}}{\mu_0 \mu_1 \ldots \mu_{k-1}} \right]$$

Likewise, the probability of servers being busy at a given time can be found from

$$P_{BUSY} = P_R(K \geq m) = \sum_{K=m}^{\infty} P_k = S^{-1} \frac{m^m}{m!} \sum_{K=m}^{\infty} e^K = S^{-1} \frac{(me)^m}{m!(1-e)}$$

And the mean queue length and mean queue time are found from

$$L_Q = P_{BUSY} \frac{e}{1-e} + me$$

$$T_Q = T_S \left[1 + \frac{P_{BUSY}}{m(1-e)} \right] \text{ where } T_S = \frac{1}{\mu}$$

For details of these and other queuing theory applications, see the previously discussed references.

To further demonstrate to the reader the usefulness of this technique for evaluating systems, an example is given in Section 17.3.

17.3   Token Bus Distributed System

17.3.1   Introduction

The token bus distributed processing system (a local computer network) consists of processors connected to interface units which, in turn, are connected by a common communication medium–the global bus. The allocation of the bus is controlled by the cyclic passing of tokens in a sequential manner from lowest-numbered interface unit (IU) to the next highest until all numbered IUs have been interrogated and serviced. The sequential numbering is determined during power up, and once steady state has been reached, it may be assumed to remain constant for modeling purposes. If an IU requires no service, control is passed to the next IU with an associated delay. The time it takes for the control to pass through the sequence completely is termed the scan time (as previously discussed).

Rather than investigating the entire token bus system per se, emphasis will be on the bus, or the IU and bus layer, for modeling purposes. The main body of the example documents the development of the analytical models, in particular, the solution of the models for the value of the average scan time. The analytic computation of the scan time allows one to further determine such interesting and practical bus parameters as average message waiting time, average queue length, and bus utilization. From the derived formulas, one can readily ascertain the effect on bus parameters of increasing the number of processors, altering the sequential placement of processors, or varying the message arrival rates.

17.3.2   Preliminary Formulations and Definitions

The message arriving at the processor is assumed to follow a Poisson distribution, in other words,

$$P(r,t) = \frac{(\lambda t)^r e^{-\lambda t}(r = 0, 1, 2, \ldots)}{r!}$$

where $P[r,t]$ is the probability that r messages arrive in time t, with each message being of the same size.

Service is required if there are one or more message arrivals in time t or

$$P(1 \ or \ more \ arrivals, \ t) = 1 - P(0, t)$$

which, in turn,

$$= 1 - \frac{(\lambda t)^0}{0!}e^{-\lambda t} = 1 - e^{-\lambda t}$$

Since the assumption is that steady state has been reached, we can let $f_\tau(t)$ denote the probability density function of the scan time t, $F_\tau(t)$. The corresponding cumulative distribution is then equal to

$$F_\tau(t) = P(\tau \le t); \frac{dF_\tau}{dt} = f_\tau; -\infty < t < \infty$$

$$F_\tau(t) = \int_{-\infty}^{t} f_\tau(\mu)d\mu$$

Let p denote the probability of an arbitrary processor requiring service during one scan:

$$p = \int_{-\infty}^{\infty} (1 - e^{-\lambda t} f_\tau(t)dt$$

If more than one arrival occurs at any processor in any scan, that arrival can be considered to be blocked. This message will then have to wait at least one scan time before it can be placed on the bus. This implies that

$$P(\text{blocking}) = P(\text{more than one arrival in scan time})$$

$$P(\text{more than 1 message requiring sevice in time t}) =$$

$$1 - [P(0, t) + P(1, t)]$$

$$1 - \left[e^{-\lambda t} + \lambda t e^{-\lambda t} \right]$$

To enable the evaluation of p, for λt, small,

$$e^{-\lambda t} \approx 1 - \lambda t$$

which implies that

$$p = \int_{-\infty}^{\infty} \left(1 - e^{-\lambda t}\right) f_\tau(t)dt = \int_{-\infty}^{\infty} \lambda t f_\tau(t)dt\lambda \int_{-\infty}^{\infty} t f_\tau(t)dt$$

which is equal to $\lambda\bar{\tau}$, by definition of expected value.

The relationship of $p = \lambda\bar{\tau}$ will be used for all the models for simplification purposes. For clarity and convenience, Table 17.1 contains the symbols and their corresponding definitions which will be used in the development of the analytical models.

Symbols and their definitions:

N Number of processors and, consequently, number of interface units because of a one-to-one correspondence in the system

T_s Time required to service a message at an interface unit

T_{si} Time required to sevice a message at an interface unit i

T_c Time delay associated with control (token) passing from an interface unit to its physically nearest neighbor interface unit

T_{ci} Time delay associated with control passing from interface unit with logical sequence number i to interface unit with logical sequence number $(i+1)$

λ Average message arrival rate at each interface unit

λ_i Average message arrival rate at interface unit i

τ Time to scan through the entire sequence of IUs

$\bar{\tau}$ Average or expected scan time

σ_i Set equal to 1 or 0 depending upon whether interface unit i has a message awaiting transmittal or not

d Distance between interface units i and $i+1$

t_s The time it takes to send the message of predetermined constant size from IU i to IU $i+1$ separated by distance d

UF Bus utilization factor

p Probability of an arbitrary interface unit requiring service during one scan

17.3.3   Analytical Modeling of the Token Bus

The analytical models developed for the token bus will be presented in an order reflecting an increasing degree of complexity and, consequently, a relaxation of the corresponding mathematical assumptions. In each of the models, a steady state, constant message size, and equal spacing between processors will be assumed. In addition, once the IU has been given control of the bus, it will be assumed that the message buffer for the interface unit will be emptied instantaneously onto the bus. The underlying specific assumptions in each case will be clearly outlined.

Case 1:

In the basic analytical model, it will be assumed that the arrival rate of messages at each of the N interface units is equivalent and is represented by λ. In addition, it is assumed that once steady state has been reached, the sequential (logical) numbering of the interface units is identical to the physical numbering (spatial numbering from left to right); that is, it follows the representation in Figure 17.6.

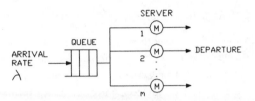

Figure 17.5   Multiple service queue.

If we let T_c denote the time delay associated with the token (control) passing from one interface unit to another, the $T_c i$ for each interface unit may be considered the same since it has been assumed that the processors are equidistant from one to another; and, consequently, the control will need to traverse the same distance from a processor to its next (with next highest sequence number) neighbor.

Another essential time parameter is the time it takes to service a message for any interface unit; in a ring topology with a token-passing scheme, one could consider T_s, which is the time required to service a processor to average out to the same value over time for all processors. This is described in Yuen, which shows that one cannot reach the same conclusion for the bus topology. Time to service a message is a function of the destination IU. Therefore, the placement of the source IU within the bus topology will affect the average time it takes to service one of its messages. For example, let $N = 3$, giving the configuration shown in Figure 17.6.

For interface unit 1 to transmit a message to processor 2, the message will have to traverse the distance from 1 to 2; for interface unit 1 to transmit a message to 3, it will have to traverse the distance from 1 to 3. If we represent the equal distance between two neighboring interface units as d and we let each of the other IUs be potential similar message destinations (that is, a uniform distribution for message destinations is assumed), then

$$E \left(\frac{T_s}{\text{source} = 1} \right) = \frac{1}{2} \left(\frac{d}{\text{velocity estimate}} \right) + \frac{1}{2} \left(\frac{2d}{\text{velocity estimate}} \right)$$

where

$$\frac{d}{\text{velocity estimate}} = t_s = \begin{array}{l} \text{time to send message} \\ \text{of the chosen size from} \\ i \text{ to } i+1 \end{array}$$

$$= \frac{1}{2}t_s + t_s = \frac{3}{2}t_s$$

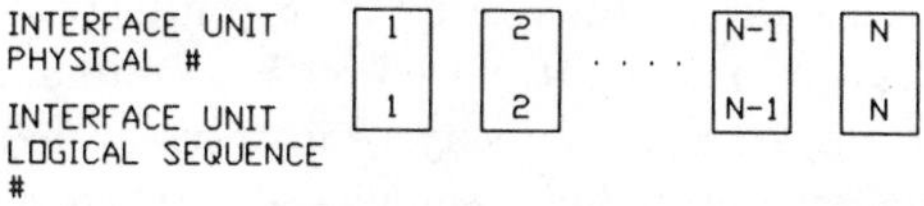

INTERFACE UNIT
PHYSICAL #

| 1 | | 2 | | . . . . | | N-1 | | N |

INTERFACE UNIT
LOGICAL SEQUENCE
#

Figure 17.6   Token bus representation.

For processor 2 as the source processor, the corresponding equation becomes:

$$E\left(\frac{T_s}{\text{source} = 2}\right) = \frac{1}{2}t_s + \frac{1}{2}t_s = t_s$$

Let T_{si} denote the time it takes to service a message at interface unit i. The time it takes for the token to pass from the ith IU to the $i + 1$st interface unit may then be expressed as:

$$\Delta\tau_i = \sigma_i T_{si} + T_c; \quad \sigma_i = \begin{cases} 1, & \text{If } IU_i \text{ has a message} \\ & \text{awaiting transmittal} \\ 0, & \text{Otherwise} \end{cases}$$

The total scan time becomes

$$(1) \quad \tau = \sum_{i=1}^{N} \Delta\tau_i \quad or \quad \tau = \sum_{i=1}^{N} (\sigma_i T_{si} + T_c)$$

Now, taking expectations of both sides of equation (1) we get:

$$\begin{matrix} \text{average value} \\ \text{of scan time} \end{matrix} = \bar{\tau} = \sum_{i=1}^{N} E\left(\sigma_i T_{si}\right) + \sum_{i=1}^{N} E\left(T_c\right)$$

$$= \sum_{i=1}^{N} E\left(\sigma_i T_{si}\right) + NT_c$$

By definition of expected value of product,

$$E\left(\sigma_i T_{si}\right) = \sum_{\sigma_i} \sum_{T_{si}} \sigma_i T_{si} p\left(\sigma_i T_{si}\right)$$

Since it was mentioned previously that T_{si} is a function of the distance that the message has to travel and since δ_i can only take on the value 0 to 1,

$$E\left(\sigma_i T_{si}\right) = \frac{1}{N-1} \sum_{k=1}^{N} |i - k| t_s p$$

where $i - k$ represents the number of interface units away from the source interface unit i, the destination interface unit k is located, and any interface unit other than i has an equally likely probability of being a destination interface unit. That is, a probability equals $\frac{1}{(N-1)}$ where p is the probability derived in the preliminary formulation.

In summary,

$$\bar{\tau} = \frac{1}{N-1} \sum_{i=1}^{N} \sum_{k=1}^{N} |i - k|\, t_s p + N T_c;$$

$$\bar{\tau} = \frac{t_s p}{N-1} \sum_{i=1}^{N} \sum_{k=1}^{N} |i - k| + N T_c$$

$$= \frac{t_s p}{N-1} \left(\frac{N^3 - N}{3} \right) + N T_c$$

$$= t_s p \frac{N(N+1)}{3} + N T_c$$

Substituting $P \approx \lambda\bar{\tau}$ into the above equation,

$$\bar{\tau} = \frac{t_s \lambda \bar{\tau} N(N+1)}{3} + N T_c$$

$$\bar{\tau} \left(1 - \frac{t_s \lambda N(N+1)}{3} \right) = N T_c$$

$$(2) \quad \bar{\tau} = \frac{N T_c}{1 - \frac{\lambda N(N+1)t_s}{3}}$$

This equation is valid, based upon the assumption and approximations if and only if

$$\frac{\lambda N(N+1)t_s}{3} \ll 1$$

Case 2:

In this model, we relax the assumptions that all the interface units having identical message arrival rates equate to λ by allowing for message arrival rates of λ for interface unit i. However, we retain the assumption of the hypothesized logical and physical configuration which, in turn, will be eliminated in the subsequent case. The relaxation of the assumptions is being done in a gradual manner to emphasize the evolutionary nature of the development of the analytical models. The relaxation of the equivalent message arrival rates will allow for a greater realm of applicability and consequently testing, but it will, naturally, complicate the ultimate formula for $\bar{\tau}$

Since each interface unit now has a characteristic message arrival rate λ, p now becomes, for interface unit i:

$$p_i = \int_{-\infty}^{\infty} \left(1 - e^{-\lambda_i t}\right) f_\tau(t) dt$$

$$p_i \approx \lambda_i \bar{\tau}$$

Equation (1) is still applicable, that is,

$$\tau = \sum_{i-1}^{N} \Delta \tau_i = \sum_{i-1}^{N} (\sigma_i T_{si} + T_c)$$

Furthermore, $\bar{\tau}$ is still

$$\bar{\tau} = \sum_{i=1}^{N} E\left(\sigma_i T_{si}\right) + N T_s;$$

where

$$E(\sigma_i T_{si}) = \frac{1}{N-1} \sum_{k=1}^{N} |i - k|\, t_s p_i;$$

$$\bar{\tau} = \sum_{i=1}^{N} \frac{1}{N-1} \sum_{k=1}^{N} |i - k|\, t_s p_i + N T_c$$

$$\bar{\tau} = \frac{t_s}{N-1} \sum_{i=1}^{N} \left(i^2 + (1+N)\left(-i+\frac{1}{2}N\right)\right) p_i + N T_c$$

Substituting $\lambda_i \bar{\tau} \approx P_i$:

$$\bar{\tau} = \frac{\bar{\tau} t_s}{N-1} \sum_{i=1}^{N} \left(i^2 + (1+N)\left(-i+\frac{1}{2}N\right)\right) \lambda_i + N T_c$$

Thus, (3):

$$\bar{\tau} = \frac{N T_c}{1 - \frac{t_s}{N-1}\left(\sum_{i=1}^{N} \left(i^2 + (1+N)\left(-i+\frac{1}{2}N\right)\right)\lambda_i\right)}$$

Case 3:

This model incorporates major modifications, which should permit the model to better reflect the actual system. In particular, it is assumed that once steady state has been reached, the logical numbering does not have

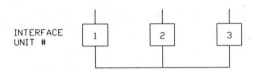

Figure 17.7   Token bus configuration.

to reflect the physical location, but in fact, the steady state configuration may be, for example, as shown in Figure 17.8.

The logical sequence numbering of the token bus system may assume any out of the $N!$ possible different choices of the steady state with an equal probability. Therefore, it is of the utmost importance to develop a model which can reflect all $N!$ of the possible combinations.

Consequently, T_c now is not a constant, but it must in some sense reflect the time it takes for the token to travel the distance from interface unit i to interface unit $i + 1$.

Let i represent the logical sequence number of the interface unit, then

$$\Delta \tau_i = \sigma_i T_{si} + T_{ci};$$

where $T_{ci} = $ time for token to traverse distance from IU with logical sequence number i to IU with logical sequence number $i + 1$. $((N + 1)$st IU becomes IU #1)

In the previous models, the logical sequence number and the physical number of the interface units were identical; therefore, it was not necessary to state explicitly the correspondence of the index i.

The total scan time is now expressed by

$$(4) \quad \tau = \sum_{i=1}^{N} \Delta \tau_i \quad or \quad \tau = \sum_{i=1}^{N} \sigma_i T_{si} + T_{ci}$$

$$\text{average value of scan time} = \bar{\tau} = \sum_{i=1}^{N} E\left(\sigma_i T_{si}\right) + \sum_{i=1}^{N} E\left(T_{ci}\right)$$

which for a known configuration is equal to

$$\sum_{i=1}^{N} E\left(\sigma_i T_{si}\right) + \sum_{i=1}^{N} T_{ci}$$

or

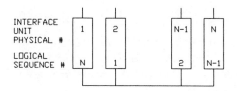

Figure 17.8 Case III configuration.

$$\sum_{i=1}^{N} E\left(\sigma_i T_{si}\right) + \sum_{i=1}^{N} |i - (i+1)| T_c$$

$N + 1$ denotes 1 because of cycling, where $T - C$ is the time it takes for the control to pass from any interface unit k to physical unit $k + 1$.

We have previously evaluated

$$\sum_{i=1}^{N} E(\delta_i T_{si})$$

and in order to take advantage of the results, the index k will denote the physical number of the interface unit, while the index i will denote the logical number of the interface unit. Combining the results and making the substitution that $\lambda_k \overline{\tau} \approx P_k$, we get

(6) $$\overline{\tau} = \frac{\sum_{i=1}^{N} |i - (i+1)| T_c}{1 - \frac{t_s}{N-1} \left(\sum_{k=1}^{N} \left(k^2 + (1+N)\left(-k + \frac{1}{2}N\right)\right)\lambda_k\right)}$$

From equation (6), one can determine the effect on the average scan time by varying any combination the variables N and k:

1. The number of interface units N
2. The arrival rates λ_k of the messages at the interface units with logical numbers k
3. Varying the logical sequential numbering of the interface units
4. Varying the distances between neighboring interface units
5. Varying the average size of the messages arriving at the interface units

The main constraint of the model is

$$\frac{t_s}{N-1} \left(\sum_{k=1}^{N} \left(k^2 + (1+N)\left(-k + \frac{1}{2}N\right)\right)\lambda_k\right) << 1$$

17.3.4   Message Number and Waiting Time

The average number of messages in the token bus distributed processing system $\bar{m}$ for the IU that are either being serviced by the bus or are waiting in the queue for service is equal to, for an average scan time, $\bar{\tau}$ and average message arrival rate λ is equal to

$$\text{average \# of messages for IU} = \overline{M} = \sum_{i=0}^{\infty} iP \text{ (\# of messages arriving } = i)$$

$$= \sum_{i=0}^{\infty} i \frac{(\lambda\bar{\tau})^i e^{-\lambda\bar{\tau}}}{i!}$$

$$= (\lambda\bar{\tau}) e^{-\lambda\bar{\tau}} \sum_{i=0}^{\infty} \frac{(\lambda\bar{\tau})^{i-1}}{(i-1)!}$$

$$= e^{-\lambda\bar{\tau}} (\lambda\bar{\tau}) \sum_{j=0}^{\infty} \frac{(\lambda\tau)^j}{j!}$$

$$(7) \quad \overline{M} = (\lambda\bar{\tau})$$

The average queue size at the IU is then

$$\text{average \# of messages in queue for IU} = \overline{M}_q = \sum_{i=1}^{\infty} (i-1) \frac{(\lambda\bar{\tau})^i e^{-\lambda\bar{\tau}}}{i!}$$

$$\overline{M}_q = \sum_{i=1}^{\infty} \frac{i(\lambda\bar{\tau})^i e^{-\lambda\bar{\tau}}}{i!} - \sum_{i=1}^{\infty} \frac{(\lambda\bar{\tau})^i e^{-\lambda\bar{\tau}}}{i!}$$

$$\overline{M}_q = \overline{M} - \sum_{i=1}^{\infty} \frac{(\lambda\bar{\tau})^i e^{-\lambda\bar{\tau}}}{i!}$$

$$(8) \quad \overline{M}_q = (\lambda\bar{\tau}) - \left(1 - e^{-\lambda\bar{\tau}}\right) = \left(\lambda\bar{\tau} + e^{-\lambda\bar{\tau}}\right) - 1$$

The total number of messages in the system for N processors, all having message arrival rates equal to λ, is then

$$(9) \quad N\overline{M}$$

The average number of messages in the system awaiting service equals

$$(10) \quad N\overline{M}_q$$

If each interface unit has a different λ, we can let

$$\bar{\lambda} = \frac{1}{N} \sum_{i=1}^{N} \lambda_i$$

Equation (7) then becomes:

$$\bar{M} = \bar{\lambda}\bar{\tau}$$

Equation (8) becomes:

$$M_q = \left(\bar{\lambda}\bar{\tau}\right) + \left(e^{\bar{\lambda}\bar{\tau}}\right) - 1$$

Equation (9) and (10) hold.

To evaluate the expected waiting time for a message in queue at each IU:

$$E(\text{waiting time}) = E(\text{number in queue})\bar{\tau}$$

or

$$\overline{M_q}\bar{\tau} = \bar{\lambda}\bar{\tau}^2 + \bar{\tau}\left(e^{-\bar{\lambda}\bar{\tau}} - 1\right)$$

Another useful measurement is the probability that the system is blocked. This is equivalent to the probability that more than one message arrival occurs at an interface unit in any scan time. Letting λ denote the message arrival rate at any interface unit, then

$$P(\text{blocking}) = P(\text{more than 1 message arrival in scan time})$$

$$= 1 - \left(e^{-\lambda\bar{\tau}} + \lambda\bar{\tau}e^{-\lambda\bar{\tau}}\right)$$

$$= 1 - e^{-\lambda\bar{\tau}}(1 + \lambda\bar{\tau})$$

The fraction of message being blocked equals

$$\frac{P(\text{more than 1 message arrival in scan time})}{P(\text{terminal requires service})}$$

$$= \frac{1 - e^{\lambda\bar{\tau}}(1 + \lambda\bar{\tau})}{1 - e^{\lambda\tau}}$$

17.3.5   Token Bus Utilization

Another practical measurement that may be determined given the previous analytical results is the bus utilization factor. This quantifies the utilization of the bus for actual message transmission. The utilization factor equals

$$\frac{\bar{\tau} - NT_c}{\bar{\tau}}$$

for a first approximation, as in Case 1, or:

$$\frac{\bar{\tau} - \sum_{i=1}^{N} |i - (i+1)| \, t_c}{\bar{\tau}}$$

where $\bar{\tau}$ as in Case 3. This equation demonstrates that as the distance between sequential neighbors increases, the actual bus utilization decreases because more time is spent in token passing. To obtain an even more precise factor, one may subtract from the numerator the estimated time allocated for transmission of the overhead bits per message.

The above example showed how the analytical model can be used to investigate the performance of a LAN for some limited aspects of its architecture. Furthermore, it provided a means to demonstate the capabilities of analytical modeling for evaluating the steady state behavior of a candidate design. The analytical techniques were shown to provide a limited breadth of coverage, though they do provide a quick basis for filtering out poor designs and alternatives early in a design or selection process. For more information, refer to the many fine books on queuing analysis and applications to computer systems listed in the references.

17.4   References

Kleinrock, L., *Queueing Systems, Vol I: Theory*, John Wiley & Sons, 1975.

—, *Queueing Systems, Vol II: Computer Applications*, John Wiley & Sons, 1975.

Kobayashi, *Modeling and Analysis*, Addison Wesley, New York, 1984.

Lavenberg, *Computer Performance Modeling Handbook*, Academic Press, 1981.

Trivedi, *Probability and Statistics with Reliability Queuing and Computer Science Applications*, Prentice-Hall, Englewood Cliffs, NJ, 1982.

18. Simulation Modeling

Beyond analytical modeling lies simulation. Simulation provides a means to visualize a system that is not yet built, to analyze a system to determine critical elements, and to act as a design assessor in order to evaluate proposals; it also can forecast possible issues in future developments or additions to a system. Simulations provide the ability to realize these benefits. Simulations take a model or description of a system and, based on this, perform experiments which enable the analyst to determine behavior of a system. The models used are typically objects, mathematical equations, relationships, or observations known about a system. We all at one time or another have used models. Models are used in all of the arts and sciences to visualize projects before they are undertaken. This is much more critical when it comes to large abstract processes and systems that we wish to analyze.

Modeling a system, though, requires much knowledge and insight into the overall design and operations of the system. This process of modeling a system can be easier if there exist physical laws that can be used to describe the system behavior, we can easily visualize the graphical interrelationships of the system, and the system is fairly stable. This is not always the case though. Typically in most systems being modeled today (LAN's distributed systems, etc.), a large volume of fundamental laws and data does not exist. There is a wide variation in operational parameters, and there is a wide variability in the human interaction variables. But all is not lost; modeling still is a viable candidate if used wisely. Remember that a model is an abstraction of a system. The extent to which this abstraction mimics the real system will dictate its success. When developing this abstraction, one must determine what aspects of the real system are most important and how

ABSTRACTIONS/REFINEMENTS

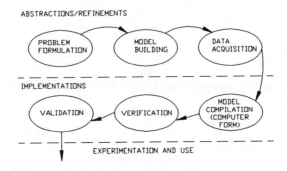

Figure 18.1   Simulation model-building process.

they interact. Simulation models or descriptive tools have been developed to assist in the visualization of models and their study.

Simulation models provide a sanitized view of a system. They provide a means to capture pertinent information and characteristics of a system with mechanisms and methodologies to experiment with these characteristics and information. In essence the simulation provides a laboratory, a place in which we can study aspects of systems under controlled conditions. Using this controlled experimental environment, a simulation model can perform design analysis, product analysis, performance assignment, or sensitivity analysis of systems.

18.1   Building the Model

To construct and use a simulation model to evaluate a system requires the six major processes or steps shown in Figure 18.1. However, interaction and fuzziness of the borders occurs between some of these steps within the entire process. Overall, each step can be uniquely defined by its major job or function.

From this figure we can see that there are three major phases that a model goes through within the overall process. They are abstraction, implementation, and experimentation or use. Abstraction refers to the period of time during which the model is defined and refined. During this phase the following three processes must be performed: problem formulation, model building, and information collection. Problem formulation is the portion of the abstraction process in which the model determines what is being modeled and what portions are most important. Model building is the phase in which this problem statement is refined into mathematical or logical relationships which describe the problem in terms amenable to analysis. The final portion of abstraction is data acquisition, which is the process in which information about the system, its components, operations, and boundary conditions are identified, specified, and collected for use in the actual model building.

The model building phase is comprised of three elements:

Model construction
Verification
Validation

Model construction, compilation, or translation is the portion of the modeling process in which the specification is turned into an operational computer program. Typically, simulation languages are used at this phase to save the modeler from all the tedious aspects of timekeeping, event control, and information management. To build the simulation model, the modeler takes the model specification previously developed, along with the operational parameters and state descriptions, and uses these to specifiy the simulation model.

Simulation models (code form) typically evolve in a top-down fashion. The modeler builds a high-level simulation and tests it. Once accepted, the detail is increased in steps until a final level of granularity is acheived. At this point the next step in the modeling process is undertaken: verification. The verification process is used as a step to determine if the computer program executes the model as intended in the specifications. Typically, this phase requires analysis of step outputs and overall results to see if the proper actions are occurring as intended.

The final portion of the implementation phase is validation. This typically is composed of running the model against a known set of inputs and expected outputs from the real system and seeing if the model provides the same output across some known range of acceptable variance. Once these steps have been done, the model can now be used to perform experimentation to study how the system will respond to stress conditions, new application area, change, failures, or a wide range of other conditions.

18.1.1   Types of Models

If one were to look at the range of programming languages available for simulation or at the breadth of models developed to examine systems, one would begin to see distinct patterns in terms of the types of models being built. These basic model types can be roughly described as discrete event, continuous transition, queing, or combined models. Each one of these types of models have characteristics fixed to that model type. For example, the discrete-event-type models tend to transition and change state only on defined event boundaries, whereas the continuous-type models are more like derivatives or integrations that change continuously at each time interval.

18.1.1.1   Discrete Models

In discrete simulation models, system objects are referred to as entities. Entities carry with them attributes which describe the entity. Actions on these entities occur on boundaries or events. Events of interest typically are arrival events, start-of-service events, and end-of-service events. The entities keep with them attributes that give information on what to do with this entity upon certain events. Only on these event times can the state of entities change. For example, only on an arrival event can a service event be scheduled, or only on a service event can an end service event be scheduled.

What this implies is that all actions within this type of model are driven by event boundaries. All things in between event boundaries are nonchanging. To build a simulation model using discrete event modeling requires definition of all events, definition of changes to state at event times, definition of all activities that the entities can perform, and the interaction among all the entities within the system. In this type of modeling each event must trigger some other event for the system to operate. This triggering provides the events' interaction and relationships with each other. For example, to model a self-service gas station, we need to define the following entities and events:

- Arrival event
- Service event
- Customer entity
- Server entity
- Departure event
- Collection event

The events guide how the process occurs and entities provide the media being acted on with the collection event. This provides a means to extract statistics from the entities. To build a simple model the following process could be used:

1. Arrival event
   a. Schedule next arrival (time now + delta T)
   b. If all pumps are busy, num waiting = num waiting + 1
   c. If the pump is idle, schedule service event
   d. End
2. Service event
   a. Num pumps busy = num pumps busy + 1
   b. Schedule service end event based on service required
   c. Take begin service stats
   d. End

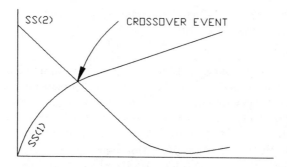

Figure 18.2 Continuous variables plot.

3. End service event
   a. Pump busy = num pump busy - 1
   b. Schedule arrival
   c. Take end service stats
   d. End
4. Entities
   a. Server–number of pumps, service ratios
   b. Customers–service requirement

To run the model using these simple events and entities requires just a call to initiate service (schedule some number of arrivals and some end conditions). The relationship of the events to each other will keep the model running, with statistics taken on the service times of the customers.

This is a very simple example and by no means complete, but it does provide a description of some of the basic concepts associated with discrete event simulation modeling. For more details of this type of modeling, refer to the Gasp IV simulation language and its associated text introduction to Gasp IV by Pritsker [1984].

18.1.1.2 Continous Modeling

Continuous modeling deals with simulation of physical objects which can be described by some set of continuously changing dependent variables that define equations. These equations are typically in the form of differential equations. The model executes and changes state based on the computation of the equations and their relationship to each other. For example, if we had two equations that produced the output seen in Figure 18.2, the following simulation event could be derived:

When SS(1) = SS(2) then begin execution of SS(3)
Else continue computation of SS(1) & SS(2)
End

This type of operation allows us to trigger new computations or adjust values of present ones based on the relationship of one continuous equation versus another. This operation of continuous simulation is a variant; that is, it includes aspects of discrete event simulation with that of the continuous type simulation.

Modeling with continuous simulation language is performed by (1) determining the different equations that define the system under study and (2) defining the significance of the interaction of the equations change based on this interaction. When taken together, one can use this methology to define a wide range of simulations of real-world systems.

18.1.1.3   Queuing Modeling

A third class of simulation is based on theoretical analysis. Queuing theory has been used for a long time to assist in the evaluation of numerous real-world systems. The problem with this form of analysis is that it is very specialized and requires extensive mathematical background to use it effectively. With the advent of simulation languages tailored for queuing analysis, the use of such analysis has been brought down to a more manageable level. For example, the simulation language SLAM by Pritsker [1984] provides a very flexible and easy way to construct queuing models of systems using graphical and/or straightforward language elements. This methodology relieves the user of the necessity to solve queuing problems. The user only needs to postulate the problems, formulate a queuing model, and let the simulation do the rest. This has provided another powerful tool to assist in the analysis of complex systems, though this is not the ultimate.

18.1.1.4   Combined Models

What is really needed are languages that integrate all of the previous model types together in order to be able to accurately model the wide range of real-world objects. Then, as we know, physics requires the use of continuous event and even queuing concepts. Having all of these concepts under one model relieves simulators from the tedious job of developing their own variants of each type within the more limited singular models. This use of combined modeling provides for much more flexible models. Simulators can initially build a model in the queuing style to quickly bring a model up. This provides the means to verify that a model at a high level will simulate the wanted real-world system, leaving details until later. Also, the use of combined modeling provides a means to more readily model a system at multiple levels of complexity. A model can have components of least interest modeled in queuing form, sections requiring continuous variables in continuous modeling form, and the sections requiring a lot of detail can be modeled in discrete form.

Details of the pros and cons of such modeling techniques are best described in [Pritsker, 1974]

18.1.2   Simulation and LANs

Within the last 10 years, simulations have been constructed to provide the means to evaluate the performance of LANs. Early work focused on singular systems and typically only one of a few aspects of the LAN. The detail was kept at high levels with possibly only the protocols evaluated in any detail. These early models provided much insight into the operational boundaries of LANs and their weaknesses, but they did not provide means to evaluate LANs against each other. The need of the business community was to have a capability to evaluate multiple LANs for their corporate requirements. Work done in the last few years has been migrating toward development of prototypical tools and first-level market tools to provide this capability. Tools developed for the general case must provide a means to tailor the input parameters easily to configure the model to evaluate LAN 1 versus LAN 2 against some fixed requirements. A tool of this caliber is described in Fortier [1979, 1980, 1983, 1986]. This tool will be summarized in the system being evaluated as an example in terms of what it is modeling, how it is modeling it, and the results of a test case (the same case as in Chapter 17).

18.2   Simulation Example

To illustrate the application of simulation to evaluate local area networks, the following example of a program developed to model networks will be evaluated.

The model is constructed to closely equate its components to that of an actual LAN under study. The major components being studied are the network link, interface unit, and host-to-interface unit connections. Additionally, the model contains components for simulation controller, data collection, event control, and post-processing support.

The network being modeled is a global bus architecture with a token-passing protocol. Control in the LAN transfers from node to node in a logical ring fashion. The major elements to be examined are scan time (time for control to cycle through its entire cycle) and average time for a message. The model will examine these parameters as they relate to variations in message size and arrival rates.

To construct the model requires first a determination of the important qualities in the network. The major elements are the link, IU, and pro-

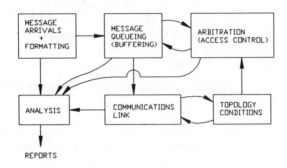

Figure 18.3   LAN model.

cessing element. Within each network, other important aspects exist. In the communications link, the important characteristics are the link capacity, the propagation delay, the number of channels per physical link, and whether the link supports separate data and control paths.

The interface unit has many more major functions with its characteristics. For example, a typical interface unit is composed of input and output drivers and receivers, buffers to hold information for input or output to bus media, control and arbitration hardware, message handling, hardware and software addressing, hardware and software, and error control hardware and software.

The final component is the processing device and its interface to the LAN interface unit. This needs to be quantized and characterized as to its buffering and special capabilities as well as to its control environment.

In order for the simulation to accurately model the real system, it must also represent all the aforementioned components. The simulation being described is a detailed model aimed at providing a means to study a wide range of distributed topologies, protocols, and components for LANs. The basic components of the model provide such a coverage (see Figure 18.3).

The message arrival component provides a means to simulate either random message arrivals to the nodes in the system based on predefined distributions or operational-system induced messages via a scenario generator. These messages represent the attached processors submitting a piece of data for transfer. The simulated message generated contains information which characterizes the message such as origin, size, destination, format, etc. During the passage of this message through the simulated network environment, historical information will be attached to enable the evaluation of its passages. This information will provide the data necessary to perform the statistical analysis of the network from when the message has

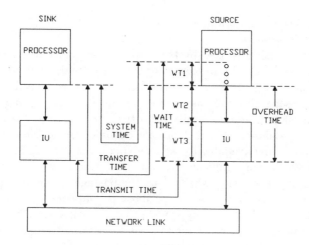

Figure 18.4 Network evaluation parameters.

"arrived." That is, it is in the buffer of the processor unit, ready to be sent to the NIU; it is modified to include any necessary formating. This process in the simulation is performed by a delay associated with the message for formatting and some additional attribute adjustments. Once this has been accomplished, the message is placed in the interface unit. It is now awaiting transmission. This portion of the simulation program provides the mechanism to simulate the waiting line of messages to be transmitted within the system. The buffer model provides the capability to simulate limited queue size to simulate overflow conditions.

The arbitration portion of the model provides a means to simulate the requesting and granting of access (control) of the communications media. For example, in a ring topology with token passing, this module would simulate control by determining the time it takes to send and receive the token at the next physical site down the line. This time is essential to compute when one looks at how long it will take for control to pass from one site to another or to tranverse a whole cycle across the system.

The communications link portion of the simulation provides modeling of link activity at the bit level. It provides for determination of propagation delays and transmission time for a message down the link. The topology package provides information to the communications and arbitration components to aid in their faithful modeling of the true system structure. In all cases as each portion of the model performs its task on the simulated message, it adjusts the attributes of the message that hold information about the state of the message.

This information is used by the analysis component to calculate some basic time statistics. These basic time statistics are derived from the major events of interest in a message transfer scheme: (1) the arrival of a message, (2) the message entering the queue, (3) the message leaving the queue, (4) the message becoming available to the interface unit, (5) the message starting transmission, (6) the message ending transmission, and (7) the message becoming available to the receiving processor.

These events are significant from a simulation viewpoint because they allow time measurements which chart the passage of the message through the system. In a LAN, one of the most primary measures of success is the speed at which accurately transmitted messages are completed. This series of time events provides for analysis of overall, as well as intermediate, delays imposed on the communications process.

The time between these basic events or checkpoints along with the various combinations of these checkpoints gives rise to some specific measures. These measures are illustrated in Figure 18.4. System time is the time between message generation at the source processor and message reception by the destination or sink processor. This measure quantifies the total delay associated with message transmission in the network.

Transfer time is the time which transpires between the emission of a message from the queue to its reception at the sink. This time represents transmission time disregarding waiting time to begin transmission.

Transmit time addresses the time a message spends in the process of physical information transmission. This measure indicates the actual timeliness of the low-level protocol and the speed of the physical transmission.

Wait time refers to the time a message spends waiting for its service turn. This measure is further broken down into four smaller quantities: WT1, WT2, WT3, and WT4. WT1 is the time a message spends in the queue. WT2 is the time interval between removing the message from the queue or buffer to the point at which the IU begins preparing the message for transmission. WT3 represents the time required to prepare a message for transmission. WT4 is the time associated with setup and begining of transmission over the link.

Overhead time equals the sum of WT2, WT3, and WT4. This time is considered the time which must be yielded to the interface unit as the price of networking or message transfer.

Other viewpoints on this stored information provide the simulator with a means to evaluate overall performance of a LAN. One can view the total volume of information versus overhead, information lost in communication, volume of overhead, and information latency and staleness.

The following list describes the evaluation parameters collected in this model (details of this model can be found in Fortier [1982]).

1. Calculated for Each Processor

a. Queue length statistics

(1) Average queue length

The time weighted average of the number of message waiting for transfer

(2) Peak queue length

The maximum number of messages which have waited in the IU queue

(3) Standard deviation of queue length

The standard deviation of the queue length from its average

b. Message size statistics

(1) Average message size

The average size of message

(2) Maximum message size

The maximum size of message

(3) Standard deviation of message size

The standard deviation of the message size froms its average

c. Waiting time statistics

(1) Average waiting time

The average time a message is required to wait for service by the IU before it is transmitted

(2) Peak waiting time

The maximum time a message was required to wait before it was transmitted

(3) Standard deviation of waiting time

The standard deviation of waiting time from its average

d. Blocking statistics

(1) Queue block

Average number of processors in queue block; maximum number; standard deviation

(2) Contention block   Average number of processors in
                                       contention block

2. Test parameters computed for the system

a. System time statistics

(1) Average system time   The average total time the message
                                      spends in the system (i.e., the time
                                      it takes to reach a destination after
                                      it originates at the source)

(2) Peak system time   The maximum time a message
                                      spends in the transfer process

(3) Standard deviation of system   The standard deviation of system
time   time from the average

(4) Messages in the system statis-   total number of packets
tics

(5) Average number of system mes-   Average number of messages con-
sages   tained in the system including
                                      those in transit

(6) Peak number of system mes-   The maximum number of messages
sages   contained in the system

(7) Standard deviation of system   The standard deviation of messages
message numbers   contained in the system from the
                                      average

b. Transfer time statistics

(1) Average message transfer time   The average time required to take
                                      messages from the origin and de-
                                      liver it at its destination

(2) Peak message transfer time   The maximum time which a mes-
                                      sage took to reach its destination

(3) Standard deviation of message   The standard deviation of message
transfer time   transfer time from the average

c. Transmit statistics

(1) Average message transmit time — The average time a message spends in physical transmission over the communication lines

(2) Peak message transmit time — The maximum time a message spends in physical transmission

(3) Standard deviation of message transmit time — The standard deviation of the transmit time from the average

d. System waiting time statistics

(1) Average system waiting time — The average time waited by all messages prior to transmission

(2) Peak system waiting time — The maximum time any message has waited for transmission

(3) Standard deviation of system waiting time — The standard deviation of message waiting for transmission from the average

e. System message size statistics

(1) Average message size in the system — The average size of all messages generated in the system

(2) Maximum message size in the system — The largest message which has been generated by the system

(3) Standard deviation of message sizes — The standard deviation of message from the average

f. Overhead time statistics

(1) Average overhead time — The average of message transfer time (message transmit time)

(2) Peak overhead time — The maximum of message transfer time (message transmit time)

(3) Standard deviation of overhead time — The standard deviation of overhead time from its average

g. Information overhead statistics

(1) Average information overhead

The average of the total number of overhead bits divided by the total number of message information bits

h. Information throughput statistics

(1) Average information through-put

The average number of information bits transferred over unit time

(2) Maximum information through-put

The maximum number of informa-tion bits transferred over unit time

i. System throughput statistics

(1) Average system throughput

The average number of information bits transmitted in unit time

(2) Maximum system throughput

The maximum number of bits transmitted in unit time

j. Message loss statistics

(1) Total messages lost

The total number of messages lost

(2) Message loss rate

The rate of messages lost

(3) Message loss because of full queue (percent)

Messages lost because of queue overflow

(4) Message loss because of bit er-ror (percent)

Messages lost because of errors in transmission

(5) Message loss because of status change (percent)

Messages lost due to loss of an IU or node

k. Time to complete statistics

(1) Probability of data late

The probability that a system mes-sage will arrive after it is set to ex-pire

(2) Average late time

The average time messages were late in the system

3. Periodic tabular data collection

a. Periodic average system throughput statistics

(1) Periodic average system throughput

System throughput sampled periodically and displayed in graphic form

b. Periodic queue length statistics

(1) Periodic system queue length

The sum of all processor queues sampled periodically and displayed in graphic form

c. Periodic messsages in the system statistics

(1) Periodic measure of messages in the system

The difference between total messages generated and total message recieved sampled periodically and displayed graphically

d. Periodic number of retransmits

(1) Periodic retransmits

The number of retransmits which occur over a period of time and displayed graphically

e. Bus resource statistics

(1) Control bus busy

Percentage of bus throughput used for control information

(2) Data bus busy

Percentage of bus throughput used for data transfer

(3) Idle time

Percentage of bus throughput that is idle time

Using the model's computed values and comparing them to the following analytical derivations yields a very close fit, illustrating the value of simulation and analytical evaluation for LANs.

The following paragraphs set up the parameters of interest; they are followed by a presentation of results of this model.

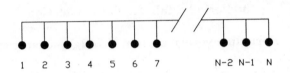

Figure 18.5 Processor numbering.

18.2.1   Average Interprocessor Distance

First determine the average number of interprocessor links from any processor i to any other processor in the system. Let the processors be numbered in sequential order as shown in Figure 18.5.

Given any processor number i, there are $(i - 1)$ interprocessor links to the left and $(N - i)$ interprocessor links to the right. So, add them and take the average. The average number of interprocessor links to the right equals:

$$(1) \quad \frac{\sum_{J=1}^{N-i} L}{(N - 1)} = \frac{(N - i)(N - i + 1)}{2(N - 1)}$$

The average number of interprocessor links to the left equals:

$$(2) \quad \frac{\sum_{J=1}^{i-1} L}{(N - 1)} = \frac{(i - 1)(i - 1 + 1)}{2(N - 1)}$$

Actually, the two directions are mirror images of one another; therefore, make the transformation $N = 2i - 1$ in the sum of equation 1 to yield:

$$(3) \quad \frac{\sum_{J=1}^{i-1} L}{(N - 1)} = \frac{(i - 1)(i)}{2(N - 1)}$$

Combine (2) and (3) to yield the average distance from any processor i to any other processor.

$$(4) \quad \frac{(i - 1)(i)}{(N - 1)}$$

Take the average number of links from any processor to any other processor by summing equation (4) over N processors and taking the average.

$$(5) \quad \frac{\frac{1}{N-1} \sum_{i=1}^{N} (i - 1)(i)}{N} = \frac{\sum_{i=1}^{N} i^2 - \sum_{i=1}^{N} i}{N(N - 1)}$$

$$= \frac{\frac{N(N+1)(2N+1)}{6} - \frac{N(N+1)}{2}}{N(N - 1)} = \left(\frac{N + 1}{3}\right)$$

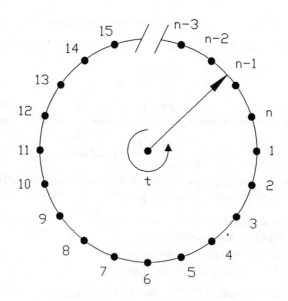

Figure 18.6 Average wait time configuration.

Given that the average interprocessor distance D is constant between processors, the average interprocessor distance (AIPD) is:

$$(6) \quad AIPD = (D)\left(\frac{N+1)}{3}\right)$$

18.2.2 Average Transmit Time (t)

The average transmit time is the average time required to send a message from one processor to another, given that any destination is equally likely and that roughly equal numbers of messages arrive at any processor in the system.

$D =$ Interprocessor distance or this distance between equally spaced processors (meters)

$N =$ The number of processors in the system

$Sb =$ The speed of propagation of bits through the system (second/meter)

Bits = The number of bits which will be transmitted in equally sized messages

$N = 1$

3 = The average number of interprocessor links; see equation (5)

The average transmit time equals the average distance bits must travel:

$$D \left(\frac{N+1}{3} \right)$$

Time the speed of a single bit through the system. Time the number of bits which must traverse the distance including overhead bits and arrive at

$$(7) \quad T = D \left(\frac{N+1}{3} \right) (Sb)(Bits)$$

The simulation parameters of the transfer time and transmit time for a packet or message is (see Figure 18.1):

PK-XFER–packet transfer time
PK-XMIT–packet transmit time
MS-XFER–message transfer time
MS-XMIT–message transmit time

In the validation run of the Hughes IR&D bus, messages are composed of a single packet. Therefore, packet and message parameters are equal. That is:

PK-XFER = MS-XFER
PK-XMIT = MS-XMIT

Since no delays representing the removal of the message from the queue, starting message transmission, or removing the transmitted message are calculated in the simulator, transfer time equals transmit time. This situation corresponds to WT2, WT3, and WT4 equal to zero. That is:

PK-XFER = MS-XFER = PK-XMIT = MS-XMIT + average transmit time (T)

18.2.3   Average Wait Time in the System

The token bus resembles n processors placed in a circle. Within this circle processors are generating messages to be sent to other processors. Processors are allowed to send their messages when it is their turn. A processor's turn is determined by a round-robin scheme, which is symbolized by a rotating pointer as shown in Figure 18.6. If the symbolic pointer doesn't encounter a message waiting at the processor to which it is pointing, the pointer immediately starts rotation toward the next processor. If a message is encountered, the control pointer stops at that processor until message transmission is complete. If no message is encountered during a rotation, the rotation time equals a constant t.

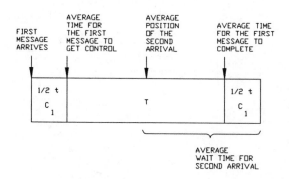

Figure 18.7   Average transmit time.

If messages arrive to an empty system (no other messages are transiting the system), it will wait, on the average, $\frac{1}{2}t$ or $\frac{1}{2}$ a rotation time. That is to say, sometimes the control pointer will arrive an instant after a message arrives, making the wait time zero, and sometimes it will have left an instant before, making the wait time t. Since wait time is uniformly distributed between 0 and t, the average is $\frac{1}{2}t$. At every minute λ (arrival rates) the likelihood of an arrival occurring to an empty system is very high and the average wait time is $\approx \frac{1}{2}t$. Assuming that we begin with an empty system, at least one message must arrive; therefore, $\frac{1}{2}t$ or C_1 will be taken as the first term in a series of wait times which will sum to the average wait time (WT):

$$(8) \quad WT = \overline{Wt_0} = C_1$$

If during the transmission of the first message a second message arrives, it will have to wait not only $\frac{1}{2}t$ for the pointer to transfer control but also whatever time remains in the process of transferring control and transmitting the first message. Since an arrival can occur anytime during the servicing of the first message, the second arrival will encounter an average wait time of $\frac{1}{2}C_2$, C_2 being the time required for the pointer to pass control to and transmit the first messages, where:

$$(9) \quad C_2 = \frac{1}{2}t + T$$

T = the average time required to transmit a message in the system. This situation can be seen in Figure 18.7. Therefore, the average additional wait time contributed by the second arrival is:

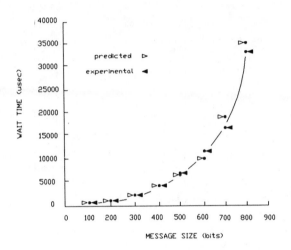

Figure 18.8 Experimental versus simulation results (wait time versus message size).

$$(10) \quad Wt_2 = \frac{1}{2}(C_1 + T) + C_2$$

Let $C_1 + T = C_2$ = average time required to pass control and tranmit a message:

$$(11) \quad \overline{WT_2} = \frac{1}{2}C_1 + C_2$$

This additional wait time occurs with a certain probability. The probability is equal to the probability of the occurrence of an arrival during servicing of the first or the probability of getting one and only one arrival during time C_2 expressed as P_x^i or the probability of getting i arrivals during time x. In this case $P_{C_2'}$. The wait time equation is:

$$(12) \quad WT = C_1 + P_{C_2'}\left(\frac{1}{2}C_2 + C_1\right)$$

A third arrival may occur during the transmission of the first or second arrival. This arrival could potentially wait to seek control as follows: The time for the first message to take control and tranmit is C_2; the time required for the second message to take control after the first one is completed is also equal to C_2. Thus, the maximum time a third arrival must wait before it can seek to take control is $2C_2$. On the average, the third arrival will not wait the maximum, but occasionally it will wait the maximum or minimum or zero. Since it is equally likely that any wait time between the

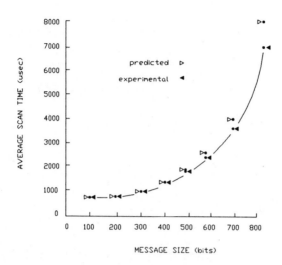

Figure 18.9 Experimental versus simulation results (scan time versus message size).

minimum and maximum is possible, on the average the wait time will be $\frac{1}{2}$ the maximum or $\frac{1}{2}(2C_2)$.

After the third arrival has waited for the previous two arrivals to complete, it must wait until the control pointer transfers control to the processor containing the third arrival C_1. Thus, the total wait time for the third arrival is on the average $(C_2 + C_1)$.

If a third arrival occurs, the average wait time which would be observed is the average of the wait time of the first and second arrivals, or:

$$(13) \quad \overline{Wt_3}\frac{1}{2}((\frac{1}{2}C_2 + C_1) + (\frac{1}{2}(2C_2) + C_1)) = (\frac{3}{4}C_2 + C_1)$$

Similar forms for $i + 1 = 4, 5, 6 \ldots$ arrivals can be derived from the following:

$$WT = \left(\frac{i+1}{4}C_2 + C_1 \right)$$

The average wait time of $i + 1 = 4, 5, 6 \ldots$ arrivals occurring over time C_2 is:

$$i = 1$$

$$Wt_1 = \frac{1}{2}C_2 + C_1 = \left(\frac{1}{2}C_2 + C_1 \right)$$

$$Wt_2 = \frac{1}{2}\left(\left(\frac{1}{2}C_2 + C_1\right) + \left(\frac{1}{2}(2C_2) + C_1\right)\right) = \frac{1}{2}\left(\frac{3}{2}C_2 + 2C_1\right)$$

$$= \left(\frac{3}{4}C_2 + C_1\right)$$

$$Wt_3 = \frac{1}{3}\left(\left(\frac{1}{2}C_2 + C_1\right) + \left(\frac{1}{2}(2C_2) + C_1\right) + \left(\frac{1}{2}(3C_2) + C_1\right)\right)$$

$$= \frac{1}{3}(3C_2) + 3C_1)$$

$$= (C_2 + C_1)$$

$$\vdots$$

$$Wt_i = \frac{1}{4}(i+1)C_2 + C_1$$

$$f_i = \frac{2}{i+1}$$

The probability of getting this average wait time is the probability of getting at least one arrival during the servicing of the first arrival plus the probability of a getting an arrival during servicing of the first or second. This boils down to two-thirds of the probability of getting two, and only two, arrivals during transmission of the first and second arrivals. The two-thirds comes from the fact that there are three possible occurrences of which only two are acceptable. The possibilities are: two arrivals during the transmission of the first, one arrival during the transmission of the second, and two arrivals after completion of the first. The only possibility which doesn't result in the average wait time above occurs if both arrivals occur after the transmission of the first. Thus, the probability of getting the average wait time, equation (6), is:

$$(14) \quad \frac{2}{3}P_{2C_2}^2$$

A similar argument can be made for the probability of getting the average wait time for configurations of $i + 1 = 4, 5, 6 \ldots$ arrivals, which turns out to be:

$$(15) \quad \frac{2}{(i+1)}P_{iC_2}^i$$

Thus, WT is now equal to:

$$(16) \quad WT = C_1 + P_{C_2}^1\left(\frac{1}{2}C_2 + C_1\right) + \frac{2}{3}P_{2C_2}^2\left(\frac{3}{4}C_2 + C_1\right) \ldots$$

Derivation of the General Form

$t = $ The time required for control return to any processor assuming no intervening arrivals

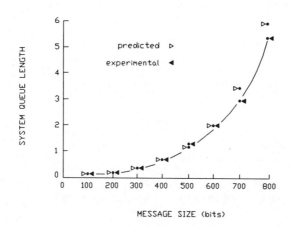

Figure 18.10 Experimental versus simulation results (system queue length versus message size).

T = The average time required to transmit a message

$C_1 = \frac{1}{2}t$ = The average amount of time required for control to be assumed by an arrival

$C_2 = T + \frac{1}{2}t$ = The average amount of time a message will be in the process of transmitting

P_x^i = The probability of i arrivals over x time

fi = The fraction of arrival patterns which will result in continuous transmission of i arrivals

$\overline{Wt_y}$ = The average wait time experienced by y continuously transmitting arrivals

$$WT = C_1 + f_1 P_{C_2}^1 \overline{Wt_1} + f_2 P_{2C_2}^2 \overline{Wt_2} + f_3 P_{3C_2}^3 \overline{Wt_3} \ldots F_n P_{nC_2}^n \overline{Wt_n}$$

Probability P_x^i of i arrivals over x time interval

Given:

$$P(i,t) = \frac{(\lambda t)^i e^{-\lambda t}}{i!} \quad (i = 0, 1, 2 \ldots)$$

Where $P[r,t]$ is the probability that r messages arrive in time t, let $t = x = iC_2$:

$$P_{iC_2}^i = \frac{(\lambda i C_2)^i e^{-\lambda C_2 i}}{i!}$$

The general form is:

$$Wt = C_1 + \sum_{i=1}^{\infty} \frac{2}{i+1} \frac{(\lambda i C_2)^i e^{-\lambda C_2 i}}{i!} \left(\frac{i+1}{4} C_2 + C_1 \right)$$

$$Wt = C_1 + 2 \sum_{i=1}^{\infty} \frac{(\lambda i C_2)^i e^{-\lambda C_2 i}}{(i+1)!} \left(\frac{i+1}{4} C_2 + C_1 \right)$$

Derivation of packet and message wait times: PK-Wait, MS-Wait

Since packet and message sizes are equal, there is one packet-message. In this case, packet and message wait times are equal or

$$PK - Wait = MS - Wait$$

The magnitude of these quantities are given in equation (31), or:

$$PK - Wait = MS - Wait = WT$$

Time a packet or message is in the system (T-PKS-SY) or (TIM-M-SY)

In the verification run of the token bus, messages are not broken up into mulitple packets, rather the message and packet sizes are the same. In this case, the average time a packet remains in the system and the average time a message remains in the system are identical. In the verification run, no system time was accumulated for moving messages from the communication system or for acknowledging the receipt of the message. Thus, the time a message remains in the system is equal to, simply, the wait time in the queue plus the transmit time.

Average time a message or packet remains in the system is T-PKS-SY or TIM-M-SY equal to the average transmit time plus the average wait time.

Derivation of average packet and message size in the system PK-SZ-SY - MS-SZ-SY and message sizes in processor 1 through processor 10, MS-SZ-P1 - MS-SZ-PX

The validation simulation uses a single message size which is equal to the input parameter CSize. Thus:

$$PK - SZ - SY = MS - SZ - SY = MS$$

$$= SZ - P1 - MS - SZ - PX = CSize$$

Derivation of message and packet overhead PK-OVERH, MS-OV (%)

Since there is only one packet per message, the percentage of overhead is equal for both messages and packets, or:

$$PK - OVERH \ = \ MS - OV \ (\%)$$

These quantities are equal to the message overhead length (input parameter length) divided by message size (input parameter (CSize)) times 100 percent, or:

$$PK - OVERH \ = \ MS - OV \ (\%) \ = \ (Length/CSize)100$$

Derivation of the average time required for control to circulate completely around the system: scan time

See Chapter 6, Section 6.3.

18.2.4 Derivation of the Number of Observations

The following parameters are calculated once per message. Therefore, the number of observations should approximately equal λ_s (system arrival rate) times the duration of the simulation.

$$
\begin{array}{ll}
T - PKS - SY & MS - XFER \\
PK - XFER & MS - XMIT \\
PK - XMIT & MS - WAIT \\
PK - WAIT & MS - SZ - SY \\
PK - SZ - SY & MS - OV(\%) \\
PK - OVERH & MS - LATE \\
TIM - M - SY &
\end{array}
$$

Message sizes MS-SZ-P1-MS-SZ-PX are calculated only when a message arrives at a particular processor. The number of arrivals to any one processor should be approximately λ_p (processor arrival rate) times the duration of the simulation or $\frac{1}{N}\lambda_s$ (system arrival rate) times simulation duration, where N_e equals the number of processors in the system. The number of scan observations equal the simulation duration divided by the average scan time.

18.2.5 Summary Data

The graphs in Figures 18.8, 18.9, and 18.10 represent the composite of all data runs performed in relation to the three validation parameters defined below:

1. AVG-WAIT-TIME. This represents the average time a message must wait from generation time to start of transmission time for all messages.
2. AV-SCAN-TIME. This represents the average time required to perform one total control cycle from beginning to end and back to beginning.
3. AV-SYS-QUEUE-LENGTH. This represents the aggregate average total queue length for all active processors in a network.

This description, with the use of a simulation program to examine a LAN's performance, can be applied much more rigorously to test out all aspects of a LAN before committing to the purchase or construction of one. This type of analysis provides the buyer or designer with the knowledge to correctly select a LAN for their uses.

18.3   Summary

This chapter outlined concepts for simulation modeling and its application to modeling local area networks. Simulations have provided a means to study the dynamic behavior of systems without incurring the cost of building and testing a real prototype. They provide a means to study alternatives and adjustments to a design or designs before a commitment is made to one. This provides the architect with a powerful tool to analyze alternatives and select a more optimal design than would be cost effectivly possible otherwise.

This chapter also outlined the basics of simulation techniques in use today and provided an example of how this technology can be applied to the analysis and study of alternative local area network architectures. Further details of this model and the basics of the simulation methodology can be found in the references below.

18.4   References

Fortier, P. J., "Generalized Simulation Model for the Evaluation of Local Computer Networks," *Proceedings of HICSS-16*, January 1983.

—, 1979.

—, 1980.

—, *Design of Distributed Operating Systems: Theory and Concepts*, Intertext, Inc., McGraw-Hill, New York, 1986.

—, 1982.

Pritsker, A. B., *The GASP IV Simulation Language*, School of Industrial Engineering, Purdue University, Wiley and Sons, Inc., New York, 1974.

—, *Introduction to Simulation and Slam II*, Systems Publishing Corp., 1984.

19. Empirical Modeling: An Example

The final method that we shall explore is empirical. In the analytical and simulation method, the emphasis was on accurately representing the network. In empirical modeling, the emphasis is on extracting the necessary information from the network without affecting the performance of the system. The method used to evaluate the data, once extracted, is relatively similar to the two previous methods. In this section, the evaluation method is derived from an analytical method commonly referred to as "operational analysis" [Wagner, 1975]. The bus evaluated is, again, the token bus.

First we will develop the evaluation parameters from operational analysis. Then we will examine the means by which the data is measured and extracted from the running system, and, finally, we will look at the results.

It should be noted that when using an analytical method of evaluation of network performance, steady state conditions are required. Therefore, the test must be designed as a series of runs that provide an analytical result at the end of each run. By plotting the results of each run, a graph is developed which represents the dynamic performance of the network under a varying workload. When evaluating an operating network as opposed to a controlled prototype, as is presented here, this method would not be applicable. Under these conditions, the measurements must be taken over a sample period of time in which the system is operating in a relatively steady state condition (i.e., constant workload). The sample periods must be adjusted to conform to the changes in the workload.

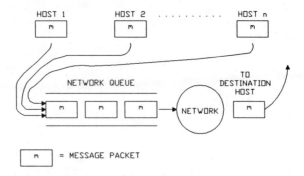

Figure 19.1 Serialization of message traffic.

19.1   Derivation of Parameters

In the R&D bus, all message packets originate within the hosts. Messages are queued in the host awaiting access to the network. Arrivals of new messages and their arrival rates are determined by each host's simulation software. The BIU is the interface to the network. All message packets enter the network via the BIU and are said to leave the network when the BIU relinquishes control of them to the host.

The subnetwork consists of the serial communications bus (i.e., the medium) together with the BIUs, which provide management and control functions. Each message packet transmitted represents, to the network observer, an atomic, uninterruptable network operation. During each packet transmission, only one BIU has control and only one packet is passed. This scheme serializes network use by the nodes.

The R&D bus evaluation system represents a single-resource queuing system in which the network provides a single-service facility. Messages originating at the hosts consist of a homogeneous set of jobs requiring the resource of the network. The hosts represent both the source and the sink for all jobs (i.e., message packets) in the system. All message arrivals enter the queue via a host and complete upon exiting the BIU at the destination node (see Figure 19.1).

The objective of the R&D bus evaluation is to gauge the overall performance of the network. That is, the R&D bus is observed as a queuing system in which the network is considered its only resource. To this resource, or server, the arrival of message packets can be considered to come from a single queue. This situation results from the serialization process performed by token passing. The queue of these packets to the network is the aggregate of message packets, ordered by time, found in the queues at each node. The queue of messages to the server is the composite of the individual queues at each node.

The arrival of message packets in the R&D bus is assumed to be a Poisson process. In any interval of time T, the probability that n arrivals occur in that interval is given by:

$$\frac{(LT)^n e^{-LT}}{n!}$$

where L (lambda) is the average arrival rate.

The Poisson arrival process is used since it corresponds to assumptions that can be made for messages transmitted by a global bus, such as the R&D bus. It is assumed that the population of packets that may request transmission is infinitely large. The R&D bus puts no constraint on the number of messages generated, other than those imposed by limits of the observation interval. Message packets arrive singly rather than in groups. The average arrival rate L is assumed to be constant.

To generate messages with a Poisson distribution, the relationship between the exponential and Poisson distributions has been used. That is, if the time between arrivals during a certain observation period is exponentially distributed, the number of arrivals per observation period is Poisson distributed.

If the probability that a message will occur during a small time interval is very small and if the occurrence of this message is independent of the occurrence of other messages, the time interval between occurrences of messages is exponentially distributed. Thus, if message packet arrivals are assumed to be Poisson distributed with a mean equal to L, the time between arrivals is exponentially distributed with mean O, where $O = \frac{1}{L}$.

The arrival of message packets to the system queue are generated from an exponential distribution. The actual interarrival times A^i are determined by message generation functions in each host. To simulate an exponential distribution, the inverse transformation of the density function is used:

$$A = -O \, log^e \, R$$

where O is the mean time between arrivals (arrival rate) and R is a random variate such that $O <= R <= 1$.

The interarrival time for a message packet at any host is

$$A^i = -O^i \, log^e \, R$$

The arrival of all message packets to the network is the sum of the arrivals at all N hosts transmitting to the network. It is

$$-(O^1 \, log^e \, R + O^2 \, log^e \, R + \ldots + O^n \, log^e \, R)$$

or

$$-(O^1 + O^2 + \ldots + O^n) \, log^e \, R$$

by the serialization process.

Operational analysis, a queuing network model, introduced by Buzen [1976], has been used to describe the measured performance of the global bus. A set of operational variables are used to characterize the system during any one run or observation period (O, T). The state of the queue at any time t, $n(t)$, represents the number of message packets awaiting transmission by all nodes. The $n(t)$ varies from O, indicating that no node is ready to transmit, to N. N defines the largest number of transmissions pending for a given observation period.

The set of all values of $n(t)$ for $O <= t <= T$ is called the behavior sequence of the system.

The behavior sequence for the R&D bus is said to satisfy the one-step assumption. That is, $n(t)$ can change only in increments of +1. Thus there are no simultaneous arrivals, completions, or coinciding arrival and completions. In general, this rule is made true by the resolution of the time increment. In this case it follows from the serialization process of the token. Each state transition from n to $n + 1$ corresponds to an arrival; each transition from $n + 1$ to n corresponds to a completion.

There are three operational quantities of interest for a behavior sequence.

$A(n)$ The number of arrivals when $n(t) = n$
$C(n)$ The number of completions when $n(t) = n$
$T(n)$ The total time during which $n(t) = n$

Grand totals are defined as

$A = A(O) + A(1) + \ldots + A(N - 1)$
$C = C(1) + \ldots + C(N - 1) + C(N)$
$T = T(O) + T(1) + \ldots + T(N - 1) + T(N)$

The flow-balance behavior sequence implies that the overall arrival rate is equal to the output rate. This is equivalent to the condition that the total number of arrivals A is equal to the total number of completions C and also to the condition that the initial state $n(O)$ is equal to the final state $a(T)$.

These operational quantities are used to derive other operational quantities which characterize network performance. Total waiting time and busy time are of particular interest.

Waiting Time   The waiting time for a message packet is the amount of time that a message spends in the system. This is the measured time between a packet arrival and its completion. The total waiting time is the summation of the waiting times for the individual message packets.

$$W = \sum_{n=1}^{N} nT(n)$$

Busy Time   The busy time is the total time that one or more message packets exist in the system. This can be thought of as the time when the server is not in the idle state, assuming that a message packet arriving to an empty queue is given instantaneous service.

$$B = \sum_{n=1}^{N} T(n) = T - T(O)$$

For this example six other performance parameters of interest exist that can be defined from the above operational parameters: arrivals A, completions C, total time T, busy time B, transmission time T^2, arrival time T^3, along with mean queue length:

1. **Mean queue length**   The average length of the queue during a test run:

$$M = \frac{W}{T}$$

2. **Response time**   The mean response time for the network is the ratio of the total waiting time for all message packets to the number of message packets transmitted:

$$R = \frac{W}{C}$$

3. **Utilization**   The utilization of the network is the ratio of busy time to total time; that is, the ratio of time that the network was used to the total time the network was available:

$$U = \frac{B}{T} = \frac{(T - T(O))}{T}$$

4. **System service time**   The overall service time, or mean time between completions, is the average amount of time that any one message packet spent in the system. Service is calculated only for that period of time during which the network is utilized (busy time):

$$S = \frac{B}{C}$$

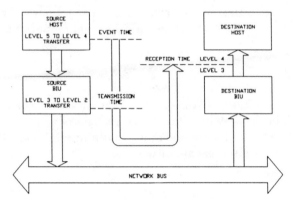

Figure 19.2 Time tagging process.

5. **Network service time**   Because the portion of the system
that is of interest, in this case, is the level 1 and 2 protocol
implemented in the network adapter, it is desirable to determine
the actual time required to transmit a packet. All other
parameters are calculated from a system point of view (i.e., from
event time to reception time), giving a view from the host. The
network service time takes the view of the packet that is next to
be transmitted (i.e., from transmission time to reception time).
Figure 19.2 depicts the reference times for the two views:

$$S^n = \frac{[(T^2 - T^3)]}{C}, \text{ for a given run.}$$

6. **Throughput**   Throughput, or output rate, of the system
reflects the number of packets transmitted during an observation
period:

$$X = \frac{C}{T}$$

These six parameters were used to characterize the operation and performance of the network.

19.2   Data Collection

The network consists of a prototype of a serial communications R&D bus
implemented on the network adapter, which together with the IOP make
up the BIU. The IOP functions as the interface between the host and the

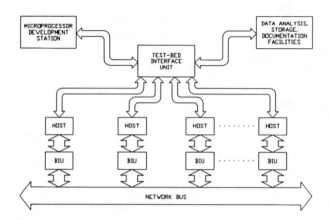

Figure 19.3 Test-bed and support systems.

bus. Since all messages are subdivided into smaller packets, only the transmission of packets is analyzed. The transmission of a message packet is defined as the measured time between a packet's arrival at the source BIU and the time the destination BIU relinquishes control of that packet to the destination host.

Each message packet is time tagged as it is routed through the system. These time tags are stored in tables within the host processor's memory for postsimulation run analysis.

Each message packet is identified by a unique message identification number. This number consists of two fields: the physical address of the source host (a unique physical address is defined for each host during system initialization) and a sequence number for the packet. For example, message number 2015 is the fifteenth packet to be transmitted by node 2.

Three time tags are associated with each message packet number: event time, transmission time, and reception time. Figure 19.2 depicts the time tagging process.

The event time is the time when the message packet enters the system. The event time is the earliest possible moment at which the packet could be transmitted; that is, the time at which the host places the packet in the transmission queue. The event time of each message is derived from the exponential distribution described above. The event time for the ith message is the sum of the event time for the $i-1$th message and the $i-1$st interarrival time:

$$\text{Event time}^i = A^{i-l} + \text{Event time}^i - l$$

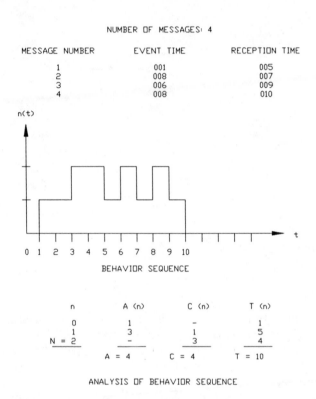

Figure 19.4   Generation of behavior sequence.

The recording of this time tag is the responsibility of transmitting host. The transmission time is the time when the message packet begins to use network resources. This time tag reflects the time when the source BIU begins transmission of the message. The recording of this parameter is the function of the transmitting BIU. The value of this parameter is passed to the host for storage.

The reception time is the time when the message packet is removed from the network and is available to the host. This time is defined as the instant the destination BIU relinquishes control of the message to the destination host and informs the host of a completed transfer. The recording of this parameter is the function of the destination BIU. The value of this parameter is passed to the destination host for storage.

Each host contains functions for the collection and storage of event times and transmission times for all transmissions by that node and reception times for all receptions at that node. Upon completion of a simulation run,

```
{BEHAVIOR SEQUENCE}
  VAR EVENT TIME [1...],      {NETWORK STARTS TRANSMISSION}
      RECEPT TIME [1...],     {NETWORK FINISHES TRANSMISSION}
      A(N),                   {NUMBER OF ARRIVALS}
      C(N),                   {NUMBER OF COMPLETIONS}
      T(N),                   {TOTAL TIME}
      n,                      {SIZE OF QUEUE}
      i,                      {EVENT TIME INDEX}
      j,                      {RECEPTION TIME INDEX}
      LAST TIME;              {LAST ARRIVAL/COMPLETION TIME}


N := 0; i := 1; j := 1;
LAST TIME := 0;
FOR EACH EVENT TIME AND RECEPT TIME DO
    BEGIN
       IF EVENT TIME_i <= RECEPT TIME_j THEN
          BEGIN
             A_n := A_n + 1
             T_n := T_n + (EVENT TIME_j - LAST TIME)
             LAST TIME := EVENT TIME_j
             n := n + 1
             i := i + 1
          END
       ELSE
          BEGIN
             C_n := C_N + 1
             T_n := T_N + (RECEPT TIME_j - LAST TIME)
             LAST TIME := RECEPT TIME_j
             n := n + 1
             i := i + 1
          END
    END
END
```

Figure 19.5   Behavioral sequence algorithm.

these parameters are transferred to an offline processing unit where they are stored for later analysis (see Figure 19.3).

A simulation run analysis begins by associating event times, transmission times, and reception times with their message identification numbers. This table is now sorted by the event time. A unique file, called the merge file for that run, represents the chronological order in which message packets arrived at the network. This order defines the arrival of message packets

packet size (16 bit words)								
200	RUN 09	RUN 19	RUN 29	RUN 39	RUN 49	RUN 59	RUN 69	RUN 79
180	RUN 08	RUN 18	RUN 28	RUN 38	RUN 48	RUN 58	RUN 68	RUN 78
160	RUN 07	RUN 17	RUN 27	RUN 37	RUN 47	RUN 57	RUN 67	RUN 77
140	RUN 06	RUN 16	RUN 26	RUN 36	RUN 46	RUN 56	RUN 66	RUN 76
120	RUN 05	RUN 15	RUN 25	RUN 35	RUN 45	RUN 55	RUN 65	RUN 75
100	RUN 04	RUN 14	RUN 24	RUN 34	RUN 44	RUN 54	RUN 64	RUN 74
80	RUN 03	RUN 13	RUN 23	RUN 33	RUN 43	RUN 53	RUN 63	RUN 73
60	RUN 02	RUN 12	RUN 22	RUN 32	RUN 42	RUN 52	RUN 62	RUN 72
40	RUN 01	RUN 11	RUN 21	RUN 31	RUN 41	RUN 51	RUN 61	RUN 71
20	RUN 00	RUN 10	RUN 20	RUN 30	RUN 40	RUN 50	RUN 60	RUN 70

Clock Increments (CI) Per Node	800	700	600	500	400	300	200	100
Nodal Periodicity (NP) $\left(CI \times \dfrac{40 \text{nsec}}{CI} \times \dfrac{1}{20} * \right)$	1.6 nsec	1.4 nsec	1.2 nsec	1.0 nsec	0.8 nsec	0.6 nsec	0.4 nsec	0.2 nsec
System Arrival Rate (AR) $\left(\dfrac{3 \text{ nodes}}{NP} \right)$	$\dfrac{3 \text{ arrivals}}{1.6 \text{ nsec}}$	$\dfrac{3 \text{ arrivals}}{1.4 \text{ nsec}}$	$\dfrac{3 \text{ arrivals}}{1.2 \text{ nsec}}$	$\dfrac{3 \text{ arrivals}}{1.0 \text{ nsec}}$	$\dfrac{3 \text{ arrivals}}{0.8 \text{ nsec}}$	$\dfrac{3 \text{ arrivals}}{0.6 \text{ nsec}}$	$\dfrac{3 \text{ arrivals}}{0.4 \text{ nsec}}$	$\dfrac{3 \text{ arrivals}}{0.2 \text{ nsec}}$

Figure 19.6   Test runs.

to the system and is independent of the source node. The network and messages represent a single-resource single-queue system.

Information in the merge file is reduced into a behavior sequence defined by the operational quantities: arrivals $A(n)$, completions $C(n)$, and total time $T(n)$. Each operational quantity is stated as a function of queue size n. Figure 19.4 illustrates the generation of a behavior sequence given four transmissions and receptions during observation period $(O, 10)$. The algorithm is given in Figure 19.5.

Parameters used to define the behavior sequence for a simulation run are then used to calculate operational quantities total waiting time W and busy time B. These quantities can now be used to calculate network operational and performance parameters. In order to verify the R&D bus prototype, these parameters should be compared with results derived independently from both an analytical model and a software simulation of the R&D bus.

In order to accurately monitor activity on the network, it is necessary to maintain consistent time throughout the R&D bus test bed system. In this case the requirement has been met by synchronizing the individual real-time clocks within each host and BIU with a central external clock. The real-time clocks are used solely for time tagging purpose; they are not used for synchronization or control of network activities.

19.3   Test Definition

The analysis which has been performed has been done to define the limits of the R&D bus. The test was defined in such a way as to evaluate the bus

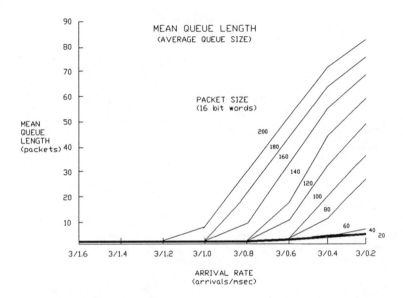

Figure 19.7   Mean queue length.

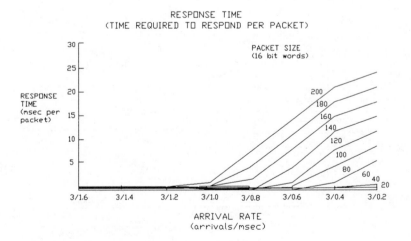

Figure 19.8   Response time.

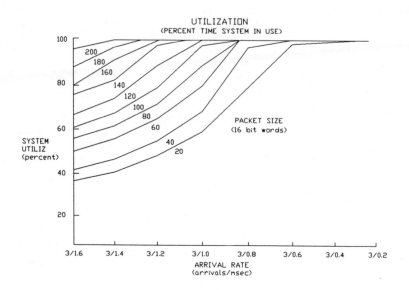

Figure 19.9   Utilization.

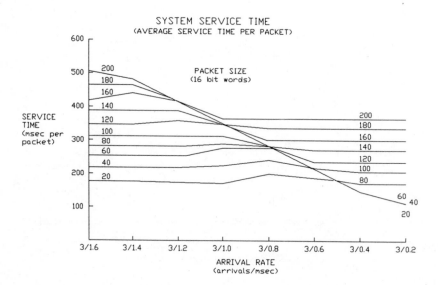

Figure 19.10 System service time.

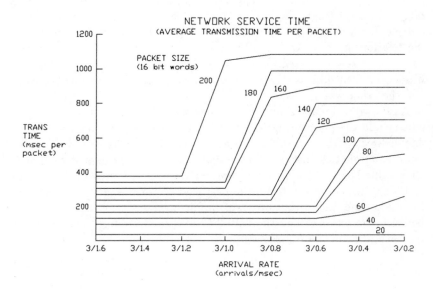

Figure 19.11 Network service time.

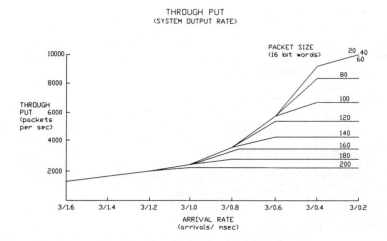

Figure 19.12 Throughput.

as it enters into saturation. The two independent parameters are arrival rate and packet length. A series of tests were conducted in which each run represented a change to one parameter. Figure 19.6 shows in matrix form the relationship between arrival rate and packet length. The performance parameters were collected for each run. The evaluation of bus performance was accomplished by analyzing data when one parameter was held constant and the other was varied.

As shown in Figure 19.6, the test runs were defined by varying the periodicity and the packet length. The packet size as shown is in 16-bit words and is directly transferrable to the analysis package. The periodicity values represent time ticks between individual message generations at each node. This value has to be scaled to represent the time between arrivals to the system. By scaling the time, the overhead of time tagging is minimized. In actual time, each tick represents 40 microseconds (μs). The scale factor between the test bed and the actual bus is 20. Therefore, the periodicity representative of the R&D bus is:

$$\text{Periodicity at each node (NP)} = \left(\frac{40\mu s}{20}\right)(\text{time ticks})$$

The periodicity for the system is the nodal periodicity divided by the number of nodes generating messages. For this test the number of nodes was three, which make the system periodicity:

$$\text{System periodicity (SP)} = \frac{\text{NP}}{3}$$

The value we wish to use to evaluate the R&D bus is arrival rate, which is the reciprocal of the periodicity. Therefore the X axis on all graphs is arrival rate and is determined as:

$$\text{Arrival rate } (AR) = \frac{3}{\text{NP}}$$

19.4   Test Results

The test results, for this example, consist of six graphs shown in Figures 19.7 through 19.12, representing the six parameters of interest previously defined, plotted as a function of arrival rate and packet size. An evaluation of the meaning of the results is provided for each graph.

Graph 1 (Figure 19.7): mean queue length. The mean queue length (M) provides a good representation of when the system enters saturation. As can be seen by the graph, the system enters saturation for the larger packets first, starting with a 200-word packet at an arrival rate of three arrivals per 1.2 ms. For the test run, it appears that the system did not enter total saturation for packet sizes of 60, 40, and 20 words; however, the system was on the edge of saturation as shall be pointed out under utilization. The mean queue length for the system prior to saturation ranges from .36 minimum for a 20-word packet to 2.1 minimum for a 200-word packet, both at an arrival rate of three arrivals per 1.6 ms.

Graph 2 (Figure 19.8): response time. The response time (RT) represents the time required for a packet to receive service. This gives a good view of the response of the system from the perspective of the packets. As the graph shows, the system response time increases as the system enters saturation. This is caused by longer wait periods in the queue; and, as a result, this plot resembles the mean queue length plot.

Graph 3 (Figure 19.9): utilization. The utilization (U) of the system provides another good indication of the system approaching saturation. As can be seen, the system approaches saturation for 200-word packet sizes at an arrival rate of three arrivals per 1.2 ms. For this case the utilization is 99 percent. For the 20-word packet size, the system reaches 99 percent utilization when the arrival rate is three arrivals per 0.4 ms. This indicates that the system is approaching saturation at this point even though the mean queue length does not have a significant buildup.

Graph 4 (Figure 19.10): system service time. The system service time (SS) gives an indication of the time required for a packet to be serviced from the system point of view. The interesting phenomenon in this instance is that the service time decreases as the system enters saturation and then levels off once the system is totally saturated. The explanation for this is that from the system view the queue fall-through time is included in the calculation of service time when the system is not saturated. When the system becomes saturated, there is always a packet available when the token arrives at a node. At this time, the queue fall-through time gets cancelled from the calculation by means of a pipeline effect for packet handling at each node.

Graph 5 (Figure 19.11): network service time. The network service time (NS) looks at the service time from the network view. In this instance, there is no appearance of increased performance caused by the pipeline effect. In fact, the opposite is true. When the system is not in saturation and the arrivals are staggered, a packet arrives at the bus and is the only one available for transmission because no other node has a message available. In this case, the NS represents the time for a message propagation across the medium plus the time for the token to scan the bus. When the system becomes saturated (all nodes have traffic in their queues), the NS represents the time for a message to propagate through the medium plus the time for each message at all the other nodes to propagate through the medium. In the case of these experiments, all the traffic for a run was homogeneous.

This gives a result when the network service time for a saturated system approximately equals the service time for a nonsaturated system times the number of nodes. In the case of these experiments the number of nodes was three.

Graph 6 (Figure 19.12): throughput. The throughput (TP) of the system represents the effective output of the system. These results show that as the system enters saturation, the throughput of the system reaches a maximum value which does not change under increased load.

19.5   References

Busen, J. P., "Modeling Computer Systems Performance," *CMGVII Conference Proceedings*, Atlanta, Georgia, 1976.

Guttman, I., et al., *Introductory Engineering Statistics*, John Wiley & Sons, NY, 1982.

Kobyashi, H., *Modeling and Analysis: An Introduction to System Performance Evaluation Methodology*, Addison Wesley, NJ, 1978.

Peebles, P., *Probability, Random Variables, and Random Signal Principles*, McGraw-Hill, New York, 1980.

Wang, E., *Introduction to Random Processes*, Springer-Verlag, New York, 1983.

PART SEVEN
Systems Management

20. LAN Operating
System Philosophies

LANs provide a service to their users. Namely, they provide a means for these users to communicate information among each other in a timely fashion. This communication concept has opened up new avenues to the users of the LAN. It has provided a means to "grow" new applications for computers in their enterprises. Partly because of this growth in applications a need has developed for more and better services from the LAN. These services are similar to those seen in early centralized computer systems with extensions to service the network and remote users.

The main function of these early operating systems was to provide a service which insulates the users from the intricacies of the underlying hardware and software. That is the operating system provided for the "systems" management of processes (user applications, etc.), memory, input/output, devices (sensors, printers, robots, etc.), and files (secondary storage) based on systemwide goals for level of service and reliability. The network has added another feature to the systems management problem, that of communications management. The management of communications between users has become an important aspect of LAN developments of late and will continue to be so.

The issue in systems management in local area networks is that of determining what level of service is required. That is, do we need a network for occasional mail transfers, are we using the network for more detailed database management processes, or do we need tightly coupled overall control because of applications that span many machines and require synchroniza-

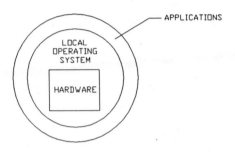

Figure 20.1   Centralized computer.

tion and sharing of each other's resources? In each case we are referring to a different class of operating system to meet the needs economically.

The centralized computer system with no network has a structure as shown in Figure 20.1. This type of system is as we all know our central computer resources to be.

With the advent of the local area network, the next class of management software evolved to that as seen in Figure 20.2. The LAN introduced a need for software to control the communications between the local hosts. This software was simple and only handled the transfer and reception of data in the global applications: from mail or file transfers. This data then would need to be interpreted and translated by the receiving nodes in order for it to become useful to them.

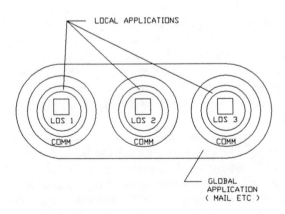

Figure 20.2   First-phase LAN system management.

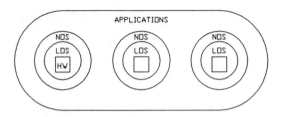

Figure 20.3 NOS view of LAN.

As the LANs progressed in complexity, so did their operating and management environments. Once users became accustomed to LANs with the communications management layer, they began to dream up new uses of the LAN and its extended resources (e.g., distributed data management to provide each user station with the entirety of the enterprise's data bank versus just a fraction of it as in earlier systems). To provide better service to this new class of user application required the addition of new features to the communications management software. The additions grew into the next class of LAN systems management software called the "network operating system." A network operating system, or NOS, provides more transparent use of the system's resources beyond that of mere communications management. A NOS allows the users to request services as in the past, but now they could be oblivious to whether it is a local or remote request. That is, the NOS would find the control process or data and institute its operation as requested by the user without the user knowing that any network interaction occurred. This is shown pictorially in Figure 20.3.

The next logical step from here is to rid the system of the local and network components and construct in their place an operating system developed with the network and user applications in mind (i.e., a global operating system–GOS). The main difference in this approach versus all the others is that there is no local autonomous operating system or network component but one singular operating system built on the hardware (see Figure 20.4).

The GOS is built on top of the bare machine; it is not an add-on to existing software. This mode of construction allows the GOS to encompass all resources without interference from old software. The GOS is comprised of the same management components except they cover all the nodes of the system versus only a single machine. The components of the GOS include:

- Process or object management
- Memory management

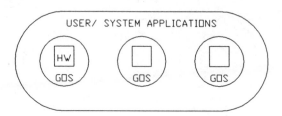

Figure 20.4 Global operating system model.

- I/O management
- Device management
- Network management
- File management

Each of these management components provides global control and management of their entrusted resource(s). These components typically are broken up into "cooperating peers" (to be discussed later) on the physical system.

The rise of networks and the need for expanded service has fueled the path of new technology. Initially there were computer networks to link mainframes and minicomputers. Then came the VLSI explosion and microprocessors, which has led to intelligent workstations to networks of computers serving a single user. As the technology progresses and the need for extended services expands, the operating systems must be developed to handle the situations and meet the needs of the users. Without this growth, the network will only be a small part of what its potential is.

20.1   Operating System Model

What is an operating system for? And why is it constructed as it is? These questions address some of the basic notions of an operating system's existence. The most basic answer to both of these questions comes from the following notions. An operating system is built to provide fundamental services to users. It is constructed to provide general solutions to user problems of managing their applications. The operating system removes the user from dealing directly with the intricacies of the hardware of the computer. For example the I/O subsystem, or disk secondary storage subsystem, would be extremely difficult to use by more than one individual if it were not for the operating system's general, complex, and dynamic solutions to the I/O and memory management problems.

An operating system is a "mechanism" that enforces application-established "policies" regarding the sharing of "system resources" by a set of users. This sharing of resources is needed since no resource has infinite service capacity. And the policy of allocating or sharing the resource is necessary since the operating system is implementing a "general" solution to the sharing of the resources that must provide probabilistic behavior and "fair" service.

The concept in delivering this service is to provide a collection of servers which provide the actual control of the underlying hardware elements. That is, for each of the jobs to be done by the operating system, it possesses a server(s) that will perform the action for it in the name of global service to all.

A server can be a single process or a group of cooperating processes, depending on the nature of services or resources. A single-server process is a single process that provides the service to the user process accessing the resources, whereas a cooperating set of processes can also be a single server. The group of processes supporting the service are operated together in a cooperative fashion to provide the wanted affect on the underlying system resource.

Servers have been typically classified as either a monitor or manager. A monitor process is used to provide service for a resource which can be accessed in a serialized manner, such as a printer or tape unit, whereas a manager process is used to provide a set of services which can be offered concurrently. The concept of these two basic server types will be better described and illustrated as this chapter progresses.

These servers provide, along with the resource(s) they control, service to user processes. The service is accessed via a uniform naming convention that provides unique global names to the servers. These names are then used by the operating system to bind the user process to a particular server for its service duration. That is, access to the underlying resource is provided by the combination of a name and the binding of the named server to the underlying resource.

The important question to ask at this point is how does the "system" manage these resources. We have seen briefly how one can access a given resource but not how this request is met by the system; nor have we seen how the system would perform the service in relation to all others on the system. What this refers to is a management style. That is, how does the system go about serving the multitude of requests it receives? Does it take the traditional approach and serve them FIFO, round robin, LIFO, etc.? In each case the system in an agreement style dictates how the requests that arise are served. The service provided by the contemporary schemes even if augmented by priorities typically will provide "fair" service though not necessarily optimal service from the system's view. The management style selected for the system must take the system's resource management into account, not each individual process. The goals must be set up to address the primary criteria of optionality set up for the system, such as:

- Highest priority first
- First in first out
- Round robin
- Shortest processing time

and perform them on a global basis rather than simply for each local entity. The major concept here is that the system manages the resources and is not driven by the individual user's needs. It is driven by the needs of the system as a whole.

20.2   Basic Concepts and Abstraction

The notion of management style is described by a combination of useful concepts such as modularity, priority, value, etc., and abstractions such as objects and operations thereof. Management style defines the policy of the system, not its mechanisms for implementing them. The policy is represented by a particular set of management algorithms and its associated decision heuristics. That is, a major portion of the operating systems policy is determined by how it goes about managing the allocation of resources in the system. The mechanism is the agency or device by which the policy is carried out. Policy and mechanism are directly analogous to the well-known concepts of strategy and tactics used by military organizations. To illustrate this concept, we will briefly describe a portion of an operating system: a scheduler. This general scheduling model is attributed to Ruschitzka and Fabray [1977]. In this model, a scheduling policy consists of three parts:

- A decision rule
- A priority rule
- An arbitration rule

The decision mode determines when a rescheduling occurs. Common examples of such decision modes are nonpreemptive, preemptive, or quantum-oriented preemptive [in which a task is allowed to run some fixed time (quantum) and then removed to allow others to execute].

The priority function, connected with a given scheduling algorithm, uses system parameters along with the offered tasks and assigns priorities or orderings to them. A priority function can be defined to support any scheduling policy such as first in first out, round robin, deadline, or rate monotonic schedulers.

The arbitration rule resolves any conflicts which may occur among jobs with equal priorities, for example, FIFO or round robin. What these show are the policies or strategies for performing the scheduling of a group of tasks or processes. It represents an abstraction of how to do the job, not the actual means to perform it. Mechanisms would be required to support the policies (i.e., implement them). In this case we would require code to time the scheduler to run based on the decision mode, to assign the priorities, and to break ties.

Other useful abstractions can make the job of designing, implementing, and managing the operating system much easier. For example, to clarify interfaces and interaction among operating systems' policies, we may wish for and, most likely, desire modularity via use of the object model of construction. Objects represent an abstraction constructor for structuring systems. The basic concept is that an object represents a resource or service that is to be managed or provided by the system. The object contains all the pertinent data it requires to manage the resource or perform its service encapsulated (held) within its boundaries. The allowable actions on the resource or the service actions are the only outside visible components of the object. This abstraction allows for clean structuring of elements of the operating system while maintaining strict adherence to modularity and clarity principles. More will be said in later sections on this construction element.

Other important concepts to address include the issue of centralized versus decentralized control. On the latter, we must also consider local versus global elements of control. Systems are built with single or replicated resource items; therefore, this is an issue in developing a management style for the LAN. These resources can be autonomous or cooperating, and various models have been used to describe them, such as the object model or process model as described in Fortier [1987].

20.2.1   Centralized versus Decentralized

In determining what type of control is wanted we must take into consideration what the users' requirements, as well as the systems' requirements, will be. For example, users will be concerned with cost and manageability considerations as well as computing requirements, whereas the system will levy requirements caused by performance, reliability and availability, and extensibility, which will drive the decision to go one way or the other.

Centralized control of a distributed LAN system may be selected based on taking the safe route. This is because the mechanisms of centralized control are well understood, they can be implemented using typically simpler algorithms, and, for cases in which computing is isolated to each machine, may offer better performance in some situations.

Decentralized control, on the other hand, would be selected to ultimately achieve higher availability, higher flexibility, better modularity, and better ultimate performance for the system. These are achieved by an operating system environment that can use the distributed assets to provide better overall service to the users.

To understand the decentralization and the control aspects, we will look at the two components of this, physical and logical decentralization, and what these mean to the problem at hand.

Physical decentralization deals with the notion of a "decentralized computer" (i.e., multiple computing nodes) physically dispersed across a LAN and without the use of any shared primary memory. An important aspect of this to keep in mind is that the processor computation rate is much higher than the interprocessor communication rate.

Additionally, with physical decentralization we have the problem that communication within the operating system is inaccurate and incomplete with respect to system state changes, and they will need some form of "best effort" decision making to perform the systems management job.

Logical decentralization refers to two aspects: degree of decentralization and multilateral resource management. Multilateral resource management refers to management decisions that are made multilaterally by a group of peers through "negotiation," "compromise," and "consensus." Degree of decentralization refers to a few factors such as the percentage of resources involved in a transaction, the percentage of decision makers which participate (this could be greater than the percentage of resources involved), the extent to which all decision makers must become involved before a decision has been completed (totally committed, occasional interaction, one-shot, etc.), the degree of equality of decision makers' authority and responsibility, and the degree of negotiation. All of these represent measures of "intensity" that the interacting elements exhibit during their decision-making processes.

20.2.2   Single versus Replicated Resources

In a centralized computer system, the notion of replicated resources is not really an issue. This is because of the central computer's operational mode. The replicant is operating on and controlled by the same processing engine as the other copy. Conversely, in the distributed case replicants become a source of major problems but also major gains. The replicated resources must be controlled and acted on by a variety of processing engines in such a way as to keep their status consistent with each other. That is, when a process acts on a replicant at one site, the same action must occur to the other replicants at all other sites in such a way that they all move to a new state acceptable by the mass. This is best described by examining the problem in distributed databases. In this case the state changes are reads and writes to the database that are viewed as correct if done in a particular manner. To read an item we must be sure that we are reading the most recent copy; otherwise we must search out the most recent. To write we must coordinate the actions of all other replicants to ensure that the database as a whole maintains its consistent and correct state. This coordination is handled by the use of cooperating peers as will be seen a bit later in this section.

The other side of the coin, in this section, is that of a single resource. With multiple replicated resources we see that one only needs to access the local copy to get serviced, whereas with a single resource, we have the additional problem of network communications and queued service by the single server associated with the resource. The single resource is easier to manage, yet it will limit flexibility and throughput; the replicated resources will provide better service to users but at an additional cost in terms of operating system management to maintain. In each case, one must weigh the benefits versus the user pools' requirements to see which best meets the needs.

20.2.3 Autonomous versus Cooperating

Associated with the above notions of single and replicated resources is that of autonomous resource or server and cooperating resource or server.

The autonomous server or resource(s) can provide its service without the need for interaction with other servers or resources. For example a printer and its server are good examples of an autonomous server and its resource. The printer server is given a job (print out file X). It does this itself by reading the file from the disk and outputting it to the fixed media (paper). Autonomous servers or resources maintain their state information locally to ensure their ability to perform their task alone. They also do not need to synchronize their actions with others, thereby allowing them the freedom to act based solely on their local view of activity in the system.

Cooperating servers or resources, on the other hand, must perform their functions in conjunction with others, not in a vacuum as in the autonomous case. The cooperating server or resource must interact with its peers to effect the operation it is designed for. For example, in the distributed database case, to update an item the database server on one site must converse with those on all sites who possess a copy, tell them of its intent to update, and get a consensus agreement in order to actually perform the update. That is, it must cooperate with all others involved to perform its intended function.

This concept of autonomous and cooperating servers is an important component of an operating system and its management style, as will be seen in Chapter 21.

20.3   Summary

This chapter addressed the concepts embodied in operating systems for local area networks. Covered were the concepts of the server and the server model for operating systems design. As part of this coverage the concepts of resource sharing and cooperating servers were defined and explained, as were the necessary abstractions of these concepts.

20.4   References

Fortier, P. J., *Design of Distributed Operating Systems: Concepts and Technology*, Intertext, Inc., McGraw-Hill, New York, 1986.

Ruschitzka, and Fabry, "A Unifying Approach to Scheduling," *ACM*, vol. 20, no. 8, 1977.

21. Server Models of
Interaction and Control

As was alluded to in Chapter 20, all operating system environments were developed for distributed computers, and, therefore, local area networks use a variant of the client server model. This chapter will examine the particulars of this and other models used in the research, development, and operations of local area networks and distributed computing systems.

21.1 Client Server Model

A related concept to that of the autonomous and cooperating server is the model used to describe their interaction with users. The client-server model is an abstraction used to better describe the interaction and relationship between the users of a service (resource) and the service.

The model is general and can fit the autonomous or cooperating entity case (see Figure 21.1). There can be one to N clients (requestors) looking for service from a particular server class (a server or group of servers providing the same functionality) as well as one to k servers providing this service and performing the service on one to n physical resources (hardware or software entity).

The client is a computational entity (a computer program that interacts with the operating system) which requests a service from a server. The server is the computational element that provides the requestor with a valid response to its request. It is the interface between the client and the resource. It provides the transparency of resource to the using clients.

The client-server relationship is a relative one since a server can itself be a client to some other server (see Figure 21.2). The model has been widely

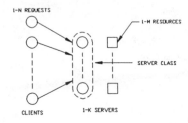

Figure 21.1   Client server model.

used in various network operating systems to structure their environments and has provided a basis for some of the work in the object-oriented systems under development now and in operation. Details of the components and concepts will follow, as will examples to better clarify the notions.

21.2   Service and Resources

What is a service in the context of a computer system? It has been described in the literature as an operation performed on a system resource, but this is not complete. The operation must be such that it is controlled and bounded so as to not violate any of the underlying structures. Service is an abstraction in this case; it represents the policy or strategy for accessing and using some underlying entity. This policy is implemented via a set of servers which represent the mechanisms for instantiating the service policies. The server model, which describes what constitutes a service, is comprised of five major elements or descriptors:

- Service class
- Service name
- Service function
- Server(s)
- Resource(s)

The service class represents a grouping of servers such that these servers provide the same functionality or service policy to the clients it services. The server name represents a means to address, access, or identify the class of service and the underlying servers. The service function describes the policy that the service is to provide (i.e., the operations that this service can perform and their affect on the resource in question).

The server(s) describe the actual entities (objects, processes) that will provide the specified service. The resource(s) represents the physical entities (hardware and software) that are being managed by this service.

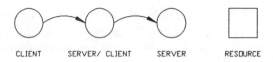

CLIENT   SERVER/ CLIENT   SERVER   RESOURCE

Figure 21.2   Server-client abstraction.

The above description describes in a generic sense the service abstraction. The basic means to provide this service in systems in existence or planned is the "server" and the "object." The server is described as a process or collection of processes that implement the service policies defined, and the object is described as an abstract data type with operations defined on it.

The major difference is that of encapsulation. The object maintains all aspects of the resource and its state within the object, whereas the process is tied to the resource but does not encase it, nor does it carry the state around with it (see Figure 21.3).

To clarify the notion of what constitutes a server (process or object based) the following examples will be discussed:

- File server
- Print server
- Administrator

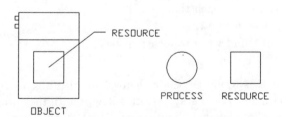

RESOURCE

OBJECT   PROCESS   RESOURCE

Figure 21.3   Object and process differences.

For a file server the structure of the server would require the following operations: open, close, read, and write as the basics. These processes would be associated to physical resources upon initialization of the requests for service via underlying system servers.

The job of the file server at the user interface boundary is to provide a simple uniform view of the underlying physical file structures. As part of this job the file server provides for logical addressing which it converts to unique IDs for use in actual accessing of files.

The server processes for this function would possibly have processes to intake the given command, open, close, read, write, and perform the action as follows:

```
Process file server (cmd, data, file, device)
Do cmd
    Function open (filename, device)
        Find filename, device
            Lock file name
            Set attributes
    End
    Function close (filename, device)
        Unlock filename
        Clear all attributes
        Release device
    End
    Function read (filename, data)
        If filename open then
            Search (Data)
            If found then output data
    End
    Function write
        If filename open then
            Search (data)
            If found write to location
    End
```

These processes would associate themselves with a given resource when put into service and would stay with this device until they are done. These processes are what is called "lightweight"; that is, no computational state (such as local data) is implicitly transferred to a process via invocation

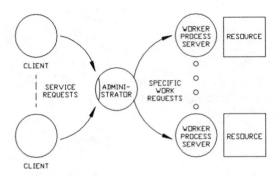

Figure 21.4 Multiple process server (administrator).

other than its formal parameters. These parameters define and steer the process toward the proper actions.

Another server example is the print server. The job of this server is to control the use of a printer resource(s). The process is again only attached to a specific printer when told to do so, not by convention such as in the object model case. The print server process must possess a means to determine what printer it will be using, how to determine its state, and how to control its actions to effectively do its job. This may actually mean that the print server is comprised of a group of servers serving the major service

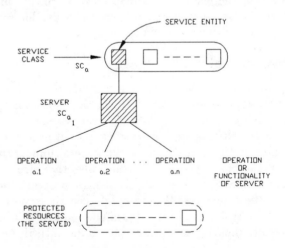

Figure 21.5 Structure of service.

```
Process server
{
PID pid;
while (True) {
    pid = Block Receive Any (message, mtag);
    Do_service (message, result);
    reply (Pid, result;
    }
}
```

Figure 21.6   Behavioral sequence algorithm.

class of print server. The print server process from a generic view would possess functions to open or associate a device, to close or deassociate a device, and to output to the device.

The final example is the administrator server. This type of server is actually a multiple process server that takes in all client requests for service, organizes them based on its functionality, and delves out the work to the subservient worker servers (see Figure 21.4).

This final example depicted the notion of having varying levels of abstraction (service) to the problem to be addressed (i.e., the management of some resources). The generic model of service is shown in Figure 21.5. This figure depicts the set of service classes available by an operating system. It then shows how the class servers map down to an instance of a class server down to the specific operations performed by this server instance (and finally to the resources) being managed.

21.2.1   Structure of Server

We have explained what a server is, that is, what the policy of building a server is. We have not as yet described the mechanisms used to realize such entities or shown a sampling of a class of server types.

The server is the basic operating system entity. It provides the functionality of the operating system and keeps the system running smoothly. The single server is the basic type of server and the other structures are built from this. The single server is essentially a single process which provides a basic service to the requestors. For example, a generic server for a requestor is show in Figure 21.6. This server takes one request at a time, services it, sends a result, then picks another, and so on until there are no more requests.

This simple single server construct can be embellished to construct a variety of server structures to meet a myriad of needs. For example, if a

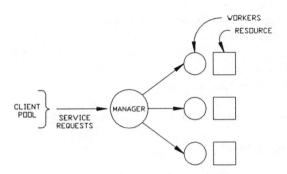

Figure 21.7   Manager server with fixed number of workers.

resource is distributed in such a way that each element function can be clearly partitioned, we may wish to construct a server which mimics this structure. This would be a functionally partitioned server or worker. The functional partitions are such that if the individual pieces are put together, a single server for the composite resource would be realized. Another variation on the single server would be a replicated server. This type of server is a single server with copies of itself at some number of sites in the LAN. The purpose of such a server type would be to manage a replicated resource on each machine (node in the LAN) with the same service entity. Issues of synchronization and coordination put aside, this too is a simple outgrowth of the single server model. A further refinement of the model would lead to an additional class of server to control clusters of resources. This would be the manager. This type of server has two subclasses or types: fixed or variable. The basic manager server is constructed as a hierarchy with the manager acting as a client to the underlying servers (see Figure 21.7).

This structure is very useful to implement many of the device servers needed in a LAN operating system. The number of devices is known and a rigid structuring of these to optimize run-time efficiency can be performed.

The variation of this structure is the variable number of worker managers. This class of management server is well suited to situations in which a variable number of resources are to be managed. An example would be a process manager or file manager in which the number and size of the underlying resources being managed vary. By allowing the management software to vary along with the load, one can better optimize the use of physical assets and time.

These servers can be physically realized via many means, although the most well-known structuring and construction methods are the procedure, message, or object-oriented paradigms.

```
/* Declarations of private data */
Type Priv_data
. . . .
/* Process declaration */
process process_module_name
{
/* Declarations of stack (i.e., auto) variables */
. . . .
type stack_data;
. . . .
/* Process body */
. . . .
}
/* Declarations of private functions and procedures*/
function type f1 (...){...};
procedure f1 (...){...};
. . . .
```

Figure 21.8 The process definition template in C.

21.2.2   Procedure-oriented Paradigm

The procedure-oriented paradigm is best described as one that uses the classical programming methodology, using the program, procedure, and function as the computational entities. The constructor to create new active elements is the fork and join operators. These provide a means to dynamically spawn off new procedures based on the state of the active procedures or a means to unite a set of executing procedures into a single procedure to synchronize some activity on multiple hosts.

The act of cooperation or interaction between procedures is the remote procedure call (RPC). This is the traditional call to a coroutine in Fortran or a procedure in Pascal. The remote procedure call accesses the other procedure, gives control to this procedure, and awaits the response to its call. This basic operation can be augmented to allow the calling procedure to continue rather than wait.

To synchronize the operations of procedures in the operating environment, this model used the semaphore [Dijkstra, 1968] or the monitor [Hoare, 1974]. The semaphore is a mechanism that allows one element to access some critical item without being bothered or interfered with by others. It is analogous to a lock-unlock in database terminology. The monitor provides additional structure to allow selectable entrances and use of resources.

```
Process Requestor
{
PID server_id;

. . .

server_id = Findpid("service_X");
Set_Up (request_message);
Request(server_id,message,result,mtag);

. . .

}
process Server
{
PID pid;

. . .

while(TRUE){
pid = Brecany( message, mtag );
Do_service ( message, result );
Reply( pid, result );
}
}
```

Figure 21.9 A solution for the nR - 1S problem.

A system that used this class of construction paradigm was mesa [Laver, 1979].

21.2.3   Message-based Paradigm

The basic constructor for the message-based paradigm is the process. A process is the data structure that defines the fundamental module of a distributed program. It is comprised of a process definition containing a process body, private data, functions, and procedures.

The process encapsulates in its private address space all the entities of the process. This implies that the components of the process (procedures, functions, etc.) cannot be directly accessed (RPC) but can only be effected via the use of the process interfaces provided. An example process structure is shown in Figure 21.8

To instantiate (i.e., bring to an active state), the message-based mechanism uses a create operand. This allows for the creation of a new instance of a process. Likewise, using the destroy, one can eliminate an instance of a process.

Processes in this model cooperate with each other using message-passing primitives. That is, the processes can only affect each other's actions through the passing of messages among each other. It is up to the individual processes to interpret and act on the messages received. They do not respond directly as in the remote procedure call case (see Figure 21.8).

The message passing can be accomplished via direct or implied interprocess communications primitives. What this says is that we can have either the processes explicitly use send-receive primitives to converse with each other or can have these embedded within the operating system. In this case the processes talk to each other as if they were in the same machine (i.e., by addressing the processes name not via invocation of an interprocess communications process).

Synchronization in the message-based mechanism is handled by message-passing primitives and the proper interpretation of these primitives by the involved processes, as will be seen in upcoming sections.

Examples of systems adhering to this type of client-server constructor are DCS [Tsay, 1981], Amoeba [Tanenbaum, 1981], and Shoshin [Toku, 1983].

21.2.4   Object-oriented Paradigm

This model of construction uses the object as the basic computational entity. The object is an abstract data type consisting of two principal parts: a specification and a body. The object encapsulates all aspects of its state within its boundary. It maintains its own state and keeps its internal elements invisible to the outside. The object's state can only be affected through the use of the externally available operations. This is the only view of the object available to the outside world.

To provide a new instance of an object requires the use of a create primitive. This causes the named object to be instantiated with a unique identifier. Multiple copies of an object can thus be created via multiple instantiations. Each will have a unique identifier and exist exclusively of the others. Likewise to rid the system of some object requires the use of a destroy primitive. This would remove the instance of an object and its linkages. An important aspect of the object constructor is its protection boundaries. The object's access is controlled via a capability or ticketing mechanism. This limits use of the object's operations to only those other objects who have been granted the rights to use them.

The interaction between objects and their cooperation is performed via the invocation of operations on the involved objects. The invocations can be organized and access granted such that we can have one-to-one, one-to-many, many-to-one, etc., clusters of objects. They can cooperate in synchronous or asynchronous fashion if designed to respond as such.

Synchronization of objects is achieved through the adherence to sequences of invocations that provide the synchronization. For example, we

```
process Root
{
 . . .
  While (TRUE) {
    Get_number (n);
    result = Call (fact, n);
    Put_number (result);
  }
}
function int Call(x, arg)
PROCESS x;
int arg,
{
  ...
  pid = Create(x, ATTACH, ANY_HOST);
  if(NotEq(pid,NULL_PID)) {
    if(Request(pid,arg,result,mtag)¿0)
    return(result);
  }
  return(0);
}
process Fact
{
  int result = 1;
  PID pid;
  ...
  Getargs(n);
  if (n > 0)
    result = n * Call(Fact, n - 1);
  Reply (Parent(), &result);
}
```

Figure 21.10 A program skeleton for computing n factorial.

could provide a transaction-based facility which would synchronize the objects based on some serializability or other synchronizing process.

Examples of such operating systems of this type include Eden [Almes, 1983], Clouds [McKendry, 1984], and Archos [Jensen, 1984].

21.2.5 Server Examples

To clarify the concept of the server fully, the following examples of servers using the message-based paradigm are provided. These examples will show the process of using messages as the synchronizing and cooperating mechanisms between the processes of the examples.

N Requesters -1 Server (nR - 1S) Problem   The objective of the $nR - 1S$ problem is to specify a process coordination in which a server process offers a service for N requestor processes. A requestor process must locate a server process which can provide a proper service, say "service_X" and send a request message; then it waits for the return of a result message. On the other hand, a server which offers service_X must perform a requested action and return a result to the requestor processes one at a time; it then waits for the next request message. The skeleton of a solution is shown in Figure 21.9.

This type of simple requestor-server structure can be derived by the object-oriented decomposition scheme or even by a control-oriented scheme. From the object-oriented point of view, the server process encapsulates a service; on the other hand, from the control-oriented point of view, we may consider that a "commonly used" routine was extracted and encapsulated in the server process. One important point is that the server process is dynamically bound to the requestor process using the reference name.

Factorial Problem   The objective of the factorial program is to specify the dynamic process activities for computing the factorial of a given number. In this problem, we assume that we can use all processors for the computational activities. One solution is to use multiple processes to compute a factorial, so as many computing processes as necessary may be created recursively. It may be less efficient than the recursive call within a single process, but the purpose is to show dynamic cooperation among the communicating processes.

Figure 21.10 shows a program skeleton which is derived from our control-oriented decomposition for this problem. In the solution, the root process is used to get an arbitrary number from a terminal and to start the actual computation by passing the given number to the fact process. The fact process then recursively creates itself until the argument becomes one; then it pops off from the recursion by returning the result value. If the fact process cannot create any more processes, it will return zero to the parent processes. When a fact process or its processor dies, its parent process can

```
process Server_0
{
  ...
  While(TRUE){
    pid = Brecany( message, mtag );
    switch( fromwho( pid)) {
    case SERVER_N:
      Reply( message.requestor,message );
      break;
    case REQUESTOR:
      Fsend(Right( myiad ), message, mtag );
      break;
    }
  }
  ...
}
process Server_i /*i = 1 ... N - 1*/
{
  PID pid;
  ...
  Setflcb( Left( myid), maxws, sizeof( message ));
  while (TRUE) {
    Brcc( Left( myid ), message );
    Do_service(message.field[myid]);
    Fsend( Right( myid ), message, mtag );
  }
}
```

Figure 21.11 A program skeleton for pipelined N servers.

receive zero as a return value. Note that the call routine should be included into each domain of processes separately (i.e., it is a private function).

$$PROCESS\ fact\ =\ "/bin/fact";$$

One important prerequisite is that the fact process can be created on demand in any processor environment. Here, because of the sequential nature of the computing process, we may not gain any parallelism or efficiency; it may not be as fast as it should be in a real implementation. However, this type of cooperation based on a demand-oriented dynamic process creation concept is useful on many occasions.

A pipelined N server   The objective of the pipelined N server problem is to construct a cooperation structure among N server processes using

```
process Manager_with_Static_Workers0
{
  Initialize0:
  while (TRUE) {
    tag = All_workers_busy0¿ WORKERTAG : HIGHTAG;
    pid = Brecany(&msg, sizcof( pid, tag );
    switch (Message_from(pid)) {
    case WORKER:
      Update_worker_status( pid, &msg );
      if( Waiting_reply0 )
        Reply_to_corresponding_process(msg);
      break;
    }
    if(Not_qempty(request_q)&&Not_busy_workers0)
      Reply_to_worker(Get_first(request_q));
  }
}
```

Figure 21.12 A program for one manager with N workers.

a pipelined scheme. In this problem, we assume that each request message must be processed by all N servers in order to complete the requested service. The key issue is how to design asynchronous communications among the servers in the most efficient manner. In the models which provide only the blocking type of send primitives (e.g., CSP), we must create a buffer process between two servers to improve asynchronous cooperation; otherwise the first server must wait for the completion of the second server. However, our model provides nonblocking send primitives, so we can simplify the interaction among processes without any buffer processes.

Figure 21.11 shows a program skeleton which is derived from our dataflow-oriented decomposition for this problem. In this solution, we used the scheme in which Server_0 receives a request and gives the result to the requestor; thus the last server must send back the result to server_0*. We also assumed that enough buffers are allocated by Setflcb0 to keep requests ongoing among N servers. If there is not enough buffer space left for Server_0, this process may block itself until a buffer becomes available at Server_1. This blocking may cause a deadlock in this solution, so we may change Server_0 in such a way that Server_1 always asks for a message by using a request primitive; then server_0 sends back a message by using a reply (nonblocking) primitive. Thus, Server_0 does not wait for the buffer area in Server_1 and can wait for a new message or result message from the server_N all the time. Note that in this way, Server_0 must keep new requests from the requestors until Server-1 becomes available. More details of this scheme will be explained in the following problem.

This is caused by the semantics of the Reply primitive in our model. The reply primitive must be invoked by the process which has already received the corresponding request message.

One manager with N workers   The problem of one manager with N workers is to design a server process which provides various service functions for requestors; the functions must be invoked concurrently. One solution is to create a worker process for every request and assign the actual task. This type of dynamic structure is attractive if the number of incoming requests is not large and its arrival rate is not high; otherwise we must create too many worker processes. Instead of the dynamic creation of workers, we can also assign a request to a set of worker processes in a systematic manner. Figure 21.12 shows one of our fundamental cooperating structures between a manager and a fixed number of workers.

In this solution, the manager process keeps a single queue for incoming requests from the requestors. The worker process first sends a request message to the manager asking for a new task and awaits the reply. If some worker is not busy and a new request is received, the manager assigns the task to the worker process by using a nonblocking send (i.e., a reply primitive). In this way, the manager never blocks on the completion of the requested actions. Furthermore, if all workers are busy, the manager process simply waits for a message from a worker by using the selective receive feature. Thus the manager does not need to worry about the size of the internal request queue.

The remainder of this section will look at these various models in greater detail and embelish the concepts embodied in them.

21.3   Process-based Model

The fundamental components of the process-based model are processes, messages, and ports. Processes represent the active elements or entities in the system. They communicate to each other via messages through their associated ports. Processes are comprised of code and data in some known state (e.g., ready, running, waiting). The collection of system service (operating system) and user applications processes constitute an operational system performing a given set of jobs. The operating system processes implement mechanisms in support of the systems management policies to control and manage the system's resources and their interactions. There is at a minimum a simple service process for each major resource in the system such as process manager, device manager, memory manager, I/O manager, and network manager, though in reality there is a multitude of servers and classes of server processes implementing the management policies of the

```
/* declaration of process */
/* declarations of private data */
_type priv_data;
/* declarations of message spaces */
_type_message_parameters
/* process declaration */
process process_module_name
{
/* declarations of stack (i.e., auto) variables*/
type stack data;
/*process body */
}
/* declarations of private functions
    and procedures */
function type FI (...){...};
  .

  .

  .

procedure PI (...){...};
  .

  .

  .

/* End of process declaration */
```

Figure 21.13 Process declaration template.

LAN system. Additionally each created user application is brought into the system as a process that uses the operating system service processes in performing their intended function.

21.3.1   Processes

In this model a process definition is the fundamental module of a distributed program and consists of declarations of a process body, private data functions, parameters, functions, and procedures. A process definition defines the structure and dynamic behavior of a process within a distributed program. A process template is defined in Figure 21.13 in a modified version of C [Kernighan, 1978].

The process declaration defines a process body, private data, message data areas, and parameters, as well as embedded functions and procedures. These, when taken together, define the static structure and dynamic behavior of the process.

The process represents the fundamental computational entity for this model. As such it is used to construct the various services required by the system to manage its resources.

The generic model of the process-oriented paradigm defines two basic categories of processes: private and public processes (services). Private processes are typically short-lived processes started up to run specific programs for users of the system. They are meant to provide service to one individual or other process and are known only to the invoking user or process. For example a user program is a private process, as is the time-driven scheduler to the operating system. Public processes, on the other hand, are system processes that are available to a wide range of users (system or individual). Examples of this type of process are a database manager process, a printer process, a mail server process, etc. Public server processes are typically long lived, accepting requests for work servicing the sending responses and then readying themselves for the next access (message).

21.3.2   Ports

The processes alone do not constitute a "system." They need to interact and exchange information to perform their intended tasks of applications execution and managing the assets of the system. To accomplish this, the concept of port or connector associated with each process has been developed. The port acts as the sole means by which processes (private or public) can converse with one another.

In the context of a processes description, the port is the parameter or message area reserved in its structure (see Figure 21.13). This area becomes the place in which incoming and outgoing information to or from the process are held and flow.

Knowledge of a port number (name) is taken as prima facie evidence that the holder has a right to use the port in question. Processes can generally determine what other processes they will give their port name to. This could be done on a system level (by a port manager) or at a process level at which the process will by design or interpretation know or determine who to give its port name(s) to. A process accepts messages from any of its ports and sends messages to any ports it knows of in the system. All protection in this model is built around how one uses and manages the ports. This concept is analogous to the holding of a capability in the object model, as we will see later.

21.3.3   Messages

As was alluded to above, the message constitutes the mechanism for processes to exchange information. No other means is provided if the process model is tightly adhered to. Messages are addressed from port to port, or process to process, based on the level of abstraction and on low-level hiding of details the operating system wishes to provide.

The passing of messages between and among the processes in the system provides the fundamental mechanisms for process synchronization, cooperation, and information exchange in the system. For example by the proper use of messages to indicate a transaction start, to block a process, and to wake up a process, we can build a database transaction system. The basic message primitives are the send and receive primitives. These can be of the blocking or nonblocking type. Using them, we can build basic and elaborate semaphore and synchronization capabilities into the system. For example, if a simple semaphore (wait, signal) is wanted, we can use the message-passing scheme as follows to construct the synchronization:

P(x)   If the semaphore is not set, I will set it (i.e., if free, acquire resource "lock"); if set, wait (wait or lock).

V(x)   Clear the semaphore (signal).

In the message-passing scheme, we would use the ports and blocking messages to perform the synchronization as follows:

Port A is associated with the process performing the semaphore isolation and containing the critical information wanted.

Port B is the port associated with the process-seeking service.

The semaphore operates as follows:

• PB sends a request block message to A and blocks itself awaiting a response.
• If A is free, it will block its port from being used and signal B.
• If A is blocked, it will reject the message.

This is analogous to the P(x) or wait semaphore action.

Once A has completed its processing for B, it will send a message to B indicating completion. B will then send a message to A to unblock it. This is analogous to the V(x) semaphore or unlock in traditional systems.

From this we can see that many forms of synchronization can be achieved through the judicious use of the ports, their conditions, and messages flowing between them.

To clarify some of these concepts, some simple examples of management elements will be described here from Shosin [Tokuda].

21.3.4   Shoshin System Server Model

In the previous sections, we have described the basic mechanisms which are provided by the process-based model. In order to provide the same functions in the LAN environment, we have developed our system server

```
process Monitor()
{
    Initialize();
    while( TRUE ) {
        pid = Brecany( &msg,sizeof(msg),ANYTAG );
        DO_service( pid, &msg, &result );
        Reply( pid, &result, sizeof(result));
    }
}
```

Figure 21.14 The basic structure of the monitor process.

model which is based on process-based encapsulation concepts. That is, a service is encapsulated by a set of servers, and resources are managed by cooperation among the associated servers. In this section we describe our server model and give an overview of the actual system servers in the Shoshin system.

In Shoshin, each type of resource, or service*, is encapsulated by a set of system server processes. Thus a process can access a resource or obtain services only by sending an explicit request to the corresponding server. In this way, it is easy to achieve "network transparent" access to resources and services.

A server can be a single process or a group of cooperating processes, depending upon the nature of services or resources. We developed three different types of servers: monitor, manager, and distributed manager. A monitor process is used to provide service for a resource which can be accessed in a serialized manner. A manager process is used to provide a set of services which can be offered concurrently. While a monitor and manager manage the resources based on local decisions, the notion of distributed manager has been devised to administer a set of resources based on global decisions. A distributed manager is not a single process in a single site; it is a group of managers that cooperate together to provide a class of service.

In the following sections, we will describe these concepts as well as cooperation structures.

21.3.5   The Monitor Process

A monitor process is used for a resource which can be accessed by only one process at a time. The basic idea is from the "monitor" concept by Hoare [1974]; similar constructs are also used in other message-passing operating systems [Manning, 1977; Cheriton, 1979]. The main point of the monitor process is that the sequence of actions on the resource must be strictly serialized. The skeleton of the monitor process, written in our modified C, is shown in Figure 21.14.

We use the terms "resource" and "service" interchangeably. Others may sometimes distinguish between a resource and service based on whether emphasis is laid on the encapsulated data (object) or the set of functions on that object.

From the requestor's point of view, the request message must be submitted by using the request primitive, and it must wait for the result. Thus, the semantics of a monitor process are identical to those of the traditional monitor module. However, there are a few differences between the two. First, the monitor process can reject the incoming request if the access is not allowed. Second, the monitor process can perform selective receive based on the request message's tag value. Third, the requestor will not block forever even if the monitor process dies before it returns the result (this is because of the communication abort mechanism in IPC). Finally, the monitor process does not need to block itself until the requestor receives the reply message. In this sense, this interaction is different from the traditional procedure invocation scheme.

21.3.6　The Manager Process

A manager process encapsulates a set of resources (or services) which can be offered concurrently. The manager performs resource management by cooperating with a set of associated worker processes. All actual actions are (independently) performed by the worker processes so that the encapsulated resource can be accessed by several requestors concurrently. The relationship between the manager and a worker process can be dynamic or static. By dynamic relation we mean that the worker is created on the receipt of a request and is destroyed after the request action is completed. The term static relation demands that all workers be created at initialization of the manager process and then wait for work from the manager. Thus, the number of workers is always fixed. (It is also possible for the manager to increase or decrease the number of workers based on the current workload.) Workers themselves are strictly serial in operation.

In the static scheme, the basic structure is that the manager process executes a loop and waits for a "service" request (submitted by a request primitive from a user process or a "give-me-a-task" request, which includes the result for the previous task and is also submitted by a request primitive) from a worker process. The manager mainly maintains request queues and the status of its workers. When a user request is pending and a worker becomes ready, the manager submits the task by a nonblocking (i.e., reply) primitive. Thus the manager never blocks to send a task to workers and is always ready to respond to an incoming request. When all workers are

```
process Manager_with_Static_Workers()
{
  Initialize();
  while( TRUE ) {
    tag = All_workers_busy()? WORKERTAG:HIGHTAG:
    pid = Brecany( &msg, sizeof(msg), tag );
    switch ( Message_from(pid)){
    case WORKER:
      Update_worker_status( pid, &msg );
      if ( Waiting_reply() )
      Reply_to_corresponding_process(msg);
      break
    case USER:
      Enqueue( request_q, pid, &msg);
      break;
    }
    if (Not_qempty(request_q)&&Not_busy_workers())
      Reply_to_worker( Get_first(request_q));
  }
}
```

Figure 21.15 The basic structure of the manager process.

busy, the manager only waits for a message from workers. This important
selective receive function is simply provided by message tagging in Shoshin.

The manager with static workers is similar to the administrator model
[Cheriton, 1979; Gentleman 1981]. However, their "administrator" model
cannot allow the manager to have an arbitrarily long requestor queue without rejecting a requestor's request. This is because of the lack of a selective
receive function in their IPC facility. In their model, the administrator
(ideally) requires the queue length to be the same as the total number of
requestors in the system; otherwise some of the requests must be canceled
because of lack of queue area. In Shoshin, the length of the request queue
depends on the number of worker processes, and the length should be at
least the same as the number of workers.

A skeleton of a simple manager with static workers is shown in Figure
21.15, in which the manager can receive a message either from user processes
(i.e., requestors) or its workers. The manager process also controls the
incoming request messages based on their message tag, using the selective
receive feature. For instance, if workers are not busy, a message of highest
priority will be selected. On the other hand, if all the workers are busy,

```
while(TRUE){
   ...
   switch( Message_from(pid)) {
   case WORKER:
   ...
   case CARRIER:
      Update_carrier_status( pid, &msg );
      if( Waiting_reply())
      Reply_to_corresponding_process( msg );
      break;
   case USER:
      ...
   }
   ...
   if(NOT_qempty(carrier_request_q)&&Not_busy_carrier())
      Reply_to_carrier(Get_first(carrier_request_q));
}
```

Figure 21.16 Modification of the manager for the carrier process.

the manager tries to receive a message only from the workers, not from the requestors.

21.3.7   The Distributed Manager Process

A distributed manager provides a class of services and consists of a group of managers which form a distributed control network (e.g., complete network, a virtual ring, a tree, etc.) using one or more workers of each manager. The important difference between the distributed manager and previous two modules is that the distributed manager tries to administer a set of resources based on global decisions instead of local decisions at a single host. One way to achieve such global decisions is to coordinate a decision step among a group of managers. Another requisite is to assign the same service class for a set of managers, so user processes must ask for a service by referring to that generic name. Without using these techniques, the requestor must find another server itself if the first server, which is given by the process binding, is not available.

Our approach is to form a control network among the managers. If the service should be provided by another server, the manager must forward the request to the proper server. For instance, by creating a "carrier" process on demand or by adding the carrier as one of the (static) workers owned by every manager, the managers can form a distributed control network.

In the case of adding a static carrier process, simple modifications, which are shown in Figure 21.16, are required in the main loop of the manager.

In order to form a distributed control network, a manager must find out the other managers' PIDs. For a complete network, all other managers' PIDs must be found, whereas a virtual ring or tree only require the predecessor's and successor's PIDs. However, because of the simplicity of adding and deleting one of the managers from the current network, we use a complete network in Shoshin.

Further details of the process-based structure of the Shoshin operating system can be found in Tokuda [1983].

21.4   The Object Model

The fundamental computational paradigm in this model is the object. Objects are generalizations of abstract data types as they relate to modeling computer system components. The data structures represent data files, executable modules, interprocess communication mailboxes, directories, applications modules, hardware resources, and their control software. Each of these items is structured and operated on as objects. As such they have fixed invariant operations that define their context within the system. Objects are totally encased; that is, they maintain their own state irrelevant to the outside world. The outside world can reference an object only by its name, not its internals; the access is through the offered services (operations) and no other way.

Objects can be passive or active. Passive objects provide a basic service but do not affect or act on any other objects, whereas active objects act on other objects in performing their designed functions. The object's structure is similar to that of an Ada program. There is a specification part and a body.

The specification part describes the external user's view of the object. It consists of a set of data types and a set of operations that other objects will use to activate the services offered by the object. This external view is all that is available to outside objects (information hiding principle). Outside objects can only use the object with these operations and no other way. For example, an elevator object can only go up and down and open or close its doors within the boundaries of the building it is in (number of floors). It cannot go sideways or around; it cannot go above the top floor or below the bottom floor. Users can only push buttons to open or close the doors and to go up and down. They have no way of knowing how the elevator is actually built (i.e., whether it is a cable system or hydraulic). They only see its operations, not its internal mechanisms. The same holds true for objects in this model of design.

Generic
   Type eltype is private;
   Package queue-P is
   Type queue (MaxQElements:Natural) is limited private;
   Procedure append(Q:in out queue;E:in elttype);
   Procedure remove(Q:in out queue;E:out elttype);
   Function is-empty(Q:in queue) return boolean;
   Function is-full(Q:in queue) return boolean;
   Procedure init-queue(Q:in out queue);
   Procedure destroy-Q(Q:in out queue);
   Full Q, Empty-Q; exception;
   Pragma inline (is-empty,is-full,init-queue,destroy-Q).
Private
   Subtype nonnegative is integer range 0..integer:last;
   type queue (max Q elts:natural)
      Record
      First-Elt,Last-Elt:Non-Negative:=0;
      Cur-Size:Non-Negative:=0
      Elements:Array(0...Max-Q-Elts)of Elttype;
      End Record;
   End Queue-P;
   Package Body Queue-P is
      Pragma Inline(Is-Empty,Is-Full,Init-Queue,Destroy-Q);
      Procedure Append (Q:in out queue;E:in Elttype) is
      Begin
         If Q.Cursive=Q.MaxQElts then
            Raise Full-Queue
         Else
            Q.Cursize:=Q.Cursive+1;
            Q.Lastelt:=Q.Lastelt+1)Mod
   Q.Max Q Ects;

Figure 21.17 Queue object example (continued on next page).

```
    Q.Elements (Q.Lastelt):=E;
  End if;
End append;
Procedure remove (Q:in out queue;E:out Elttype) is
Begin
  If Q:Cursive=0 then
    Raise empty-Queue;
    Else
    Q.CURSIZE:=.CURSIZE-1;
    Q.FIRSTELT;=(Q.FIRSTELT+1)
MOD
    E:=Q.ELEMENTS(Q.FIRSTELT);
    END IF;
    END REMOVE;
FUNCTION IS-EMPTY(Q;IN QUEUE)RETURN BOOLEAN IS
BEGIN
  RETURN Q.CURSIZE=0;
END IS-EMPTY;
FUNCTION IS-FULL(Q:IN QUEUE)RETURN BOOLEAN IS
BEGIN
  RETURN Q.CURSIZE=Q.MAX-Q-ELTS;
END IS-FULL
PROCEDURE INIT-QUEUE(Q:IN OUT QUEUE) IS
BEGIN
  NULL;
END INIT-QUEUE;
PROCEDURE DESTROY-Q(Q:IN OUT QUEUE) IS
BEGIN
  NULL;
END DESTROY-QUEUE;
END QUEUE-P;
```

Figure 21.17 Queue object example.

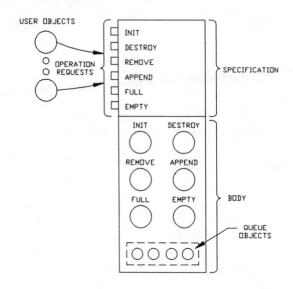

Figure 21.18 Queue object representation.

The body of an object consists of descriptions of private abstract data types, private operations, and private objects and processes. All objects must, as a minimum, have one process encased in it; all other items are optional. The private information encased in the object is only visible to processes within the object.

Procedures defined within the object determine the access rules for the encapsulated data, handling of mutual exclusion, or providing dirty access if wanted. As an example of an object, a specification for a queue is developed.

One of the most common data structures is the queue. It is used in all facets of computer and algorithm design. The behavior of any queue (for example, FIFO) can be defined using four operations (create, destroy, append, remove). The first one would be used only once, to create or initialize a queue, initializing its state; for example, the create operator would fix the relevant parameters of the queue, such as the number of elements in the queue, start point, and name. Once a queue has been created, the other three operations, append, remove, and destroy, can be invoked by the creators who wish to use this data structure. In the following example, only the procedures implementing the four operations would be able to alter the state of the queue. Synchronization of actions necessary to preserve queue invariants will be found in the code bodies of the procedures implementing the append and remove operations.

Server Models of Interaction and Control 419

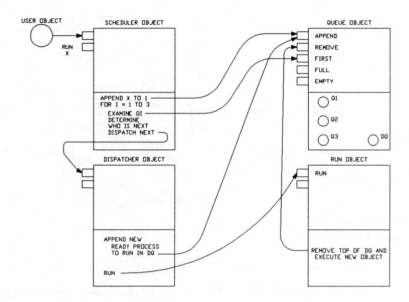

Figure 21.19 Cooperating objects.

The general package queue shown in Figure 21.17 provides a finite queue object for use by requesting objects. Each instantiation of the package requires a type parameter that specifies the type of the queued elements. After instantiation, any number of queues may be declared by using the type queue.

To create a queue Q the invocation INIT-QUEUE must be made once. This invocation must precede any use of the active operators append and remove. Additionally, to make this a useful construct for applications development, we must have additional operators to check the state of the data structure. These are is-empty and is-full. These operators provide the capability to determine if there is something in the queue or if it is full. Finally, once a queue is no longer needed, DESTROY-Q should be performed to restore the memory to the system's memory pool. Additionally, for a queue to have usefulness to designers, it must have boundaries; it must have dimension to be realistic. Therefore, a descriminant called "max-Q-elements" is used to specify a minimum requirement on queue size in terms of number of items.

Semantics of append and remove operations must also be included for the handling of conditions in which, if the specified queue is empty and a call to remove is made, an exception must be raised signaling an invalid use

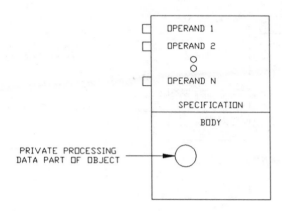

Figure 21.20 Simple object.

of the data structure. If, conversely, the queue is full and a call to append is made, an exception also must be raised, signaling an invalid use of the data structure.

What this example shows is a simple nonprotected instantiation of an object, a queue. The object has a data structure that can change only in specific ways; that is, it can be added to or removed from either the end or from the head of the data structure. The object has provided state information (the is-empty or is-full operator) and manipulation operators (append, remove, init-, destroy). These provide the external view that any user function has of this object (see Figure 21.18). The object encapsulates (protects) the actual manipulation code and data structure within its body. The body has an internal form comprised of private, protected code and data. These in themselves can also be objects.

This generalized queue object provides to requestors a means to create N queue objects that all have the same qualities, structure, interface, and operations while still providing for a variety of simple data structures to be stored in the queue (integer, real, character, abstract, etc.).

What the above description provides is a basic view of what constitutes a single object. To build anything truly useful in order to do an end-processing job requires the use of many simple objects. Even within an object, other simpler objects may be used or may be part of the object in order to provide the requisite service. As a result, the object model provides generic components that can be combined in various fashions to provide the service necessary. This implies that the object model represents a way of building systems that is much different from that shown in the

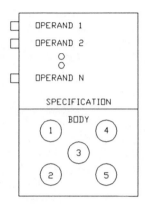

Figure 21.21 Complex object.

process model. The process model uses large processes, albeit a few, to construct a system, whereas the object model uses numerous simple structures linked together to provide the requisite services. The object model services are more generic and simple, while the process models are specialized and complex.

But building a system using the object model requires the linkage of numerous objects. The object model is a structuring tool; it provides easy mechanisms and policies for linking objects. It does not imply any particular design technique; that is, it can easily be used with top-down or bottom-up design techniques. In top down, the designer defines high-level system operations on abstract components and iteratively defines the lower-level structures as necessary. In bottom up, the system designer defines the lowest-level constructs, such as queues, lists, trees, data manipulators, etc., and using these, continues to "build up" to a full system. These concepts describe design philosophies that provide to the designers only what they need at a particular time and that allow them to ignore unnecessary details. The designer focuses on the specifications (operations) and implementations (data structures) of the objects with their interactions, devoid of any other implementations.

For example, to build a scheduler the designer may deem it necessary to use top-down development and defines a scheduler object that examines three levels of queues containing ready-to-execute objects. The scheduler then selects one of the entries from the tree, extracts it, and inserts it in the dispatcher queue. The dispatcher, in turn, removes items from its queue, in the order in which it was designed, and places them in the running

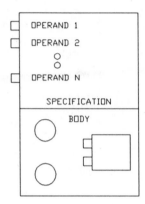

Figure 21.22 Complex object with shared data object.

state, that is, on the physical hardware. Pictorially, this is shown in Figure 21.19. This is a high-level example; but it does show how, through the combination of disjointed objects, each with their own unique function, operating systems can be built. In more general terms, objects interact through requests for service and responses to service. Objects can be nested within objects. For example, (1) an object could be comprised of a single process (see Figure 21.20), (2) an object could be comprised of multiple processes (see Figure 21.21), (3) an object could be comprised of multiple processes and shared objects (see Figure 21.22), and (4) an object could be composed of multiple processes, shared objects, and nested objects (see Figure 21.23).

Constructing useful systems entails the selection and binding of the objects together, using the requestor server capacity of the objects. The problem with this simplistic view is that it does not take into account conflicts for the objects' use. In order to operate properly, actions on objects must happen completely and accurately or not at all. This implies that objects support failure atomicity. This term, like its use in database systems, implies the serialized, nonconflicting operation of the objects' operations among each other in the system; that is, actions on objects will occur in a given order that provides a proper and correct sequence of state changes on the underlying objects.

21.4.1   Capabilities

To provide this type of service, the object model requires mechanisms that control the interaction and access to the objects comprising the system. The

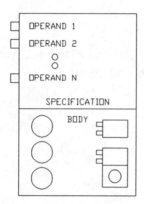

Figure 21.23 Complex object with shared data and nested objects.

scheme for providing this is composed of the capability and its semantic use. The concepts involved deal with protection, authorization, and precedence. Controlled use of resources (objects) is essential in order to provide logical, efficient, and accurate use of the computer system. For example, certain actions are permissible on physical and logical resources such as CPUs, memories, and peripherals. CPUs can only be executed on; memories can be read or written; disks can be read and written; tapes can be read, written, or rewound; programs can be read, written, or executed; data files can be opened, closed, read, written, created, or deleted.

To guarantee the proper use of these objects in the system, they must be controlled to allow users access only to those server objects they have been authorized to access. Additionally, at any point in its execution, an object should be able to access only those resources that it currently requires to complete its execution. This requirement levied on systems is typically referred to as the need-to-know principle. This principle is necessary to limit the amount of mischief a damaged or faulty object can cause to the system. The object model, through its structure, provides some of this protection.

The specification part is the only part known and accessible to the outside world, while the internal part or body is the protected part; that is, the body part is inaccessible by outside forces. Users can request services but cannot actively process the objects' internals. Structure alone, however, will not guarantee the integrity of an object; it cannot guarantee that unwanted users will not access it. Any object could request any other object.

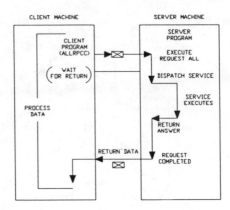

Figure 21.24 Client-server RPC model.

To correct this lack of control, a concept referred to as a "protection domain" is introduced. A process (the active portion within an object) operates within a protection domain or environment, which specifies what resources and rights to it a process may access. Each of those domains provide a definition of the objects and the operations allowable on this object and by whom. These "rights" provide the protection.

The major means of achieving this in object-based systems is the capability. Capabilities are stored as a list with each object. If an object possesses the capability ticket for another object, it can use it. If it does not possess a capability, it has two options; it can go away since it has no rights to the wanted object, or it can attempt to acquire a capability for an object. This mechanism of capability protection and use has been very successful in systems built using this model of design.

Synchronization in this model can be achieved in many ways. The basic means is to build traditional semaphore-like synchronization primitives into the objects. Another scheme, described in Sha [1984], postulates building synchronization mechanisms around the concept of transactions. By the use of database-like transaction interaction concepts, object interaction and synchronizations can be achieved. Details can be found in Fortier [1986] of the object model and examples of use in operating systems.

21.5   Remote Procedure Call Model

Also referred to as the procedure-based paradigm, the remote procedure call model has as its basic computational entity the program procedure and function. These are, as we all are familiar with, in conventional programming languages (i.e., the subroutine call or procedure call). The variation is that the calling and called procedures need not be resident at the same machine for it to work.

As in the previous cases, this mechanism is based on the policy of client and server. The procedure wishing to perform some remote task acts as the client, and the remote procedure controlling the service acts as the server. The RPC mechanism works as in the traditional case: the requestor forms a call to the remote procedure and passes the parameters necessary to perform the task at the remote site. The remote site receives this request and, as in the central computer case, acts on it by invoking the wanted action.

In principle, one can see that this is a very simple concept and can be easily provided within a local area network. The problem comes in how to handle multiple requests from many sites. The issues would be (1) to allow the individual procedures to provide their own form of sequencing through multiple requestors or (2) to allow a system service (interprocess communication service) to provide the sequencing of items (requests) to the other procedures. Each of these alternatives have good and bad points. In the first case, the burden of how to perform the sequencing task is removed from the system and dropped on the lap of the individual programmer. This is good for the system programmers but terrible for the average "Joe." The problem is that much redundancy of solutions will ensue and resources may be inefficiently used. The second case puts the burden on the system to develop a general solution. In this case the system can determine, based on a fuller view, which item to send on next for service while the others remained blocked.

The RPC mechanism is simple, yet it provides a powerful means to build distributed systems. The use of this mechanism puts the burden on users to know more about system structure but provides flexibility to build any needed application. This is a fall out of the Unix method of providing all things needed for a programmer to get in trouble to build an elegant system.

As an example, let's look at the Unix RPC mechanism. The basic unit of operation is the call RPC( ). This call is used to perform the remote access for service through the XDR (external data represent) and related routines. The client program issues a call RPC( ) to initiate a request (see Figure 21.24). This translates to a message being sent to the remote machine with the RPC embedded. On reception, the remote machine will extract the RPC from the message and forward it to the proper procedure. The remote procedure will be initiated, will perform the wanted service, and then return an answer based on the performed service. The result will be packaged into the proper parameters (typically the RPC's parameters are handled on a value-result fashion), then shipped back to the caller as return parameters from a procedure call. By using the RPCs properly, we can build any operating system mechanism we wish. The RPC is a powerful mechanism that, if handled properly, can provide processes the means to build distributed processes and systems.

21.6   Summary

This chapter provided a review of the basic models of construction used in building distributed operating systems. Covered were the major classes of models: the object model, the process model, the remote procedure call model, and the generic process server model.

21.7   References

Almes, G., et al., "The EDEN System: A Technical Review," *TR* 83-10-05, University of Washington, October 1983.

Cheriton, D. R., "Thoth a Portable Real-Time Operating System," *Communications of the ACM*, vol. 22, no. 2, February 1979, pp. 105-115.

Dijkstra, E., "Cooperating Sequential Processes," in *Programming Languages*, Figenuys (ed.), Academic Press, New York, 1968, pp. 43-112.

Fortier, P. J., *Design of Distributed Operating Systems: Concepts and Technology*, Intertext, Inc., McGraw-Hill, New York, 1986.

Gentleman, W. M., "Message Passing Between Sequential Processes: The Reply Primitive and the Administrator Concept," *Software Practice and Experience*, no. 11, 1981, pp. 435-466.

Hoare, C. A. R., "Monitors: An Operating System Structuring Concept," *Communications of ACM*, vol. 17, no. 10, October 1974, pp. 549-557.

Jensen, E. D., and N. Pleszkoch, "ARCHOS: A Physically Dispersed Operating System," *Computer Science Department Working Memo*, Carnegie Mellon University, Pittsburgh, 1984.

Kernighan, B. W., and D. M. Ritchie, *The C Programming Language*, Prentice-Hall, Englewood Cliffs, NJ, 1978.

Laver, H. C., and E. H. Satterthwaite, "The Impact of Mesa on System Design," *Proceedings of the 4th Conference on Software Engineering*, Munich 1979, pp. 174-182.

Manning, E., "A Homogeneous Network for Data Sharing," *Communications, Computer Networks*, vol. 1, no. 4, 1977, pp. 211-224.

McKendry, M. S., "Clouds: A Fault Tolerant Distributed Operating System," *I.E.E.E. Distributed Processing Technical Committee Newsletter*, 6/SI-2, 1984.

Sha, L., "Modular Concurrency Control and Failure Recovery," Ph.D. dissertation, Carnegie-Mellon University, Pittsburgh, 1984.

Tannenbaum, A. S., "An Overview of the Ameoba Distributed Operating System," *ACM Operating Systems Review*, vol. 15, no. 3, July 1981, pp. 51-73.

Tokuda, H., "Shoshin: A Distributed Software Testbed," Ph.D. dissertation, University of Waterloo, Ontario, Canada, 1983.

Tsay, D., "Mike - A Network Operating System for the Distributed Double Loop Computer Network," Ph.D. dissertation, Ohio State, 1981.

22. Resource Management in Local Area Networks

22.1 Systemwide Resource Management

The previous chapters have looked at the various basic issues in management of resources in a local area network environment or in distributed computing environments. The techniques and concepts developed in these chapters will become clearer as we look at further issues in the management of system assets and the goals of the more interesting issues in LAN management, such as naming and binding management, load balancing, scheduling, and information management as they relate to the overall LAN operating systems area.

22.1.1 Naming and Binding Management

In a LAN, as in any system, when a process, object, or procedure is created or wants to converse with some other process, object, or procedure, it must possess a name or identifier through which it can be recognized. In the LAN this name is used in determining what the process, object, or procedure is and where it is located. The selection of a name can be done in various ways in a LAN environment. For instance, the user name given to a process can be used in conjunction with a user ID and system node name to give a unique systemwide name. Another alternative is to have a global name manager that provides a unique name to new processes when asked.

Typically, in systems names exist at two levels: the user level and the system level. This implies that there are two distinct name spaces. At the upper level (human), there are typically global symbolic names. Symbolic names are those that are more convenient for human users; therefore, they have definition to the users. For example, we may have a process identified as printer or disk server, mailbox, network I/O, etc. This name space is supported by a catalog which provides the mappings (bindings) between the symbolic names that people use and the global unique identifiers that the system uses to actually access the objects.

The global unique identifiers reside in a "catalog" that defines the actual parameters necessary to acquire and access an object (bindings to storage, etc.). Binding protocols, or levels, are used to define in a logical and physical way how the namings extend down into physical realizations in a hierarchical fashion. More will be said on this in later sections.

22.1.2   Load Balancing

Another important systems management issue is that of load balancing. When the computers in the LAN become overloaded, there needs to be mechanisms to detect this condition, determine corrections, and carry them out. Load balancing is the process of taking the processing loads on the network and in some fashion partitioning it so that the nodes are uniformly loaded. The problem is how does one do this, and what mechanisms can be utilized to realize these policies?

22.1.3   Scheduling

Associated with load balancing is the scheduling issue. If the initial scheduling phase is handled at a more global level, loadings can be better controlled. If this occurs, load balancing as a separate entity is not required. Therefore, we examine some issues in scheduling processes in a LAN environment and look at solutions used and postulated.

Finally, information management is examined as it relates to the LAN environment. This aspect of system management is very critical in the sense that enterprises (companies) live or die based on how good their information is. Timely and correct information provides the basis for sound decisions. Therefore, it is a critical issue in LANs that there be sound mechanisms for information management.

22.2   Naming and Binding Management

22.2.1   Naming

The problem addressed here is that of how to find out a servers' identity or name in a system so that it can be used to perform its job. As was said previously, this is the problem of naming and name management. To address this, we will examine the techniques applied to some existing LAN operating systems. In particular we will look at three well-known examples from the research world: Cronus, Shoshin, and Mike. The techniques used in these are indicative of most commercially available mechanisms.

In Cronus names exist at two levels: a relatively high symbolic name level and a relatively low global unique level. At the highest level, Cronus allows users to use symbolic names that provide for convenient use to humans. These symbolic names are managed by a Cronus catalog manager. This process maintains a mapping of the symbolic name to the global unique identifier (name). The lower level uses unique identifiers at the systems level to provide a means to differentiate all objects in the system. These in turn are formed into UID tables which describe the actual physical realization of the names object (i.e., its bindings).

In Mike there is a hierarchical scheme for names. At the global level only the "administrators'" (guardian) names are known. This provides for a level of abstraction and information hiding. Names in Mike are logical names that do not have any connotation to their physical locations.

The guardians on Mike have a unique systemwide name, while processes encased within these guardians exist and have names only at the local level. The names of the guardians are formed into a nonhierarchical set, with their subparts named in relation to them. For example (stack, push, si, temp) implies that the stack guardian is to push item temp onto stack si. As in the previous example, Mike uses a two-tiered approach. That is, it possesses human-oriented names and machine-oriented names. The global unique identifiers are built as the concatenation of a node identifier and local unique guardian name. Those taken together provide a global unique identifier.

The Shoshin test-bed system also uses a similar naming mechanism. It uses a hierarchy of names to uniquely define items in the system. The breakdown is shown as service class name, instance name, and host name. This provides a way to uniquely address any service, instance of a service, and the location of this service in the system. As in the other cases, it will require a mapping mechanism to actually perform the binding, although in this case bindings can be done dynamically versus statically. Details are in Tokuda [1983].

The V system implements several levels of names. At the lowest level, each process has a process identifier. Next each server process has a symbolic name such as LPR (line printer), DSK (disk), etc. The symbolic names are mapped via a kernel table to the PIDs. Again, as in the previous examples, the names are associated as a symbolic (human) version and a system version (PID).

22.2.2   Bindings

The binding of names to physical realizations is very critical and often over-looked. The binding can be done at process definition, process compilation, process loading, or process run time. Each have unique aspects that restrict users to what can or cannot be accomplished with their entity.

Binding performed at definition time has been done in the past. This implies that when the designer is coding the process, a unique ID is provided. This in turn is used to map the process to its identifier for use in the future. This type of binding is extremely limiting and not used in any reasonable system.

Binding at compile time is an option that has been used in past systems. It requires the compiler or compiler manager to know the present mappings and be able to allocate a UID for this process. A more useful means is to do mappings at load time. This again, however, is not too flexible, but it does provide a means to better use UIDs in the system. When a process is initialized, it is given a UID to have and use until it dies. When it exits, the UID is returned to a pool to be reused. This is okay if no other process will use the UID directly to address a process; otherwise, when a new process is initialized using this UID, erroneous control flows and processing will occur.

Finally, bindings can be done at run time. This implies a dynamic binding mechanism that will cause the given name to be bound to a UID only during run time. And even more, it could change during run time. Examples of these binding classifications can be found in Tsay [1981], Tokuda [1983], Schantz [1981], and Tanenbaum [1981].

22.3   Load Balancing

The issue of load balancing in distributed systems has many flavors. One could look at this as one of two basic flavors: monitoring or scheduling. The two have totally different connotations. The monitoring version looks at load balancing as an after-the-fact problem. That is, let overloads occur, then fix them. In the scheduling case we look to provide load schedules so that the overloads will not occur. That is, we fix the problem before we even have one. One is like detection and recovery in a database system, and the other is like avoidance. In each case something different is required.

Another analogy is congestion in local area networks or even more so in wide area networks. In these cases we look at means to either detect and fix congestion situations or avoid them. Load balancing is the same problem, just restated with some different connotations. The function of load balancing is to maintain some level of loading within predefined boundaries, at each host within the network. The problem is one of how to do this without having a major impact on the run time system. This is essentially the problem of detection and action in distributed systems or, stated differently, that of decentralized control.

The problem in load balancing is how to determine when a node is beyond some acceptable value, and how to indicate this to other nodes. This is essentially the problem of decentralized control. The problem is that there is no "centralized" decision point, no implicit "global" clock, and no simultaneous accurate or complete system state available.

As an example of a decentralized control algorithm we will discuss the virtual ring algorithm. This could be used to test each node for its load level. Those exceeding their limit could ship out excess on the ring; those with spare capacity could take the jobs off and perform them. This is one version of a load balancing algorithm.

The virtual ring is composed of n cooperating servers formed into a virtual ring (circular server). In the virtual ring for each server si there exists a unique predecessor $\text{Spred}(i)$ and a successor $\text{Ssucc}(i)$. A single control token is on this ring. When a server receives the control token, it performs a task (in this case the load balancing job). When it completes its task, it passes the token on to its successor. If the token is lost, it is regenerated using some resolution algorithm.

If we were using this method for load balancing, the algorithm could be sketched as follows:

```
Load balance server_i;
   begin
   {initialize local data}
   while (active) do
   {received message from any node}

   R msg:= receive (any);
   case rmsg.tag of

   Local_request: {new job for this node i}
      begin
      {enter request into request queue;}
      enterQ (req_q, rmsg);

   token_arrival
      begin
      {determine state}
      if spare capacity and rmsg
```

```
        contains jobs to do then
        {extract job(s) and put in queue}
        else if capacity exceeded
        {shed work }
        temp:=dequeue {job};
        token out:= rmsg.token + temp;
        and if
        send_token (succ(server_i),token out);
    endcase;
    od;
end;
```

This is one of many decentralized control algorithms that could be applied to the load balancing problem. Other schemes include:

- Voting algorithms
- Best effort algorithms
- Transaction algorithms
- Byzantine generals

22.4   Scheduling

Scheduling is the system management component that controls what runs when and where. The policies of this function that provide this operation are the decision mode, priority function, and arbitration rules [Ruschitzka and Fabry, 1977].

The decision mode provides the policy to determine when a rescheduling occurs (i.e., nonpreemptive, preemptive, quantum-oriented, etc.). The priority function associated with a given algorithm uses system parameters to aid in computing and assigning priorities to jobs. The arbitration rule provides a policy to break ties or conflicts between jobs of equal measure. The mechanisms to realize these are broken up into two major classes: the binding mechanism and the invoking mechanism.

The binding mechanism relates to the policy functions defined above. That is, it defines how a scheduler determines when to schedule and where. For example, periodic and using first fit, random fit, best fit, or best-effort fit. The invoking mechanisms defines how the actual service is invoked at the determined site(s).

The scheduling problem for LANs is basically that of how to pick what job will run where and when. Scheduling in most systems works by planning to have sufficient resources available for the worst-case operation of processes. Therefore, when examining to see if an offered job can be added to a present load, the scheduler will look at its worst-case operation, add

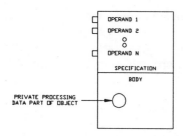

Figure 22.1 Arobject.

this into its present load, and determine if it can fit. If not, the job is either rejected or offered to another node for service. In any case, the computer system is asked to make a decision in order to manage the resources. These management decisions (scheduling) must be made on the basis of information regarding the state of the computation, the user requirements, and the goals to be achieved. In a LAN, communications of this information is slow relative to the rate of system state change. That is, the individual nodes' conditions will change faster than these changes can be propagated to all the nodes in the system. Therefore, the resulting system state information used on any node is inaccurate and incomplete.

Based on this fact we cannot expect that traditional scheduling mechanisms will work appropriately in LANs. Decisions for resource management must be made by best-effort means. That is, we must formulate solutions based on a fuzzy, incomplete view of what is going on. These solutions draw their basis from related research in nonmonotonic logic, fuzzy logic, Bayesian decision theory, and applied AI.

Nonmonotonic logic involves formal logic. Formal logic is based on three basic entitites:

- Axioms. They describe facts assumed to hold. Inference rules. They describe rules for the manipulation of the axioms.
- Theorems. They describe facts which may be deduced from axioms using the inference rules.

In nonmonotonic logic we can express new axioms that can negate previous deductions. Additionally we can use beliefs, conjectures, and probabilistically known information to assist in the decision process.

Fuzzy logic consists of rules for deducing the truth of statements defining fuzzy set membership, in which fuzzy sets are defined by predicates whose truth is known approximately (e.g., the set of young people). The

```
Aerobject Sample Specification
begin
    CToperation opr-name(arb,...)  => (result);
    EToperation opr-name(arg,...)  => (result);
    . . .

end;

arobject Sample body
begin
    var DataObject; –shared data objects among processes
    . . .

    process INITIAL();

    begin
        Accept(AnyOperation, ReqMsg);
        . . .
        result = DoComputation(ReqMsg);
        . . .
        Reply(Req.TrasId, result);

    end INITIAL;

    end Sample;
```

Figure 22.2 A skeleton of arobject declaration.

use of fuzzy set theory provides us with a way of describing the degree of membership of an element in a particular set.

Bagesian decision theory assumes that a decision must be made without knowledge of the state but that the probability of any particular state occurring is known.

Artificial intelligence mechanisms use best-effort decision mechanisms to evaluate available information, attempt to draw justifiable conclusions from this information, identify the most probable set of solutions from this, and, using this information, generate possible solutions and test them against goals (value to system) to provide the best decision based on the known information and rules.

These type techniques are now being applied to the solution of scheduling problems in LAN environments. We will not find many off the shelf

```
arobject ResourceMap specification
  begin
    CToperation GetResource()
      =>(ResourceId:integer,Status,Boolean);
    net effect:allocates one unit of resource and
      returnsitsresourceidand status
    EToperation ReleaseResource(ResourceId:integer)
      => (Status:boolean);
    net effect: releases the specified resource into
      the map as an allocatable resource.
    CompensationOpr CompGetResource(ResourceId:integer)
      for GetResource =¿(Status:boolean);
    net effect:ReleaseResource(ResourceId:integer)
      returns the specified resource into the
      map as an allocatable resource.
  end ResourceMap;
```

Figure 22.3 Resource map states and specifications.

products yet, but those that exist will continue to evolve towards these techniques.

Algorithms to perform this scheduling in LANS include:

- Guess fit
- Random fit
- First fit
- Best fit
- Best-effort fit

You can see by inspection that these are presented in order of complexity and optimality from simplest and lowest to most complex and optimal.

We will examine random, first, and best-effort fits. In random fit the scheduler acts in total isolation. It receives the request for service, generates a random number, and sends the schedule request (creation) to the corresponding resource manager. This algorithm does not concern itself with system load and therefore can be very unpredictable.

In the first fit scheduler, a request for creation is sent (a request to run this process) to all sites. The first site that responds with a "reasonable" bid for the job is assigned its operation. Reasonable refers to a site's ability to serve this job with adequate resources.

In the best-effort scheduler, we look at selecting a schedule based on a best guess of what is optimal for the system. This guess is based on present knowledge and past history of the run-time environment. The scheduler

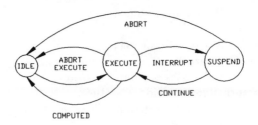

Figure 22.4 State transition diagram for arobjects.

attempts to schedule each process to maximize the total system value function. That is, the measure of optimality is that each process's completion "value" is taken into account in constructing a sequence of values that will provide the largest return to the system. That is, each process value function's (curve) density is computed by the selection of interactions that provide the most completions of these possible and within the highest possible densities (area of curves), we can construct fairly optimal schedules. Details can be found in Locke [1986].

22.5   Management of Resources

In LANs the important aspect of system management from the user view is that resources are available for use by their processes. Therefore, the important aspect of the operating system is how it manages resources for the users.

As an example of a mechanism for management of resources, the following example from Archos is described. The Archos system is based on the object-oriented paradigm. This model also makes the assumptions that

FLAG	RESOURCE ID	OWNER ID
0/1	R_1	O_i
0/1	R_2	O_j
$\vdots$		
0/1	R_N	O_k

Figure 22.5 Resource map.

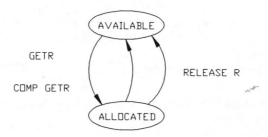

GETR

COMP GETR

RELEASE R

Figure 22.6 State migration.

these objects need not be located at a single node; there is no master-slave relationship between a caller and callee, invocation of operations on objects can be performed at any node, and operations can be invoked concurrently by creating separate processes.

The principal components of Archos is a set of arobjects (objects). These consist of a specification (set of operations) and a body (private data objects, atomic data objects, permanent data objects, normal data objects, processes) (see Figure 22.1).

The Archos operating system uses the concept of transaction to control the interaction of arobjects in the system. As such all operations are controlled via the transactionlike interaction of their operations on the arobjects. This is analogous to the database transaction with its serializable actions and noninterfering operations on the controlled data items. The transaction processing facility provides the commands for transactions and locks. The transaction management operations are:

SelfTid () => mytid   Returns its own transaction id.

ParentTid (tid) => parent-tid   Returns its parents transaction id.

AbortTransaction (tid) => status   Aborts the specified transaction and its children.

TransactionType (tid) => transaction-type   Returns a type of transaction.

IsCommittee (tid) => status   Checks whether the specific transaction is committed or not.

IsAborted (tid) => status   Checks whether the specific transaction is aborted or not.

The lock management operations are:

SetLock(ObjectName, lock-mode)   Obtains a lock for the specific object; returns true if the lock is obtained.

TestandSetLock(ObjectName, lock-mode)   If the specific lock for
the object is not held then obtains it and returns true; otherwise
returns false.
IsLocked(ObjectName, lock-mode)   If the specific lock for the
object is held, returns true; otherwise false.
ReleaseLock(ObjectName, lock-mode)   Releases the lock on the
specific object.

All objects in the system migrate through three states: idle, execute,
suspend (see Figure 22.4). These provide for the transaction states and
transitions necessary to provide the interactions wanted.

Using this as a model, we can build any type of resource manager we
wish. As an example, we show a resource map in Figure 22.5. This shows
how the system can provide objects to manage a group of resources. The
resources exist as a set of resource IDs and owners along with their state.
The resources can migrate from state available to allocated as shown in
Figure 22.6 using the GetR, releaseR, or comp Get$ commands as specified
in Figure 22.3.

What this shows is a way, through using the object model, in which
resource managers can be constructed.

Details and further references for constructing operating systems and
resource managers for distributed computer systems can be found in Fortier
[1986].

22.6   Summary

This chapter addressed various technology issues related to the construction
of systems management policies and mechanisms for local area networks.
Included were concepts for developing management styles for LANs, what
constitutes various styles, the basic building blocks of managers (client-
server model), and various examples of components of operating systems
for LANs. These represent the "core" elements of a LAN operating system,
though they do not represent a complete compilation. Other important aspects include data management system monitoring, fault isolation, recovery
management, and many other topics that are out of the intended context
of this chapter. These issues are addressed in other texts and papers in the
specific areas.

22.7   References

Fortier, P. J., *Design of Distributed Operating Systems: Concepts and
Technology*, Intertext, Inc., McGraw-Hill, New York, 1986.

Locke, E. D., "Time-Driven Scheduling for Real-Time Systems," *IEEE Computer Society Workshop on Real-Time Operating Systems*, Boston, February 1986.

Ruschitzka and Fabry, "A Unifying Approach to Scheduling," *Communications of the ACM*, vol. 20, no. 8, 1977.

Schantz, R., et al., "Cronus, a Distributed Operating System," *ACM Operating Systems Review*, vol. 15, no. 3, July 1981, pp. 51-73.

Tanenbaum, A. S., "An Overview of the Ameoba Distributed Operating System," *ACM Operating Systems Review*, vol. 15, no. 3, July 1981, pp. 51-73.

Tokuda, H., "Shoshin: A Distributed Software Testbed," Ph.D. dissertation, University of Waterloo, Ontario, Canada, 1983.

Tsay, D., "Mike - A Network Operating System for the Distributed Double Loop Computer Network," Ph.D. dissertation, Ohio State, 1981.

PART EIGHT
Examination of LANs in Use

23. Elements of Local Area Network Architecture

This section examines some of the commercial and special-purpose local area networks that are in use today. The networks to be discussed here span a wide range of intended application areas from low-speed personal computer links to high-capacity, real-time, space-based communication systems. Before looking at specific implementations, however, let's establish the criteria under which we will view the different implementations and review some of the basic LAN concepts which are germane to the networks considered in this section. These criteria are discussed here so that the reader can develop an appreciation for the subtle terms and techniques which can differentiate seemingly identical networks.

The view of networking taken in this chapter is admittedly simplistic in that it overlooks many important issues such as network addressing, routing, monitoring, end-to-end service protocols, and security. Rather than take the more comprehensive treatment of networking issues, the emphasis has been placed on those issues that will allow the nonexpert to compare and evaluate different network implementations for a particular application. For those who would like more details on the topics discussed in this chapter, the references provide an excellent source of additional information.

23.1 The Question of Topology

In a discussion of LAN interconnection, the question of physical versus logical topologies should be addressed. The physical topology of a system refers to the pattern of interconnection formed by the actual connecting medium. Logical topology, on the other hand, refers to the picture you

445

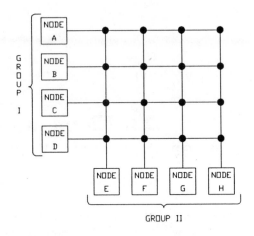

Figure 23.1   A 4-by-4 crossbar switch connecting two processing groups.

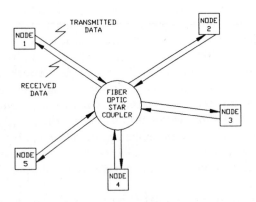

Figure 23.2   Logical bus topology implemented using star wiring and a star coupler.

would get if you drew the possible connection paths between the various communicating nodes in a network. For some types of networks, the physical and logical topology are identically described. For example, the use of the crossbar switch shown in Figure 23.1 gives a precise definition of which nodes may connect to which. Other system configurations are more deceptive as to their actual logical configuration. The technology currently used in fiber optic communications, for instance, allows only point-to-point links without any intermediate tap points along the way. In order to implement a logical bus using this medium, a fiber optic star (which splits the light from a channel and sends it down several other channels) is used; hence an apparent contradiction in interconnection terms. Figure 23.2 illustrates this concept.

23.2   Elements of a Protocol Discussion

To discuss the characteristics of a LAN, the type and implementation of its protocol must be addressed. Several issues which characterize protocols are important. Among the most telling of these are the contention access mechanism that controls the electrical connectivity to the communication medium, the next level access methods that control which of the network nodes gets to transmit data, the limits on message and/or packet size on the network, the handling of retransmission and error conditions, and the dependency of the protocol on the physical network topology. Each of these issues is discussed in the following paragraphs to set the stage for the discussion of specific network implementations later in the chapter.

Discussions of contention access schemes can vary from low-level hardware schemes such as the DOT-OR method to higher-level software schemes of virtually any level of complexity. In any case, the contention mechanism, if present in a network design, does much to define the order and type of access that can be achieved. Most contention mechanisms fall into level two of the ISO protocol model. Since contention mechanisms control access to the physical medium, the analysis of network response time and access fairness will concentrate on this area of the protocol. For example, priorities for the various nodes and messages in a LAN can be used as an input to the contention access mechanism, an important consideration when designing real-time networks. Also, contention mechanisms define portions of the performance characteristics of a LAN and, hence, are important when arriving at reliable predictions of network response time and throughput under specific conditions.

Lastly, the complexity of the contention access method directly affects the complexity and level of implementation of the network interface unit for a particular LAN. For example, the IEEE 802.3 protocol standard requires a collision detection mechanism that must be implemented in the front-end

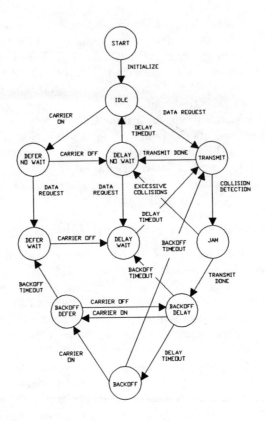

Figure 23.3 Simplified state transition diagram for the CSMA/CD protocol.

hardware of the network interface components in order to ensure the timely detection of a collision situation.

On top of the contention protocol layer—if the contention layer does indeed exist for the LAN under consideration—are the "next level" access layers. As with contention access methods, these mechanisms generally fall into the data-link layer of the ISO model. The characterizing features of protocol discussions on this level are mainly the transfer of blocks of information between two network stations. This layer generally performs the detection of errors at the physical (ISO level one) layer and often provides an error recovery scheme such as retransmission. The elements of the protocol that are important here are the meanings of the bits on the physical medium, the control signals made up of special bit patterns, and the sequences of control patterns as they appear on the transmission medium.

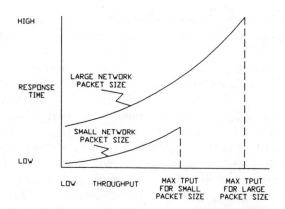

Figure 23.4 Typical response time versus throughput curve.

The specific implementation details at this level are often expressed in a state transition diagram. As an example, the state transition diagram for the transmit part of the CSMA/CD protocol is shown in Figure 23.3.

Limits on message or packet sizes directly affect network performance in the areas of response time, network efficiency (the percent usable traffic as compared to total traffic), and utilization (the percentage of the total available network bandwidth that is usable for data transmission). Response time can be defined as the interval between the message ready signal from the host and the message accepted for transfer signal from the network interface unit. Response time can also be defined at the network interface unit as the time from a ready-to-transmit state until actual message transmission. This measure is often specified on a packet basis and is more meaningful when expressed this way because a message may consist of many packets, and the response time of the initial packet can create a deceptively good message response time. Also, as the ratio of network overhead to packet size on the network decreases, the throughput of the network increases. Unfortunately, an increase in packet size may also mean an increase in average response time. Thus, network protocol designs must maintain a balance between throughput and response time as appropriate for the network's intended application. Figure 23.4 illustrates the response time versus throughput for the general case.

In any LAN implementation, transmission errors will occur with some nonzero probability. Admittedly, the chance of a network error may be small, but its occurrence may place the network into a state that can only be recovered from by a reset. It is desirable to avoid this, however, since the error condition would require human intervention, which is both costly and time consuming. Some level of error detection is, therefore, usually necessary.

There are many potential sources of error in a local area network. Wire transmission media is susceptible to electro-magnetic fields, and perturbations of transmitted data can occur. Fiber optic cables may suffer from attenuation caused by misaligned connectors or failure of send-receive optical components. Digital information errors resulting from memory errors can cause anomalies in transmitted data. Combinations of the above may result in unanticipated situations that are not specifically dealt with in the protocol. In order to protect against these anomalies, most protocols rely on some sort of error recognition and recovery activity. Some of the most commonly used techniques for error detection include the check summing of data blocks on the network, transmission feedback and comparison (such as the collision detect mechanism of Ethernet), and error detecting and correcting codes (for highly reliable systems). Corrective actions occupy a range of possibilities from packet level retransmission to redundant data paths to error-correcting circuitry. These facilities, therefore, perform an important role in the operation of any LAN.

As mentioned earlier (the question of topology), certain topological factors affect the choice of applicable protocols. The reverse situation, the influence on the topology by the choice of a particular access protocol, also occurs. The CSMA/CD protocol, for example, must be implemented on a medium in which every node hears every transmission. Ring protocols such as the IEEE 802.5 token ring rely upon the fact that a repeater mechanism (register insertion) is available so that the control token can be recognized and altered as it passes a station. Master-slave types of implementations may rely on a hierarchical structure of communicating nodes. The important point in all of this is that the various technologies and protocol techniques can often dictate other portions of a LAN's design. It is important, therefore, to understand these interrelationships so that careful consideration can be given to each design decision. Even the order in which design decisions are made becomes important if initial choices impose rigid requirements on subsequent ones. We will see some examples in which the desire to use certain technologies has directed, and sometimes limited, the design of other system components.

Summarizing, we can see that a discussion of the protocol features of any particular LAN involves considerably more than just the access mechanisms. In the discussions of specific LANs and implementations that appear in Chapter 24, an attempt is made to highlight some of the more novel approaches of protocol use where they appear.

23.3   Performance Characteristics Comparisons

One question frequently asked when discussing the merits of any local area network implementation is: How fast is it? Perhaps the most standard and misleading reply to this is the basic data rate of the medium. For example, the Digital/Intel/Xerox (DIX) Ethernet LAN is specified at a 10-Mbps data rate although the actual amount of message traffic that it can carry is much less than that. In fact, it is often difficult to give a specific number for the actual message-carrying capacity of a network because of the different operating conditions and total applied load. It is useful, therefore, to discuss network performance in several different ways. The basic measures of performance that will be applied to the network implementations discussed in this chapter will include the basic signaling rate of the medium, the raw capacity of the medium in a particular configuration, the effect of the protocol on the network performance under various loading scenarios, and the impact on performance because of packet or message size.

The definition of the basic signaling rate for a LAN is simply the clock speed at which transitions on the physical medium can take place. This measure is usually expressed in megahertz (MHz) and is representative of the absolute upper bound on data transmission speed.

If every transition on the medium could represent a single bit of information, the basic data rate and the signaling rate would be equal. This situation, however, assumes that there is also a clocking signal that is sent along with the data to maintain synchronization between sender and receiver. While this may be true for some network implementations, it is not usually the case since it requires additional conductors or conduits to carry the clock information. A more common method involves the incorporation of clocking information into the data stream, thereby making the transmitted data "self-clocking." One such scheme is the Manchester encoding method. Another is the 4B/5B scheme. The Manchester scheme is 50 percent efficient in that half of the available bandwidth is used for timing information. Thus, a system with a 10-MHz signaling rate would have a maximum data rate of 5 Mbps using Manchester encoding. The Manchester technique is discussed later in the chapter. For the 4B/5B scheme, four (information) are encoded into a 5-bit code to achieve an 80 percent efficiency for data transfer. The same 10-MHz network, using the 4B/5B scheme, would achieve an 8-Mbps maximum data transfer rate. The 4B/5B encoding scheme is also explained later in the chapter.

Another interesting and important measure of network performance is the calculation of the maximum use of a particular network implementation. This calculation is based on the propagation speed of a signal on the network

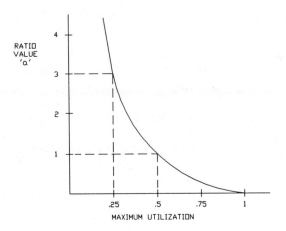

Figure 23.5 Ratio value a versus maximum use.

and the length of a data packet. The following calculations are based on those given in Stallings [1984].

The maximum use is defined as the maximum usable portion of the available network bandwidth. Maximum use is calculated as a function of the bit length of the network (the number of bits in transmission on the network at any given instance in time), the maximum signaling rate of the network (in MHz), the propagation speed of a signal on the medium, and the packet size. The bit length of the medium is defined as follows:

$$\text{bit length (bits)} \; = \; \frac{(\text{length of medium } (m))(\text{signaling rate (bps)})}{\text{propagation speed } \left(\frac{m}{s}\right)}$$

Next, a measure of the fraction of a message that is in transit at any one time (a) is given as:

$$a(\%) \; = \; \frac{\text{bit length (bits)}}{\text{packet size (bits)}}$$

Finally, the maximum use is given as:

$$\text{maximum use } (\%) \; = \; \frac{1}{(1 + a)}$$

Intuitively, this measure says that if the ratio of bit length to packet size remains small, there is effectively little "dead time" after a message transmission when compared to the total time required for the packet. Dead time is loosely defined as the time between the completion of a message transmission onto the medium and the reception of the final bit at the receiver. As an example, let us assume that we have a typical network (10-MHz signaling rate, 500-m length and 2E8-m/s propagation speed) which has a bit length of 25 bits. Further assume that the packet size on the network is 1K bytes (8K bits). The ratio of bit length to packet size is 0.00305 and the maximum use of the network is 99.6 percent. Thus, for a 10-MHz signaling rate on a LAN with the above characteristics, the maximum data rate that can be achieved is 99.6 percent of 10 MHz, or 9.96 MHz. Now let's see what happens if we increase the ratio of bit length to packet size by using a packet size of 64 bytes. The ratio value a becomes 0.0488 and the maximum use drops to 95.3 percent. Figure 23.5 shows a plot of the ratio value a versus the maximum use. From this plot we can see that approximately two-thirds of the total area is contained within the space defined by the values $0 <= a <= 3$. For $0 <= a <= 1$, there is almost one-third of the total area under the curve. These measures indicate that the value of a must increase dramatically to yield a maximum use of under 50 percent. In fact, most of the networks that we will examine will exhibit maximum use of 95 to 100 percent. Keep in mind, however, that this upper limit on use does not account for further bandwidth loss caused by the encoding schemes mentioned above. For the first example (99.6 percent maximum use), the actual data rate using Manchester encoding would be half of the maximum data rate, or 4.98 Mbps.

Another characteristic that is useful for catagorizing and discussing local area networks is the method used to actually modulate the data onto the transmission medium. There are two methods of accomplishing this: baseband (sometimes called carrier band) and broadband (also called wideband) transmission. Both of these techniques apply equally well to fiber as to wire transmission media. It is important to note here that the choice of protocol is a separate issue which is not affected by the transmission technique. Baseband transmission in a LAN refers to the practice of applying the unmodulated signal directly to the transmission medium. In this case, a transition on the line actually represents a bit of information (which could be encoded by one of the methods mentioned earlier).

Baseband-type transmission systems can be implemented on virtually any type of transmission cable (twisted pair, coaxial, fiber) and usually support a basic signaling rate in the 10-MHz range. In contrast, broadband communication uses a high-frequency (approximately 300 MHz) coaxial or fiber optic cable as a frequency multiplexed transmission medium. The basic digital data that forms the LAN communication packets is modulated onto a carrier signal within a specified frequency range. In this arrangement, LAN communications are usually mixed in with other types

454   Handbook of LAN Technology

of transmissions (voice, video, or even other LANs) using separate carrier
frequencies.

The local area networks we will examine will employ a variety of the
above techniques in both homogeneous and heterogeneous fashion. In fact,
the consistency of use of either broadband or baseband transmission techniques often determines the degree of interoperability of different networks
using the same protocol.

23.4   Interfacing with the Network

Once we have the lower-level protocols and communication medium in
place, a suitable access method for user program interface is required. There
are basically three types of interface possible: memory based, direct access,
and executive service requests. These three options are discussed below.

Memory-based network interfaces operate on the concept of using shared
memory as a common repository for message and control information. A
typical network setup using this kind of host to interface unit communication has three main components: the message memory buffer area, the
transmission control information area, and the reception control information area.

The first of these components, the message buffer area, is where outgoing
messages are built by the host and where incoming messages are dumped
by the interface unit. The management of this buffer area must be such
that the integrity of message data that is stored there is preserved. The
situation in which good message data is overwritten before it is used by
either the host or interface unit must be prevented. This protection is
usually provided through the use of a buffer pool that contains pointers to
chunks of memory that are available for outgoing and incoming message use.
The buffer pool is maintained on a list which is either controlled centrally
by the host (using a request and allocate scheme) or maintained in tandem
by the host and the interface unit through a semaphore mechanism.

Other methods typically associated with memory management by traditional operating systems are also quite suitable for providing message buffer
management. The critical issue in the management of any type of buffer
scheme is to ensure the availability of buffer space for incoming messages. If
no space is available upon message reception, either older message data will
be overwritten or the new data will be lost. The lack of buffer memory for
an outgoing message is not as critical, as the impact is usually experienced
as a delay rather than lost data. Even with interface units that provide
internal buffering, some scheme such as this is needed to provide overflow
storage.

The second portion of a memory-based network access scheme is the
transmission control information area. A typical implementation of this

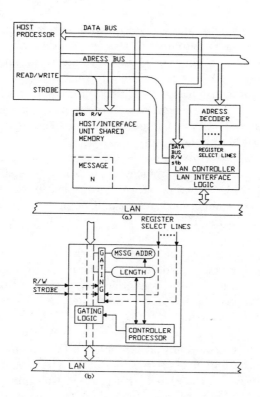

Figure 23.6 (a) Host-LAN controller interface and (b) controller block diagram.

portion of the communication service is done using what are called transmission control buffers (TCBs). These buffers contain information such as the location of the message data in the buffer memory, the length of the message, the destination address of the message, the sending process ID, the message priority, the limit on the number of retries, and whether or not an acknowledgement of message transmission is required from the receiver.

The TCB is built by the sending process and passed along to the interface unit after the message has been located in the message buffer memory area. The network interface unit then uses this information as control parameters to effect message transmission. As with the message buffer management scheme, TCB access must also be controlled. The methods used for message buffer management are appropriate here also.

The third component of a memory-based host-interface unit access method is called the reception control information area. This function is typically implemented using a mechanism called a reception control buffer

(RCB). A RCB contains information similar in nature to that contained in the TCB, such as message source ID, message length, error indicators, time of reception, address of message in buffer memory, message priority, and destination process ID. The RCBs are filled in by the interface unit upon message reception and released to the host processor. As with the buffer memory and TCB management, care must be taken to avoid conflicts in RCB allocation and access. Of course, the methods used for buffer and TCB management apply here.

The underlying principle for all three of these components, buffer memory and TCB and RCB management, is the ability to manage and share pieces of memory. One method of implementation for this requirement is through the use of a buffer queue containing pointers to the actual memory buffers, TCBs or RCBs. Figure 23.6 shows the use of this scheme for buffer memory TCB and RCB management.

The second type of commonly used network access method is the direct access method. For this type of interface, the host and interface unit have a master-slave relationship. The interface processor is hooked to the host as a memory mapped or I/O device would be. Communication with the controller, then, is accomplished through the use of host address decoding to several registers that reside in the NIU interface hardware. Typically, these registers contain information that is similar to that found in the transmit and receive control buffers of the memory-based interface. The information for the set of registers associated with message transmission includes the message address in memory, the length of the message, and an address for the return of transmission status to the host.

On the receive side, the information deposited by the host in the controller reception registers would include the address into which the interface unit can deposit the message. On the interface unit side, the controller would be expected to supply the received message length, a reception status, indicators as to the nature of the message (e.g., point to point, broadcast, directed broadcast) and possibly some status on the general health of the transmission link. Figure 23.6 shows a block diagram which is typical for this type of implementation.

In operation, this type of interface is somewhat simpler than the memory-based scheme because there is no need for the memory-based semaphore lock on transmit and receive control buffer areas. Instead, the hardware associated with I/O access on the host to interface bus acts to arbitrate the contention for the register resources. To orchestrate the transmit and receive sequence with the associated status and message information return from the interface unit, either a polling or interrupt scheme can be used. In polling, the host periodically checks the status registers of the interface unit by issuing a normal I/O read. The results of this operation are then

```
transmit$message$interface: procedure (mssg$address,mssg$lngth,
  mssg$priority..other parameters) public;

   /* check to make sure that the interface is free */
   if not(input(IO$command$reg) = transmitting) then
   begin
      output(xmit$address$reg) := mssg$address;
      output(xmit$lnght$reg) := mssg$lngth;
      output(xmit$priority$reg) := mssg$priority;

      .
      .
      /* other implementation specific information */

      .
      .
      /* enable transmission */
      /* the 'transmitting' flag is reset by the */
      /* interface unit after transmission is complete */
      output(xmit$command$reg) := xmit$enable;

      /* indicate a message transmission is in progress */
      xmit$in$progress$flag := true;
      /* enable the status return interrupt */
      enable status$int;
   end;
end transmit$message$interface;



transmit$status$handler: procedure interrupt status$int public;
   transmit$status := input(xmit$status$reg);
   xmit$in$progress$flag := false;

   .
   .
   /* other housekeeping code */

   .
   .
end transmit$status$handler;
```

Figure 23.7 Interrupt-driven host transmission interface (in PL/M-style code).

```
receive$mssg$interface:  procedure interrupt receive$int public;
incoming$mssg$address := input(receive$address$reg);
message$status := input(receive$status$reg);
message$priority := input(mssg$priority$reg);
.
.
.
/* other reception parameters */
.
.
.
end receive$message$interface;
enable$message$reception:  procedure(mssg$buffer$address) public;
/* tell NIU where to put an incoming message */
output(receive$address$reg) := mssg$buffer$address;
/* enable the message reception interrupt */
enable(receive$int);
end enable$message$reception;
```

Figure 23.8   Interrupt-driven host reception interface (in PL/M-style code).

interpreted to determine the action to be taken. For interrupt-driven systems, the specific interrupt or interrupt vector word directs the host to the appropriate interface service routine. In either the polled or interrupt-driven case, the completion of a transmit-status or receive-accept message cycle is indicated by the host action of reading or writing one of the control registers.

For transmission, the first read access of a valid status register would typically signal the end of a transmission cycle. Here, a valid status is one which pertains to the most recently transferred message. For reception, the act of supplying a new reception buffer address indicates the completion of a reception cycle. Figure 23.7 shows a sample implementation of interrupt-driven transmit and transmission status routines. Figure 23.8 shows the interrupt-driven message reception routines. These routines would execute in the host processor and form part of the host side of the host-NIU interface for a direct access interface.

The third type of network interface to be discussed here is that which uses executive service requests. This type of network access is useful in implementing higher-level communication protocols such as Ada-style rendezvous and CSP-style [Hoare, 1978] input and output commands. Certain mechanisms impose restrictions on the lower-level connection implementa-

RECEIVE SIDE

		single		multiple	
		wait	no-wait	wait	no-wait
S E N D	S I N G L E				
S E N D		wait	A	B	A	B
S E N D		no-wait	B	C	B	B
S I D E	M U L T I P L E				
S I D E		wait	A	B	A	B
S I D E		no-wait	B	C	B	C

Figure 23.9 Communication classes for the executive service request type of communication interface.

tions. CSP, for example, implies a message-based interconnection which makes it appropriate for use in a distributed system implementation but which also imposes a certain style of network usage. The Ada-style task synchronization mechanisms use a hybrid interconnection model which takes a message-based approach on the output side and a shared memory paradigm on the input side.

The various interconnection models can be specified in terms of a kind of generic set of higher-level network access facilities. Although many variations are possible on this basic set of primitives, those discussed below are those found in many existing systems. There are actually two aspects to this problem, that associated with the waiting to send or receive a message and that which arises when the same communication involves several parties. Figure 23.9 shows a range of options that may be available for higher-level network access commands. In this figure, the single identifier indicates that the sender or receiver consists of only one logical process. Contrasting this is the multiple case which indicates a broadcast type of send operation and a logical sink process for a receive operation. Waiting for a send or receive operation implies a synchronization of the communicating processes with the underlying message transfer service, thus, a process that waits for a communication block until the action actually occurs. A process specifying the no-wait type of communication would simply check some sort of indicator that contains information on the availability of the network service. A busy indication does not block the inquiring process; it simply queues the process request or requires that the process try again at a later time.

The various combinations of wait and no-wait and single and multiple message participant types results in different situations in terms of perfor-

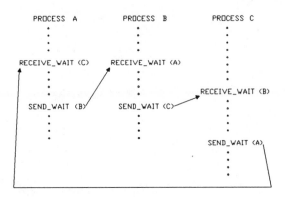

Figure 23.10 Deadlock of three communicating processes.

mance and complexity of the interface mechanism. Also, some combinations are not easily implemented on certain types of lower-level protocols. The following paragraphs discuss the usefulness, restrictions, and problems associated with the various classes of interface access methods. In Figure 23.9, the letters within the matrix indicate the class of communication session that is created when choosing the corresponding row and column entries. Single message indicates that there is only one sender or receiver of the message (i.e., the physical source or destination field contains the identifier for a single, uniquely identified process). Multiple messages, on the other hand, are either of the directed broadcast type (a message to a class or group of processes) or of the collection node type (multiple messages directed to a single receiver).

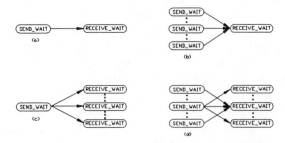

Figure 23.11 Fully syncronized communications. (a) One to one, (b) N to one, (c) one to N, and (d) N to N.

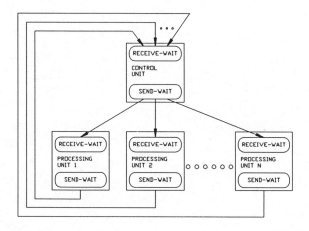

Figure 23.12 Fully synchronized communication in a parallel processor.

Class A communication as shown in Figure 23.9 is referred to as fully synchronized. In this case, a process executing a send or receive type of message is blocked until the other communicating process executes the receive or send counterpart. The benefit of this type of facility is that two communicating processes can be forced to synchronize (to a tolerance which is limited by the time it takes to get a message through the network) at prespecified execution points. One danger in this type of service is the possibility of deadlock of the communicating processes because of process failure or resource limitations. Figure 23.10 illustrates the deadlock of three communicating process. Deadlock is possible when two or more processes are waiting for corresponding messages in a predecessor-successor fashion. Then there is a circular dependency among the processes. In the figure, no process can proceed beyond it's corresponding receive command until the corresponding sends are executed. The sends, however, are conditioned by the execution of the preceeding receive commands, thus deadlock occurs.

Figure 23.11 shows the various combinations of single and multiple send-receive operations for fully synchronized communication. Figure 23.11b and c shows one to N (or N to one) multipoint synchronization. Here, a single sender or receiver and N receivers or senders all use the wait type of communication operators. The involved processes are synchronized when all of them have executed their corresponding communication operations. All processes, therefore, come together at a common point and are then released simultaneously (to a time within the network communication delay time). This type of communication is useful for controlling multiple, cooperating

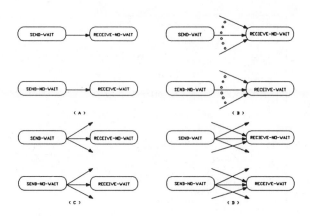

Figure 23.13 One-sided synchronization. (a) One to one, (b) N to one, (c) one to N, and (d) N to N.

processes that work on parts of a problem in parallel and then synchronize to combine the partial solutions into a whole. Figure 23.12 illustrates this operation for an N-processor multiprocessor. In the figure, the controller executes a single send-wait with the operation to be performed on the local data of each of the processors. Each processor executes a receive-wait for the reception of this operation command. After the computation is completed, each of the N processors uses a send-wait to the controller with the results of the partial computation. The controller handles these messages with a single receive-wait command. Thus, the entire multiprocessor operates in lock step for each interation on a set of N data items.

The final facet (N to N) of fully synchronized communication is shown in Figure 23.11d. Actually, this option is a combination of the one to N and N to one cases. All communicating processes executing wait-type operations must have the corresponding operations performed before execution can resume. As the other communication classes are introduced, note that arbitrarily complex communication and synchronization schemes can be constructed by combining the various high-level operators of Figure 23.9.

Class B communication is referred to as "one-sided synchronization." In this form, one of the communicating entities uses a wait type of operation and the other uses a nonwait type. Synchronization of two processes using class B communication occurs at the time when both communicating processes are present at the communication interface. Figure 23.13 shows the possible configurations for one-sided synchronization. As an example, a sender using a send-wait operation will block until the receiver executes a receive-no-wait command. At that time, the sender is freed and may proceed with its processing. Thus the sender knows when the receiver reaches the synchronization point. This communication class is useful for situations in which the unsynchronized process (the one using the no-wait operation) cannot afford to block for synchronization. This process, then, can periodically issue a no-wait command and use the returned status to control further processing.

For one-sided, N-to-one (or one-to-N) synchronization, the process executing the wait type of command will block until all of the corresponding processes have executed their companion operations. Figures 23.13b and 23.13c illustrate this communication class. In Figure 23.13b, two situations are depicted. In the first, the sender is blocked until the receive command is executed. The receiver, however, is not blocked because a no-wait operation is being used. The information generated here is the same as for the one-sided, one-to-one case: the sender knows when the receiver has reached a certain program execution point. The second situation shows a sender using a no-wait operation and the receiver using a wait operation. In this case, the receiver will block until all of its input messages have been received. The sender will not block at any time. When the receiver becomes unblocked, it knows that each of the sending processes has reached a given execution point.

One-sided, one-to-N communication is depicted in Figure 23.13c. A blocked sender (waiting) in this scenario will remain blocked until all accompanying receives have been performed. The sender, therefore, has to wait for N processes to each reach their desired states. A blocked receiver, however, only needs its one sender process to complete the synchronization (see the second case of Figure 23.13c).

The N-to-N case of process synchronization with N blocked receivers and N nonwaiting senders is the same as for the N-to-one case for N blocked receivers and a single, nonwaiting sender (Figure 23.13b). In both cases, the blocked receiver is waiting for input from N senders, at least one of which is executing a no-wait type of send operation. For the case of N to N with a blocked sender and a nonwaiting receiver, the situation is similar to that of one blocked sender to N free receivers (Figure 23.13b). Thus, one-sided, N-to-N synchronization satisfies the same conditions as for N-to-one and one-to-N synchronization, but it involves more processes. By examining Figure 23.13d in comparison to Figure 23.13b and c, one can see the similarities.

Class C communication, unsynchronized, occurs when there are two or more nonwaiting processes executing send and receive operations. Using this type of service, the sending process drops off its message at the communication point (with the send operation) and continues processing. On

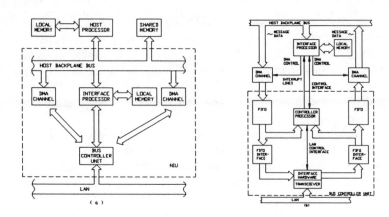

Figure 23.14 (a) Basis structure of a node and (b) block diagram of the NIU.

the receiver side, a receive operation is executed periodically to check for an incoming message. If no message is present, the receiving process simply continues performing other tasks. When the reception poll indicates a message has been received, the appropriate reception operations are performed. This type of communication is useful for applications in which the relationship between communicating processes is incidental (i.e., the communication does not in any way control or precondition the execution of the involved processes). An electronic mail system is an example of an application in which this type of communication service would be useful because the operations of sending and receiving mail can be independent. The arrival of a correspondence does not necessitate an immediate action by the receiver, and reading one's mail can be done periodically or when a threshold on the number of messages has been exceeded. Thus, the two systems can operate independently and autonomously if mechanisms are in place to provide intermediate storage of transaction data.

This concludes the overview of some of the basic principles and techniques used in network implementations. With this setting, we will now look at some existing and proposed networks. These examinations are difficult to conduct at a consistent level because different networks offer (and advertise) a wide variety of services and capabilities. Also, some of the networks to be discussed are end-user products with a full range of communication support while others are bare bones, experimental systems. Nevertheless, a broad spectrum of network systems will be scrutinized, from low-speed office-oriented systems to high-speed fault-tolerant networks for scientific and military use.

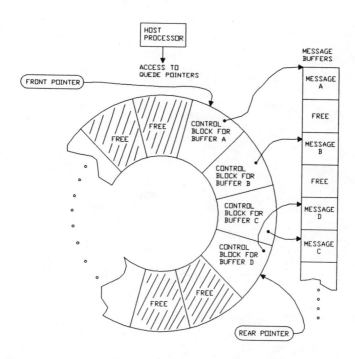

Figure 23.15 Circular queue buffer management scheme.

23.5   Research Token Bus

This section is included as an in-depth example of the implementation of a network interface unit (NIU). The NIU is composed of two processors, the bus controller and the interface processor, which implement the lower three levels of the ISO model. Attached to the NIU is a host processor which implements levels four and five of the ISO model. The LAN, to which the NIU is attached and implements the protocol, is a Manchester encoded token bus that operates over a coaxial cable at speeds up to 1 Mbps. The following section will discuss the implementation and function of each of the three NIU components, the bus controller, the interface processor, and the host. Figure 23.14a gives the overall structure of a node on the bus. Figure 23.14b illustrates the components which comprise an NIU.

The bus controller unit of the NIU contains a microcontroller and some special-purpose hardware to perform bus-specific functions. In Figure 23.14 dotted lines are used to outline the configuration of the control unit. The major responsibility of the bus control unit is to manage all functions associated with the physical use of the transmission medium. This includes

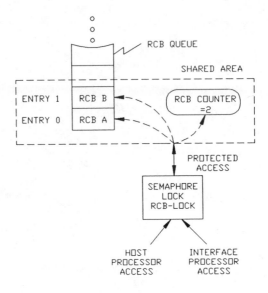

Figure 23.16 Reception control block interface.

protocol handling (token generation and recognition), message recognition, error detection (parity and Manchester code), data encoding, message status generation, and transfer of message data to and from the interface processor. These responsibilities are allocated to the various pieces of the controller as shown in Figure 23.14. The bus controller and interface processor interface consists of a set of I/O-addressed registers for the transfer of specific information such as DMA starting address, message length, and message status. The bus controller processor polls the incoming registers for information from the interface processor while the reverse path (from the bus controller to the interface unit) is interrupt driven.

The interface processor is responsible for controlling the message interface between the host and the NIU. The main functions that are necessary to perform this job are the programming of DMA devices to transfer message data between the host and NIU, the monitoring and control of the bus controller's operation, message-flow monitoring, and transport-level error checking and status reporting.

In the host processor, network software provides the functions necessary for message packetizing and unpacketizing and the management of message and control buffer memory. Also, procedures which allow application processes to access the network are provided.

host_RCB-interface: procedure interrupt RCB_int public;
    /* wait for the interface processor */
    /* to release the semaphore and then acquire it */
    do while lockset(@RCB_lock,1);
    end;
    /* fill in the empty RCB queue rear locations */
    /* if there are less than 2 RCBs left in the queue */
    do while RCB_count ¡ 2 and RCB_available
    /* get new RCB from buffer manager */
    call buff_manager (@new_RCB);
    /* add RCB to the queue and update */
    /* the RCB counter */
    RCB_que(RCB_count) := new_RCB;
    RCB_count := RCB_count + 1;
    end;
    /* release the semaphore lock */
    RCB_lock := 0;
    /* enable interrupts and return to interrupted processing */
    enable;
    return;
end host_RCB_interface;

Figure 23.17 Host sides of the RCB interface.

To illustrate the interaction between the host and the NIU, the following section discusses the implementation and operation of the host-NIU interface. The interface is memory based and the terminology used to describe it is consistent with that used in Section 23.5.

The circular buffer scheme for message buffer use in the research token bus is set up such that the host processor manages the creation and deletion of buffers (see Figure 23.15). A portion of the available shared memory is segmented into pieces of contiguous storage (usually of a constant size). The circular buffer itself contains pointers to chunks of memory that have been set aside for message buffer use. Two additional pointers, queue front and queue rear, keep track of the next available buffer and the last available buffer. The entries between the two pointers (inclusively) contain pointers to available message memory buffers for use in transmission or reception. For transmission, the host process acquires a message memory buffer from the queue and then updates the queue front pointer by one toward the rear of the queue. The message is then built in the acquired buffer by the host process. The number of buffers available for use in the message buffer pool can be dynamically adjusted by the host. All that is required is a notification of the new queue length to the host's buffer acquisition routines. After a message has been built in the buffer, a TCB must be acquired and filled in by the host process. A pool of available TCBs is managed by the host exactly as for message buffers. It is necessary, however, to protect the ready TCBs from simultaneous access by both the host and interface processor's processes. To accomplish this, an additional queue, the work queue, is maintained to provide a pipeline of available work to the interface processor. The ideal implementation for this interface would be a FIFO mechanism, wherby the host would feed TCBs into one end where they would flow down the pipe and be removed by the interface processor at the other.

Since we are dealing with a memory-based scheme, however, pointers to the data versus the actual data itself are what "flows." TCBs containing ready messages for transmission are placed in the rear of the work queue by the host and taken out of the front of the work queue by the interface processor. Figure 23.16 shows the corresponding situation for the RCB interface. The action of adding or removing from the work queue includes the contention for a controlling semaphore and access to the work queue front pointer. The essential feature of this technique is that once the host releases the TCB into the work queue, it is available for use by the interface processor. The case for the management and control of RCBs between the host and interface processor is identical. Available RCBs must be generated and maintained in a pool by the host, and they must be ready for use when needed by the interface processor. The critical data section (where data is shared by the host and interface processor) is that section of memory in which the count of available buffers and the actual queue entries are located. Note, however, that there actually are two queue systems used here; one is used to manage a pool of buffers (the circular queue) and the other is used to implement the host-NIU interface (the work queue mechanism).

In order to ensure the availability of an RCB for the interface processor and to allow efficient operation of the queue mechanism, only a small number of the frontmost work queue entries should be designated as "shared" entries. One method of implementation, which works equally well for both the transmission and reception portions of the host-interface processor interface, is explained in the following text. Figure 23.16 illustrates the general operation of this scheme for an RCB interface. In this scheme, the two frontmost entries in the queue are designated as shared data areas. At initialization time, the host places at least two RCB addresses in the front of the queue for use by the message reception mechanism. Also, the host updates a counter indicating how many RCB addresses are contained in the queue. A semaphore flag is used to protect access to the counter and to

```
interface_processor_RCB_interface: procedure public;
    /* check for available RCBs in the queue */
    if RCB_count <> 0 then do;
        /* disable interrupts in the critical section */
        disable;
        /* contend for the semaphore lock and acquire it */
        do while lockset(@RCB_lock,1);
        end;
        /* copy the first entry from the RCB queue */
        RCB_pointer := RCB_que(0);
        /* move the next queue entry down to the front */
        RCB_que(0) := RCB_que(1);
        /* decrement the RCB counter */
        RCB_count := RCB_count - 1;
        /* release the semaphore lock */
        RCB_lock := 0;
        /* enable interrupts */
        enable;
        /* program the input DMA device with */
        /* the RCB information */
        in_DMA.address := RCB_pointer.address;
        in_DMA.length := maximum_message_length;
        :
    end;
    /* no RCBs available */
    else call take_overflow_action;
end interface_processor_RCB_interface;
```

Figure 23.18 Interface processor sides of the RCB interface.

the first two queue locations (also called registers). Each time the interface processor receives a packet or data from the network, the following actions occur:

1. The interface processor checks to determine if a message reception area has been set up. If one has, proceed to step 2. If a buffer area has not yet been set up and if an RCB is available, remove it from the queue and use the parameters to set up the message buffer. If an RCB is not available, the interface processor takes whatever action is necessary to deal with the overflow (drop message, overwrite last message, etc).

2. The interface processor initiates transfer of the packet data into the message buffer memory. Message-packet reception status and housekeeping (i.e., message size) is performed by the interface processor as the data is transferred into the message buffer memory.

3. The interface processor informs the host (either via interrupt or memory flag) that a reception has occurred and provides the address of the appropriate RCB to the host.

4. The host obtains the semaphore lock for the RCB counter and queue and, based upon the value of the counter, places one or two new RCB pointers into the queue and updates the RCB counter. The semaphore lock is then released. The host then performs the functions necessary to complete the message reception and passes the information along to the receiving process.

This method attempts to ensure that the interface processor will not have to wait for the host to supply message buffer address information upon a message reception. The determination of the number of queue front locations that are contained in the protected locations affects both the interface processor's wait time for a new RCB address and the host's delay in acquiring the RCB semaphore. A short protected queue length will provide the least delay when executing code in the critical section (e.g., between the acquisition and release of the semaphore lock) but could result in the loss of data when message receptions occur in rapid succession. A longer protected queue length may experience problems with the execution time within the critical section although it will be less prone to the depletion of available RCB pointers. An intermediate solution to the queue length problem must be derived based on the speed of the interface and host processors, the expected interarrival times of network packets, and the time required to receive a single packet. Fast execution or long packet interarrival times warrant a longer queue length. Slower packet processing or short interarrival times indicate the need for a shorter queue.

As mentioned earlier, the construction of the TCB interface can be accomplished using the same techniques as for the RCB interface that is explained above. In this case, the TCB counter will signal the interface processor that messages are awaiting transmission. Successful transmission of a message is indicated to the host by a status word in the TCB which is filled in by the interface processor. The TCBs are returned to the host for recycling in the same way as for RCBs.

Figures 23.17 through 23.20 show sections of PLM code that implement the host and interface processor sides of the RCB and TCB interfaces. On the host side of the RCB interface, the RCB count flag is checked to

host_TCB_interface: procedure interrupt TCB_int public;
    /* contend for and acquire the semaphore lock */
    do while lockset(TCB_lock,1);
    end;
    /* fill in the empty TCB queue front locations */
    do while TCB_count < 2 and TCB_available;
    /* adjust TCB queue pointers */
    TCB_que(TCB_count) := new_TCB;
    end;
    /* release the TCB lock on the front of the queue */
    TCB_lock := 0;
end;

Figure 23.19 Host side of the TCB interface.

determine the need for additional RCB pointers. If the count is below the specified threshold (set at network initialization time), the host contends for the locking semaphore. The next section of code is critical in that it must be executed as fast as possible to ensure a minimum lockout time for the RCB queue area. After filling in the empty RCB slots, the host releases the lock and moves onto other management tasks. Note that the host only has to fill in the required number of RCB slots; it does not have to copy data from slot to slot. Again, this is done to minimize the amount of time that the interface processor is locked out of the critical shared data area. The host can either poll the RCB count to determine when to add new RCB pointers or it can be interrupted by the interface processor whenever an RCB is used.

On the interface processor side of the RCB interface, an interrupt is generated by the detection of an incoming message. In an attempt to always keep one step ahead of incoming messages, the interface processor acquires an RCB and sets up the necessary DMA even when no incoming message is pending. This is accomplished by polling the RCB counter and using one if there is one available. In the case in which the interface processor is not prepared, however, the actions associated with setting up for an incoming message must be done on the fly. After contending for and acquiring the semaphore lock, an RCB for the incoming message is taken from the RCB queue. The information in the RCB is used to program a DMA device for transfer of the message contents. If the front buffer area (the locations protected by the semaphore) is not empty, the remaining RCB buffers are copied down into the frontmost positions. The lock on the RCB queue is then released and the interface processor moves on to other tasks such as determining the message length and generating a reception status.

Since the interface processor carries the burden of copying the RCBs to the front of the queue, the length of the protected queue area may affect the interface processor's response time to an incoming message. This effect would be noticed if the amount of time to copy the RCBs were greater than the time required to complete a message reception and back-to-back messages were received.

For the TCB interface, the host maintains a queue of TCBs which contain information on messages ready to be transmitted. As with the RCB interface, the first few locations in the queue are protected by semaphore access (see Figure 23.16). When the host generates a new message and associated TCB, it checks the TCB counter and determines if the critical data area at the front of the queue is full. If it is, the host simply adds the new TCB to the rear of the queue and continues processing. If the critical area is not filled with TCBs, however, the host then contends for the semaphore lock and places any ready TCBs into the critical queue locations. Again, care is taken to minimize the amount of code that must be executed between acquiring and releasing the semaphore lock. It is important to note, however, that the delay caused by the host action on the TCB queue is not as time critical as that performed on the RCB queue. Here, if the interface processor is temporarily locked out of the TCB queue, no data is lost. The outgoing message is merely delayed until the host releases the semaphore lock.

One point to note in both the RCB and TCB interfaces is the emphasis on speed in the critical section. For example, the contents of the next queue location is always copied to the front of the queue even if there is not a valid control block pointer in that location. This saves the overhead of having to perform test and branch logic on the control block counter. The moral here is that writing less sophisticated code for use in a critical area may actually provide better performance of the interface. In general, it is even allowable to produce critical section code that can commit errors in processing, as long as the errors can be compensated for by code in a noncritical section. An example of this might occur because the interface processor does not check the number of valid control buffers in the queue before moving the pointers down to the front of the queue. Thus, the host software must figure out if the RCB addresses that were moved were valid ones or not and fill in the appropriate entries. Also note that in both the RCB and TCB interfaces, the interface processor only works with the critical locations at the front of the work queue. The host processor is free to manage the

```
interface_processor_TCB_interface: procedure public;
    /* check for TCBs in the TCB queue */
    if TCB_count ¡¿ 0 then do;
        /* acquire the TCB lock */
        do while lockset(@TCB_lock,1);
        end;
        /* copy the TCB from the front of the queue */
        TCB_pointer := TCB_que(TCB_que_front);
        /* copy down the next TCB in the queue */
        TCB_que(TCB_que_front) := TCB_que(
        (TCB_que_front + 1) mod TCB_que_size);
        /* decrement the TCB counter */
        TCB_count := TCB_count - 1;
        /* release the TCB lock */
        TCB_lock := 0;
        /* program the output DMA devices */
        out_DMA.address := TCB_pointer.address;
        out_DMA.length := TCB_pointer.length;
        .
        .
        .
    end;
end interface_processor_TCB_interface;
```

Figure 23.20 Interface processor sides of the TCB interface.

remainder of the queue in any way that is appropriate, possibly even with the circular queue method discussed earlier.

23.6   References

Hoare, C. A. R., "Communicating Sequential Processes," *Communications of the ACM*, vol. 21, August 1978, pp. 666-677.

Stallings, W., "Local Network Performance," *IEEE Communications Magazine*, February 1984.

24. LAN Implementations

To provide a better feel for the LANs available, this chapter will examine example networks from each of the major topologies and control mechanisms described throughout this text. The topology, access method for the media, performance characteristics, interfacing methods, and adherence or conformance to the ISO standard protocol levels will be described for each LAN.

24.1 Ethernet by Xerox

Perhaps the most popular local area network of recent years is the Ethernet. Xerox began development of the Ethernet system in early 1973 to support the interconnection of its new personal computer, the Alto. The initial impetus for a broadcast-type network was provided by the success of the University of Hawaii's Aloha radio network which was refined with the addition of a collision-detection mechanism. After several years of development and use, Ethernet was modified and adopted by the Intel and Digital Equipment Corporations for inclusion in their equipment. This modification is called the DIX (for Digital, Intel, and Xerox) Ethernet and is discussed in this section.

As it exists, Ethernet is a passive broadcast system. This means that the network itself is powered by the connected nodes (the passive part) and that all nodes can hear every message transmission (the broadcast part). The Ethernet protocol, CSMA/CD, is that of the IEEE standard 802.3 and in fact is the basis for that standard. The network operates at speeds up to 10 Mbps at distances up to 2.5 km. One of the most appealing features of Ethernet is its protocol simplicity and relatively low-cost implementation. Also, there are a plethora of Ethernet equipment manufacturers who supply

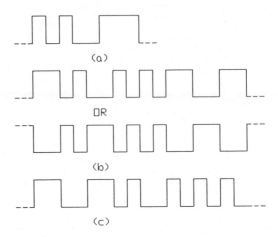

Figure 24.1 Encoding schemes for 10100111. (a) Binary representation, (b) differential Manchester encoding, and (c) straight Manchester encoding.

everything from cables to custom communication software. On the negative side, Ethernet does not perform well under high-load conditions and is not deterministic in its response time (a problem for some time critical applications).

Ethernet's 10-Mbps transmission represents the data capacity of the network. The actual data transmission rate (not counting overhead and access volume) will be somewhat less depending on the average message length and average intermessage time. As mentioned earlier, a 10-Mbps baseband Ethernet actually has a signaling rate of 20 MHz because of the use of Manchester encoding. The form of encoding used for Ethernet is differential Manchester. Digitally transmitted data is a series of binary digit representations on the transmission medium. A serial transmission is broken into slots, called bit times, each of which conveys a binary 1 or 0 of information. Normal binary transmission allows 1 bit of information for every bit time, provided the sender and receiver are synchronized for the length of the transmission. This is important so that the receiver can decide when to sample data on the line and, therefore, detect the correct binary pattern (i.e., the one that was sent).

This implies one of the following: (1) the sender and receiver are synchronized frequently so that their relative clock drift does not affect data reception, (2) there is a separate clock signal that accompanies the data, or (3) the clock signal is somehow encoded in the data transmission. The first

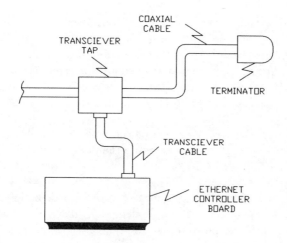

Figure 24.2   A typical Ethernet implementation.

type, frequent synchronization, is commonly used for RS232-type communications in which synchronization occurs at the beginning of every short bit string (usually 8 bits). The second type, using a separate clock signal, requires another data path and thus is not really serial data transmission. The third type, encoding the clock with the serial data, is commonly used in LAN implementations.

Differential Manchester encoding is of the third type, and it essentially uses 2 bit times to transfer 1 bit of information and a clock signal. In order to recover the clock information from the transmitted signal, differential Manchester guarantees that there is at least one signal transition on the line for every 2 bit times. This transition serves to reset a receiver clock which counts the time remaining in a 2-bit-time window. The number of transitions in two consecutive bit times defines the transmission of a binary 1 or 0. For a binary 0, there is an additional transition at the center of the 2-bit window. A binary 1 is characterized by the absence of a transition at the center of the 2-bit window. Thus, there are actually two frequencies being transmitted, one at half of the basic signaling rate (10 Mhz) for a string of binary 1s and one at the signaling rate (20 Mhz) for a string of binary 0s. Differential Manchester encoding, therefore, is also called frequency modulated (FM) encoding.

Figure 24.1 shows a binary waveform and the corresponding Manchester encoded waveform. As a note, differential Manchester encoding is different from straight Manchester encoding, in which the direction of the transition on the line (positive or negative going) determines the presence of a binary 1 or 0. An easy way to separate the two is the fact that, for differential Manchester, it is possible to look at a random interval in a bit stream and precisely determine the binary string being transferred. This is not possible for straight Manchester because the detecter must maintain synchronization on 2-bit boundaries. Figure 24.1c shows straight Manchester encoding for comparison.

Ethernet uses the carrier sense multiple access protocol with collision detection (CSMA/CD) to control access to the physical medium. CSMA/CD, as explained in Chapter 4, involves listening to the communication medium before attempting to transmit a message. CD indicates that the transmitting station will detect the presence of two or more simultaneous transmissions on the network. A simple detection mechanism for collisions is to exclusively OR the incoming and outgoing digital signals at the transmitter. A difference in the outgoing and incoming signals will result in a transition of the exclusive OR output, thus signaling a collision.

The physical medium for baseband Ethernet consists of standard 75-ohm coaxial cable, the associated terminators, transceiver cable, and the transceivers used to tap into the cable. A typical Ethernet configuration is shown in Figure 24.2. An Ethernet implementation allows a maximum segment length of 2.5 km (without repeaters) and allows taps at approximately 1-m intervals.

In addition to the baseband Ethernet, several broadband implementations also exist. In this case, broadband coaxial cable is used and the message information is modulated onto the cable. A typical broadband cable has several frequency channels that are used for different data transmissions. This Ethernet construction requires different connector technology and modulation-demodulation facilities from the baseband version, but it is otherwise functionally equivalent to the baseband Ethernet.

In relation to the ISO reference model, Ethernet implements the physical link and a portion of the data-link level. Error recovery mechanisms as specified in the ISO data-link layer are partially implemented in that a message can be retried a number of times in the event of a collision. Higher-level end-to-end error checking is not specifically implemented in the Ethernet system, although this capability can be, and usually is, provided by additional system-specific software.

Since all nodes are connected to a common medium, there is no routing required as specified in the ISO network layer. An exception to this, which is not discussed in this chapter, occurs when multiple Ethernet systems are connected via bridges and gateways. Higher-level functions vary greatly depending on the hardware used to implement the Ethernet and on the software used to implement the upper ISO layers. Two examples of different degrees of service are the Intel-supplied Ethernet communication boards and the DECnet equipment. In the Intel product, the user is supplied with enough hardware to implement the Ethernet protocol and with software that allows low-level access to the bus (e.g., allows direct buffer management, address manipulation, etc.). In the DECnet case, Ethernet is bundled into a total distributed environment in which users can logically address destination processes and do not even need to be aware of the network. This range of implementations of the higher ISO levels can make it difficult to interface off-the-shelf components without a significant software effort.

Many studies have been done to analyze and rate the performance of Ethernet type protocols; some even claim contradictory conclusions. This section will not, therefore, attempt to produce an in-depth evaluation of such a LAN's performance. For performance analysis discussions, the methods and conclusions presented in Strole [1983], Limb [1984], Stallings, and Takagi [1985] should be read.

There is a general consensus that under light loading, Ethernet provides very good response time because of the simplicity of its protocol and corresponding low overhead. Before continuing this discussion, let us first calculate the maximum utilization as defined in Stallings. This will give a feeling for the raw capacity of the network without considering the protocol implications. Define the maximum throughput as the product of the bus bandwidth and the maximum utilization of the bus (a percentage of its usable bandwidth). The maximum utilization is calculated as a function of the bit length of the network (as number of bits in transmission at any one instant in time), the maximum signaling rate of the network (in bits per second), the propagation speed of the medium and the network packet size. For Ethernet, the bit length for a 10-Mbps 500-m network with a propagation speed of 2E8 m/s is given as

$$\text{bit length} = \frac{(\text{length})(\text{signaling rate})}{\text{propagation speed}} = \frac{(500 \text{ meters})(10E6bps)}{2E8 \ m/s} = 25 \ bits$$

The maximum utilization of the network for a 1K-byte packet size is

$$\text{max utilization} = \frac{1}{1+a}$$

where

$$a = \frac{\text{bitlength}}{\text{packetsize}} = \frac{25\text{bits}}{(1024\text{bytes} x 8\text{bits/byte})} = .00305$$

so

$$\text{max utilization} = \frac{1}{1 + .00305} = 0.996$$

The maximum throughput that the network can support is defined as

$$\text{max throughput} = (\text{max utilization})(\text{signalingrate})$$
$$= (0.996)(10E6 \; bps) = 9.96 \; Mbps$$

See Stallings for a complete derivation of the above calculations.

The maximum throughput and utilization figures calculated above represent an upper bound on the performance of an Ethernet system with the described characteristics. The actual throughput will depend also upon the number of nodes in the network and the amount of traffic being contributed by each node.

The performance of an Ethernet-type bus is heavily dependent on the load applied to the bus. The probability of a collision occurring during a message transmission is proportional to the number of simultaneous transmissions (which is a function of the applied system load) and, to some extent, on the length of the bus segment. When a packet does collide during transmission, the actual bus throughput declines because of the time wasted during the collision. At high bus loads, the throughput of an Ethernet-type bus becomes unstable (that is, it begins to decline) as more and more packets become involved in collisions. The throughput of Ethernet can also be shown to be a function of the number of active stations on a network segment. As the number of stations increases, the likelihood of a message becoming involved in a collision increases. This occurs because the presence of more stations, each with a given workload, decreases the probability that only one station will attempt to access the medium within any given transmission slot. In fact, it is theoretically possible to move the entire network into such a state that the throughput drops to zero, even if no new load is presented to the system.

A transmission slot is defined as the worst-case time for the first bit of a packet to propagate the length of the medium. The packet length used for transmission also has an affect on the maximum attainable throughput. For larger packet sizes, the amount of data transferred for each successful bus access increases while the collision overhead remains constant. Thus, the bus spends a greater percentage of the available bandwidth transferring actual message data than it does for shorter messages. Longer messages, however, increase the amount of time between idle periods and therefore increase the average response time for a waiting transmission. A thorough analysis of CSMA-type protocols can be found in Takagi [1985].

24.2   DSDB by IBM

The IBM DSDB local area network was developed in the early 1980s to support real-time computationally intensive applications [Fortier, 1984]. Some of the target applications for this type of communication bus include space-born computing systems such as that used on the U.S. space shuttle program and also for real-time control systems. The DSDB communication bus is a contention-based, priority allocated, broadcast bus that can contain multiple transmission paths interconnected with system bridges.

The communication bus itself is logically split into three separate buses: the signal bus for bus contention, the token bus for destination buffer reservation, and the data communication bus for actual message transfer. Each of the above logical buses is broken up into fixed time slots that occur simultaneously on all three buses. A signal, token, and data transfer are allowed to occur during each slot. The basic bus contention scheme for all three logical buses uses message priority and a wired logical OR connection to allocate bus usage for the next time slot. The contention scheme operates as follows:

1. Each bus frame on each of the three buses (signal, token, and data) is signaled by a synchronization pattern supplied by one of the nodes connected to the bus. At the start of the frame, a node wishing to access one of the buses on the next time slot outputs that node's physical address and message priority, 1 bit at a time.

2. Simultaneously with the address and priority output, the node monitors each bit output to the bus and decides if the bit level that is present on the bus is the same as that transmitted.

3. If the bit was the same as transmitted, the next bit is output and step 2 is repeated. If the bit level is different, the node stops contending (stops sending bits), returns to step 1, and waits for the next cycle.

With the above scheme, the node with the longest string of consecutive 1s will have the highest priority and win control of the bus for the next cycle. Bus contention, therefore, is overlapped with the actual use of the bus and the associated overhead is hidden (just like a two-stage pipeline, one stage for contention, the second for transfer). Also, there can be one transfer in each bus frame. Each bus time slot allows the transfer of one signal, one token, and one data message.

The signal bus is used to alert a destination node of the intention to transmit and the type of message that follows. Message types are defined in terms of periodic and aperiodic messages. Periodic messages have the property that they can be specified a priori; therefore, they allow a node's

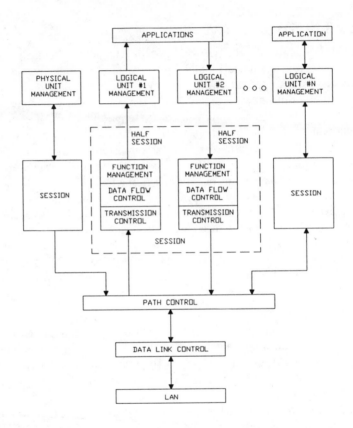

Figure 24.3   SNA node (noncontrol type).

buffer management algorithm to be statically determined. Aperiodic messages, however, do not have this property and they require special handshaking to ensure adequate resources at the receiving end. This is the main purpose of the token bus.

A token on the token bus is used to verify that there are sufficient resources at the destination node to accept the aperiodic message transfer. This is not a token in the 802.4 or 802.5 sense in that it does not allocate control of the bus (this is done in the contention part). Instead, the token serves as a kind of message header that is transferred separately from the message. This header contains information as to the size and criticality of the message to be sent, and it gives the receiver a chance to either allocate buffer storage and prepare for arrival or to indicate that the message will not be accepted. In this way, a rejected message will not tie up a whole bus frame that could be used for a more critical message.

In reference to the ISO model, the facilities described thus far make up the physical link and data-link layers. The next level, the network function, is implemented in each network node and bridge. The remainder of the data-link level is implemented at each node and consists of packet sequence checks and message retry facilities.

Message routing follows a predetermined connection path to its destination. These paths are set up dynamically at run time but remain in place until a change in the network configuration is forced (e.g., failure or node addition).

On top of the network level resides a single network traffic scheduling and management controller that implements a function analogous to the ISO transport layer. This function attempts to schedule a predetermined message load to attain maximum throughput and minimum response time for all nodes on the network. The schedules are determined at network startup and do not change unless the status of the network changes.

Since the DSDB is an IBM product, it is interesting to note the correspondences to the SNA model. The data-link control and physical levels are implemented by the contention mechanism. SNA sessions are embodied in the buffer allocation protocol which is implemented through the token mechanism. The network traffic scheduling and message routing algorithms form the basis for a system services control point (SSCP) node. Also, a DSDB node has several functions that correspond to the PU and LU sections of an SNA node. Thus, although the DSDB was not intended to be used for the same type of applications as the SNA architecture, the influence of SNA is definitely evident. Figure 24.3 shows the general configuration of a noncontrol-type SNA node.

For comparison with the Ethernet system, the following calculations reflect the maximum utilization and throughput for a DSDB-type bus. Assumed here are a single 500-m bus, a propagation velocity of 2E8 m/s, a signaling rate of 64 Mbps, and a packet size of 1K bytes.

$$\text{bit length} = \frac{(\text{length})(\text{signaling rate})}{\text{propagation speed}} = \frac{(500m)(64E6bps)}{2E8 \ m/s} = 200 \text{ bits}$$

The maximum utilization of the network for a 1K-byte packet size is:

$$\text{max utilization} = \frac{1}{1+a}$$

where

$$a = \frac{\text{bit length}}{\text{packet size}} = \frac{200 \text{ bits}}{(1024 \text{ bytes})(8 \text{ bits/byte})} = .0244$$

so

$$\text{maximum utilization} = \frac{1}{1 + .0244} = 0.976$$

The maximum throughput that the network can support is defined as:

$$\text{maximum throughput} = (\text{maximum utilization})(\text{signaling rate})$$
$$= (0.976)(64E6)bps = 62.46\,Mbps$$

Because the contention for bus resources is overlapped with actual message transfer, the bus should theoretically be able to support the maximum throughput calculated above. This would be the case if we had a situation in which the receivers all had unlimited buffer space. Because of the high speed of the medium, however, this does not occur and some degree of buffer management is required. This is the reason for the a priori network scheduling of periodic messages.

Since there are no collisions possible on the bus, there will always be a packet transferred if there is one available for transmission. The loss of contention does not mean that data is not sent; it merely means that the losing node must wait another frame and contend again. Correspondingly, the actual number of messages transferred in a given amount of time is simply a function of the original offered load.

Under these assumptions, therefore, the throughput of the DSDB bus is a linear function of the original load, up to the maximum utilization as calculated above. This would indicate that a DSDB with overlapped bus contention and separate buses for contention and data transfer would allow total use of the data path and would perform significantly better than Ethernet for the heavy-load applications.

Let's now look at a slightly more realistic case in which the bus contention is not overlapped with actual data transfer. The contention takes a fixed percentage of the total available frame time. In this case, every data frame must pay an overhead equal to this fixed percentage. Contention is synchronized among all nodes on a network segment, and there is a fixed packet size used for all transmissions. For any percentage of offered load, then, the overhead will be a fixed amount and will proportionally decrease as the offered load increases.

Overall, then, the contention-type bus offers an improvement over the CSMA/CD protocol in that it remains stable at high loads. One disadvantage, however, is the fact that the network response time may be less than for CSMA/CD under light load. The response time increase in the DSDB case occurs because a node must wait until the start of the next frame to contend for the bus and then wait another frame to transmit. In the CSMA/CD case, there is no such waiting time. An additional consid-

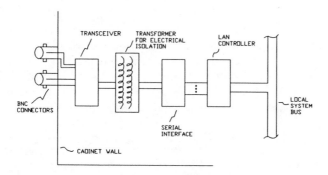

Figure 24.4   A typical Cheapernet implementation.

eration is the added complexity involved in implementing the three logical bus protocols in a single node.

24.3   Cheapernet

One of many Ethernet clones, Cheapernet evolved from the desire to provide a less expensive, slightly less capable network implementation. Like Ethernet, Cheapernet uses the CSMA/CD protocol operating on a 10-Mbps cable. The Cheapernet uses a thin, 50-ohm coaxial cable that limits the segment length to approximately 80 m. A minimum of 0.5 m is specified for internode spacing. Up to 30 nodes may be placed on a single cable segment, and segments can be connected for a maximum network span of 420 m. A total of 1024 nodes are possible with the use of multiple segments. The physical connectors for a Cheapernet system consist of standard BNC connectors which are daisy chained between nodes to form a network segment. The major cost savings of the Cheapernet system over a traditional Ethernet implementation are attributed mainly to the integration of the transceiver function into the data terminal equipment (DTE) and to the use of thinner, cheaper coaxial cable. The physical connection to the medium is accomplished without the use of special transceiver hardware and, as mentioned earlier, uses only standard BNC connectors. A typical Cheapernet node implementation is shown in Figure 24.4. Note that the interface unit typically resides on the system backplane bus of the host computer and thus does not require any external components other than the cable interfaces. This is in contrast to the Ethernet implementation which uses external transceivers to make the physical node connection. The disadvantage with the Cheapernet system, however, is that portions of a system must be recabled whenever a node is added or deleted from the network.

24.4   Ungermann-Bass Net/One

The Ungermann-Bass Net/One LAN is actually a set of products that implement a variety of network configurations. Included in this set are baseband and broadband Ethernet compatible LANs, a thin wire CSMA/CD LAN, a fiber optic Ethernet implementation, a token ring system and network software, and network management products.

24.4.1   Ungermann-Bass Net/One Ethernet Baseband

The Net/One Ethernet Baseband product is compatible with the DIX Ethernet 2.0 standard and the IEEE 802.3 local area network standard. Operating at 10 Mbps, Net/One Ethernet baseband allows segments of 500 m and, with repeaters, up to 2500 m for a total network span. Up to 100 transceivers are allowed on a single segment with a minimum transceiver separation of 2.5 m and a maximum transceiver cable length of 50 m (see Figure 24.2 for an illustration of a standard Ethernet configuration). Multiple network repeaters may be used to create multidimensional configurations. There are some restrictions on the use of a network involving repeaters, however, in that no more than two network repeaters are allowed in the transmission path between any two transceivers. This limits the usable end-to-end length of an all-wire system to 1500 m. The insertion of a fiber optic segment in a network, however, allows the attainment of the full 2500-m span. These limitations are caused by the end-to-end signal propagation time of 9.6 μs maximum. The bit error rate of the network is specified at one error in every billion bits transferred.

Two interesting features, which are part of almost every Ethernet-type LAN, are the watchdog timer and the collision presence test. The watchdog timer serves to stop run-on transmissions (i.e., a transmitter that is stuck on) and prevent network lock up. It does this by automatically disabling the NIU's transmission output if the preprogrammed time (usually set to slightly more than the maximum packet size) is exceeded. The collision presence test is used to ensure proper operation of the collision detection circuitry. This test essentially simulates a collision situation to enable the testing of the collision response mechanisms.

As intimated earlier, the various Net/One baseband CSMA/CD products (standard, thin wire, and fiber optic Ethernet) can be interconnected to form hybrid networks with segments consisting of different types of transmission media. This is done by using network repeater units hooked up, via transceivers, to the various types of interconnection cable. Thus, the characteristics of the type of physical cable used for a particular implementation are not known except at the transceiver hardware level. The other CSMA/CD products are described below.

24.4.2   Ungermann-Bass coaxial baseband CSMA/CD

The Net/One thin coaxial cable LAN operates at 10 Mbps using the CSMA/CD protocol. The network is compatible with the Ethernet version 1.0 specification. The thin cable is less expensive than other coaxial media, but it does present some limitations. The maximum segment length for thin coaxial cable baseband is 200 m with up to 30 transceivers per segment. This is significantly better than the Cheapernet distance of 80 m, even though the Net/One approach uses BNC connectors also. The segment length is not, however, as long as for the heavier coaxial cable that has even better signal attenuation properties. Thus, this implementation represents a middle ground for an Ethernet-type LAN implementation. For the thin wire system, the minimum separation between network transceivers is 1 m, and there can be no more than two network repeaters between any two transceivers. The maximum span of a thin wire network using only thin wire coaxial cable is 600 m. The use of a fiber optic link increases this distance to 1600 m. As with the Net/One Ethernet LAN, the maximum transceiver cable length is 50 m. The Net/One thin wire transceivers are DTE interface compatible with the other Net/One CSMA/CD transceivers so that the same DTE equipment can be used in different network configurations. Physical segments of the thin wire cable are made using BNC connectors. The transceiver attaches to a segment with a BNC T connector.

24.4.3   Ungermann-Bass optical fiber

The Net/One optical fiber LAN uses light-emitting diode (LED) light sources and PIN photodiode detectors to communicate over a single mode fiber cable. An optical star coupler is used to split and distribute an incoming signal to all attached nodes on the network. Each attached station has two fiber connections, one for data transmissions to the star coupler and one for data receptions from the star coupler. A single optical segment may contain up to 64 nodes, the maximum number of ports available on the star coupler. Multiple optical segments may be connected with an electrical repeater which regenerates a signal from one optical segment to another. The maximum span of an optical network is limited by the end-to-end signal propagation delay. This is a function of the total cable length and the number of repeaters in the transmission path. The transceivers used are Ethernet (version 1.0) compatible on the DTE interface. On the optical side, the transceiver connects with the incoming and outgoing fibers. Circuitry converts electrical signals to light waves and vice versa. A repeater unit consists of two transceivers and signal regeneration circuitry. Operating at 10 Mbps, the operation of the network's CSMA/CD protocol is

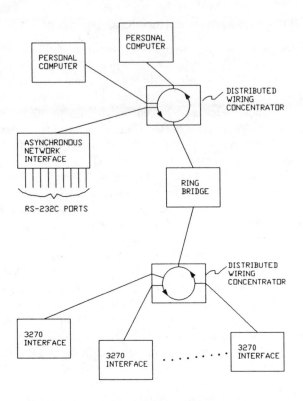

Figure 24.5   A typical Intro/Net configuration.

identical to other Net/One CSMA/CD products. The fiber system's low bit error rate of one error for every million bits transferred is attributable in part to the environmental and electrical immunity of fiber optic transmission cable. Since the interface at the transceiver cable is identical for all three Net/One CSMA/CD products and the networks all operate at 10 Mbps, the same controlling software can be used for all three applications.

24.4.4   Ungermann-Bass broadband CSMA/CD

The Net/One broadband LAN uses standard cable TV transmission hardware within a building complex. Operating at a 5-Mbps data rate per channel, the system can support five different channels within a single network segment. The nature of broadband communication equipment is such that a station transmits data at one modulated frequency and receives at another. This scheme requires a translation which remodulates the transmitted sig-

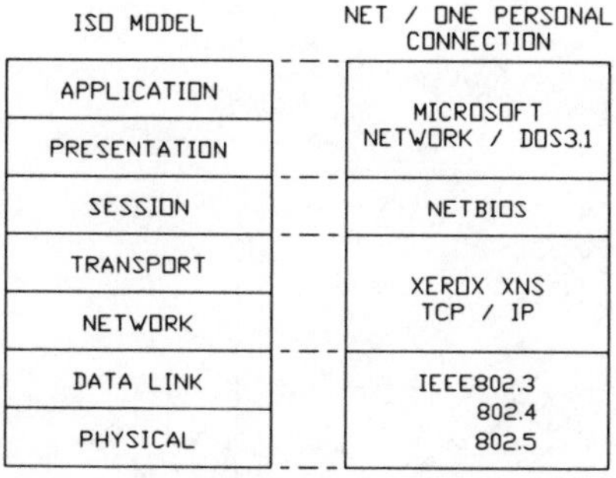

```
        ISO MODEL          NET / ONE PERSONAL
                              CONNECTION

      APPLICATION
                              MICROSOFT
      PRESENTATION         NETWORK / DOS3.1

      SESSION                 NETBIOS

      TRANSPORT
                              XEROX XNS
      NETWORK                 TCP / IP

      DATA LINK              IEEE802.3
                               802.4
      PHYSICAL                 802.5
```

Figure 24.6   Net/One personal connection correspondence to the ISO reference model.

nal so that the receivers can detect it. This translation is accomplished in a device called a "head end." Each network segment must have a head end to provide frequency translation for the nodes in the segment. The Net/One broadband system conforms to the EIA and IEEE 802 guidelines for broadband LANs. Specifically, this means that each 5-Mbps channel should have a 6-MHz width with a 192.25-MHz offset between the transmitting and receiving frequencies. For example, a station might transmit using a carrier frequency channel of 59.75 to 65.75 MHz and receive on a channel of carrier frequency 252 to 258 MHz. Modulation of the data signals is done using the duo-binary, AM/FSK technique. The Net/One implementation specifies five channels in the frequency range of 59.75 to 89.75 MHz for transmission (each channel being 6 MHz wide) and five channels in the frequency range of 252 to 282 MHz for reception (again, each channel is 6 MHz wide). Each of the 5-Mbps channels uses the CSMA/CD access protocol. The bit error rate for this type of network is specified at approximately one error in every 100 million bits transferred.

24.5   Ungermann-Bass Token Ring: Intro/Net

The Intro/Net LAN is a token ring system that works with IBM and compatible token ring system equipment. The LAN operates at 4 Mbps using a token ring protocol which is similar to that specified in the IEEE 802.5 standard. There are three types of network interface units for Intro/Net: one which allows up to eight asynchronous devices to connect using RS-232 interfaces, a card that fits allows IBM PC and compatibles to interface directly to the ring, and a unit which provides IBM 3270 information system compatible interfaces. Also, a ring bridge is offered which allows multiple rings to be interconnected. The Intro/Net system takes an interesting

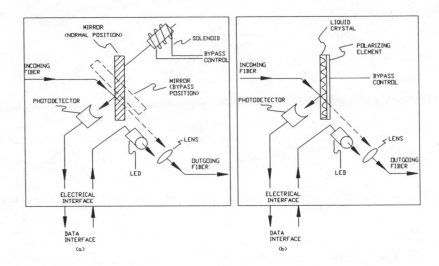

Figure 24.7 (a) Mechanical and (b) solid state optical bypass switches. Solid lines indicate normal light path, dotted lines indicate bypass light path and bypass position for the prism.

approach to the problem of interconnecting the different nodes in a ring implementation. Instead of providing links between neighboring network nodes, the Intro/Net uses a distributed wiring concentrator which allows the connection of up to 10 of the network interface units mentioned above. The user can mix and match NIU types using a single wiring concentrator. A cable length of up to 20 ft is allowed between network interface units and the wiring concentrator. Thus, the ring has a logical ring implementation with a fixed diameter ring. Figure 24.5 shows a typical Intro/Net configuration.

24.6   Ungermann-Bass Net/One Networking

Ungermann-Bass provides two types of network software; one for network management in the CSMA/CD environments and one for network file and data sharing on IBM PCs and compatibles connected via an arbitrary LAN. The CSMA/CD network management software builds on the basic capabilities of a Net/One LAN installation to provide some commonly used functions. It executes on an attached personal computer and provides services such as program downloading, network configuration, data-link monitoring, network debugging, port control, and a broadcast function. The software also allows remote access to the supplied functions that permits a network

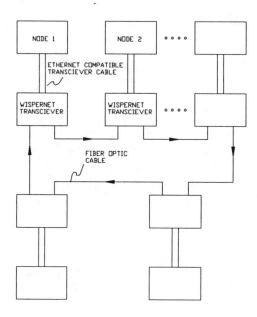

Figure 24.8 Fibercom's Whispernet LAN network.

to be automatically configured and started up. Also, the use of the debugging and configuration functions from the host personal computer permits monitoring and testing of a system under development.

The Net/One personal computer connection consists of a set of software services and a communication processor board which helps to provide communication and resource sharing for a network of IBM PCs or compatibles. Operating in conjunction with Microsoft DOS version 3.1 and the Microsoft Networks Software version 1.0, the communication processor board (called the personal network interface unit) allows the sharing of directories, network print services, remote application loading, redirection of print and file requests, the obtainment of network status, and support for the IBM Netbios interface definition. The facilities provided span the range of the ISO reference model, and, in some instances, several choices for a particular ISO service level are possible. Figure 24.6 shows the correspondence between the ISO model and the Net/One personal connection software.

24.7   Fibercom's Whispernet

Another Ethernet-compatible system available in the marketplace today is Fibercom's Whispernet. Operating at 10 Mbps, this network is completely

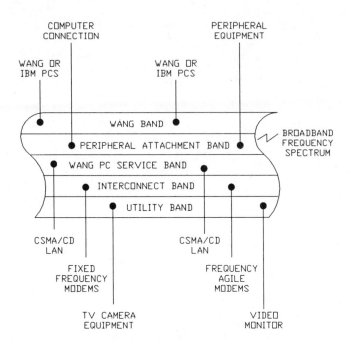

COMPUTER   PERIPHERAL
CONNECTION   EQUIPMENT

WANG OR   WANG OR
IBM PCS   IBM PCS

WANG BAND

PERIPHERAL ATTACHMENT BAND   BROADBAND
                                              FREQUENCY
                                              SPECTRUM
WANG PC SERVICE BAND

INTERCONNECT BAND

UTILITY BAND

CSMA/CD   CSMA/CD
LAN   LAN

FIXED   FREQUENCY
FREQUENCY   AGILE
MODEMS   MODEMS

TV CAMERA   VIDEO
EQUIPMENT   MONITOR

Figure 24.9   The Wangnet bands and their usage.

compatible with the Ethernet 2.0 and IEEE 802.3 standards at the transceiver cable interface. The physical layer, however, does not use the traditional multitap cable and the usual collision detection protocol. Instead,
the physical layer is implemented using a fiber optic ring. One ring can
have up to an 8-km circumference and up to 100 nodes per segment with a
2-km maximum node spacing and with no minimum spacing requirement.
A network may contain up to 1024 nodes total and up to 101 different ring
segments. Nodes in a segment are strung together with a single-strand fiber
optic cable.

In the case of a transceiver failure or a power loss in one of the network
nodes, an optical bypass switch is used to form a direct optical connection
from the transceiver's input fiber to its output fiber. There are currently
two types of bypass switches available, mechanical and solid state. The
mechanical one uses a solenoid and an attached prism to refract the light
to the appropriate interface. The solid state bypass has no moving parts
but instead uses an electric-field sensitive, liquid crystal material which is
light reflective when polarized in a particular direction. Figure 24.7 shows

simplified drawings of the two bypass switch types. The Interlan transceiver uses the mechanical type of bypass switch.

An interesting aspect of this particular LAN is the implementation of the CSMA/CD protocol on the fiber optic ring. The procedure for accessing the fiber is as one might expect for a CSMA/CD system: a station listens for an inactive medium before transmitting. Attached to the front of every transmitted packet, however, is a bit pattern that uniquely identifies the transmitting station in the network. In this way, the transmitting station is responsible for removing its own transmitted packets from the ring when they have made a complete revolution of the ring segment. If, however, the first unique identifier to come back to a transmitter after a message transmission does not match the one sent with the transmittal, a collision situation is detected. This occurs because another station began transmission while the first message was in transit but not yet at the other transmitting station. The signaling of a collision causes a jamming signal to be broadcast to ensure that the ring clears properly. The involved stations then back off and try again according to the Ethernet protocol specification. Receiving nodes that detect a collision while in reception discard the packet that is currently being accepted. The combination of the above features allows the implementation of a logical CSMA/CD-type bus on a physical ring structure. A typical Whispernet implementation is shown in Figure 24.8.

24.8   Wang's Wangnet

The Wangnet, produced by Wang Laboratories Inc., is a broadband system that provides several services over a series of frequency bands (9.1 to 400 MHz). The physical medium used in Wangnet is dual coaxial broadband cable, one for transmission and one for reception. Each network contains a loop device which provides frequency translation (as with a head end) and signal transfer from the transmission cable to the reception cable. Five different frequency bands, each offering a characteristic service, occupy the Wangnet frequency spectrum. They are the Wang service band, the peripheral attachment band, the Wang band, the interconnect band, and the utility band. Figure 24.9 illustrates the bands and the equipment that typically uses each of the bands. The following section will discuss each of the band's characteristics and usage.

The Wang band is used to provide a LAN type of service between minicomputer equipment. The Wang band occupies a frequency range of 216 to 276 MHz on the Wangnet. It supports a LAN implementation that operates at 10 Mbps and uses the CSMA/CD access protocol. Connection to the band is made via a cable interface unit (CIU), which implements the CSMA/CD protocol. The interface between the CIU and the attached computer equipment uses the high-level data-link control (HDLC) block protocol and allows variable length data packets. The Wang band can also support an IEEE 802.3 (Ethernet) compatible service. Up to five independent 10-Mbps 802.3-compatible LANs can operate simultaneously within the Wang band. The 802.3 adapter provides for the modulation of up to five baseband 802.3 signals and can support up to eight 802.3-compatible connections from user devices. The connections are completely 802.3-compatible at the transceiver cable interface, and the use of broadband communication is completely transparent to the connected equipment. Thus, the devices connected to an adapter can use any of the five 802.3-compatible LANs via any of the eight provided connections. The 802.3 networks are completely independent, however, and connected equipment cannot dynamically switch between any of the five networks. A system which implements all five of the 802.3-type networks, however, must forfeit a portion of the peripheral band capability to support the networks.

The peripheral attachment band of Wangnet is used to reduce the cabling requirements for computer to peripheral equipment. The band is separated into 19 channels, each of which can implement a peripheral subsystem. Each device that is capable of direct hook up to the peripheral band has a logical identifier which enables it to respond to data from the master device (usually a computer). Thus, computers (masters) and peripherals (slaves) can be placed on the network in arbitrary locations since the attachment is formed on a logical rather than a physical basis.

The Wang PC service band is used for interconnecting Wang professional computers by using up to four independent LAN channels. Each channel allows up to 255 Wang PCs and each operates at a 2.5-Mbps rate. Packets on a channel are of varying lengths from 15 to 512 bytes. Each of the four channels uses a token-passing scheme to arbitrate access to the network. Although the Wang PC service band is part of the total Wangnet system, it can be configured as a separate network. In the Wangnet configuration, the maximum cable distance between a transmitter and receiver pair is 12.9 km. The four channels are allocated to the 29.1- to 44.1-MHz band of the Wangnet spectrum, and each has an error rate of one bit in every 100 million bits transmitted.

The interconnect band provides a substitution for typical telephone circuits that are used for local data transfer. This band is broken up into four groups. Each group contains a number of channels and is dedicated to low-, medium-, or high-speed data communication interfaces. The low-speed group allows point-to-point RS-232C interface communications at speeds up to 9600 bps. Up to 256 such interfaces are modulated onto the cable using frequency agile modem equipment. The medium-speed band provides 64 dedicated RS-232C-compatible channels at speeds up to 9600 bps. These interfaces may be either point to point or multipoint and are attached to the cable using fixed-frequency modems. The third channel group has 16 dedicated high-speed channels which provide RS-449-compatible interfaces in either point-to-point or multipoint configurations. Each of these channels can transmit up to 64 Kbps. The fourth utility band service supplies a 50- to 19200-bps asynchronous shared channel for connecting computers and peripheral equipment. The channel is allocated using the CSMA access protocol and can support up to 2000 devices in a single configuration.

The final Wangnet band, the utility band, supports special-purpose functions such as video signal transfer. Seven channels, each with a 6-MHz capacity, are each capable of transmitting a full motion video signal.

In addition to the services supported for the five Wangnet bands discussed above, Wang also offers several other networking products that operate on the Wangnet cable. One of these is the PC-Net adapter, which supports IBM's PC-Net for IBM Personal Computer and compatible products. The interface at the network adapter cable for the PC-Net adapter is identical to that used by PC-Net products, and so the use of the Wangnet with non-Wang equipment is transparent. The Wang PC-Net adapter operates at 2 Mbps, and it merely remodulates the PC-Net signal to a new frequency (134.875 MHz) for transmission on the Wangnet.

24.9   Syteck's Localnet 20 and Localnet/PC

The Localnet 20 system is a single-cable broadband system with a total bandwidth of 440 MHz. The network is broken into 120 channels, each operating at a speed of up to 128 Kbps. The Localnet 20 channels use two 36-MHz bands in the frequency spectrum, one for transmission and one for reception. A transmitter operates in the 70- to 106-MHz range on one of the 120 channels. Each channel occupies 300 kHz of the 36-MHz band. A head end frequency translator converts the transmitted signals to the receive band, which operates in the 226- to 262-MHz range. The remainder of the cable's bandwidth is unused by Localnet 20. Each of 120 Localnet channels uses the CSMA/CD access mechanism to arbitrate the use of the medium. Thus, many devices (hundreds) may use a single channel. Access to a channel is provided via an adapter which allows up to eight RS-232C connections, each operating at speeds up to 19.2 Kbps. Using the vendor's adapters, speed matching between devices is made possible by using a buffering scheme within the adapters. The end-to-end error rate of the network is specified at 1 bit in every 100 billion bits transferred. This error rate appears significantly better than for the other networks discussed, and it is achieved through the use of cyclic redundancy checks on data packets and by allowing the retransmission of packets in error. In actuality, the impressive error rate is made possible by the redundancy

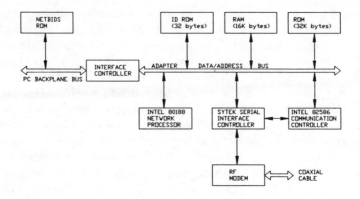

Figure 24.10 Block diagram for the PC–Net adapter card.

checks and retransmission and, therefore, does not actually represent the basic error rate of the transmission medium. The basic error rate can be expected to be the same as for the other broadband systems that have been discussed in this chapter, around 1 error in every 100 million bits transferred. This example illustrates, however, the improvements possible through the intelligent use of simple error detection and correction schemes.

In applications in which the number of devices on a channel cause the channel to be used to near full capacity, an interchannel bridge is used to spread out the load of the attached devices over two channels instead of one. The Localnet 20 system, therefore, provides the facilities for connecting computers and their peripheral equipment over relatively low-speed communication links. Room is available in the broadband spectrum, however, to implement additional local area network services. One such service is Sytek's Localnet/PC network. Operating on the Localnet broadband cable, the Localnet/PC network implements a 2-Mbps CSMA/CD network which is compatible with IBM's PC–Net. The architecture can accommodate up to 1000 nodes on a network at distances up to 10 km. Data packets are routed at the network level between the different link-level channels of the basic Localnet system. Two types of transport protocols are supported, reliable stream and datagram. In reliable stream, a virtual circuit is created with full end-to-end checking and flow control. Datagram service offers a packet-switched connection and no guarantee on the delivery of data packets. Upper-level functions (in terms of the OSI model) are also provided that support session management, logical naming, and network diagnostics. These services are explained in Section 24.10.

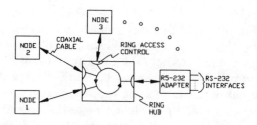

Figure 24.11 The Arcnet ring.

24.10   IBM's PC Network

The PC-Net is a broadband 2-Mbps broadcast bus that uses the CSMA/CD access protocol. The broadband medium uses the frequency shift keying (FSK) modulation technique and transmits in a 6-MHz channel centered at 50.75 Mhz. The transmitted signal is translated to the 6-MHz receive band, centered at 219 MHz, by a head end called the "translator unit." The architecture of PC-Net is based on the Sytek Localnet/PC services. The Localnet protocols, described in the previous section, provide services up to the session level of the ISO reference model. The protocols for the physical through transport layers are as described earlier. The session layer contains four choices for various types of session control. The user datagram protocol (UDP) allows datagram exchanges between users identified by logical names. The name management protocol (NMP) allows a process to attach to logical names which are used as logical network addresses. Session management is provided by the session management protocol (SMP) that handles the packetization and depacketization of messages for the applications. Finally, a diagnostic and monitoring protocol allows the gathering of network statistics and status. These session services are available to applications through the IBM Netbios command interface. In the PC-Net implementation, the Netbios provides the user interface to the network adapter card, which plugs into the PC backplane and handles all network-specific tasks. Thus, the user interface is of the executive service type as described earlier in this chapter. A block diagram of the PC-Net adapter card is shown in Figure 24.10.

24.11   Arcnet: SMC Corporation

The Arcnet local area network is a baseband implementation of a token-passing ring. Operating at 2 Mbps, the network uses a single baseband coaxial cable as the physical medium. Arcnet equipment, supplied by Standard Microsystems Corp., allows connection to the network via a PC expansion card or RS-232C interface. Equipment that is concentrated within a limited area can be cabled to a ring hub which forms the actual physical ring. Thus, the physical ring is contained within a box, and the connecting nodes interface via single coaxial cables and BNC connectors. The resulting configuration is shown in Figure 24.11. In the Standard Microsystems equipment, the hub is active (e.g., it requires power), and it handles all of the token ring protocol. Up to eight attached devices are supported on the hub, and multiple hubs may be interconnected to allow large networks that can span up to 20 kft. A passive hub is also supported and it allows a 3-to-1 port expansion for ports on the active hub. Thus, each active hub can ultimately have up to 24 nodes on it with the use of passive hub expanders. Connecting RS-232C equipment to the network requires the use of an adapter which supports data rates of 1200 to 19200 bps. The logical ring address of the attached device is switch selectable on the adapter. For IBM Personal Computers and compatibles, a controller card plugs into the backplane and provides the necessary Arcnet interface. The PC card supports enough logical addressing for 255 nodes per network segment.

Software support for a network of PCs is provided by Standard Microsystems' Vianet software. Vianet is an application program that resides on each PC in the network and is under the control of the PC's operating system (Microsoft's DOS). Network commands are attached to the operating system so that they can be accessed from a program just like any other operating system function. The Vianet software interprets application commands and then programs the attached network adapter. Thus, the Vianet/Arcnet system supports executive service request-type access to the network. Specific Vianet services include naming and identifying network resources, controlling simultaneous access to resources, and network configuration utilities. In addition to the Vianet software, networking software from Novell Inc. also works with the Arcnet equipment. The Novell software provides facilities for distributed file sharing, file locking, and record locking.

24.12   Map Bus: GM

An example of a LAN implementation that adheres to the IEEE 802.4 token bus standard is the Manufacturing Automation Protocol (MAP) bus. MAP was developed by General Motors Corporation with the hope that factory equipment from multiple vendors could be interconnected with a common communication environment. Current MAP implementations operate on a broadband cable at 1-, 5-, or 50-Mbps rates. The physical topology is a bus that allows the medium to be strung along assembly lines and between production areas. The bus uses the IEEE 802.4 token-passing protocol which helps to provide fair access to the bus, a requirement for urgent messages that must be guaranteed a chance on the bus. Because the cable is broad-band, taps cannot be made arbitrarily along the network as they can in a baseband network. Careful set up of the cable system, however, can avoid these problems. GM is taking a five-step approach to achieve full MAP implementation on its factory floors: (1) GM will configure a centralized network, (2) a local area network will be developed to allow distributed communication, (3) application services will be developed for devices on the network, (4) now the development of low-cost hardware for LAN implementations will be encouraged, and (5) a fully functional cost-effective network will be implemented. Current MAP implementations are supplied in the form of board-level products and VLSI controller chips. Also, several companies offer MAP (IEEE 802.4) protocol testers and network debuggers to aid in network configuration.

24.13   Appletalk: Apple Computer

Apple Computer, in an attempt to provide a low-cost network connection between Apple, McIntosh, Lisa, and non-Apple computers, developed a bus called Appletalk. Physically, the bus consists of a shielded, twisted pair cable and the associated connection boxes. Each node on the network connects via a short cable from a serial port on the computer to a connection box. The signals to and from the LAN cable are coupled on and off with a transformer within the connection box. Thus, a network consists of a series of connection boxes that are strung together with the shielded, twisted pair cable. The electrical characteristics of the bus limit the total number of nodes (e.g., connection boxes) to 32 per network segment. The actual interface to the bus conforms to the RS-422A interface, which has a maximum data rate of 230.4 Kbps. A single network segment can span up to 300 m. The use of up to 15 bridges allows multiple segments to be interconnected. The Synchronous Data Link Control (SDLC) protocol is used to define the bits of the transmission stream. Data on the cable is encoded using the Manchester technique, which reduces the effective bandwidth on the cable to 115.2 Kbps. Access to the physical layer is controlled with the CSMA/CA protocol. The collision avoidance (CA) variant of the basic CSMA protocol is used because the Appletalk hardware does not contain any collision detection circuitry. In collision avoidance, a device must wait for a clear bus, then wait for an additional, pseudo-random time delay before attempting transmission. By assigning different pseudo-random ranges to each node on a segment, collisions can be avoided (at the cost of wasting available bandwidth waiting for the random time to expire). The disadvantage of this arrangement is that the nodes become prioritized based on the average length of each node's pseudo-random delay time. Theoretically,

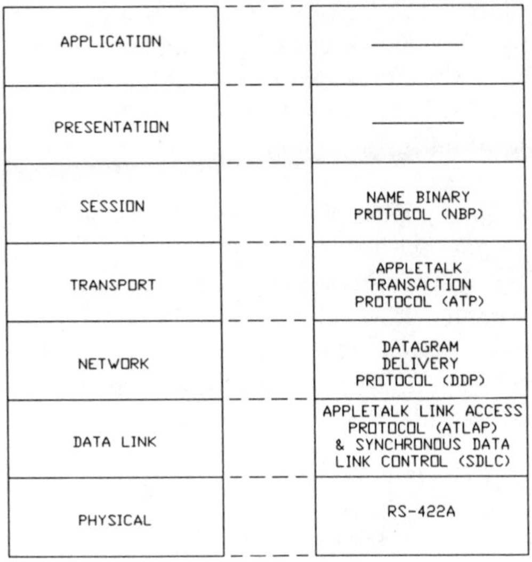

APPLICATION		_____
PRESENTATION		_____
SESSION		NAME BINARY PROTOCOL (NBP)
TRANSPORT		APPLETALK TRANSACTION PROTOCOL (ATP)
NETWORK		DATAGRAM DELIVERY PROTOCOL (DDP)
DATA LINK		APPLETALK LINK ACCESS PROTOCOL (ATLAP) & SYNCHRONOUS DATA LINK CONTROL (SDLC)
PHYSICAL		RS-422A

Figure 24.12 Appletalk protocol level comparison with the ISO model.

therefore, a node can be kept off the bus indefinitely if all nodes of shorter average pseudo-random delay time have a large amount of traffic.

The Appletalk bus also provides message framing and address control. A data frame may contain from 1 to 600 bytes of data. Address control is provided via a unique 8-bit ID for each node on the network. Node addresses are not fixed, however; they are generated at startup time and are guaranteed to be unique within a segment. The uniqueness guarantee is provided by using an inquire-acknowledge sequence in which a node essentially asks if any other node is responding to the proposed address. A positive answer results in a new address being generated and the process repeated. The above three functions are provided in a protocol layer called the Appletalk Link Access Protocol (ATLAP). Above the ATLAP level resides the Datagram Delivery Protocol (DDP), which provides service for datagrams of up to 588 bytes in length. Information such as source and destination addresses and source and destination node ID numbers are the types of data in the datagram header. On the next higher level, the Appletalk Transaction Protocol (ATP) guarantees proper packet transfer via an acknowledgement scheme. This level also allows three types of operations: a transaction request, a transaction response, and a transaction release. A transaction is typically a read or write request on a network resource such as a disk unit.

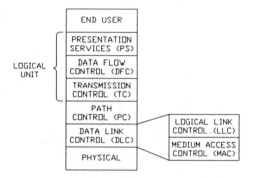

Figure 24.13 SNA structure.

The top layer in the Appletalk protocol hierarchy is the Name Binding Protocol (NBP). This service allows users to attach character names to addresses so that network resources can be logically accessed. The layers just described and their correspondance to the ISO reference model are shown in Figure 24.12.

24.14   Token Ring: IBM

The widespread use of IBM products that use the SNA structure has been expanded with the announcement of the IBM token ring. The token-passing ring is designed to fit into the general SNA model and, therefore, maintains compatibility with equipment and systems which use that framework. The network operates at 4 Mbps and is available to support several different versions of media interface hardware. This allows the ring to be run on twisted pair telephone and data-grade cables, baseband and broadband coaxial equipment, and fiber optic links. Up to 72 nodes may be configured on a twisted pair ring, up to 256 on the other media. The actual serial data stream is Manchester encoded for receiver synchronization. IBM uses the wiring closet concept to physically interconnect the nodes on the ring. The wiring closet concept houses the actual physical ring and devices called wiring concentrators. The wiring concentrators contain connection points for attaching nodes and other wiring concentrators. It also contains a series of electronic relays that allow a node to be removed from the ring without affecting the ring's operation. A ring adapter within each node performs the necessary ring communication functions, such as frame buffering, token generation, frame recognition, and routing of frames to the appropriate process address. Error checking and link fault detection are also performed here. Data frames on the token ring are variable in length.

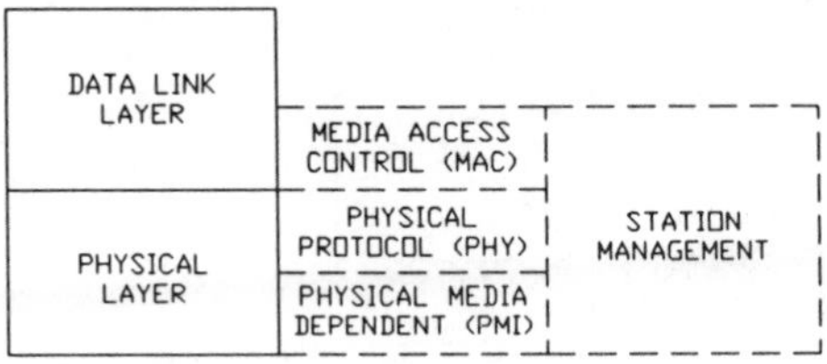

Figure 24.14 FDDI standard coverage.

The structure of the token ring protocols relative to the SNA model shown in Figure 24.13 is explained below. The physical layer contains the fundamental operations which generate the signal and provide Manchester encoding. The data-link control level is subdivided into two parts, media-dependent functions and media-independent functions. The medium access control (MAC) subdivision handles the media-dependent functions that deal with token access and generation, frame error checking, and address recognition. The logical-link control (LLC) subdivision handles media-independent functions such as byte-level protocol links (i.e., HDLC) which are established between nodes. At the next higher level, called path control (PC), network flow control and message routing take place. In a single token ring domain, routing has no significance. This function is provided, then, for multiple ring systems that are interconnected via bridges. The next three levels up, transmission control (TC), data flow control (DFC), and presentation services (PS), combine to form what is called a logical unit. There is a logical unit for each end user in the network, and multiple logical units may coexist on a single node. By using the SNA structure within the token ring system, a degree of compatibility among different IBM networking equipment is maintained, especially in the higher protocol layers (i.e., logical unit to logical unit protocols).

24.15   Fiber Distributed Data Interface (FDDI)

The American National Standards Institute (ANSI), in an effort to provide standards for high-speed LANs (more than 50 Mbps), convened the X3T9.5 committee. The work of this committee has focused on the fiber distributed data interface (FDDI), a 100-Mbps token ring LAN. The current FDDI standards cover the physical and data-link layers of the ISO reference model. Figure 24.14 illustrates the applicable standards. Although there are no absolute limitations on the length of the network fiber or the number of nodes, an assumed system would have approximately 1000 nodes spaced at distances of up to 2 km over a total fiber length of 200 km. In

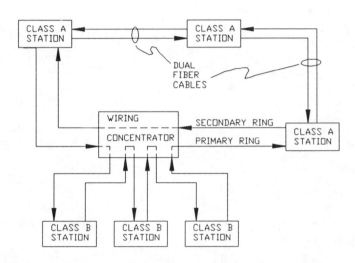

Figure 24.15 FDDI implementation.

fact, these figures are used to calculate some of the default values that are present in the standards. A bit error rate of 2.5E-10 is specified for a ring implementation. In order to provide increased fault tolerance, the configuration of a dual counterrotating ring is possible. In this case, each ring (one designated primary and the other secondary) operates separately at 100 Mbps over separate paths. Normally, there are two dual-fiber cable connections attached to each node in a dual ring implementation. The first dual fiber cable connection carries the incoming signal for the primary ring and the outgoing signal for the secondary ring. The second connection carries the outgoing signal for the primary ring and the incoming signal for the secondary ring. Primary and secondary connections are defined so that normal traffic uses the primary ring. The secondary ring is redundant and is used for fault recovery. Each of the rings follows the IEEE 802.5 token protocol standard.

FDDI allows two types of network stations (nodes) on the ring, class A, which can connect to both the primary and redundant rings simultaneously, and class B, which can connect to only one ring at a time. Class A stations use the dual connection configuration described earlier. Class B stations, however, use a single connection to carry both the incoming and outgoing lines of a ring. Figure 24.15 illustrates the station classes and their connection in a typical configuration. Note that, because of the dual fiber cable configuration, class B and class A stations can only interconnect through a device called a wiring concentrator. The wiring concentrator

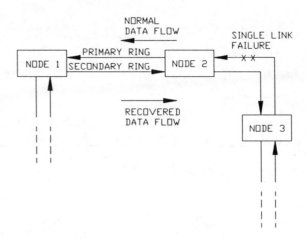

Figure 24.16 Type 2 error and recovery.

provides connection points into the primary ring that are suitable for class B connections.

The dual, counterrotating rings of the class A configuration provide a degree of fault tolerance that is not commonly found in a LAN environment. This characteristic is highly desirable for a LAN that is used in a real-time environment in which the LAN's reliability and availability are critical. In the FDDI system, there are three distinct levels of failures from which the system can recover. The first involves the loss of a node processor attached to a network interface unit. In this case, an optical bypass (as shown in Figure 24.7) can configure to its bypass state, which will enable data to flow through the disabled station's NIU. Thus, the ring in use is still operational, but with the loss of the attached station's processor. The second type of failure, a fatal link error in the primary ring in a dual ring configuration, causes the loss of communication on that ring. In this case, all data transfers are moved to the secondary ring, and the use of the failed primary ring is halted. Notice, however, that this action effectively removes all class B stations from the previous ring environment. Thus, class B stations are intended for use only for noncritical network connections. This failure type is shown in Figure 24.16.

The third failure type occurs when a NIU is lost, the dual rings between the two NIUs both fail, or a NIU is isolated because of multiple link failures. Each case is shown in Figure 24.17. Recovery for the third type of failures involves the loop back feature, which routes all incoming data back along the other fiber in the same cable. In this situation, then, each station

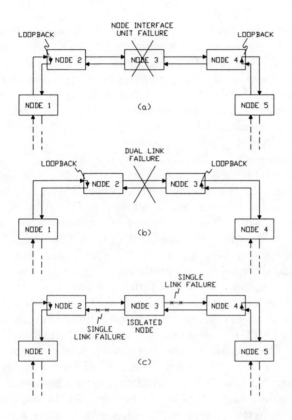

Figure 24.17 Class 3 failure modes and recovery using loopback. (a) Node interface failure, (b) dual link failure, and (c) isolated link failure.

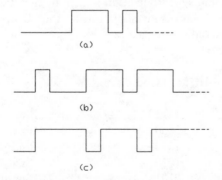

Figure 24.18 FDDI encoding scheme. (a) Binary representation of 1A hex, (b) 4B/5B encoding of (a), and (c) NRZI encoding of (b).

(except at the loop back points) will have two connections to the same ring, and the protocol must recognize this fact and adjust its operation accordingly. Thus, each NIU (except at the loop back points) will see the same message twice, once on each ring connection (primary and secondary). It is also possible that the failure typified in Figure 24.17c could cause the isolation of more than one node on the ring. In this case, two independent rings, with no common interconnection, would be formed. For class B stations, only type 1 failures are recoverable, since there is no redundant communication path for class B stations.

Data-link-level communication in the FDDI system uses the 4B/5B encoding scheme. In this scheme, each group of 4 data bits is encoded in a 5-bit code group called a symbol. This encoding yields 80 percent efficiency since it takes 5 bits to convey 4 bits of information. Symbols are defined for the hexadecimal numbers 0 through F and also for a number of communication-specific functions. Table 24.1 shows the symbols used and their 4B/5B encoding. As mentioned above, 4B/5B is a self-clocking serial data transmission scheme. As such, the 5-bit symbols are selected so as to guarantee a line transition at least every 3 bit times on the medium. The actual transmission of the data is accomplished using the nonreturn to zero inverted (NRZI) transmission scheme rather than normal binary transmission. NRZI essentially means that the presence of a binary 1 causes a change in the level of the transmitted signal whereas a binary 0 does not. The presence of a transition at the beginning of a bit time indicates that a binary 1 should be decoded at the receiver. In the 4B/5B encoding of Table 24.1, no symbol has more than three consecutive zeroes. This ensures the transmission of a 1 and, hence a line transition, at least every 3 bit times. These transitions are used to synchronize the receiver's clock recovery circuitry and synchronization is thereby maintained. Figure 24.18 shows an example of data transmission using the 4B/5B encoding method with NRZI transmission.

Symbol	4B/5B encoding	Use
Hex 0	11110	Binary 0000
Hex 1	01001	Binary 0001
Hex 2	10100	Binary 0010
Hex 3	10101	Binary 0011
Hex 4	01010	Binary 0100
Hex 5	01011	Binary 0101
Hex 6	01110	Binary 0110
Hex 7	01111	Binary 0111

Hex 8	10010	Binary 1000
Hex 9	10011	Binary 1001
Hex A	10110	Binary 1010
Hex B	10111	Binary 1011
Hex C	11010	Binary 1100
Hex D	11011	Binary 1101
Hex E	11100	Binary 1110
Hex F	11101	Binary 1111
H	00100	Halt, forces system break
I	11111	Idle, no data transmitted
J	11000	Token, message and beacon frame start signal
K	10001	Token and beacon frame start signals
Q	00000	Quiet, no signal transmitted
T	01101	Terminate, end signal for Token, message and beacon
S	11001	Not a transmitted symbol except in status frame or token, also denotes logical one (set)
R	00111	Not normally sent in data, also denotes logical zero (reset)
V or H	00001	Invalid/halt, illegal symbols
V or H	00010	Interpreted as halt (H)
V or H	01000	.
V or H	10000	.
V	00011	.
V	00101	.
V	00110	.
V	01100	.

Table 24.1 4B/5B encoding

24.16   Summary

This chapter described a sampling of networks in existence that implement concepts discussed in this text. The various LANs addressed represent a small portion of those in existence. A larger listing is found in Part 2. This is only a listing of the networks, not an in-depth discussion. To get further information on these and other networks, refer to the vendors listed in the Appendix.

24.17   References

Fortier, P. J., "A Communication Environment for Real-Time Distributed Control Systems," *Proceedings of the 1st ACM Northeast Regional Conference*, 1984.

Limb, J. O., "Performance of Local Area Networks at High Speed," *IEEE Communications Magazine*, August 1984.

Strole, N. J., "A Local Communications Neetwork Based on Interconnected Token Rings: A Tutorial," *IBM Journal of Research and Development*, September 1983.

Takagi, H., and L. Kleinrock, "Throughput Analysis for Persistent CSMA Systems," *IEEE Transactions on Communications*, vol. Com-33, no. 7, July 1985.

Appendix A: Vendors

LAN Vendors

3M, 3920 Varsity Dr., Ann Arbor, MI 48104, 313-973-1500.

Able Computer, 3080 Airway Ave., Costa Mesa, CA 92626, 714-979-7030.

Apple Computer Inc., 20525 Mariani Ave., Cupertino, CA 95014, 408-996-1010.

Applitek Corp., 107 Audubon Rd., Wakefield, MA 01880, 607-246-4500.

Asher Technologies, 1009 Mansell Rd., Roswell, GA 30076, 404-993-4590.

AST Research Inc., 2121 Alton Ave., Irvine, CA 92714, 714-863-1333.

Codex Corp., 20 Cabot Blvd., Mansfield, MA 02067, 617-374-2000.

Communication Machinery Corp., 1421 State St., Santa Barbara, CA 92101, 805-963-9471.

Complexx Systems, Inc., 4930 Research Dr., Huntsville, AL 35805, 205-830-4310.

Concord Data Systems Inc., 297 Williams St., Marlborough, MA 01752, 617-890-1394.

Corvus Systems, Inc., 2100 Corvus Dr., San Jose, CA 95124, 408-559-7000.

Cyb Systems, Inc., 2215 West Braker Lane, Austin, TX 78758, 512-835-2266.

Data General Corp., 4400 Computer Dr., Westboro, MA 01580, 617-366-8911.

Datapoint Corp., 9725 Datapoint Dr., San Antonio, TX 78284, 512-699-7000.

David Systems, 701 E Evelyn Ave., Sunnyvale, CA 94086, 408-729-8000.

Digital Equipment Corp., 200 Baker Ave., Concord, MA 01742, 617-264-1420.

Digital Microsystems Inc., 1840 Embarcadero, Oakland CA 94609, 415-261-1034.

Digital Products, Inc., 600 Pleasant St., Watertown, MA 02172, 617-924-1680.

Equinox Systems, 12041 S.W. 144 St., Miami, FL 33186-6108, 305-255-3500.

Exelan, Inc., 2180 Fortune Dr., San Jose, CA 95131, 408-434-2237.

Fibercom Inc., P.O. Box 11966, Roanoke, VA 24022-1906, 703-342-6700.

Fox Research Inc., 7005 Corporate Way, Dayton, OH 45459, 513-433-2238.

Gandalf Data Inc., 1020 S. Noel Ave., Wheeling, IL 60090, 312-541-6060.

General DataComm Inc., Route 63, Middlebury, CT 06762, 203-758-1118.

Honeywell Information Systems Inc., 200 Smith St., Waltham, MA 02154, 617-895-6000.

IDE Associates, Inc., 35 Dunham Rd., Billerica, MA 01821, 800-257-5027.

Infotron Systems Corp., 9 North Olney Ave., Cherry Hill, NJ 08003, 609-424-9400.

Intercontinental Micro Systems Corp., 4015 Leaverton Ct., Anaheim, CA 92807, 704-630-0964.

Kee Inc., 10739 Tucker St., Beltsville, MD 20705, 301-937-4740.

Magnolia Microsystems, Inc., 4039 21st Ave., West, Seattle, WA 90199, 206-0285-7266.

MicomInterlan, Inc., 155 Swanson Rd., Boxborough, MA 01719, 617-263-9929.

Molecular Computer, 1983 Concourse Dr., San Jose, CA 95131, 408-434-9500.

Motorola Semiconductor Products (Microsystems), 2900 S. Diablo Way, Tempe, AZ 85282, 602-438-3501.

NCR Corp., 1700 S. Patterson Blvd., Dayton, OH 45479, 513-445-5000.

Nestar Systems Inc., 2535 East Bayshore Rd., Palo Alto, CA 94303, 415-493-2223.

Network Development Corp., 81 Great Valley Pkwy., Malvern, PA 19355, 215-296-7420.

Novell Inc., 1170 North Industrial Park Drive, Oren, UT 84057, 801-226-8202.

PC LAN Technologies, Inc., 5780 Lincoln Dr., Suite 106, Minneapolis, MN 55436, 612-935-7509.

PerkinElmer, Corp. Data Systems Group, 2 Crescent Place, Oceanport, NJ 07757, 201-870-4500.

Phoenix Digital Corp., 2315 N. 35th Ave., Phoenix, AZ 85009, 602-278-3591.

Prime Computer, Inc., Prime Park, Natick, MA 01760, 617-655-8000.

Proteon, Inc., 4 Tech Circle, Natick, MA 01760, 617-655-3340.

Quantum Software Systems, Ltd., 215 Stafford Rd., W., #104, Nepean, Ontario, K2H 9C1, Canada, 613-726-1893.

Siecor Corp. Research, P.O. Box 13625 , Triangle Park, NC 27709, 919-549-6571.

Stearns Computer Sys, P.O. Box 9384, Minneapolis, MN 55440, 612-829-0361.

Teltone Corp., 10801 120th Ave., NE, Kirkland, WA 98033, 206-927-9626.

Tienet, Inc., 2300 Central Ave., Suite F, Boulder, CO 80301, 303-444-2600.

Wang Laboratories, Inc., One Industrial Ave., Lowell, MA 01851, 617-459-5000.

Western Telematic Inc., 2435 S. Anne St., Santa Ana, CA 92704, 714-979-0360.

Westwind Computer, 1690 65th Street, Emeryville, CA 94608, 415-652-3222.

Xerox Corp., Xerox Square, Rochester, NY 14644, 716-423-5078.

Xyplex, Inc., 100 Domino Dr., Concord, MA 01720, 617-371-1400.

LAN Software Vendors

Applied Information Systems, Inc., 500 Eastowne Dr., Chapel Hill, NC 27514, 919-942-7801.

Applied Intelligence Inc., 1043 Stierlin Rd., Mountain View, CA 94043, 415-967-3512.

AST Research, Inc., 2121 Alton Ave., Irvine, CA 92714, 714-863-1333.

Auscom (A KMW Systems Co.), 2007 Kramer Lane, Austin, TX 78758, 512-836-8080.

Communication Machinery Corp., 1421 State St., Santa Barbara CA 93101, 805-963-9471.

Communications Solutions Inc., 922 S. Saratoga, Sunnyvale Rd., San Jose, CA 95129, 408-725-1568.

Corvus Systems, Inc., 2100 Corvus Dr., San Jose, CA 95124, 408-559-7000.

Cosi, 313 N. First St., Ann Arbor, Mi 48103, 313-665-8778.

Data General Corp., 4400 Computer Dr., Westboro, MA 01580, 617-366-8911.

Datapoint Corp., 9725 Datapoint Dr., San Antonio, TX 78284, 512-699-7000.

Digital Equipment Corp., 200 Baker Ave., Concord, MA 01742, 617-264-1420.

Excelan, Inc., 2180 Fortune Dr., San Jose, CA 95131, 408-434-2300.

Intel Corp., 3065 Bowers Ave., Santa Clara, CA 95051, 408-987-8080.

Linkware Corp., 77 Rumford Ave., Waltham, MA 92154, 617-894-9330.

Motorola Semiconductor Products (Microsys), 2900 S. Diablo Way, Tempe, AZ 85282, 602-438-3501.

Nestar Systems, Inc., 2585 E. Bayshore Rd., Palo Alto, CA 94303, 415-493-2223.

Network Systems Corp., 7600 Boone Ave., North, Minneapolis, MN 55428, 612-425-2202.

Novell, Inc., 748 N. 1340 West, Orem, UT 84057, 801-226-8202.

Pacer Software, Inc., 1227 Pearl St., La Jolla, CA 92037, 619-454-0565.

Pathway Design Inc., One Apple Hill, P.O. Box 8179, Natick, MA 01760, 617-237-7722.

PerkinElmer Corp., 2 Crescent Place, Oceanport, NJ 07757, 201-870-4500.

Proteon Inc., 4 Tech Circle, Natick, MA 01700, 617-655-3340.

Spartacus, Inc., One Lowell Research Ctr., 847 Rogers St., Lowell, MA 01852, 617-275-4220.

The Software Link, Inc., 8601 Dunwoody Place, Suite 632, Atlanta, GA 30388, 404-998-0700.

The Systems Center Inc., 1320 Greenway Plaza, 214-659-9318.

Technology Concepts, Inc., Old County Rd., Sudbury, MA 01776, 617-443-7311.

Torus Systems, Inc., 495 Seaport Ct., Suite 105, Redwood City, CA 94063, 415-363-2418.

Transaction Data Systems Inc., 7061 Grand National Dr., Orlando, FL
32819, 305-351-1210.

Unipress Software, Inc., 2025 Lincoln Highway, Edison, NJ 08817, 201-
985-8000.

Appendix B: Bibliography

Abrams, M. D., and I. W. Cotton: Introduction to Computer Networks: A Tutorial, Computer Network Association, 1978.

Agrawal, R., et al.: "Deadlock Detection is Cheap," SIGMOD Record, vol., 13, no. 2, January 1983.

Agrawala, A. K., et al.: "The Slotted Ring versus the Token-Controlled Ring: A Comparative Evaluation," Proceedings of Computer Software and Applications Conference, Chicago, November 13-16, 1978.

Aho, Hopcroft, and Ullman: Data Structures and Algorithms, Addison-Wesley, Reading, MA, 1984.

Akin, T., et al.: "A Prototype for an Advanced Command Language," Proceedings of the 16th Annual Southeastern Regional ACM Conference, April 1978, pp. 96-102.

Akkoyunlu, E., et al.: "Interprocess Communication Facilities for Network Operating Systems," IEEE Computer, June 1974 pp. 36-55.

Akoka, J.: "Optmization of Distributed Database Systems and Computer Networks," MEITM Wo 916-77, March 1977.

Albrecht, H. R., and L. C. Thomason: "IO Facilities of the Distributed Processing Programming Executive (DPPX)," IBM System Journal, vol. 18, no. 4, 1979, pp. 526-546.

Alsberg, P.: "A Principle for Resilient Sharing of Distributed Resources," Proceedings of 2d International Conference on Software Engineering, October 1976.

Anderson, G. A., and D. E. Jensen: "Computer Interconnection Structures: Taxonomy, Characteristics, and Examples," Computing Surveys 4, December 1975, pp. 197-213.

Anderson, R. R., et al.: "Simulated Performance of a Ring-Switched Data Network," IEEE Transactions on Communications, vol. COM-20, no. 3, June 1972 pp. 576-591.

Anderson, T. and P. Lee: Fault Tolerance Principles and Practice, Prentice-Hall, Englewood Cliffs, NJ, 1981.

Aoki, M.: "Control of Large Scale Dynamic Systems by Aggregation," Tutorial: Distributed Control, IEEE cat. no. EHO 152-7, 1979.

Arora, A. K.: "WCRL: A Data Model Independent Language for Database System," University of Hamilton, Ontario, Canada, 1980.

Ayling, and Moore: "Main Monolithic Memory," IEEE Journal of Solid-State Circuits, 1971, pp. 276-279.

Bachman, C.: "Data Structure Diagrams," ACM Conference on Data Bases, Summer 1969.

— and M. Canepa: "The Session Control Layer of an Open System Interconnection," COMPCON Fall 78, September 1978, pp. 150-156.

Baer, J.: Computer Systems Architecture, Computer Science Press, Rockville, MD, 1980.

Balzer, R. R.: "PORTS - A Method for Dynamic Interprogram Communication and Job Control," AFIPS Conference Proceedings, vol. 38, 1971 Spring Joint Computer Conference, pp. 485-489.

Bannerjee, J., et al: "DBC Software Requirements for Supporting Network Databases," Ohio State University, Columbus, Ohio, 1977.

Baskett, F., and A. Smith: "Interference in Multi-Processor Computer Systems with Interleaved Memory," Communications of the ACM, no. 19, June 1976, pp. 327-334.

Baskin, H. R., et al.: "PRIME–A Modular Architecture for Terminal-Oriented Systems," AFIPS Conference Proceedings, vol. 40, 1972 Spring Joint Computer Conference, May 1972, pp. 431-437.

Bedford, G., and E. Grapa: "Setting Clocks 'Back' in a Distributed Computing System," The 1st International Conference on Distributed Computing Systems, October 1979 pp. 612-616.

Bell, and Newell: Computer Structures: Readings and Examples, McGraw-Hill, NY, 1971.

Bernard, D.: "Intercomputer Networks: An Overview and a Bibliography," Master's Thesis, University of Pennsylvania, May 1973.

Bernstein, P. A.: "Concurrency Control in Distributed Data Bases," Computing Surveys, vol. 13, no. 2, June 1981.

— et al.: "Analysis of Serialiazability in SDD-1: A System for Distributed Databases (The Fully Redundant Case)," Technical Report CCA-7 7-05, Computer Corporation of America, Cambridge, MA., June 15, 1977.

— et al.: "The Concurrency Control Mechanism of SDD-1: A System of Distributed Databases (The General Case)," Technical Report CCA-77-09, Computer Corporation of America, Cambridge, MA, December 15, 1977.

Bhandarkar, D.: "Analysis of Memory Interference in Multiprocessors," IEEE Transactions on Computers, no. 24 September 1975, pp. 897-908.

Bieber, J., and S. Florek: "A Performance Tool for Design and Installation Support of Distributed Database Systems," The 1st International Conference on Distributed Computing Systems, October 1979, pp. 440-447.

Biochot, P.: "Score IV, Distributed Checkpointing in a Distributed Data Management System," August 1981.

Boebert, W. E., et al.: "Kernel Primitives of the HXDP Executive," Proceedings of Computer Software and Applications Conference, Chicago, November 13-16, 1978.

—: "Decentralized Executive Control in Distributed Computer Systems," Proceedings of Computer Software and Applications Conference, Chicago, November 13-16, 1978.

Bonczek, R. H., et al.: "Information Transferral within a Distributed Database via a Generalized Mapping Language," Paper no. 577, Krannert

Graduate School of Management, Purdue University, West Layfayette, IN, November 1976.

Bosc, P.: An Overview of Freres: A System to Interrogate Distributed Data, Irisa-Rennes, January 1980.

Boudenant, J.: "Score III, The Consistency and Concurrency Control in SIRIUS Delta," 1981.

—: "A Reliable Distributed Data Management Algorithm, A Case Study: SIRUIS-Delta," Santa Monica, June 1982.

Bray, Olin, H.: Distributed Data Base Management Systems, Lexington Books, Lexington, MA, 1982.

Brinch Hansen, Per: "Distributed Processes: A Concurrent Programming Concept," Communications of the ACM, vol. 21, November 1978, pp. 934-941.

Brooks, F. P.: "The Mythical Man-Month," Datamation, December 1974.

Burkhard, W. A.: "Partial-Match Hash Coding: Benefits of Redundancy," ACM Transactions on Database Systems, 1979.

Cabanel, J. P., et al.: "A Decentralized Control Method in a Distributed System," Proceedings of the 1st International Conference on Distributed Computing Systems, October 1979, pp. 651-659.

—: "A Decentralized OS for ARAMIS Distributed Computer System," Proceedings of the 1st International Conference on Distributed Computing Systems, October 1979, pp. 529-535.

Cady, G. M., and G. Luther: "Trade-off Studies in Computer Networks," IEEE Computer Conference, 1973, pp. 147-150.

Caine, S. H., and E. K. Gordon: "PDL - A Tool for Software Design," Proceedings of the National Computer Conference, 1975.

Calculon Corp.: Distributed Data Base Technology, State of the Art Review, Rome Air Development Center, Rome, NY, 1980.

Canaday, R. H., et al.: "A Backend Computer for Data Base Management," Communications of the ACM, vol. 17, no. 10, October 1974, pp. 575-582.

Cardenas, A. F.: "Evaluation and Selection of File Organizations - A Model and System," Communications of the ACM, September 1973.

Case, P. W., et al.: "Solid Logic Design Automation," IBM T. J. Watson Research and Development, vol. 8, no. 2, April 1964, pp. 127-140.

—: "The Recording, Checking, and Printing of Logic Diagrams," IBM Corp. Technical Report No. TR00.01110.672, November 1958.

Casey, R. G.: "Allocation of Copies of a File in an Information Network," Proceedings of the Spring Joint Computer Conference, AFIPS Press, vol. 40, 1972, pp. 61-625.

Cellery, W., and O. Meyers: "A Multi-Query Approach to Distributed Processing in a Relational Data Base System," 1980.

Champine, G. A.: "Six Approaches to Distributed Data Bases," Datamation, May 1977, pp. 69-72,.

Chandy, K. M., and J. Misra: "A Distributed Algorithm for Detecting Resource Deadlocks in Distributed Systems," Proceedings of ACM SIGACT-SIGOPS Symposium on Principles of Distributed Computing, August 1982.

— et al.: "Distributed Deadlock Detection," ACM Transactions on Computer Systems, vol. 1, no. 2, May 1983.

—: "File Allocation in Distributed Systems," Proceedings of the International Symposium on Computer Performance Modelling, Measurement and Evaluation, 1976.

Chappelli, S. G., et al.: "LAMP: Logic Circuit Simulators," Bell System Technical Journal, vol. 53, October 1974, pp. 1451-1476.

Chen, K. A., et al.: "The Chip Layout Problem: An Automatic Wiring Procedure for LSI," Proceedings of the 14th Design Automation Conference, 1977, pp. 289-302.

Chin, W. N.: "Some Comments on Deadlock Detection is Cheap," SIGMOD Record, vol. 14, no. 1, March 1984.

Chow, T. S.: "Analysis of Software Design Modeled by Multiple Finite State Machines," Proceedings of Computer Software and Applications Conference, Chicago, November 13-16, 1978.

Chu, W. W.: "Optimal File Allocation in a Multiple Computer System," IEEE Transaction on Computers, vol. C-18, no. 10, October 1969.

Ciampi, P. L., et al.: "Control and Integration of a CAD Data BAse," Proceedings of the 13th Design Automation Conference, 1976, pp. 285-289.

Clark, D. D., et al.: "An Introduction to Local Area Networks," Proceedings of the IEEE, vol. 66, no. 11, November 1978, pp. 1497-1517.

— and Liba Svobodova: "Design of Distributed Systems Supporting Local Autonomy," COMPCON Spring 80, February 1980, pp. 438-444.

Clark, Jon: Data Base Selection, Design, and Administration, Preager, New York, 1980.

Codd, E. F.: "A Relational Model for Large Shared Data Banks," Communications of the ACM, vol. 13, no. 6, June 1970, pp. 377- 387.

"The Many Faces of Simulation." Computer Magazine, April 1977.

"Learning with Simulation," Computer Magazine, October 1979.

"Analytical Queuing Models," Computer Magazine, April 1980.

"Distributed Processing," Computer Magazine, January 1978.

"Circuit Switching," Computer Magazine, June 1979.

"Fault Tolerant Computing," Computer Magazine, March 1980.

"Network Protocol," Computer Magazine, September 1979,

Cook, Robert P.: "The STARMOD Distributed Programming System," COMPCON Fall 80, September 1980, pp. 729-735.

Date, C. J.: "Locking and Recovery in a Shared Data Base System: An Application Programming Tutorial," Very Large Data Base Conference, October 1979.

—: An Introduction to Data Base Systems, 3d ed., Addison-Wesley, Reading, MA 1981.

Davies, D. W., et al.: Computer Networks and Their Protocols, John Wiley, New York, 1979.

Davis, C. G., and C. R. Vick: "The Software Development System," IEEE Transactions on Software Engineering, January 1977.

Deitel, H. M.: An Introduction to Operating Systems, Addison-Wesley, Reading, MA, 1984.

Denning, Peter, J.: "Operating Systems' Principles for Data Flow Networks," IEEE Computer, July 1978, pp. 86-96.

Denoia, L.: "Performance and Timeliness in a Distributed Data Base," Ph.D. Thesis, Brown University, 1980.

Derning, P. J., and J. L. Peterson: "The Impact of Operating Systems Research on Software Technology," in Peter Wegner (ed.) Research Directions in Software Technology, MIT Press, Cambridge, MA, 1975, pp. 490-513.

DesJardins, Richard, and George White: "ANSI Reference Model for Distributed Systems," COMPCON Fall 78, September 1978, pp. 144-149.

Dijkstra, E. W.: Cooperating Sequential Process, Technological University, Eindhoven, Netherlands, 1965.

Doll, D. R.: "Telecommunications Turbulence and the Computer Network Evolution," IEEE Computer, February 1974, pp. 13-22.

Draffan, I. W., and F. Poole: Distributed Data Bases, Cambridge University Press, Cambridge, England, 1980.

Duerr, J.: "Data Communications Testing Overview–Protocol Analysis," Computer Design, February 1979, pp. 10-22.

Eckhouse, R.J., Jr.: Minicomputer Systems Organization and Programming (PDP-11), Prentice-Hall, Englewood Cliffs, NJ, 1975.

— et al.: "Issues in Distributed Processing - An Overview of Two Workshops," IEEE Computer, January 1978, pp. 22-26.

Elam, J. J., and J. Stutz: "Some Considerations and Models For the Distribution of a Data Base," University of Texas, Austin, Center for Cybernetic Studies, Research Report CSS 279, May 1976.

—: "A Model for Distributing a Database Working Paper," Department of Decision Sciences, Chmu of Pennsylvania, Philadelphia, PA, 1978.

Elson, M.: Concepts of Programming Languages, Science Research Association, Chicago, 1973.

Enslow, P. H., Jr.: "Multiprocessors Organization," Computing Surveys, no. 9, March 1977, pp. 103-129.

— (ed.): Multiprocessors and Parallel Processing, John Wiley, New York, 1974.

—: "What is a 'Distributed' Data Processing System?," IEEE Computer, January 1978, pp. 13-21.

—: "What Does 'Distributed Processing' Mean?" School of Information and Computer Science, Georgia Institute of Technology, Atlanta, Georgia, 1976.

Farber, D. J.: "A Ring Network," Datamation, February, 1975, pp. 44-46.

—: "Distributed Data Bases - An Exploration," University of California at Irvine.

—: "The Design of the Distributed Computer System," University of California at Irvine.

— and F. R. Heinrich: "The Structure of a Distributed Computer System - The Distributed File System," Proceedings of the International Conference on Computer Communications, October 1972, pp. 364-370.

— et al: "The Distributed Computing System," COMPCON Spring 73, February 1973, pp. 31-34.

—: "Software Considerations in Distributed Architectures," IEEE Computer, March 1974, pp. 31-35.

Feldman, J. A.: "High Level Programming for Distributed Computing," Communications of the ACM, June 1979, pp. 353-368.

Ferran, G.: "Distributed Checkpointing in a Distributed Data Management System," Real-Time Systems Symposium, Miami, December 1981.

Ferrier, A.: "Heterogenity in a Distributed Database Management System," VLDB 82, Mexico, September 1982.

Finkel, R. A., and M. H. Solomon: "Processor Interconnection Strategies," IEEE Transactions on Computers, vol. C-29, no. 5, May 1980.

Fischer, Michael, et al.: Optimal Placement of Identical Resources in a Distributed Network, IEEE, 1981.

Fitzgerald, A. K., and B. F. Goodrich: "Data Management for the Distributed Processing Programming Executive (DPPX)," IBM System Journal, vol. 18, no. 4, 1979, pp. 547- 564.

Fletcher, J. G.: "Several Communication Protocols Simplify Data Transmission and Verification," Computer Design, July 1978, pp. 77-86..

Flowers, J.: "Digital Type Manufacture: An Interactive Approach," IEEE Computer, vol. 17, no. 5, May 1984.

Fortier, P. J.: "A General Simulation Model for the Evaluation of Distributed Processing Systems," 14th Annual Simulation Symposium, March 1981.

—: "A Reliable Distributed Processing Environment for Real-Time Process Control," Proceedings of HICSS-18, January 1985.

—: "Generalized Simulation Model for the Evaluation of Local Computer Networks," Proceedings of HICSS-16, January 1983.

—: "A Communications Environment for Real-Time Distributed Control Systems," Proceedings of ACM Northeast Regional Conference, March 1984.

Foster, D.: "File Assignment in Memory Hierarchies," Proceedings of the 2d International Symposium of Measurement, Modelling and Analysis of Computer Systems, Stresa, Italy, October 1976, pp. 119-128.

Franck, A., et al.: "Some Architectural and System Implications of Local Computer Networks," COMPCON 79 Spring, February 1979, pp. 272-276D.

Franta, W.: "Hyperchannel Local Network Interconnection through Satellite Links," IEEE Computer, vol. 17, no. 5, May 1984.

Fraser, A. G.: "On the Interface Between Computers and Data Communications Systems," Communications of the ACM, vol. 15, no. 7, July 1972, pp. 566-578.

Freeman, P.: "Software Reliability and Design: A Survey," Proceedings of the 13th Design Automation Conference, June 1976.

—: Software Systems Principles, Science Research Association, Chicago, 1975.

Garcia-Molina, H.: "Performance Comparison of Update Algorithms for Distributed Databases, Crash Recovery in the Centralized Locking Algorithm," Progress Report no. 7., Stanford University, 1979.

Gardarin, G., and W. W. Chu: "A Distributed Control Algorithm for Reliably and Consistently Updating Replicated Databases," IEEE Transactions on Computers, vol. C-29, no. 12, December 1980, pp. 1060-1068.

— and —: "A Reliable Distributed Control Algorithm for Updating Replicated Data Bases," IEEE, 1979.

Gligor, V. D, and S. H. Shattuck: "On Deadlock Detection in Distributed Systems," IEEE Transactions on Software Engineering, vol. SE-6, no.5, September 1980, pp. 435-440.

Gonzalez, M. J., and B. W. Jordan: "A Framework for the Quantitative Evaluation of Distributed Computer Systems," The 1st International Conference on Distributed Computing Systems, October 1975, pp. 156-165.

Gordon, G.: System Simulation, Prentice-Hall, Englewood Cliffs, NJ, 1969.

Gray, J. N.: Notes on Database Operating Systems; Operating Systems - An Advanced Course, Springer-Verlag, Berlin, Heidelberg, 1978.

Gretton, W. P.: "Distributed Database Network Architecture," 1981.

Guillemont, M.: "The Chorus Distributed Operating System, Design, and Implementation," Proceedings of AFIP TC 6, April 1982.

Haas, L. M., and C. Mohan: "A Distributed Deadlock Detection Algorithm for Resource-Based System," IBM Research Report RJ3765(43392), 12583.

Hamacher, V. C., and G. S. Shedler: "Performance of a Collision-Free Local Bus Network Having Asynchronous Distributed Control," IEEE, 1980, pp. 80-87.

Hannan, J., and L. Fried: "Should You Decentralize?," Computer Decisions, February 1977, pp. 40-42.

Hanson, B.: Operating Systems Principles, Prentice-Hall, Englewood Cliffs, NJ, 1973.

Harris, M. J.: "A Prototype Ring Interface for the NPS Data Communications Ring," Master's Thesis, Naval Postgraduate School, Monterey, CA, June 1974.

Hays, G. G.: "Computer-Aided Design: Simulation of Digital Design Logic," IEEE Transactions on Computers, vol. C-18, January 1969, pp. 1-10.

Heart, F. E.: The ARPA Network, Bolt Beranek and Newman, Cambridge, MA.

Herman, D., and J. P. Verjus: "An Algorithm for Maintaining the Consistency of Multiple Copies," The 1st International Conference on Distributed Computing Systems, October 1979, pp. 625-631.

Hert, K. A.: "A Prototype Ring Structured Computer Network Using Micro-Computers," Naval Postgraduate School, Monterey, CA., December 1973.

Hevner, A.: "The Optimization of Query Processing on Distributed Data Base Systems," Ph.D. Dissertation, Purdue, December 1979.

Hightower, D. W.: "A Solution to Line Routing Problems on a Continuous Plane," Proceedings of ACM-IEEE Design Aids Workshop, 1969, pp. 1-24.

—: "The Interconnection Problem–A Tutorial," Proceedings of 10th Design Automation Workshop, 1973, pp. 1-12.

Ho, G. S., and C. V. Ramamoorthy: "Protocols for Deadlock Detection in Distributed Database Systems," IEEE Transactions on Software Engineering, vol. SE-8, no. 6, November 1982.

Hoare, C. A. R.: "Communicating Sequential Processes," Communications of the ACM, vol. 21, August 1978, pp 666-677.

Hoffman, M. G.: "Hardware Implementation of Communication Protocols: A Formal Approach," IEEE, 1980, pp. 253-263.

Hopper, K., et al: "Abstract Machines Modelling Network Control Systems," Operating Systems Review, vol. 13, January 1979, pp. 10-24.

Hsiao, D. C., et al.: "Operating System Security: A Tutorial of Current Research," Proceedings of Computer Software and Applications Conference, Chicago, November 13-16, 1978.

IEEE Computer, Special Issue on Architectures for Array Processors, September 1981.

IEEE Computer, Special Issue on Computer Architectures for Image Processing, January 1983.

INFOTEC: Distributed Data Bases, vol. 1 and 2, INFOTECH International, Ltd., Maidenhead, Berkshire, England, 1977.

IRAN "A Model for Combined Communications Network Design and File Allocation for Distributed Data Base," 1st International Conference on Distribution, DB, Huntsville, 1979.

Isloor, S. S., and T. A. Marsland: "System Recovery in Distributed Data Bases," IEEE COMPSAC, Chicago, Nov 6-8, 1979, pp. 421-426.

— and —: "The Deadlock Problem: An Overview," IEEE Computer, September 1980, pp. 58-70.

Jafari, H., et al.: "Simulation of a Class of Ring Structured Networks," IEEE Transactions on Computers, vol. C-29, no. 5, May 1980, pp. 385-392.

Jagannathan, J. R., and R. Vasudevan: "A Distributed Deadlock Detection and Resolution Scheme Performance Study," 3d International Conference on Distributed Systems, IEEE, 1982.

— and —: "Comments on Protocols for Deadlock Detection in Distributed Database Systems," IEEE Transactions on Software Engineering, vol. SE-9, no. 3, May 1983.

Jensen, E. D.: "The Honeywell Experimental Distributed - An Overview," IEEE Computer, vol. 11, no. 1, January 1978, pp. 23-38.

—: "The Influence of Microprocessors on Computer Architecture: Distributed Processing," ACM '75 Proceedings of the Annual Conference, Minneapolis, October 20-22, 1975.

— and G. A. Anderson: "Computer Interconnection Structures: Taxonomy, Characteristics and Examples," ACM Computing Surveys, vol. 7, no. 4, December 1975, pp. 197-212.

— et al.: "The Impact of Wideband Multiplex Concepts on Microprocessor-Based Aeronic System Architecture," February, 1978, AFAZ-TR-78-4, Honeywell Systems and Research Center, Minneapolis, MN.

— et al.: "A Review of Systematic Methods in Distributed Processor Interconnection," IEEE International Conference on Communications, June 14, 1976, Philadelphia, PA.

— and: "Slides on Partitioning and Assignment of Distributed Processing Software," Honeywell System and Research Center, Minneapolis, MN

Johnson, D. E.: "FAST: A Second Generation Program Analysis System," Proceedings of 3d International Conference on Software Engineering, Atlanta, May 1978, pp. 142-148.

Jones, M. N.: "HIPO for Developing Specifications," Datamation, March 1976, pp. 112-125.

Kaneoko, A., et al.: "Logical Clock Synchronization Method for Duplicated Data Base Control," The 1st International Conference on Distributed Computing Systems, October 1979, pp. 601-611.

Keller, T. W., et al.: "A Tool for Network Design; The Automatic Analysis of Stochastic Models of Computer Networks," Texas A&M.

Khokhan, K. H., and A. M. Patcl: "The Chip Layout Problem: A Placement Procedure for LSI," Proceedings of the 14th Design Automation Conference, 1977, pp. 291-297.

Kiely, S. C.: "An Operating System for Distributed Processing - DPPX," IBM System Journal, vol. 18, no. 4, 1979, pp. 507-525.

Kim, K. H.: "Strategies for Structured and Fault-Tolerant Design of Recovery Programs," Proceedings of Computer Software and Applications Conference, Chicago, November 13-16, 1978.

Kimbelton, S. R.: "Data Sharing Protocols: Structure, Requirements, and Interrelationships," COMPSAC 78, pp. 270-276.

— and Mandell, R. L.: "A Perspective on Network Operating Systems," AFIPS Conference Proceedings, vol. 45, 1976, National Computer Conference, pp. 551-559.

Kleinrock L.:" Queuing Systems: Volume I and Theory 1975, Volume II:" Computer Applications, John Wiley Inter-Science, New York, 1976.

—: "On Communications and Networks," IEEE Transactions on Software Engineering, vol. C-25, no. 12, December, 1976, pp. 1326-1335.

— et al.: "A Study of Line Overhead in the ARPANET," Communications of the ACM, vol. 19, no. 1, January 1976, pp. 3-13.

Knuth: The Art of Computer Programming, vol. I, 1968; vol. II, 1969; vol. III, 1973.

Kobagashi, A.: Modeling and Analysis: An Introduction to Systems Performance Evaluation Methodology, Addison Wesley, Reading, MA, 1980.

Korenjak, A. J., and A. H. Teger: "An Integrated CAD Data Base System," Proceedings of 12th Design Automation Conference, 1975, pp. 399-406.

Kuhns, R. C., and M. C. Shoquist: "Serial Data Bus System for Local Processing Networks," COMPCON 79 Spring Digest of Papers, February 1979, pp. 266-271.

Kumar, B.: "Performance Evaluation of Highly Concurrent Computers by Deterministic Simulation," Communications of the ACM, November 1978.

Kurii, T. L., and K. M. Kurii: "An Architecture for Evolutionary Database System Design," COMPSAC 78, Chicago, 1978, pp. 382-386.

L'Archeveque, J. V. R., and G. Yan: "On the Selection of Architectures for Distributed Computer Systems in Real-Time Applications," vol. NS-24, no. 1, February 1977.

Lam, S. S.: "A Study of the CSMA Protocol in Local Networks," Proceedings of 4th Berkeley Conference on Distributed Data Management and Computer Networks, San Francisco, August 1979.

—: "Congestion Control Techniques for Packet Networks," 2d International Conference on Information Sciences and Systems, Patras, Greece, July 1979, in D. Lainiotis and N. Tzannes (eds.), Advances in Communications, D. Reidel, Holland, 1980.

—: "Data Link Control Procedures,"

—: "Multiple Access Protocols," in W. Chou (ed.), Computer Communications, vol. 1; Principles, Prentice-Hall, Englewood Cliffs, NJ, 1981.

—: "On Protocols for Satellite Packet Switching," Conference Recordings, International Conference on Communications, Boston, June 1979.

—: "Packet Switching in a Multi-Access Broadcast Channel with Application to Satellite Communication in a Computer Network," University of California at Los Angeles, School of Engineering and Applied Science, April, 1974.

—: "Queuing Networks with Population Size Constraints," IBM Journal of Research and Development vol. 21, July 1977.

—: "Store-and-Forward Buffer Requirements in a Packet Switching Network," IEEE Transactions on Commununications, vol. COM-24, April, 1976.

— and L. Kleinrock: "Dynamic Control Schemes for a Packet Switched Multi-Access Broadcast Channel," National Computer Conference, Anaheim, CA, May 1975, AFIPS Conference. Proceedings, vol. 44, 1975.

— and —: "Packet Switching in a Multi-Access Broadcast Channel: Dynamic Control Procedures," IEEE Transactions on Communications, vol. Com-23, September 1975.

— and M. Reiser: "Congestion Control of Store-and-Forward Networks by Input Buffer Limits," Conference Records, National Telecommunications Conference., vol. 1, Dec 1977, in W. W. Chu, (ed.), Advances in Computer Communications and Networks, Artech House, Dedham, MA, 1979.

Lann, G.: "Consistency Issues in Distributed Data Bases," Proceedings of On-Line Conference on Distributed Data Bases, London, March 1981.

Larson, James A.: Data Base Management System, Lexington Books, Lexington, MA, 1982.

Larson, R. E.: Tutoriral: Distributed Control, October 1979, IEEE cat., no. EHO153-7.

Lavenburg, S.: Computer Performarnce Modeling Handbook, Academic Press, New York, 1983.

LaVoie, P.: "Distributed Computing Systematically," Computer Decisions, March 1977, pp. 44-45.

Lawson, J. T., and M. P. Mariana: "Distributed Data Processing System Design - A Look at the Partitioning Problem," Proceedings of Computer Software and Applications Conference, Chicago, November 13-16, 1978.

Lee, C.: "An Algorithm for Path Connections and Its Applications," IRE Transactions on Electronic Computers, vol. EC-10, no. 3, September 1961, pp 346-361.

—: "Queuing Analysis of Global Locking Synchronization Schemes for Multicopy Databases," IEEE Transactions on Computers, vol. C-29, no. 5, pp. 371-384, May 1980.

Leham, R. S.: Computer Simulation and Modeling, Lawrence Erlbaum Association, Hillsdale, NJ, 1977.

LeLann, G.: "A Distributed System for Real Time Transaction Processing," IEEE Computer, vol. 14, no. 2 February 1981.

—: "An Analysis of Differenct Approaches to Distributed Computing," IEEE, 1979, pp. 222-232.

Levin, D.: "Organizing Distributed Data Bases In Computer Networks," Wharton School of Finance and Commerce, University of Pennsylvania, September 1974.

Levin, K. D.: "Optimal Program and Data Locations in Computer Networks," CACM, vol. no. 20, 1977, pp. 315-321.

— and H. L. Moran: "Optimizing Distributed Data Bases - A Framework for Research," Wharton School, University of Pennsylvania, January 1975.

Li, Victor: "Performance Models of Distributed Data Base Systems," MIT, Cambridge, MA, 1981.

Liebowitz, B. H.: "Multiple Processor Mini-computer Systems - Part 2: Implementation," Computer Design, November 1978, pp. 121-131.

Lien, Y. E., and J. H. Ying: "Design of Distributed Entity- Relationship Database System," Proceedings of Computer Software and Applications Conference, Chicago, November 13-16, 1978.

Lientz, B. P., et al.: "A Model for Performing Trade-offs in Computer Communication Networks," University of California at Los Angeles Graduate School of Management, December 1975.

Liesey, J.: "Interprocess Communication and Naming in the Mininet System," IEEE COMPCON, Spring 1979, pp. 222-229.

Lindsey, B. et al.: "Notes on Distributed Data Bases," IBM Research Division, no. RJ2571, 71479 San Jose, CA.

Liskov B.: "Primitives for Distributed Computing," 7th ACM Symposium on Operating Systems Principles, 1979.

Litwin, W.: "Sirius Systems for Distributed Data Management," 2d Information Symposium on Distributed Data Bases, Berlin, September 1982.

Liu, M.: "The Design of the Distributed Loop Computer Network," Proceedings of the International Computer Conference, 1975.

Lorin, H.: "Distributed Processing: An Assessment," IBM System Journal, vol. 18, no. 4, 1979, pp. 582-603.

Maccabe, A. B., and R J. LeBlanc: "A Language Model for Fully Distributed Systems," COMPCON Fall 80, September 1980, pp. 723-728.

Mahmoud, S.: "Optimal Allocation of Resources in Distributed Information Networks," ACM Transactions in Data Base Systems, vol. 1, 1976, pp. 66-68.

Mariani, M. P. and D. F. Palmer: "Tutorial: Distributed System Design," IEEE cat. no. EHO151-1, October 1979.

—: "Distributed Data Processing (DDP) Technology Program, vol. I, Final Report," TRW and Burroughs Corp., December 31, 1977.

Martin, J.: Computer Data Base Organization, Prentice-Hall, Englewood Cliffs, NJ, 1975.

—: Principles of Data Base Management, Prentice-Hall, Englewood Cliffs, NJ, 1976.

Maryanski, F. J., et al.: "Usability and Feasibility of Back-end Minicomputers," Department of Computer Science, Kansas State University, Manhatten, KA, June 1975.

—: "A Survey of Developments in Distributed Data Base Management Systems," IEEE Computer, February 1978, pp. 28-37.

Meadow, C.: The Analysis of Information Systems, John Wiley, New York, 1967.

Menasce, D. A., and R. R. Muntz: "Locking and Deadlock Detection in Distributed Databases," IEEE Transactions on Software Enginerring, vol. SE-5, no. 3, May 1979.

Metcalf, R. M., and D. R. Boggs: "Ethernet: Distributed Packet Switching for Local Computer Networks," CACM, vol. 19, no. 7, July 1976, pp. 395-404.

Mills, D. L.: "An Overview of the Distributed Computer Network," Proceedings of AFIPS Conference, VV1. 45, National Computer Conference, 1976, pp. 523-531.

—: "Dynamic File Access in a Distributed Computer Network," University of Maryland Department of Computer Science, Technical Report TR-415, Feb. 1976.

Miranda, S.: "Specification and Verification of a Decentralizaed Controlled Locking Protocol (DPL) for Distributed Data Bases," I.E., R.I.S.S., University des Sciences De Toulouse, February 1979.

Mitchell, D.: "Distributed Algorithms for Deadlock Detection and Resolution," ACM 3d Proceedings on Distributed Computing, August 1984.

Mockapetris, P. V., et al.: "On the Design of Local Network Interfaces," University of California at Irvine, Department of Information and Computer Science and IFIP, 1977.

Mohan, C.: "Distributed Database Management, Some Thoughts and Analyses," University of Texas at Austin, TR-129, May 1979.

Morgan, D. E., et al.: "A Computer Network Monitoring System," IEEE Transactions on Software Engineering, vol. SE-1, no. 3., September, pp. 299-311.

Morgan, H. L., and L. K. Dan: "Optimal Program and Data Locations in Computer Networks," Communications of the ACM, vol. 20, May 1977, pp. 315-322.

Moto-Oka, T., et al.: "Logic Design System In Japan," Proceedings of 12th Design Automation Conference, 1975, pp. 241-250.

Moulinoux, C.: Messidor: A Distributed Information Retrieval System, ACM & BCS, Berlin (RFA), May 1982.

Moulton, P. D., and R. C. Sancier: "Another Look at SNA," Datamation, March 1977.

Mullery, A. P.: "The Distributed Control of Multiple Copies of Data," IBM Thomas J. Watson Research Center, Yorktown Heights, NY, August 1975.

Nelson, D. L., and R. L. Gordon: "Computer Cells - A Network Architecture for Data Flow Computing," COMPCON Fall 78, September 1978, pp. 296-301.

Nguyen, G. T.: "Distributed Architecture and Decentralized Control for a Local Network Database System," ACM International Computing Symposium, Iondres, March 1982.

Nize, J. H., and J. G. Cox: Essentials of Simulation, Prentice-Hall, Englewood Cliffs, NJ, 1968.

Obermarck, R.: "Deadlock Detection for All Resource Classes," IBM Research Report RJ2955.

— and C. Mohan: "A Distributed Data Base Manager," Transactions on Computer Systems, February 1984.

Ousterhout, John K.: "Partitioning and Cooperation in a Distributed Multi-processor Operating System: Medusa," Ph.D. Thesis, Carnegie-Mellon University April 1980.

— et al.: "Medusa: An Experiment in Distributed Operating System Structure," Communications of the ACM, vol. 23, February 1980, pp. 92-105.

Pactel: Distributed Data Base Technology, NCC Publications Manchester, England, 1979.

Palmer, D. F., and W. M. Denny: "Distributed Data Processing Requirements Engineering: High Level DDP Design," Proceedings of Computer Software and Applications Conference, Chicago, November 13-16, 1978.

Parnas, D. L.: "On the Criteria to be Used in Decomposing Systems into Modules," Communications of the ACM, December 1972.

Peebles, R., and T. Dopirak: "ADAPT: A Guest System," COMPCON Spring 80, February 1980, pp. 445-454.

— and E. Manning: "System Architecture for DistributedData Management," IEEE Computer, January 1978, pp. 40-47.

Patton, P. C., and A. Franck, (eds.), "Proceedings University of Minnesota Workshop on Local Computer Networks," September 16-17, 1976, October 13-14, 1977, and October 23-24, 1978, University of Minnesota.

Peterson, and Wesloychu: "Centralized and Distributed Data Base Systems," Tutorial, IEEE Computer Society, 1979.

Peterson, J.: Operating Systems Concepts, Addison Wesley, Reading, MA, 1983.

Piatowski, T. F., et al.: "Inside IBM's System Network Architecture," Data Communications, February 1977, pp. 33-48.

Pierce, R.: "Network Operating Systems Functions and Microprocessor Front End," IEEE COMPCON, Spring 1977.

Popek, G., & S. Miranda: Specification and Verification of a Decentralized Controlled Locking Protocol (DLP) for Distributed Data Bases, C.E.R.I.S.S., Toulouse, France, 1979.

Postel, J. B.: "A Graph Model Analysis of Computer Communications Protocols," University of California at Los Angeles, School of Engineering and Applied Sciences, January 1974.

Pouzin, L.: "Critical Evaluation of New Data Networks."

Pritsker, A. B.: Introduction to Simulation and Slam II, Systems Publishing, 1984.

—: The GASP IV Simulation Language, School of Industrial Engineering, Purdue University, John Wiley, New York, 1974.

Rahimi, S. K., and W. R. Franta: "A Postal Update Approach to Concurrency Control in Distributed Data Base Systems," The 1st International Conference on Distributed Computing Systems, October 1979, pp. 632-641.

Ramsey: "The Placement of Relations on A Distributed Relational DB," Distributed International Conference on Distributed Data Bases, Huntsville, AL, 1979.

Reitman, J.: Computer Simulation Applications, John Wiley, New York, 1971.

Ritchie, D. M., and Thompson, K.: "The UNIX Time-Sharing System," The Bell System Technical Journal, vol. 57, July-August 1978, pp. 1905-1929.

Roch, C.: "Am Implementation of Capabilities on the PDP 1145," Operating Systems Review, vol. 14, 1980, pp. 22-32.

Rosenfield A., and Kak A.: Digital Picture Processing, Academic Press, New York, 1971.

Rosko, J. S.: Digital Simulation of Physical Systems, Addison-Wesley, Reading, MA, 1972.

Ross, D. T., and K. E. Schoman, Jr.: "Structured Analysis for Requirements Definition," IEEE Transactions on Software Engineering, January 1977.

Ross, R. G.: "Data Base Systems; Design Implementation and Management," AMACON, New York, 1978.

Rothnie, J. B.: "Distributed DBMS No Longer Just A Concept," Data Communications, January 1980, pp. 61-67.

— and N. Goodman: "An Overview for the Preliminary Design of SDD-1: A System for Distributed Data Bases," Computer Corporation of America, Technical Report CCA-77-04, Cambridge, MA, March 31, 1977.

—, —, and P.A. Bernstein: "The Redundant Update Methodology of SDD-1: A System For Distributed Databases (The Fully Redundant Case)," Computer Corporation of America, Technical Report CAA-77-02, Cambridge, MA, June 15, 1977.

Sadt, T., et al.: "Structured Analysis for Requirements Definition," Proceedings of 2d International Conference on Software Engineering, San Fransicso, CA., October 13-15, 1976.

Samari, N. K., and G. M. Schneider: "The Analysis of Distributed Computer Networks Using MDR and MM1 Queues," The 1st International Conference on Distributed Computing Systems, October 1979, pp. 143-155.

Saponas, T. G., and P. L. Crews: "A Model for Decentralized Control in a Fully Distributed Processing System," COMPCON Fall 80, September 1980, pp. 307-312.

Sarfati, J.: "Measures on the SIRIUS-DELTA Distributed Data Prototype," February 1981.

Sauer, C., and K. M. Chandy: Computer Systems Performance Modeling, Prentice-Hall, Englewood Cliffs, NJ, 1981.

Scheuermann, P.: "Assimulation Model for Data Base Systems," Ph.D. Dissertation, State University of New York at Stony Brook, 1976.

Schupe, C. F.: "Automatic Component Placement in the NOMAD System," Proceedings of 12th Design Automation Conference, 1975, pp. 162-172.

Schwartz, M.: Computer Communication Network Design and Analysis, Prentice-Hall, Englewood Cliffs, NJ, 1977.

Seguin J.: "A Majority Consensus Algorithm for the Consistency of Duplicated and Distributed Information," 1st International Conference on Distributed Computing Systems, October 1979.

— et al.: "A Majority Consensus Algorithm for the Consistency of Duplicated and Distributed Computing System," October 1979, pp. 617-624.

Senko, M. E.: "Details of a Scientific Approach to Information Systems, Data Base Systems," Courant Computer Science Symposium, 1971.

Severino, E. F.: "Using Distributed Processing," Computer Decisions, May 1977, pp. 46-50.

Shipman, D.: "The Functional Data Model and the Data Language Daplex," ACM Transactions on Data Base Systems, vol. 6, no. 1, March 1981.

Shirey, R. W.: "Management and Distributed Computing," Computer World.

Siler, K. F.: "A Stochastic Evaluation Model for Data Retrieval Systems," Communications of the ACM, February 1976.

Sincoskie, W.: "The Series I Distributed Operating System," IEEE COMPCON 1980.

Sinha, M. K., and N. Natarajan: "A Distributed Deadlock Detection Algorithm Based on Timestamps," 4th Conference on Distributed Systems, IEEE, May 1984.

Small, D. L., and W. W. Chu: "A Distributed Data Base Architecture for Data Processing in a Dynamic Environment," IEEE COMPCON Spring 1979, pp. 123-127.

Smith C.: "Performance Specifications and Analysis of Software Designers," Proceedings of ACMSIGNMETRICS Conference on Simulation Measurement and Modeling of Computers Systems, Boulder, CO, 1979, pp. 173-182.

—: "Aspects of Software Design Analysis: Concurrency and Blocking," Proceedings of Performance '80, Toronto, May 1980, pp. 175-186.

—: "Modeling Software Systems for Performance Predictions," Proceedings of Computer Measurement Group X, Dallas, December 1979, pp. 175-196.

Smith, R. G.: "The Contract Net Protocol: High-Level Communication and Control in a Distributed Problem Solver," Proceedings of the 1st International Conference on Distributed Computing, October 1979, pp. 185-192.

—: "The Contract Net Protocol: High-Level Communication and Control in a Distributed Problem Solver," IEEE Transactions on Computers C-29, December 1980, pp. 1104-1113.

Smoliar, S. W., and J. E. Scalf: "A Framework for Distributed Data Processing Requirements," IEEE COMPSAC, Chicago, November 608, 1979, pp. 535-541.

Sorenson, P. G.: "Distributed Data Base Query System Based on a Forms Interface," Inf. Proceedings Society of Canada, 1979.

Stepczyk, F.: "A Case Study in Real-Time Distributed Processing Design," Proceedings of Computer Software and Applications Conference, Chicago, November 13-16, 1979.

Stone, H.: Introduction to Computer Architecture, SRA Inc., 1980.

—: "Introduction to Computer Organization and Data Structures," McGraw-Hill, New York, 1972.

—: Microcomputer Interfacing, Addison-Wesley, Reading, MA, 1982.

Stonebraker, M.: "A Formal Model of Crash Recovery in a Distributed System," IEEE Transactions on Software Engineering, vol. 1, SG-9, no. 3, May 1982.

Strom, C. S., and R. K. Walker: "Distributed Computer - Communications Networks," Symposium on Computer Communications Networks and Teletraffic Polytechnic Institute of Brooklyn, April 4-6, 1972.

Sunshine, C.: "Interprocess Communication Extensions for the UNIX Operating System: I. Design Considerations," Rand Technical Report R-20641-AF, June 1977.

Swan, R.: "The Implementation of the CM* Microprocessor," Proceedings of AFIPS National Computer Conference, 1977, pp. 645-655.

— et al.: "CM*–A Modular, Multimicroprocessor," AFIPS Conference Proceedings, vol. 46, 1977, NCC pp. 637-644.

Tajibnapis, W. D.: "A Correctness Proof of a Topology Information Maintenance Protocol for a Distributed Computer Network," Communications of the ACM, vol. 220, no. 7, July 1977, pp. 447-485.

Takizawa, M.: "Query Translation in Distributed Data Bases," Information Proceedings 80, Tokyo, Japan, 1980.

Tang, C.: "Cache System Design in the Tightly Coupled Multiprocessor System," Proceedings of AFIPS 1977 National Computer Conference, 1977, pp. 749-753.

Tannenbaum A.: Computer Networks, Prentice-Hall, Englewood Cliffs, NJ, 1981.

—: Structured Computer Organization, Prentice-Hall, Englewood Cliffs, NJ, 1976.

Taylor, R., and R. Frank : "Data Base Management Systems," Computing Surveys, vol. 8, no. 1, March 1976.

Teichroew D., and H. Sayani: "Automation of System Building," Datamation, August 15, 1971, pp. 2503.

—: "A Survey of Languages for Stating Requirements for Computer Based Information Systems," Proceedings FJCC, 1972, pp. 1203-1224.

— and E. A. Hershey, III: " PSLPSA: A Computer-Aided Technique for Structured Documentation and Analysis of Information Processing Systems," IEEE Transactions on Software Engineering, January 1977.

Teng, A. Y., and M. T. Liu: "A Formal Approach to the Design and Implementation of Network Communication Protocol," Proceedings of Computer Software and Applications Conference, Chicago, November 13-16, 1978.

Thomas, R. H.: "A Majority Consensus Approach to Concurrency Control for Multiple Copy Data Base," Bolt Beranek and Newman, Report 3733, Cambridge, MA, December 1977.

— et al.: "Network Operating Systems," Bolt Beranek and Newman, Report 3796, Cambridge, MA, March 1978.

Thornton, J. E., et al.: "A New Approach to Network Storage Management," Computer Design, vol. 14, no. 11, November 1975, pp. 81-85.

Thurber, K. J. and H. A. Freeman: "Architecture Considerations for Local Computer Networks," Sperry Univac, St. Paul, MN.

—: "Distributed Processing Communication Architecture: A Tutorial," IEEE cat. no. EHO152-9, October 1979.

—: "Tutorial: Distributed Processor Communications Architecture," IEEE cat. no. EHO152-9, October 1979.

— and—: "A Bibliography of Local Computer Network Architectures," Computer Architecture News, vol. 7, no. 5, February 1979, pp. 22-27 and Computer Communication Review, vol. 9, no. 2, April 1979, pp. 1-6.

— and —: "Local Computer Network Architectures," COMPCON 79 Spring, February 1979, pp. 258-261.

—: Data Structures and Computer Architecture Design Issues at the NWSW Interface, Lexington Books, Lexington, MA, 1979.

Towsley, D. F., and K. M. Chandy: "Models for Parallel Processing Within Programs: Application to CPU:IO and IO:IC," Communications of ACM, vol. 21, no. 10, pp. 821-831.

Trivedi, K.: Probability and Statistics with Reliability, Queuing and Computer Science Applications, Prentice-Hall, Englewood Cliffs, NJ, 1982.

Tsichrotzis, D. C.: Data Management Systems, Academic Press, New York, 1977.

Ullman, J. D.: Principals of Data Base System, Computer Science Press, Potomac, MD, 1980.

Unger, E. A., et al.: "Design for the Integration of a Data Base Management System into a Network Environment," IEEE, 1979.

van Cleemput, W. M.: "An Hierarchical Language for the Structural Description of Digital Systems," Proceedings of the 14th Design Automation Conference, 1977, pp 337-385.

Van Duyn, J.: Development of a Data Dictionary System, Prentice-Hall, Englewood Cliffs, NJ, 1982.

Viemont, Y. H.: "A Distributed Concurrency Control Algorithm Based on Transaction Commit Ordering," Fault Tolerant Computing Symposium, Los Angeles, June 1982.

von Issendorff, H., and W. Grunewald: "An Adaptable Network for Functional Distributed Systems," IEEE, 1980, pp. 196-201.

Von Neumann, in Computer Structures Readings and Examples, McGraw-Hill, New York, 1971.

Walden, D. C.: "A System for Interprocess Communication in a Resource Sharing Computer Network," Communications of the ACM, vol. 15, no. 4, April 1972, pp. 221-230.

Ward, S. A.: "TRIX: A Network-Oriented Operating System," COMPCON Spring 80, February 1980, pp. 344-349.

Wasserman, A. I.: "Information System Design Methodology," Journal of the American Society for Information Science, January 1980.

Wasserman, I., and P. Freeman: "Software Engineering Education: Status and Prospects," Proceedings of the IEEE, August 1978.

Wasserman, S.: "A Specification Method for Interactive Information Systems," Proceedings of Specifications of Reliable Software, April 1979.

Watson, R. W.: "Network Architecture Design for Back-End Storage Networks," IEEE Computer, February 1980, pp. 32-48.

Weidermold, G.: Data Base Design, McGraw-Hill, New York, 1977.

Weinstock, C. B., and M. W. Green: "Reconfiguration Strategies Rot the Sift Fault-Tolerant Computer," Proceedings of Computer Software and Applications Conference, Chicago, November 13-16, 1978.

White, G. W.: "Message Format and Data Communication Link Control Principles," IEEE Transactions on Communications, vol. COM-20, no. 4, June 1972, pp. 678-684.

Whitley-Strevens, C.: "Towards the Performance Evaluation of Distributed Computing Systems," Proceedings of Computer Software and Applications Conference, Chicago, Nov 13-16, 1978.

Whitney, V.: "A Study of Optimal File Assignment and Communication Network Configuration," Ph.D. Dissertation University of Michigan, 1970.

Wiederhold, G.: "Knowledge and Database Management," IEEE Software, vol. 1, no. 1, January 1984.

Wilms, P.: "A Qualitatiave and Quantative Comparison of Update Algorithms in Distributed Data Bases," Imag. Grenoble, France, March 1980.

Wirth, N.: "Program Development of Stepwise Refinement," Communications of the ACM, April 1971.

Wong, E.: "Decomposition - A strategy for Query Processing," ACM Transactions on Data Base Systems, vol. 1, no. 3, September 1976.

—: "Retrieving Dispersed Data from SDD-1: A System for Distributed Databases," Computer Corporation of America, Technical Report CCA-77-03, Cambridge, MA., March 15, 1977.

Wong, P. K. M.: Performance Evaluation of Data Base Systems, UMI Research Press, Ann Arbor, MI, 1981.

Wood, L.: "A Cable Bus Protocol Architecture," Proceedings of Datacom, November 1979.

Wulf W.: "C.MMP - A Multiminiprocessor," Proceedings of AFIPS, 1972 Fall Joint Computer Conference.

Yajima, S., et al.: "Labolink: An Optically Linked Laboratory Computer Network," IEEE Computer, November 1977, pp. 52-59.

Yee, J. G., and S. Y. H. Su: "A Scheme for Tolerating Faulty Data in Real-Time Systems," Proceedings of Computer Software and Applications Conference, Chicago, November 13-16, 1978.

Yuen, M. L. T., et al.: "Traffic Flow in a Distributed Loop Switching System," Symposium on Computer-Communications Networks and Teletraffic, Polytechnic Institute of Brooklyn, April 4-6, 1972.

Zucker, S.: "Interprocess Communication Extensions for the UNIX Operating System: II Implementation," Rand Technical Report R-20642-AF, June 1977.

"Performance Analysis and Evaluation: The Connection to Reality, in Peter Wegner (ed.), Research Directions in Software Technology, MIT Press, Cambridge, MA, 1979, pp. 557-583.

"Structured Design, Information Systems Design, 1979.

"A Critical Overview of Computer Performance Evaluation," Proceedings of 2d International Conference on Software Engineering, San Francisco, November 1976.

"Computer Networks: A Tutorial," IEEE cat. no. EHO127-1, 1978.

"Data Management in Engineering," Proceedings of Society of Engineering Science, Hampton, VA., October 1976, pp. 775-790.

"Deadlock Problem in Computer Networks," Technical Report MITTR-185, Laboratory of Computer Science, MIT, Cambridge, MA, September 1977.

"Local Area Networking," in Ira W. Cotton (ed.), Report of a Workshop Held at the National Bureau of Standards, August 22-23, 1977, U.S. Department of Commerce National Bureau of Standards, April 1978.

"Proceedings of the 2d Berkeley Workshop on Distributed Data Management and Computer Networks," Berkeley Laboratory, University of California, May 25-26, 1976.

"System R: A Relational Data Base Management System," IEEE Computer, May 1979.

Tutorial on Distributed Processing, 2d ed., IEEE, New York.

Computer Corporation of America: "A Distributed Data Management System for Command and Control Systems," January 1979.

COMPCON 79 Spring, February 27-March 2, 1979.

Distributed Processing Seminar, IBM Federal Systems Division, March 23, 1979.

"Distributed Processing," 2d ed., IEEE cat. no. EHO127-1.

International Conference on Very Large Data Bases, IEEE Computer Society: 1st, Framingham, MA, 1975; 2d, Brussels, Belgium, 1971; 4th Berlin, Germany, 1978; 5th Rio de Janeiro, Brazil, 1979; 6th, Montreal, Canada, 1980; 7th Cannegi, France, 1981.

Proceedings of the 5th Berkeley Conference on Distributed Data Management and Computer Networks, University of California, Berkeley, CA.

Proceedings of the 7th ACM Symposium on Operating Systems Principles, 1979.

Proceedings of the 3d Berkeley Workshop on Distributed Data Management and Computer Networks, August, 29-31, 1978.

Proceedings of the 1st International Conference on Distributed Computing Systems, Huntsville, AL, IEEE cat. no. 79 CH 1445-6C, October 1-5, 1979.

Proceedings of the Computer Networking Symposium, IEEE cat. no. 78 Ch1400-1C, December 13, 1973.

Trends and Applications: Computer Networks, November 1976, IEEE cat. no. 76 CH1143-7C.

Proceedings: Trends and Applications, IEEE cat. no. 79 CH1402-7C, May 1979.

Index

A

abstraction, 338
adaptive routing, 15-16
add algorithm, 194
addressing, 208, 226-228
administrator model, 413
Almes, 404
Alvin, 63
American National Standards
    Institute (ANSI), 236
amplitude modulation (AM), 7-8,
    78-79
analog transmission, 78-79
analytical modeling, 308-309
    queuing models, 308-309
Anderson, 127, 134
Appletalk, 499-501
Arcnet, 497-498
Arpanet, 5-6, 10, 139
asynchronous communications, 78
automated topology generation,
    191
    availability, 198-199

capacity, 199-200
complexity, 202-203
expansion capability, 201-202
graph theory, 191-195
performance, 200
recoverability, 201
reliability, 197-198
simulation techniques, 195-196
topology analysis, 196-197
availability, 27
average interprocessor distance,
    352-353
average transmit time, 353-354
average wait time in system,
    354-361

B

back-off algorithm, 222
Bahl & Tang algorithm, 194
Balenson, 289
baseband cable, 60-61
Bauer, 289
biconical alignment, 62